NINE LIVES

One Man's Insatiable Journey Through
Love, Life And Near Death

An Autobiography By David S Gill

Set in 11pt Palatino

Designed by HSP MILNERS, Ironworks Road,
Barrow-in-Furness, Cumbria LA14 2PG

Printed and bound by
CPI Group (UK) Ltd, Croydon CR0 4YY

Hardback ISBN: 978-0-9570645-0-8
Paperback ISBN: 978-0-9570645-1-5

First published in the UK 2011 by
DSG Publishing Limited.

I would like to dedicate this book to my very special children Hari, Kadi, Toba and Indi They are the focus of my life and I hope they will carry on with my mission and passion and take it all to greater heights and achievements.

Disclaimer

This book is the summary of my life up to this point. personal recollection which made up to this point. memories and experiences described the following stories of view. No names have been changed my own personal point intended to breach any privacy, cause any these are not stories business or damage any particular person or other individuals or simply stories of how I experienced certain people son – they are can make no apology for the truth as I see it.

Contents

PART 3

"It is not the critic who counts: not the man who points out how the strong man stumbles or where the doer of deeds could have done better. The credit belongs to the man who is actually in the arena, whose face is marred by dust and sweat and blood, who strives valiantly, who errs and comes up short again and again, because there is no effort without error or shortcoming, but who knows the great enthusiasms, the great devotions, who spends himself for a worthy cause; who, at the best, knows, in the end, the triumph of high achievement, and who, at the worst, if he fails, at least he fails while daring greatly, so that his place shall never be with those cold and timid souls who knew neither victory nor defeat." Theodore Roosevelt 1897

Foreword

David Gill is one of my best friends. I have known him for the past eight years and through time we have built an incredible working relationship and a close personal bond.

We first met during an EAZA congress in 2004 where he was representing his outstanding South Lakes Wild Animal Park in Cumbria, and I the owner of Bioparc Zoo de Doue la Fontaine in France.

We started to discuss the possibility of working together. It was immediately apparent that David was not the average zoo owner. For one thing he chose to spend time with the French! It was clearly not the preserve of the average Englishman. It was a very pleasant surprise to be able to share time and humour with him and it was here that we started to cultivate a working relationship and partnership.

Principally we were both interested to share our ideas and experiences about what we as zoo owners could do to protect endangered species. I soon realised I was very lucky to have found David as he not only wanted to help animals, but remote and indigenous people too.

Together we would put measures in place that would restore the population of giraffes in Niger, West Africa as well as provide water wells for people throughout a small community in the country. David also joined me in the other conservation projects I was involved with at the time, protection of lemurs in Madagascar and spectacled bears in Peru.

When I first travelled to Niger to meet with Omer Dovi, a passionate Nigerien with whom we developed the Association to Safeguard the Giraffes of Niger, I asked how we could save the giraffes, who were on the verge of extinction. His answer was very clear that we could only save the animals by supporting the people sharing the same territory.

I was not sure David would be sensitive to this way of working; after all I did not know him very well at the time. After a short discussion it became very clear that he was indeed the perfect person to work with on such a project and he committed to travel with me to all three conservation projects. Along with our assistants and workers in each territory we shared a special philosophy, one which was uncommon at the time. We involved each and every local community to work in harmony with us in our endeavours to protect each species. Within a few weeks David and I were travelling together, sharing the emotions, physical problems and often danger that accompanies such outlandish trips. We have been in some remarkable and frightening positions where we could have drowned amongst many other pitfalls. For me, the most dangerous situation we encountered was in Way Kambas, Sumatra where we were so pre-occupied with bites from leeches that we were relatively oblivious to the set of fresh tiger footprints that surrounded our camp.

When the fear had subsided I realised how very similar David was to myself, though he seemed to go even further. While he is indeed aware of the danger he places himself in he somehow remains unafraid of the wildest elements of nature and his surroundings in situations which would frighten 99 per cent of human beings. He always retains a remarkable calm in any predicament. I have seen him bothered by a situation but never out of control. I admire his natural intelligence, analytical qualities and his supreme calm.

When you consider the problems he has faced in his family life it is all the more impressive that David is a genial, humorous person. He has been weakened in some respects by the issues that have prevented him from having a regular family life; in fact he has had to spend many years away from his children who he loves with all his heart. I have never seen a father like him. He has actually brought his children on many of the trips we have had together over the years, taking tremendous care of them despite the elements or difficulties we have encountered. He also somehow manages to balance the parenting necessities with being an insatiable adventurer.

Despite his personal problems, whenever I see him he is always the same person totally dependable, adaptable and courageous. He is also a great humanitarian. When he first visited the desperately hot, poverty stricken wasteland of Niger he confided to me that the experience changed his life.

This was a turning point where he used his place in the zoo world and his generosity to begin to change the lives of peoples in trouble.

He can be very proud to have changed the lives of so many natives of Madagascar, Niger and Peru. Here, together, we have helped people improve their quality of life and along the way, taught them to respect and work in tandem with the animals they have in their midst.

Thanks to David's tremendous analysis and financial support the conservation projects have increased in their capacity and efficiency.

Along with the local communities we have managed to achieve amazing results for each of the endangered species we sought to protect.

I feel that in every aspect of my life David has been supportive and I am very thankful to have met him. He has changed my life, and so many others, for the better.

Pierre Gay, Bioparc Zoo de Doue la Fontaine, November 2011.

Prologue

Zimba the rhino was lying in the bottom of a ditch in one of the fields of my animal park. His jaw was broken, he was squealing, bleeding, his jaw bent right back. It was horrendous, he was in so much pain, and there was no chance he could survive his injuries or come out of that hole alive.

I called the police and everyone else I could think to involve. How could I get this rhino out of the hole he had fallen into? He was so badly injured that I just could not see a way. When the police arrived the first question they asked was, "Can we get anyone here to dart him?"

The nearest person who could have done it was miles away. Out of instinct I had grabbed my gun. All we had, I told the police, were weapons to kill the rhino, and I couldn't see an alternative.

Zimba was squealing in pain, almost upside down in a hole.

"Even if you could get a crane, you would never get the straps under him without killing him.

Look everybody there is no way that this is going to happen, this animal is in pain, he is suffering, what are we going to do? I know what I have to do; I do not have an alternative.

I have got to shoot him."

"Are you sure, are you sure?"

"Look, even if we rang the guy to sedate him, he is an hour and a half away from here even if he could come *right* now."

"Yeah, yeah."

"I am sorry but this is my choice, this is my rhino, he is on my land and I am making the decision. I am saying I am sorry but I have to shoot this rhino because he has to be put out of his misery."

I was crying my eyes out the entire time.

I stood there and loaded the rifle up with three bullets and shot them straight into his head, bang, bang, bang!

Then I loaded up with three more bullets and went bang, bang, bang into his head.

The first one would have killed him, no doubt about it, but I just wanted to make absolutely sure.

He laid there and I just looked at him.

It had all happened in minutes.

I moved to sit on a bank, in complete and utter shock, still holding my rifle. A policeman came over to me and quietly and carefully pulled the rifle from my hand.

It didn't cross my mind at the time, but I now know he believed I was going to shoot myself.

I was absolutely distraught.

Nothing in my life has ever given me the same feeling as that day and I have led a life of amazing highs and terrible lows.

You are about to read of them all.

My name is David S Gill and I want to take you on the journey of your life.

This is my story.

PART ONE

Chapter 1
In the beginning.....and a house fire

South Lakes Wild Animal Park, the 'conservation focused zoo' I own, sits in the ancient town of Dalton-In-Furness, close to the larger and better known industrial town, Barrow-In-Furness. Dalton is best known as the birth place of the artist George Romney, there is a junior school named after the famous painter.

The Norse people eventually claimed Dalton as their own and the second generation of Norse were farmers from Ireland. Today, the area is still a famous farm town. I was born virtually round the corner from where the Animal Park is today, at 32 Cleator Street, in Dalton, which was then in Lancashire, rather than Cumbria. I tend to go by the name David S Gill, my middle name is Stanley though I never use it, which I was christened after my father and grandfather.

The houses were all terraced which was typical of the area. I was born upstairs at home on May 26, 1961 and was one of the last people to be a home birth in Dalton. There will not have been many home births since then as most people went to the hospital which was in Barrow.

My mam, Edith Annie Atkinson, was born in Shap, further up into the Cumbrian countryside. She was a country girl at heart but her mam and dad moved down to Askam-in-Furness because he got a job in the iron works there. There was a large smelting place, where they used to refine iron, from the iron ore mines. The iron industry was huge in this area, everything grew around iron ore and it was one of the richest seams of iron ore anywhere in the world at the time.

My dad's full name was Edward Stanley Gill but he was always known as Stanley Gill. The Gills lived in Dalton, my granddad worked as a plumber for the railway. He fought in World War I where he had been shot through the wrist. His brother John also served during the War and died on the battlefields of Northern France. When I was a very small boy my granddad gave me his brother's penknife that he had been given along with his uniform. I have treasured the knife, which still has its original string tied to it, ever since. Whenever I look at it I think about John Gill being killed when he was just eighteen. I have fond memories of my grandparents. They had all lived a very traditional life, something I inherited, very basic in essence.

It was so different to now. One of my early memories is of playing out on the beach because my mother's mother lived right by the beach. We used to go there for our holidays. Our annual holiday was a visit to Askam-in-Furness, three miles on the red 'Ribble' bus, which was a huge thing then. It looks so tiny, anyone now would wonder how on earth that could be our annual holiday. But to us, to travel just down the road on the bus, it was a big journey.

Nana used to sit us on the side of the sink and scrub us until we bled with a scrubbing brush. "Till you're bleeding, you can't be clean", she would say. I always felt as if she was going to take the top of my ear off. She was lovely though; we all loved her and Granddad. They spoke a different language. My granddad spoke Cumbric - a local dialect - which many people now could never ever understand because they used completely different words.

My father's parents were very strict, but they'd always give you a big kiss, I always remember my nana giving me a big kiss and she always had a bit of a moustache. Granddad was a little bit frightening in some respects, he was a big man and he was bald but he used to make us laugh because he only had three hairs on the top of his head so he'd part one in one direction, then he'd part one the other and he used to say, "I can't make up my mind about this one!" We bought them a budgie one year which Granddad absolutely loved.

They were immensely traditional and old fashioned, straight from the 1800s basically. I think nana was quite a loving lady but

Granddad was stricter. He was from the hard but fair school, something I recall fondly. Granddad would give you a clip around the ear if you answered him back, he wouldn't think twice, and you usually deserved it. His favourite phrase when admonishing a child was to call them a 'little twerp!'

There were five kids in our family, all fairly quickly produced between 1959 and 1968. Alison was the oldest, I was the second. Karen came thirteen months after me, and then there were my two brothers Michael and Colin. I was always a very adventurous child, very independent, though when I was small I didn't realise that. I think it came from the fact that from early on I was replaced by one child after another. I only had thirteen months of attention before Karen took over and had all the focus from my parents. And then of course, my brothers arrived. Thus, by the age of seven I had already learned independence.

Our mam nearly died having our Colin, she had a blood haemorrhage. As a consequence, a lot of energy and attention was placed upon the younger children but it left me feeling ostracized. My dad started in the shipyard in Barrow as an office junior, making the tea amongst his duties as I recall. He certainly was a hard worker. He also worked in the evenings so we never saw much of Dad. He went out before we got up in the morning to go to work and we barely saw him at night because he would be at night school. To give him his due he became a draughtsman and engineer and had a lot of letters after his name. It was frustrating though because I loved to learn but we learned nothing about his work or his other interests.

Mam and Dad were both interested in road safety and home safety. He would run certain committees and he oversaw Cycling Proficiency for all the kids in the Dalton area and ran the *Tufty Club* which focused on teaching kids how to cross the road safely. He also ran the Junior Accident Prevention council. I would take part in all the things my dad wanted me to so I took my cycling proficiency, and got 100%. I became an instructor myself and I was also on the Junior Accident Prevention Council. Eventually I became the Chairman which was a sure thing to happen with my dad being in charge.

Mam was really involved with Girl Guides. She was a guide captain and then later became a commissioner. Girl Guides was her focus. The way it seemed to me was that my parents spent a lot of time with other people's kids but very little with some of their own. In hindsight I was screaming for attention all of the time. From day one I was clambering to say, "Mam take some notice of me, Dad take some notice of me, I'm here, please don't forget me." In those days photographs were only taken at special times, such as at Christmas or a birthday, because film was expensive to process and we were poor, so money was hard to come by. But even on these special occasions, in every photograph of me, I was either crying or you could tell I had been crying. You were forced to smile in those times, and if you didn't you would get a clip round the ear. In those photos I am always immaculately dressed but I was always upset. I have memories of laughing with my family but no photographic record.

My earliest memory is of riding on the back of an elephant at the old Belle Vue zoo in Manchester. I must only have been two-years-old but it is etched into the hard drive of my brain somewhere, it must have stirred something within me given the work I have done as an adult.

Another of my earliest memories I have is going to school for the first time. I remember very clearly that at four-years-old Mam took me to school but I didn't really want to go. I was crying my eyes out and I ended up in Miss Butterfield's class. It was terrifying for me. I remember the dinner ladies, the hall and the ropes dangling down from the ceiling and it looked so huge, it was like a castle. I hated school, there were very few days where I enjoyed going. I think my mam would say that I had to be almost forced to go to school because I just hated it, though there was no particular reason for it.

Obviously she had a lot of kids to get ready in the morning and sometimes I felt I was on my own. Consequently I was a very shy child and I had a strange phobia about visiting other people's houses. One time I was meant to go to a friend's house, we called her Aunt Sissy (though she wasn't related) and I totally refused to go in the house. I ended up sitting outside in my stroller because I wouldn't go in. I would just refuse to go into other people's houses. I also had a phobia about eating other people's food; I would nearly throw up at the thought of eating food from somebody else's house that they had made. As a consequence, I would never go to another kid's party and if I did I would cry because I didn't want to be there. When I had my own birthday party, all I ever remember is crying, I didn't enjoy it, I was always so upset, I hated things like that. It makes me smile now because I can remember doing it but I don't know why.

I have talked with my sister Karen about all of these early memories and neither of us can come up with a reason as to why I was like this. Today I am very close to Karen but when we were younger she was my nearest rival so we fought like cat and dog.

There's a definite clarity to certain things though. For instance Alison and Colin, the oldest and the youngest, were certainly the favourites in the family. I understand that with Alison it was because she was the first born and she was a girl. Yet with Colin I have never understood it, maybe it is because he was the last one. Colin just seemed to get everything, all the stuff we never had he seemed to get. As he grew up he developed epilepsy and after that he could do no wrong, he could get away with anything that we would be hammered for, and he still does to this day. Dad has never kicked a football with me in my life, never played a game with me in his life and never spent any time with me that I can remember. Other boys might spend time with their dads fishing or going for a walk, but my dad never did this. I don't remember a single thing he ever did with me or shared with me. I learned to swim but it was through my friend, Michael Field's dad. I used to go to the cinema with Colin Steel and his dad. It was always other people's fathers who spent time with me and took me through the important steps in my life.

My parents had no money, we were very poor. Yet Mam, who was a confectioner by trade, was really good with food. It was very basic fodder: mash, liver and onions, kedgeree - nothing fancy but it filled you up and I loved that food. It still gives me happy memories. It is probably surprising but not one of us was ever over-weight. A lot of the food I make today is based on the stuff she made when I was a kid.

Money was always tight but it wasn't extreme poverty, I just rarely kept up with other children. I'd get 10p from my nana to spend when we saw her but I would never get anything from my parents, though Mam would knit most of my clothes. Regardless of the weather I wouldn't wear a coat, it would be a huge baggy knitted aran jumper that Mam had made, and it certainly did the job, kept me warm on all my adventures. She seemed to enjoy knitting us everything.

My brothers and I shared a tiny room yet it somehow contained two bunk beds and a wardrobe. I will never know how on earth they fit all the furniture in the little box room. I have seen the house recently and could not believe it. It could only have been six-by-four-and-a-half-feet. I had the top bunk because I was the oldest, Michael and Colin top and tailed on the bottom and that's what it was like until I was about thirteen. We three lads had to slum it whereas my sisters were treated to a bigger room which was built as an extension on the house, with a gorgeous view of Dalton. Fortune favoured the girls!

I don't mind admitting that one of my faults was jealousy, which didn't help when kids around me seemed to have everything I wanted but couldn't afford. One lad in our class was the first to have a digital watch, when they first came out. He showed it to everybody and I was sick as a parrot, I didn't have a watch, never mind a digital watch.

Our presents were often handmade and I could never keep up.

Michael Field got a Hornby train set once and I was so jealous of him, all I wanted was *that*. It must have taken a lot but my parents eventually saved the money so I could get one but when we finally went to this toy shop they didn't have one. I ended up buying all separate parts, but at least I had a train set. I developed an interest in model trains and eventually I built a huge model railway.

My parents would save up so we could go on holiday once a year. We would buy a 'Runabout Ticket' on the railway. You could visit anywhere in the North West for a whole week. So we would go through places in the Lake District, like Grange-Over-Sands, as well as coastal resorts like Blackpool, Southport and Morecambe. My dad was stuck in his ways; we would always visit the same places.

To us it was still wonderful; we had some great days out. We would take packed sandwiches for dinner, salmon paste and cucumber sticks in my memory, but then we would go out for tea and have something like fish and chips, before coming home on the train.

One of my first major adventures into the dangerous parts of the world, where death is facing you but you never realise it, was when myself and Michael Field climbed out onto the roof of our terraced house and sat by the chimney. I know I did it just for attention, which I certainly got once my neighbour Mr. Mills saw us. Everyone was panicking but we were very confident that we weren't going to fall. I remember getting ostracized for it. It was fun to us though and we couldn't understand what all the fuss was about. I can remember it so clearly, there was a good view up there and you could see all the steam trains going all the way from Dalton station from that viewpoint! The last regular steam drawn trains ran in 1968. This was my first real adventure and it started a trend. I would do something out of the box, totally against the rules but yet challenging myself to do something that was terrifying. Even at seven-years-old it was like I said to myself, 'Just get it out of the way, you can do it.'

One thing I accidentally accomplished was a front page appearance in the local paper, the *Evening Mail* in Barrow. It was to be a precursor to many future appearances but this one was apparently heroic. There was a fire in our house one night. I woke up in the night, all I could hear was crackling and banging and then I just suddenly smelled the smoke, saw the smoke and looked across the room to see my brothers' bed on fire. The walls were just smothered in fire and flames.

I didn't wear pyjamas as a child, it was perhaps just another little rebellion, but I hated to wear them and always slept in my birthday suit, a tradition I carry on to this day. Ironically, I was very lacking in confidence and wasn't comfortable with my body, but nevertheless, I flew across to Colin's bed and saw that he wasn't there. Michael was still in bed however, so I picked him up and carried him to the top of the stairs before throwing him down to the bottom. I think he woke up as he hit the floor. He somehow avoided breaking his neck.

I saved Michael's life, via a second near death experience for him, but the funny thing was, when I started running down to Mam and Dad screaming that the house was on fire, they didn't believe me. This was probably because I had a history of sleepwalking and would often shout out strange things. Naked as the day I was born, I would walk into my parent's room and say, "Mam, Mam, I've lost me chicken, where's me chicken?" I don't know the reason for this, all I knew as a kid in my sleepy haze was that I was desperately trying to account for this lost chicken and my mam had to calm me down and get me back to sleep. So on the occasion where there was something actually happening they thought I was having another eerie sleepwalking episode.

"THE HOUSE IS ON FIRE, THE HOUSE IS ON FIRE!" I shouted, totally starkers.

"Now then son, come on, let's go back to bed."

Half way up the stairs Mam realised that the house really was melting. Total panic ensued and we eventually all got out into the street while the fire brigade came to try and salvage the house, taking out half the building in the process. In fact after that we had to sleep in different places around the house and make do with no roof on the place for a while. But I was a hero because I had rescued my brothers. It was my first claim to fame. It was very traumatic afterwards though because I was absolutely petrified that the house was on fire during the night. I would have a complete panic attack thinking I could hear crackling noises. My mam cried because I was so scared and this seemed to go on for a long time.

I felt out of place at home but I certainly had a little community that I was part of in my local street. No one had a mobile phone so you didn't travel to meet people, your life consisted of whoever was on your street and your communication was essentially determined by how far you could shout. The end of the street seemed such a long way away. Going to Askam seemed like the end of the world. When you think about the world now, visually it is so different to the way it was in that era. Cars make it that way. We didn't own a car back then, very few people did, and in fact my dad never even learned to drive. Michael and Stephen Field lived just across the road from me at 17 Cleator Street. I actually bought their house quite recently, initially for my daughter Amy to buy, but this story comes later.

I would see Michael to say hello to now and again over the years, he lived near to me still but he went down a very different road to me. Sadly I spoke with Michael recently and he revealed he had terminal cancer. He has since passed away tragically. Our gang back then included Michael and Stephen Field as well as Martin Clarke and a lad called Paul Greenaway, though he was more on the periphery. We were typical boys getting into all sorts of little adventures, naughty things really. In the autumn we always raided the neighbour's orchard in their garden and we'd pinch their apples and then wonder what we were going to do with them so we'd throw them over the wall into the school yard which was behind our garden. We were always pulled up for it but would always feign ignorance. It was never us even though we had probably been seen doing it.

There was a plumber's yard in the back street where we used to hang around the old scrap cars. Once, we found a huge tyre and we would just roll it up and down the street, with us sitting in it! Nowadays Health and Safety nonsense would completely stop this, as it was so dangerous. We would go down there at 100mph in the huge wagon tyre, if anyone walked into it they would have been killed and it could easily have carried on rolling right onto the main road. We seemed to make a habit of pretending we were doing no wrong, we actually didn't think we were. One time something happened which always tickles me when I think back.

My dad bought a garage and a garden from a neighbour at one stage - up until then we just had a back yard with an outside toilet. It was a little strange because it meant our garden wasn't directly behind our house like everyone else's, it was about three houses away. We had a lot of things stored in this wooden garage, including a wind up gramophone complete with 78 rpm records. We would go into to the garage to listen to old records, like *The Laughing Policeman* which just went on and on as we laughed with it. My dad didn't smoke but he used to always be given cigars as presents at Christmas, everyone was back then. One day I took a box of these cigars from my dad's wardrobe and took them down to the garage thinking he would never notice because he never smokes them anyway. Michael and I were in the garage and we lit up and almost killed ourselves! The garage was totally foggy with smoke, you couldn't see a thing. Suddenly there was a huge bang as my mother came storming into the garage. Out of fright we just chucked the cigars somewhere in the garage.

"What's going on in here?"

"Nothing. Nothing."

"What Are You Doing?"

"What do you mean?"

We still denied it even though you couldn't see through the garage for the smoke. So at the grand old age of seven I had my first smoke, it really put me off I felt so ill.

Those memories were fun, with my sisters dressing up in the garage while we listened to records. But the parents were never involved, anything fun like that was always just us kids. On a deeper level I was hurting. I felt as if no matter what I did I was never told I was good at anything and I never received a pat on the back for anything I might have been good at. I believe I was a very good reader, the moment I started reading I was reading newspapers, which was way ahead of my age group. Other kids were still reading *Peter And Jane* and I was reading the *Daily Telegraph*. I wasn't bad at maths either, and was always top of the class - my teachers acknowledged I was bright. One of the things I particularly remember about infant/primary school was Mrs Crayston.

If you weren't listening in her class you soon knew about it because you would have the blackboard rubber thrown right at you. That thing really hurt. But I would recommend it for anybody because it did not do me any harm whatsoever. Mrs Crayston needed to keep respect and order and so she ruled with an iron rod over her class of thirty kids. We were all absolutely terrified of her because she was so strict, but I actually remember it in a nice way, not as something nasty. I believe that as young kids you need to know where the line is, where the respect is and if you don't get it at school and you get away with it there, then parents have no chance.

Perhaps I developed certain skills that other kids didn't because I didn't play as much. My mother would probably say that I wasn't as unhappy as I think. Albeit in a loving motherly manner, I was always being told, 'you get on with this, I've got a baby to deal with, I've got tea to make, I've got the washing to do, I've got the ironing to do, you get on with that.' So I was pushed away. Yet this is what created my complete independence. Through this I found an ability to make my own decisions, to make my own way in life, rather than rely on others because I did it from day one. It was a skill that would come in very useful later on.

Chapter 2
My first pets and growing up

My first foray into the world of animals was when we got our first small pets.

We had a little fish tank with some goldfish in the front room and my siblings and I all had a fish each. My mam and dad also bought us some tortoises when we were very small which we kept in the back yard. The first one was called Willamena, if I recall, but she died the first winter because nobody knew then how to look after tortoises. The next year we had another tortoise which became Willamena II. That one died too but then we seemed to get the hang of it, the two we got after that lasted much longer. In fact, one of them, Joey, died in 2011 after 45 years.

After that we moved onto rabbits and guinea pigs which started to become my responsibility. I was allowed to develop a rapport with animals. We didn't have a cat or a dog but we had plenty of other animals. I would gradually become the one who would go in and clean them all out and feed them. I also developed a fascination for nature, plants and insects. Anything to do with the outdoors interested me and I started to cultivate my interest in the practical side of life. I loved being in our garden even though it was small, besides it seemed large to me at the time - we still had a flower garden as well as a vegetable plot and blackcurrants amongst other things. There was also a greenhouse where Dad grew tomatoes.

Later we would move house and we had our own private garden. It was here that I started to develop my belief that animals should be free. Right from the beginning I had a problem with animals being stuck in cages. Whenever my dad wasn't around I would let the rabbits out of the hutches. The problem was they would just hop all over his bedding plants, digging up all the seeds he had planted. I was certainly reprimanded strongly, despite my now familiar protestations that I had nothing to do with anything that went wrong.

I felt a deep joy at seeing the rabbits jumping and hopping right up into the sky, just running around and having fun. It would give me a thrill watching them and I didn't like them in their little cage, looking at me with a sad expression. I hated it. Today I still can't abide animals being locked up.

If they are locked in a tiny little place where they cannot express themselves in that way, jumping and moving the way they want, I hate it, I couldn't do it. I don't do that with my animals, it is the whole ethos of South Lakes Wild Animal Park that animals should be allowed to express themselves in a comfortable, familiar environment. In general the zoo fraternity has not warmed to me and a big part of it is that I am very anti-traditional zoo. I don't like traditional zoos and I think they should be either closed or changed. That's what I've been trying to do, help a few zoo's change but I cringe sometimes. Some zoo bosses are merely collectors of animals, it's more about the amount of different species they can accumulate, it's not about whether those animals are having a wonderful time, in an environment where they are protected and they have no fears from predators because you take that away from them. Are they able to express themselves? In many zoos around the world I doubt it very much. Since my childhood I have always been adamant that animals should be able to express themselves. I used to let the hamsters and gerbils roam freely around the house.

My hamsters would often misbehave, not that they knew any better. I had hooked up some makeshift speakers to an old radio for myself in my bedroom and one night the hamster chewed right through both speaker wires. The hamster would end up giving me a real fright. Lying half asleep in bed I felt something soft and furry climbing up the inside of my leg. Feeling an absolute cold terror I looked very tentatively under the covers and saw the hamster crawling towards me. I had every right to be frozen with fear given I had nothing on and he was half way up the bed. Hamsters have very sharp teeth.

We also had Patch, a black and white Dutch rabbit and Rexeena who was a natural coloured rabbit from the wild. My granddad fell across her one night and brought her to us in a box - but she never really quite tamed. Still, she remained alive, and uneaten. I didn't realise for many years that my mam had been serving us rabbit, which she occasionally bought from the butchers. She had always told me it was chicken whenever I asked, but one night she revealed the truth - I was eating rabbit. As quick as I could I ran outside to check the number of rabbits in our hutches because I instantly thought, to my terror, that I was eating my own rabbit. I had no conception that people could, or would, buy rabbits to eat; to me they were just something in our hutch. After that it was really hard to eat it thinking of the poor, fluffy rabbit being served up on a plate. Mam should have just kept on the con that we were eating chicken.

This need to free animals always put me in bother with my parents because I persisted. Regardless of the punishment dished out, I persisted in letting them out because I just wanted to see them enjoying themselves. At one point we got a Yorkshire Terrier cross called Kerry and I used to take her for walks. I would walk for miles and miles in the countryside with that poor little dog. She was shorter when we finished than it was when we started because I wore her little legs out.

As I got older I learned to appreciate a few of the typical family traditions. For our family it was bonfire night and Halloween. We always played bobbing for apples on Halloween where we would all get soaking wet, getting pushed under the water while trying to grab the apples with our teeth. It was always wonderful on bonfire night. We always had a small box of standard fireworks; it was nothing like today where people have enormous displays. I hate what goes on today because from my animal's perspective it causes a nightmare.

When I was younger the biggest noise would come from a tiny banger although we did not ever have these ourselves. We would have a small firework display in the back garden so it was more personal. Every time my dad lit a box of fireworks, we had a little bonfire and we'd put our tatties in, cooking them on the bonfire while Mam always made a dark treacle toffee and soup. I have great memories of that time of year. These days it is not the same as many people go to big displays instead of the traditional family night at home. We have organised a bonfire at the park in the past and though we had potatoes and hot dogs it is still not the same as having your own family with a little box of fireworks, doing your own little thing in your back garden. Now I dream of having all my kids with me with just a little box of fireworks, a little bonfire, cooking that same comfort food, experiencing a traditional bonfire night. More of the reason why later in the story. You might expect Christmas would hold some special significance or enjoyment to me but in reality I don't have too many good memories associated with that time of year.

For Christmas my granddad would always build me something by hand which I didn't truly appreciate at the time. In his spare time Granddad Gill would gather stuff up from a joinery shop where he worked after he retired, and use all the off cuts of wood to build me things. I would get anything from a fort to a garage or a farm, all of which he painted up to look worthy of any shop window. When I look back they were really fantastic things he made for us, all in wood and paint and something you wouldn't get now. He didn't say a lot but he was still very thoughtful.

At about seven-years-old and through my early years, I was more concerned with playing with my little gang, which wasn't a thug type thing like it is now. Then again we were very naughty. We used to all go down the fields to play, we called it 'Damming The Beck' where we would breach the dam, swing and climb on trees. We'd put one rope up in a big tree overhanging the stream but I didn't know someone had untied it. I jumped right onto it but of course it came straight off and I went head first down into the beck (stream). I will never know how I didn't die that day because I came from such a height and hit the ground with such tremendous force, the fall could easily have killed me. I had no idea where I was but all my mates were laughing.

We also got into a fair few scrapes playing down near the local railway line. One time we found a stack of detonators on a road next to the tracks. We soon worked out what they were and found a method of making them explode. They had straps on them which would attach to the tracks but we used to tie them to things and throw stones at them to make them explode. Although my favourite subjects at school were physics and chemistry, Stephen Field was a bit older and more of a science swot. After some research he gave us an idea of how to create our own little explosive fireworks, pocket dynamite as it were. So we went to the local chemists and bought all the raw materials; simple items such as weed killer, but when mixed together it was all potent. Nowadays this would be seen as a terrorist plot!

We mixed the chemicals together, then a group of us thought a safe place to conduct this experiment would be the local cricket club. We thought setting this thing off in the concrete outside toilet building would be safe enough. So we lit the touch paper and decided to run like hell, only we ran across the biggest expanse of open space in the whole of Dalton. We were sprinting right across the cricket pitch! This thing made the most enormous bang and a cloud of smoke which just enveloped the whole pitch. We were only halfway across the cricket ground when the noise and smoke erupted. It was like something out of a cartoon because there was a big flash and smoke. There we all were in the middle square of the pitch suddenly lit up like rabbits in the headlights!

Everyone was in the cricket club in the bar at the time because it was a really wet night; they were watching telly or playing darts. They all looked out and there we were halfway across. We ran like hell and had to go under the beck and then the bridge to escape at the far end. I could not believe it made such a noise. We didn't stop at that though, in fact, we perfected how to make a small firework which would make a big eruption. We used to go down to the railway and plant the explosives in the small tunnel which led the beck under the railway.

One time we lit one of these bangers in the middle of the tunnel, but there was so much smoke from it we couldn't get out fast enough. We were choking on the smoke, we couldn't see the end of the tunnel, couldn't see anything at all. When we got out we just collapsed on the side of the track but the wind was blowing the smoke right into our faces.

Chapter 3
A Life changing event and discovery of my "gift"

It was while we were on one of our adventures that I came upon the person who was to change my life forever. When I was nine-years-old in April of 1971, the gang and I were pedalling down St. Helens hill, on the outskirts of Dalton, on our bikes, searching out new life forms and new ground to cover.

Suddenly we hit upon a diversion I'd not seen before.

"We've got to go down that road, we've never been down there, I wonder what's waiting," I said.

As we rode we saw a man in a field, cutting a huge hedge down and then piling up all of the hedgerow, the trees and branches to make a bonfire.

We all stopped in our tracks and shouted over,

"Can we help you, do you want a hand?"

"Yes you can if you want, put all these branches over there."

We were only little but we were cutting his work load right down and dragging everything he needed moving – if we could lift it we helped.

At the end of the day we said to him, "Are you going to be doing this again, do you want any help tomorrow?"

"Sure do, this will take me months".

His name was Keith Howson and he had just taken over at St. Helens farm after the previous farmer had completely neglected it and let it go to rack and ruin. No hedges had been laid and there were gaps in everything, it was in a terrible state. Keith had a huge job on his hands trying to set off laying all the hedges to make it secure for any stock that he had. The next day we went back to help him again but this time we were down to two - just me and Colin Savage wanted to go back and help him out.

Colin got fed up of the work himself after a couple of weeks and from that point on it was just me. I loved it. I would ride down on my push bike and help Keith out. I'd get a cup of tea and a sandwich and quickly Keith and I built a bond together. He was courting his future wife Janet at the time but he had endured tragedy in his life and had gone off to Canada just to escape the world. After a while he came back home to make a new life. He was a lovely man. I would spend my whole weekends at the farm with Keith. His method of making a living was very traditional and hard working. He would start work at 5am, and go through until 6pm. Thirteen hours a day, seven days a week. I don't think my mam even knew I'd gone out but I would leave the house at 5am and cycle up to Keith's.

I would be the one to get the cows in, which I loved. Some of them were so big I couldn't even reach around their necks. Keith would also let me feed the cows while he would put the milking units on, huge old fashioned type urns that I could barely carry. Eventually I learned how to take the unit off and became strong enough to carry it by myself, it was an art to carry it without spilling any. It was often cold outside but in the shed with the cows it was warm, I loved it in there and learned every one of the cow's names. I would get tea or coffee in a big tin mug, so hot you would burn your mouth on the side of it. I started to follow Keith and changed my habits from having sugar in everything to none at all, all he ever added was honey.

I became something of a surrogate son to Keith and Janet, even after they were married, I'd be there having breakfast with them in the morning and because my dad didn't have time for me I definitely had a craving for love and attention. I didn't expect money for helping Keith out, having a bit of food and drink, and the company was enough for me. Money didn't even ever cross my mind. I had a paper round during the week days when I was a child and always had the ethic instilled in me that if I wanted anything I had to work for it myself. So I would get a little bit of money for myself that I'd earned. It was all about working hard and I learned very early on that you get something out of life if you put something into it. If you want something you have to put the effort in because I didn't get anything any other way. Asking for it didn't do any good, working for it did. Regardless of the weather you had to get up early - cold, wet, windy, you had to do it and it wasn't easy work, nor were you paid well for the work involved. But I got used to it, the responsibility of work is it doesn't matter what the situation is, you still had to do it. My mam or dad wouldn't have got up and done my paper round if I said I had a headache or something like that, there was just no way. You could have two broken arms, two broken legs and a broken neck and you'd still get kicked out. I've seen parents doing paper rounds for kids now if they can't, or won't, do it and you think, 'what the heck is that all about?'

Even when my dad got a better job, the kids saw no extra rewards for it. He became a manager but there was nothing extra. I didn't ask for anything. I got a bike one Christmas but it turned out to be a little embarrassing more than anything else. We were given these little bikes which had to last us until we were sixteen, Gemini 22 if I remember correctly. By the end the seat and handlebars had no more room to extend and they just popped out, so I had to ride this little bike with tiny wheels. I'm sure it looked really stupid but it got me about at a time when everyone else was riding Choppers.

It was the work with Keith that I truly loved. I loved achieving something but more than that I was striving for somebody to recognise me, to see me as someone a little more special and that's what Keith did. After all the other lads had stopped helping him out it was just me and that meant I received full focus from him. I was the person who got a pat on the back: "Good lad, well you've worked hard, haven't you?" It was the first time I had experienced that and it was just what I needed, everything that had been lacking at home. My response was to work even harder, which gave me a focal point, I had a focus to do better and achieve because Keith recognised me.

One day as I was bringing the cows in, he said to me the most important words that have ever been said to me in my life, words that mean more to me than anything else. Now I completely understand what he meant though at the time I couldn't see it. Keith took me to one side.

"You," he said,

"Have a gift with animals."

"Gift?"

I was only young.

What did Keith mean, I have a gift?

The Howsons had a sheep dog named Jen and Keith likened me to this accomplished shepherd.

"You have a gift because you are like a sheepdog."

Keith hardly said a word to her, barely whistled; yet Jen knew what to do. She knew when to stop, to start, to get down, to get up, to move closer, to move back, to get those cows to do what they had to do.

"You have a gift, you have a sense of being able to know exactly when to stand, when to move back, when to come forward."

Keith went on, "Some people don't pick that up in a lifetime and you've got it at eleven-years-old. You know what to do, you never take that extra step."

Unbeknownst to me, Keith had been watching me. He was not only a hard worker and a terrific farmer, but a sharp observer. Today I understand what he meant. People often take that one step too far with animals and it will make them bolt. Or they'll not go close enough so the animal won't take any notice of them or generally they'll crowd an animal which panics it. But I seem to know, and I've always known. I used to look into their eyes and seem to have some sort of communication going on that said, "I know what you're going to do next," and I pre-empted it by moving one way or another or, if necessary, standing back. Those words from him were extremely important, and that encouragement did spur me on, though I didn't appreciate the magnitude of what he had said at the time.

But he was right; I did have a gift with the animals. If I was at the farm alone, I would know exactly what to do. Sometimes I could go into the field and I would fall asleep leaning on a cow. I remember old Annie, she was an Ayrshire and I could lie down on her back, with my head on her belly and fall asleep and she wouldn't even move. I could do that with a number of them in fact. I had relationships with the cows shall we say. Now there are friends of mine who might raise an eyebrow at that statement, but I had relationships with those cows and they *were* relationships because it was like you could talk to them and honestly, they could talk back to you.

Now of course they weren't speaking directly to me, there were no words involved, but we communicated. I can sense what they feel, what they are thinking, I relate to them and they relate to me. Today, without speaking a word, I can do exactly the same with a rhino as I could do back then with a cow. I can walk in, they won't budge, they don't see me as a threat, I can lie down and I can play with my rhino's. I am accepted as a family member - no fear from them or from myself. I now realise that Keith was so right when he said I had a special gift, it is an unbelievable relationship I enjoy with animals.

It is also pronounced with the giraffes. Often my staff at the park can have real trouble trying to get the giraffes to go outside. They can have been at it for hours sometimes and then they'll finally relent and ask me. I can walk in, I look at them and I basically say to them, 'Come on, stop messing, it's better for you out there than in here,' and they look at me and it is as if they think, 'Well, yeah, fair enough' and they just turn around, walk straight out and I don't have to do anything further. It doesn't work 100% of the time, but certainly 90%.

The staff sometimes don't realise that it isn't about shouting at the animal or trying to do what you want them to. They don't communicate with the animal properly to let them know what they want them to do. The way I communicate with the animal is to make them realise they need not be frightened, that everything outside is okay for them. The bottom line is the animal needs to believe it is their decision to do something, they have to want to do it themselves.

If you push it too quickly, too fast or you try to make it do something it doesn't really want to do, it's going to react badly against you. That is where problems occur with animals because people don't look ahead to see any potential fears or problems from the animal's perspective. It's impossible to teach. I have never seen anybody else who's worked for me yet who's got the same ability, one or two have a gift but not on the same level also some have shown special talents, which we will get to.

Some people might think it is just bravery (or stupidity!) to go into a group of rhinos but it isn't a case of being fearless - many times I am very cautious myself. It is healthy respect which the animals also pick up on. You can't be blasé or cocky. Every time I go in with rhinos I am watching exactly what I do and I'm pre-empting what can potentially go wrong. There are plenty of potential accidents and it wouldn't necessarily be my fault, it could be somebody else banging a crisp bag or something and if I'm the wrong side of a rhino, the rhino could swing round and flatten me.

I would never be at the bottom of a hill looking up at a rhino because the speed he can come down it is ten times faster than the speed he can come up.

You've also got to have a natural ability to know what's dangerous and what isn't. Again it's something you can't just teach someone. Some people can play the piano and some people are pianists. Some people can paint a picture and some people are artists. Some people can act and other people are just totally natural and it just oozes from them and you can see other people have to force it. People can work at it but some are entirely natural, they don't have to put any effort into it because it's there. Some people work with animals and some people have a gift and I do believe without any shadow of a doubt I've got a gift.

It doesn't just apply to animals who already know me, the same goes for any animal even if I have not encountered them before. I can calm animals down better than anyone and my staff rarely want an animal to arrive without my being there. I've only ever made a mistake with judging an animal once in my life, it was a horrible one but I made that mistake.

Generally I can do things with animals other people could never get away with. Recently we had to introduce two jaguars together, they'd never met each other and one was twice the size of the other, and I really thought the big one would kill the smaller one as soon as he saw it. So I went in to look at them, they were in separate pens. I thought to myself, 'he's big but he's not aggressive, she is small and she's searching for love somehow'.

I went away to have a cup of tea and I thought about it. I came back in and looked at them again. I started speaking to them, though not out loud.

I asked them, 'Are you going to be alright, are you going to kill her or not?'

I looked at them and somehow or other I decided they would be safe together. Most people would have thought I was insane for putting these two together straight away, they would normally have weeks to get used to each other. But the very day that they arrived I put them together and they've been absolute best buddies ever since, they just went perfectly together.

I've done that with so many animals I know my staff are astounded sometimes. Most of the time, even when putting tigers together, things have gone fine. But the one time it did go wrong it went spectacularly wrong. I had a young lioness that I had to introduce to two older ones as well as a male and after months of close housing I finally got it introduced to the male and everything went perfect and I thought, 'fantastic, that went perfectly.'

After a little while I decided it was the right time to try one of the females on her own, the quietest of the two. Everything seemed to be fine so we opened the slide and the female ran in, grabbed her by the back of the neck and killed her. I never saw it coming, didn't read it correctly. It was all over so quickly there was nothing I could do but it was devastating.

Chapter 4
School , first crush and early education

My very first crush in life was Mrs Whiteley. I had moved to an all boy's school right behind my home, called Broughton Road School and here I was, my first teacher, a gorgeous female straight out of university. I know she was straight out of uni as I've met her since and she explained to me. She also told me that I was a very special person in her class. At the time I think she knew she was special to me as well. She was a young lady back then, just 22 or so, though that seems light years away when you are only eight yourself.

I worked like crazy for Mrs Whiteley. I was top of the class for spelling, for maths, for everything. I really wanted to prove something to her and I remember there were about five David's in our class, so I had to stand out. If anyone shouted 'David' about five people turned their heads at once. It was a popular name in 1961.

My affection for Mrs Whiteley had broader implications. I always gravitated towards women rather than men. My next year teacher was symbolic of this. Mr Morgan was a big moustachioed brute and I did not like him one bit. I certainly believe that a key to learning is to like your teacher because in his class I dropped right back. It was the mark of a real change in me - I suddenly did not want to go to school, I was just so unhappy.

The following year I had a male teacher called Mr Riley. He was short, loud and bearded and was reminiscent of the dwarf king from the *Lord Of The Rings* films.

In Year Four I was happy again because I had a female teacher, Mrs Berry. I adored her and excelled under her. The problem I seemed to have with males in my life had all started with my father. Because I felt rejected by my dad, I thought all males were just people, I never felt a love from them, like I wanted them near me or they wanted me to be near them. From then on I seemed to always have a problem with men, something which continues at a lesser level to this day. My three best friends are male funnily enough, but beyond that, I prefer to associate with women, I'm much more comfortable in their company. This is one of the reasons I have more female than male staff at the Park, though I'll be the first to say that in general women work much harder than men.

Though I did well in Mrs Berry's class I was constantly blighted by school reports which said I had the ability but must 'try harder'. My son Hari actually has the same thing today - his reports are identical to mine. I didn't feel that I had to try too hard at school, most of it came naturally to me. But my teachers knew that and thought I should try to make the best of my abilities. At the time however I was more interested in working on the farm. I went to school all week, then I went to the farm at the weekends. It was as if I didn't exist in my own family.

It's funny how the male influence seemed to all come from Keith Howson, and though he was a male we got on. He was a strong farming man but there was also a gentle quality about him. A devout Christian, he always treated me very well. He just knew I had ability and he encouraged it. It was a wonderful thing to do, from a wonderful man. It wasn't long after I started working for Keith that he developed Brucellosis. It hit the cows first and after they all had to be put down he caught it himself and he nearly died. Brucellosis was a bacterial disease which was as serious as Foot and Mouth, so as soon as Brucellosis appeared in your herd, every single animal had to be shot and burned. Keith had to cull all the cattle on the farm and disinfect everything. Then the disease got hold of his blood and seeped into his brain, he was lucky to survive. One redeeming feature that instantly altered was that all his hair turned completely white, he had plenty of hair but it just turned ghostly almost overnight.

When Keith and Janet had their first baby, Michael, I recall buying flowers and a ceramic vase as a present for Janet when she came out of hospital. As happy as I was for them the arrival of a new child on the scene was difficult for me to handle. Up until then it was as if I had been their son and suddenly they had their own baby, so although they still let me tag along I did feel a little pushed out. I'd been searching for love and to feel special and I had found it with Keith and Janet. I wasn't close to my parents, I was hardly close to my siblings either, I would never actually play with my brothers, they were never a part of the team, they were never out doing the silly things I was. My brothers never knew about it, they were totally different to me.

I was always different at school as well. Most of the teachers seemed to like me but in hindsight I would have been regarded as one of the geeky crowd by the other kids. I was never a sporty person and have always felt that academic achievement should mean more than whether you are good at hitting a cricket ball. Yet all those who were good at sport seemed to get the kudos. It's still the same today.

Being interested in farming when I attended a school in the town was seen as strange by many children. They thought I must be odd because I was interested in cows and sheep. I probably didn't help myself either because I would rarely take part in group activities and I also deliberately rebelled. I've never been a conformist. The greatest football team of the time was Leeds United–in the late 1960s and early 70s they were the most successful club and most kids supported them.

But I didn't want to conform, I never wanted to be the same as everyone else, I had never supported a football team in my life. But suddenly I decided I would support a team myself, only it wouldn't be Leeds, it was going to be Stoke City. There was no basis at all for this, after all, Stoke never won anything, so it wasn't about being successful or a glory hunter, it was about being different. Mike Field was on my bandwagon and fell in love with the Potters too. I wanted to stand out, I wanted some attention, so Stoke City it was.

This led to gentle ribbing to which I would always have a reply, though I was never a fighter. By senior school I wished I was as I started to get bullied, to the point where I was scared to go into school. I played truant a lot because of it, I didn't want to go to school and I daren't tell anybody. I rarely got hit but there were a lot of threats - I wasn't allowed to go to certain places or do certain things or I would be threatened with a kicking. Sometimes I think if they had hit me it would have been better to get it out of their system but they never did. The ringleader was a guy called David Bradford but one day he got his comeuppance. There was a lad I got on well with in my class, John Rawlinson, a tall, stocky lad from a farm. One day I inadvertently told John about David Bradford and that I had to walk a certain way home to avoid him.

"I don't like him either," John said. "I'll sort him out for you." He completely leathered this kid and told him never to go near me again, and he didn't.

Whatever happened at school however, I always remained in the top stream for every subject. Somehow I managed it, and that was without even doing my homework. As far as I was concerned I didn't have time for homework, I was busy working on the farm. Yet my parents never even noticed, and Parent's Evening was more like Parent Evening because only my mam would ever go, never my dad. Even with homework, they never even knew I had it, much less forced me to do it. I was just left to my own devices. I had free reign to be out of the house for the whole of the weekend, they weren't bothered. I would already be out of the house in the morning when they got up and then just casually come back in at tea time. I'd be an absolute mess when I came in and typically; my dad hated me being on the farm. In particular he hated the smell I would be carrying. Looking back it was understandable but they made me strip in the porch, right down to my underpants, before I could even come in the house. I never noticed the smell of course, the same way South Lakes' rhino keepers do not realise they are carrying the pungent stench of rhinos with them at all times, the rhino smell sticks with you forever. It was like that for me at Keith's farm.

My father never encouraged me in any way whatsoever and I always thought he was against my chosen pastime. It seemed as if Dad wanted me to go left and I was always going right. I remember hellish arguments with him. I often went completely out of my way to annoy him because I wanted attention from him. Though I was hungry for their acceptance and encouragement, in hindsight they did me a favour with their way of handling the family. Though I was very rebellious and had little time for getting my head down into academic work, I could certainly read and retain information well enough. This actually meant that a lot of the time I would pass exams even though I hadn't exactly 'revised' for the test. I just remembered it the first time around. I was always interested in mechanics and science, things that perhaps I might have expected my dad could tell me more about. Instead I was given Ladybird books which at the time had a series of books explaining how various things worked. Consequently I amassed a huge amount of information on different subjects that I was interested in, something which would come in very handy later on.

I was fascinated with everything–how a petrol engine works, how a tractor works, how does milk get to us. I had a variety of books which explained all of this and then there were books on volcanoes and geology as well as space and a whole host of scientific subjects. Most kids would leave these huge books on the shelf but I ate it all up and learned a tremendous amount about nature because it interested me.

An example might be that at one point I learned all about grass, not the herbal variety, but the grass you walk on. I heard them talking on the farm about species of grasses one day and learned that, contrary to most people's beliefs that grass is just grass, and it's green, there were all types of different grasses: long grass, short grass, broad leafed, thin leafed, ones with high sugar, ones with low sugar, ones with protein and I was fascinated by all this, this variety of life. I would also read through the *Farmers Weekly* when Keith had finished with it, always learning and developing more knowledge about the work going on around me.

My reading didn't stop there either. I also loved the Enid Blyton books, such as *The Famous Five* and *The Secret Seven*. The *Ring O' Bells Mystery* was my absolute all time favourite, I read that I don't know how many times. A lot of the time I read adventure stories and this fed my imagination. I didn't have a television in my room or visit the cinema so I created worlds in my imagination just from reading. Every night before bed I would read and then put the paperback under my pillow. I was into a lot of fantasy adventure material, like most boys really, but predominantly I liked to learn about things I would see in front of me.

For Keith it must have been quite annoying really.
How?
Why?
How?
Why?
When?
Tell me.

Then there were the practical skills which most lads learned from their father. I learned these from Keith. Simple things which were a practical goldmine, such as how to brush the floor correctly. There is not just one way to do it, if you do it properly you can use half the energy and half the time. He taught me all sorts of useful information regarding hammers, nails, nuts, bolts and threads, even how to mix concrete. I will forever be greatly indebted to Keith because there is no way I could have done the things I have since without him.

One of the happiest times of my childhood were spent at my Aunt Betty and Uncle Jim's house in a small village called Priest Hutton, near Carnforth. They were not strictly our aunt and uncle but we referred to them as such, and they may as well have been. My brother Michael and I were sent there for our half term holidays in October when I was ten. The week we spent there seemed to last forever and I wished it could have. It was an escape from home and we had some wonderful adventures in the country. Additionally I was shown a lot of attention from my aunt and uncle. Jim worked for the railway and was also a small time farmer with a few beef cattle which was perfect for me. It was in Priest Hutton that I experienced my very first real romance and crush on a girl of my own age.

I fell head over heels in love with Diane Bainbridge in just a week. We played together and visited her home, a rambling farm house in the village. When I had to leave she gave me a yellow handkerchief which I have kept all these years. Unfortunately Betty and Jim have long since passed, but I still chat with their daughter Jean and husband Jeff recalling all the things we got up to. Diane is often mentioned, so it was a memorable romance for everyone. But it wasn't just the relationship with Diane that makes me recall those times with fondness - it is the fact that I was loved and cared about.

We went on this holiday about three times each October if I recollect. I always loved the connection I had with my extended family and continued to visit as soon as I got my own wheels. I once rode all the way on push bikes along with Mike Field, a distance of some 36 miles.

I still see Jean, Jeff and their daughter Rachel today, often having them round at Christmas. I have only ever seen Diane once again in my life at Uncle Jim's funeral and she was still as good looking then over 30 years on.

I realised at senior school - once the girls joined up with the boy's school - that another thing I was quite good at was pulling the girls. My very first girlfriend was Natalie Hopkins and she was the object of every young male's desire in the school, perhaps because she had developed at a faster rate than her peers. Everybody wanted to go out with Natalie so it was like a little challenge, I wondered if I could be the one.

One night I donned my best bright multi-coloured tank top with my flared trousers, a combination that would probably see you shot today, and went down to the 10p Friday night disco at the local cricket club. You were supposed to only be allowed to have soft drinks but some kids used to sneak in cigarettes, most of which were quickly extinguished by the supervisors who would come around and take them away from you.

I started to ingratiate myself with Natalie, sitting next to her and chatting her up. I noticed quickly that if I was to be accepted I'd have to smoke like she did. Given I was only twelve it was quite a surprise that I managed to buy a pack of ten Embassy Regal but after jumping that hurdle I decided I would have to light one up and stroll in smoking it. I lit one up, swaggered up to Natalie, took a big drag on it and threw up. I was sick as a dog, it did not sit well with me at all and it was clear this particular approach certainly did not work. I learned right there and then that swaggering in and being somebody you're not is not the best ploy in life to get a woman.

The first thing Mam said to me when I got home was, "Have you been smoking?" I must have stunk of smoke every night I went to that place because it used to be full of it. "No I haven't," I answered but she knew - "Yes you have," she said, to which I promptly threw up. I must have been green around the gills, she knew straight away.

In the end though I managed to get together with Natalie Hopkins, without the aid of cigarettes and I had plenty of kisses with her. I was bored after a while though, I wasn't exactly thinking long term. My first kiss had come shortly before when we had been playing 'Truth or Dare' in the backyard of Mike Field's house and they had an outside toilet. Here we would be dared to kiss a girl. The girl in question was some five years older than us which was some gap, and some achievement. The kiss itself was less impressive though. As the door to the romantic confines of the outside toilet closed she leaned over and gave me a sloppy kiss in the dark, a kiss which tasted like fish and chips.

By the time I was fourteen I was having more and more input on the farm with Keith, once it was legal he even let me drive a tractor though he was always very sensible and reluctant to let me do anything remotely dangerous, especially as Keith knew my taste for adventure and exploration. Despite my insistence on pushing the boundaries, I was always a respectful child and had been raised to speak properly and politely. Keith was no exception, there was never a profanity uttered in his household, they were good Christian folk. My parents never swore either. I myself was inadvertently religious, given I was part of the choir and every Sunday I would attend church with my family two or three times. It gave me a good grounding in morals and respect.

There were also bible classes at Keith and Janet's. Their Christian ethics really manifested in their relationship, which was something that seeped into my character. I wanted to grow up to emulate their sterling example of how a family should run. They had ups and downs like every couple but they always stuck together and I truly admired their love and dedication for each other. This is where the Christian morals came in; you can work your way out of problems if you live by the code of ethics in The Ten Commandments. The rules are designed that way–that you shouldn't get into trouble in the first place, but if you do, there is a way out. So I had no problem attending bible classes at their house.

I became a choirboy mainly because we had a church organist living next door to us. The family were wonderful people, Mr and Mrs Warton. Mr Warton was a charming old man and his wife was one of the nicest people you could ever possibly meet. She was a chest hugger, always giving me enormous cuddles, in fact that was the first time I almost drowned, in Mrs Warton's chest. She was the grandmother everyone would dream of having.

Church was a regular commitment for myself and the family, all of my siblings were in the choir at some point. Personally I loved the singing. At one point however I decided I didn't want to spend all day in church on a Sunday, I wanted to be at the farm. My dad argued with me about it but the insistence on trying to make me go only stopped me from actually doing so. My whole belief was, and is, shouldn't God be the only person to question what you are doing? The whole concept of Christian faith and almost every other faith is that you don't hold grudges against people, you forgive and forget and you have peace. It is the basis of just about every religion there is.

The first time I ever experienced profanity was when Keith and I went up to the farm of a fellow named Richard Parker. When we got to the kitchen in this household I couldn't believe it, Richard and even his wife and kids punctured every sentence with the f-word. I think there were only three other words used the whole time I was there. It was while at this farm that I first rode on a tractor. My role was simple, I had to drive the tractor in a low gear in a straight line while several of the lads at the farm would throw bales of hay onto the back of the tractor. What no one had realised was that when I was supposed to turn around, I didn't have enough weight to control this huge vehicle, and unbeknownst to me, there was a steep drop at the end of the field. I rolled down the hill at a deadly speed, all the while in possible danger of jack-knifing and killing myself instantly. At the time I didn't realise I was in much danger at all but later Keith confided to me how frightening the whole episode was and just how close I had been to death that day. The tractor could have rolled at any time but I managed to keep it upright until being rescued by all the other workers. From then on Keith was even more careful about my four-wheel escapades.

Later on I also helped out at another farm, Dick's Stables, where this time I was paid a small amount of money. My overriding memory of that place, aside from loving every second I spent there, was of eating tomato and salt sandwiches. As unpleasant as it sounds now, those sandwiches would taste like nectar, big thick bread and a flask of tea. Perhaps because I would be so hungry after all the work I had put in, those sandwiches went down like a perfectly cooked Indian meal might today.

For me the emphasis was always on putting in the effort, to be rewarded, not by money, but by recognition. Whenever I was asked to do something I would give every ounce of my effort, and then delve into the extra reserves of energy and effort I could muster. I would always go that step further because I wanted to be recognised for putting that effort in. when praise did come on those farms where I helped out, I would feel ten feet tall. The recognition was beautiful but all it made me do was to work even harder. It was perhaps this insatiable thirst for praise that led to my becoming a workaholic in later years, though I was already on that path as a teenager. The constant need for encouragement or acknowledgement meant in some ways I could never be satisfied. As a consequence of this, even after all Keith had done for me, I couldn't be satiated by the wonderful treatment I had working for him and his family. In the end Keith couldn't give me all I wanted. There were no girls working at the Howson farm.

Chapter 5
Adolescence and the urge to travel.

The greatest thing you can be given in life, especially as a child, is an opportunity. The key to your life, your entire future is in being given the chance to show your worth, to show what you are made of. With opportunity you can make something happen. Keith Howson was the first man in my life I saw as a person who cared about me and helped me to achieve things and gave me that opportunity. What he couldn't give me however was the freedom to become a fully-fledged teenager. It was in that midst of pubescent adolescence, after five years in Keith's company, that I did something I am certainly not proud of, I let Keith down to start working for Wilf Rigg at Elliscales Farm. There were two reasons, one was the sheer indifference to any form of authority that Rigg harboured and the other was his daughter Julie. I fancied Julie a lot, she had soft, flowing hair and a beautiful broad smile. In my eagerness to make Julie my girlfriend I began to walk home from school via the Rigg farm. In hindsight, the way I treated Keith was terrible. After all he had done for me, to just leave him that way was incredibly unfair and selfish, but I was still thinking with my young teenage brain.

Ironically Wilf Rigg had, like Keith, been to Canada and then returned to rent the Elliscales that was formerly run by his Father, Benny. For the time and in the local area, Wilf was very progressive. He was the first person in the area to grow maize, which would be fed to the cattle and for the locality this was a truly progressive development. I warmed to his methods and became very interested in the whole methods behind growing the corn, and often took it home myself to eat fresh corn on the cob.

There was one problem with Wilf, he was an alcoholic. It didn't help that he was a chain smoker as well, given my hatred of smoking. Wilf would head down to the off license to buy the largest possible containers of ale that he could, huge seven pint tins. Still, he was certainly a progressive thinker - not to mention a friendly fellow - and there were many factors to like about the Rigg set up, not least of which was his gorgeous daughter. Wilf's car was a white Vauxhall but he had an 8-track cassette player, something clearly straight from North America, and he would often listen to Johnny Cash and other country music, perhaps sowing the seed for my own love of country which came much later.

Wilf's lack of parental guidance over me allowed me to get away with far more than I could on Keith's farm, in fact I could pretty much do anything I wanted, including drive a tractor as much as I liked. Wilf allowed me to do everything on the farm, while he and his mates would spend time in his workshop drinking. I'd be left to milk the cows, alone morning and night. It was particularly irresponsible because I had no grasp of the technicality behind how a farm ran, I didn't understand the energy they needed in order to feed, that would come later. All I knew was you put food in front of the cows, they ate it, and went quiet. You put the unit on and when you felt that there was no milk left in the bag you took the unit off and emptied it in the tank. After that they would need mucking out. At the end of the day, Wilf would ask me,

"Have you finished?"

"Yes," I would answer, "everything's finished."

Wilf would then head in for his dinner having not done a thing all day!

My modus operandi, to impress Julie, was quietly working however, something that kept me going day after day. I wouldn't just work the day shift, I would stay late to make sure Julie knew I was there. Her dad wasn't too keen but regardless, I managed to start a relationship with Julie. In my mind at the time I was in love with her, and it helped that she became the first girl who let me explore her body - holding, touching and feeling in that innocent, naïve way that kids do. Julie was lovely but it wasn't the longest courtship and after a short while we split.

One night after we had split up Julie had a party up at the farm. On the farm grounds was an old cottage which was fairly run down but it had an upstairs room which she used as a den and one night she had a party which for some reason I wasn't invited to. This irritated me because I had no idea why, though my mind turned as to whether she might have a new boyfriend. In the spare room in the cottage there was enormous amount of junk but I found a way through to a view point, a keyhole through to the bedroom, the makeshift den. To my dismay, and amazement I saw a group of girls sitting in a circle, playing strip poker. This cold spare room of the cottage got warmer and warmer as I witnessed them all keep going and going, taking off all of their clothing before they were down to underwear. Eileen Jinks, a girl I really fancied, drew the short straw and was supposed to take her bra off. Suddenly Eileen developed a case of shyness though she was being egged on by the others.

Eileen was having none of it and soon screamed, before jumping up to run out of the room, the problem being she ran right towards the door where I was peeping through the keyhole. Like a scene from *Benny Hill* I had to try and gain some composure and get well away from the door. Luckily they had locked the door which bought me a few seconds, though as I fell over on my way to try and get out of the house, my escape was hardly smooth. I stumbled over all the junk, before jumping out of the window and nearly fell ten feet to the roof. I ran and ran, thinking they were bound to have seen or heard me. Given I had almost broke my neck in all the pandemonium I presumed they definitely knew I was there.

The next day I saw the girls and began to ask them whether they had had a good party, teasing them a little. Eventually though my sarcasm dropped me in it when I said something only a peeping tom at the scene of the party would have known. It turned out to be quite amusing in the end, with them threatening that if I told their dad, they would also tell him I was there watching and I'd be in just as much trouble.

Eventually, working on Wilf Rigg's farm, the inevitable happened - I was offered a drink of beer. Personally I never liked the taste and still don't today, but I started to drink the beer he gave me and would be milking the cows high on alcohol. It was a thrill at first and I'm sure Wilf thought he was making me feel good about myself by thinking I could drink beer at fourteen, but in the end I decided I really did not like the buzz of alcohol. To this day alcohol affects me quicker than other people, I must have some non native blood within me because it goes straight to my head, I can only drink so much. At such a young age, being exposed to large amounts of beer was bad news. It certainly was for Wilf as his persistent alcohol consumption and smoking would contribute to his death.

Even in my adolescence I would come to my senses and realise the good things about working for Wilf were far outweighed by the bad and I missed being around Keith. So after two years working with Wilf I went back to Keith. Being the gentleman he is, Keith seemed to understand, despite being upset at my disloyalty. It would never quite be the same, they do say 'never go back', but I was still working hard and developing my interest in farming and hard work as I always had.

Once I was back at Keith's I developed a very strong bond with his daughter Rachel. There was an instantaneous attachment to his little girl and I would take her everywhere with me, giving them a break every afternoon. I even took her on a motorbike which I used to ride around the farm by the time she was four-years-old, though she was always sworn to secrecy. Janet would have gone ballistic. Later she found out and revealed she would have had a heart attack if she had known at the time!

By the time I was eighteen I was extremely close to Rachel, it was really like having a child of my own. I still have photographs of us building snowmen and going for walks on the farm. Rachel began to share my love for nature and we would go on long nature trail walks, watching the swans with their cygnets and looking for foxes and other animals. Today it is very different. Sadly, there is a great big bypass over that whole area. Rachel now has a few children of her own and she and her mother visit the zoo year after year. It is always wonderful to reminisce with them.

During the times with Rachel I had my first experience of a death in the family, the first time anyone I knew had died. It was my nana. One night she had had a stroke, from which she never truly recovered, when she had her second stroke it killed her. I helped carry the coffin with my brothers. The day of the funeral my granddad told everyone: "I want to die, I want to go with her."

He was determined to die and stopped eating. Within the year, by Christmas time, he looked more like a refugee in a concentration camp than my granddad. He was just skin and bone. After 60 plus years of being with his wife he couldn't face life without her. He would tell me all through the year that he just wanted to die. He started to lose his faculties and many times he would talk to me thinking I was my dad, or someone else, though sometimes he could remember who I was. But quite often he would tell me stories as if I were a stranger. I would sit with him often, though it was a very strange, almost macabre situation. Here I was listening to my granddad, whom I loved so dearly, telling me his life story before knowing he was about to go to be with my nana. I had a yearning to listen to him and spend the time with him, knowing there was not long left. I admired Granddad's dedication to his wife, she was his life, the immense devotion to one person, and one person alone.

In effect their expectations were nothing fancy and they never saw outside their insular box. That was it, that was their life, there was nothing else. Their love was everything. They would do their shopping at the Co-Op and come home and watch one of the two channels on their television - it was a very simple, yet beautiful, life.

After a while Granddad was given his wish to die, I think his medication was stopped leaving him to go peacefully and naturally. On Christmas Eve that year he passed away. It wasn't as sad as it could have been however because we all knew that he was where he wanted to be, it was almost like a perfect Christmas present. Yet there was a huge swathe of conflicting emotions, he was in the right place for him but I desperately didn't want to lose him.

My Nana and Granddad Atkinson would also pass not long afterwards. It was a sober development to suddenly be faced without all of my grandparents. In the past there had been many parties to go to at Christmas time, and suddenly they weren't there. The funny thing is I have no idea how our entire family used to fit in their houses. I had to go to my nana's house after she died to help empty it and I could not believe just how tiny this place was. I couldn't work out how you got mam and dad with us five kids, uncle Jim and aunty Dorothy with their two kids, uncle Frank and aunt Marjory with two kids and Nana and Granddad and we all sat down to tea. It was like something out of *Doctor Who* - a tardis, but somehow it all worked.

We would all play games around the table though I'm sure we must have been greased in order to all fit alongside each other because we must have been tucked in like sardines. I also helped carry my granddad's coffin, it was something of a tradition that I always took part in. My granddad had spent a life in industry and smoked a pipe, it was angina that got him in the end, though sadly he would go on a relative's Ruby wedding night. After that it was my nana who faded away, and she became diabetic, another skeleton. It was all the more poignant because we had always called her Super Gran.

As for me, it was becoming all the more obvious which direction my life was taking, even if I had no concrete plan at the time. One thing was for sure, a life of academia was not for me. If anything proved that it was the time of my exams at school. Here I was, after going all through school at the top of the class, a sure-fire prediction for Grade A's all the way. And yet, when it came to the time of the exams I lost all of my impetus and just could not be bothered to try. It just didn't seem important to me, nobody pushed me, my parents didn't push me, nobody seemed to care except one or two teachers who really thought I was throwing my life away. Nevertheless, I didn't revise a thing, I just went straight to the exam rooms without doing a thing. I lost it, especially in the last year, I just didn't want to be in school at all.

All I wanted was to be in the outside world working on a farm. As much as my dad could be disappointed about my choice in life, he certainly decided he wasn't impressed at my choice of career - I was a yokel and had no promising future. My mam did at least understand where my heart lay and gave me an element of support. She knew I had to work in nature and not in a shipyard. If Dad had any aspirations for me at all in life then it would have been for me to become an engineer, to follow his steps in a shipyard. But I didn't want to do that, I wanted to be out there working on the farm. I absolutely loved it, it was my life, I didn't do anything else. I didn't play football, I didn't play rugby, I didn't play cricket. I tried to play tennis.

I had a friend called Bertrand Park, Bertrand was an absolute star. In fact he went on to study at both Oxford and Cambridge and became a neurosurgeon. He always was a contradiction to me because Bertrand was the most intelligent person I've ever met in my life, and yet he smoked! I couldn't understand how a neurosurgeon who knew all about the human brain could poison his body with cigarettes. It didn't stop him being a superhuman tennis player however. We would play tennis, near my childhood bombsite at the cricket club. He always thrashed me, it was just depressing, he never ever *let* me win, he used to keep me there as a partner because I got so depressed I didn't want to play.

"I'm not doing this anymore."

6-0, 6-0, 6-0.

Game, set and match Bertrand Park.

He was that good I could barely return his serve.

"Come on, just serve a few soft ones so I can at least get on the scoreboard."

But he never did.

During my childhood years I had a fascination for railways, I started train spotting, whilst to many it may seem a geeky thing to do, it was actually a wonderful way to build friendships and travel the country. It became a bit of an obsession and I used to spend a lot of my spare time at the railway station at Dalton to see specific trains come through and collect the numbers of the engines. This hobby expanded many aspects of my life at the time away from the farm. I still have all my books from that time in my little historic library. My love for trains led me to travel all over Europe in the future and to own my own steam railway eventually.

My first true travelling adventure came when I was sixteen. I decided I needed a holiday so I saved up all the money I could from my paper round. I wanted to combine my love for trains, which was only on the increase, and get out there somewhere. I ended up buying a Scottish rail ticket and going off to Scotland for a week on my own. I literally toured the length and breadth of the country which looks small but when you start to traverse the Highlands and beyond, it is quite vast. I didn't have a lot of money so I had to spend my nights sleeping on the trains. That meant that each journey needed to be long enough that I would have time to sleep, so it was often from one end to the other, one diagonal extreme to the next.

I travelled as far as John O'Groats and then to other parts such as Aberdeen. It was while in Aberdeen, a notorious fishing port, that I had a particularly foul experience. As I was out searching for Aberdeen Loco Sheds I accidentally got splashed with rancid fish water one day. As I recall, a vehicle drove into a puddle and the pungent water soaked my trousers completely. Unfortunately I had no spare clothes with me. I tried to wash them but it made no difference so I had the embarrassing stench etched into me everywhere I went, which was especially unpleasant when I would be on a train with the heating on. The smell was so horrific that I actually came home just to have a bath and get a change of clothes, and then I was back out again.

There was never an issue at home, they didn't even know where I was going or what I was doing. Mam encouraged me to be independent, though I was completely different from my siblings, none of them ever did anything like that. In the past I had gone for weekends away with a few other lads but I did so on my own.

I traversed the whole of Scotland though a lot of the time I would hang around the railway station of wherever I was. Much of my time was spent on the train because what I learned was, if you can get a train that leaves Edinburgh at 11 o'clock at night and lands in Thurso at 6 o'clock in the morning you'd be able to sleep as the trains were often quiet at night. So I would have a sandwich and a cup of tea, usually with a full seat to myself, and just rest that way.

As well as trains I always had a fascination with motorbikes, many years later I would own a Harley Davidson. Yet, the two-wheeler would be the reason that my first, more serious relationship, wouldn't last. There was a beautiful red haired girl who started coming to Keith and Janet's bible classes, Elaine Walker. She was a year younger than me but I fell for her charms, luscious long, red curly hair and a figure to die for. She was shy to begin with but after a while she allowed me to start taking her out and we started to ride motorbikes together. I had my trail bike and she bought a little 125cc and we often went off driving together. We moved on to a more serious relationship quite quickly, where I felt I wanted to settle down with her. Unfortunately her mother did not share my enthusiasm, she always disliked me for some reason. Perhaps it was the fact that I was a rebellious person who was coercing her daughter into fast, dangerous motorbikes. Her mother became rather aggressive towards me, leaving me in no doubt as to her feelings about me. It led to a lot of sneaking around between myself and the red haired beauty. In the end, she was probably too nice and pure– she proved that by marrying a vicar I think some time later.

She ended up moving to a flat in Morecambe and went to Art college there, so I would often travel down to be with her but at the time I was experiencing a rather nomadic existence for me. I'd lost focus in my life, if I had ever had it, and didn't really have any idea where I was going. It would still be a long while before I would come to the right direction in life. I saw her for the first time in 32 years only a few weeks ago when she attended the zoo as a paramedic. Amazing how life turns these things up out of the blue, we said hi and smiled.

Chapter 6
Italy, football and romance

0.0943%.

1 out of 106.

Those figures are indelibly etched into my mind.

That was the result I attained in my first A-level for pure maths. I was honoured - no one in Ulverston Victoria High School had ever achieved such a record low score. I got the one mark because I thankfully remembered my name and managed to record it perfectly on the page. It was no wonder I got such a great score though, when the papers were handed out it was like a different language - I had no idea what the questions referred to, possibly because I hadn't actually been to a lesson.

I enrolled in the sixth form in order to further my educational career, though I had no idea why really. I had no interest in school and I still hated it. Nevertheless I had, for some reason, decided to continue at school and undertaken pure mathematics, applied maths, economics and biology. Amazingly, I only ended up failing algebra (pure maths) and passed the first year of all my other subjects, even though I had no idea what to do in my future. But I came to my senses and realised that I should be furthering the work which I was really interested in, and that meant working with nature. So I left Ulverston and enrolled at Myerscough College in Lancashire, where I joined a Practical Agriculture course. It wasn't studying for a degree as such but these days it would amount to the same thing.

During my time in college one of the most memorable events was entering the Mighty Three Peaks race, where one had to climb the three highest peaks in the Pennines as fast as possible. I entered along with two lads I knew, Tom and Andy. The weather on the tops was terrible, the peat bogs were wet, deep and suction that ripped our boots clean off. It was an epic run, that turned into a walk or even crawl in some places. We entered a very respectable time of eight hours to complete a race that I happily would never enter again. I have been on some crazy walks since in the name of wildlife conservation but never to compete for 'fun'. I had the pleasure of meeting Tom at the park some time later when he brought his family for the day. We reminisced about the race amongst other things and it was a pleasure to see him again after 29 years.

Ironically at this point I also ended up in the shipyard, just like my dad would have wanted. I needed some cash so I took a summer job, in the x-ray department in Barrow shipyard. In hindsight I was doing quite a dangerous job, something not many people would probably fancy, working with gamma and x-rays and so on. Maybe there is something lurking in my body now, you never know, but I'm not concerned about it - in fact several of the people I worked with are still alive now! It was just a job, working with radiation for about six months. It was interesting to a point but I still wanted the outdoor life and here I was stuck inside. I knew I didn't want to be in a typical job that everyone else was in, I didn't want to work in the shipyard or be an electrician or a plumber or anything like that, I wanted to be different, I *knew* I wanted to be different.

My thirst for adventure led me to join the Royal Air Force when I was still a teenager. There was no solid reason for me doing this other than a deep respect and interest in the military. It fills your soul and makes you proud to watch the Trooping Of The Colour for instance. I have long been impressed with the bravery of the military, and there is no prouder job than serving your country.

It was partially a practical decision to look towards a more lifelong career. I had long sought only to become a farmer but my economics training led me to a very obvious realisation. With property prices going through the roof at the time I admitted to myself that I would never be able to afford a farm for myself and would be destined to work my behind off for someone else. Yes, I might be able to work in the industry I loved, but how would I ever progress?

I decided to apply for the position of Aircraft Engineering Technician which meant I would also be able to attend university, attaining a degree and getting paid at the same time. So, I went off to Swinderby in Lincolnshire to join the scores of other blokes who were attending basic training. For me, being the type who prefers female company it was a rude awakening to be surrounded by nothing but alpha males in an almost exclusively male dominated environment. I was terrified and instantly I missed my mother. I'd gone out of my way to escape my home life but when placed in such a difficult environment I was yearning for that comfort. Nevertheless I was very proud when I first wore my uniform. Polished boots, tie and cap all perfectly positioned, I certainly didn't look as if I were scared or doing the wrong thing, I looked as if I was ready to serve my country. The basic training was very hard and discipline was paramount, but I put my soul into it. There were medicals in each week and at one I failed the hearing test, it was a very specific test to ascertain high frequency ability because with jet engines this was important. I was brought back for further tests and told it was not possible for me to continue with the position that I had applied for. They suggested a different role but it was not for me and I made a decision to get out of the situation.

There were certainly elements of being in the forces that I liked - the physical side of it, the shooting, the basic training, the marching and the parade drills, but given it was so early in my RAF career they did the honourable thing and gave me a free pass out of the services.

I was already in admiration of the forces but having been in the beginnings of a career in that side of things I am full of respect for those who do that job to their full commitment and serve in Afghanistan and other dangerous situations. I acknowledge that they are very special people.

Everything happens for a reason, so they say and it would prove to be so very true for me.

When I got to 18 years old I started to go out on a Friday and

Saturday night as most kids of my age did. We would go round the pubs of Dalton one night and Ulverston the next. A group of around 8 lads all out for a good time and they could drink ! I reckon that they drunk between 8 and 10 pints of beer each on a typical night, getting inebriated in the process. I could not keep up at all after 2 pints I was not happy and feeling out of control of myself a feeling I never liked or enjoyed. They used to rib me a bit and eventually I just decided that this life wasn't for me. I still went out with them but decided to drink orange juice or Coke, you can imagine the resulting barrage of jokes and abuse I got from the lads and not long after I stopped all together .

The joke was on them though as I decided to save all my valued funds and invest them in travelling abroad, so when they all went to Blackpool for a weekend drinking for their holidays I was visiting all the culture capitals of Europe and I never ever have looked back since refusing to conform to the accepted norm.

During this time I picked up a more useful skill - I managed to learn basic Italian. My inspiration was simple - I was writing to a girl from Torino, Italy. This association came from a trip I made in 1980. I had a friend from Ulverston, from our train spotting days who was about three years younger than I was, I got on well with his family, they moved to Italy for his dads work as an interpreter and I went to stay there for a holiday, which I combined with attending the 1980 European football championships which were being held there. I was never particularly a football fan but it was obviously a huge event and it peaked my interest.

I met up with Andy Murray (not the tennis player, or Bertrand Park in disguise!) who lived down the road from Juventus' stadium, he and his family were all big fans of the club. One of the matches we managed to get tickets for was England versus Italy, but with him being based in Torino (Turin), we had tickets for the Italian end. I will always remember when Kevin Keegan hit the post with a shot and out of 80,000 I was the only one who shouted 'Wooooaaahhhh'. Andy promptly told me to sit down, somehow I got away with it. Given football hooliganism was a real problem at

Italy, football and romance

the time it was probably even luckier.

I also managed to get tickets for England against Belgium which became a very famous match for the events that unfolded. This time I managed to get into the England end though I wished I hadn't. We were soon being pelted with all sorts of makeshift missiles raining down upon us. You could smell the violence in the air. Eventually a fight broke out behind England goalkeeper Ray Clemence's goal. The fight escalated to the point where riot police and soldiers became involved, firing teargas in every possible direction. It was horrendous, I could hardly breathe. There was no distinction by the authorities over who was actually causing trouble, if you were there you were hit. We, luckily managed to avoid this, but it was very close. Suddenly the wind turned and the tear gas was being blown onto the pitch. The gas started to affect Ray Clemence, his eyes were streaming, and they had to stop the match. Altogether I was completely terrified. The match itself was fairly humdrum and the score was a disappointing 1-1.

Worse still we had to remain in the Stadio Comunale for hours after the match. When we were finally let go we were walking down a road that was like a war zone, there were tanks and armoured vehicles everywhere. They were trying to escort us away with the other England fans but of course, Andy lived in the city knew the area well so in perfect Italian he eventually managed to explain and we got through the barricade.

The trip itself was amazing however, travelling to Venice and Rome and other exotic destinations. Andy was studying at a private American school in a small village called Pecetto Torinese,which he took me to. Given I was a little bit older I seemed to get a lot of attention from all of the girls at the school, I don't know what it was but they all seemed to want to talk to me. Three of the girls were especially beautiful and one, Monica Jona, stood out in particular. She was tall with long jet black hair and a stunning figure. I ended up writing to all three girls as pen pals afterwards (I recently found all the letters when searching for old photos for this book). The writing continued until such time as I managed to save up and return there a year or so later. So, for my 19th birthday I spent my time at Monica's family house up in the mountains. They were rather well to do folk, their house had extensive gardens and a private tennis court. My birthday present from them was an album I have treasured ever since, *The Eagles - Hotel California*. In fact The Eagles are one of my favourite bands to this day.

From the top of their mountain home you could see over many miles of beautiful Italian countryside all the way to the Mediterranean coastline. One night we watched a thunderstorm from the sanctuary of her house, it was a poetic, moving experience to see the lightning illuminate the sky from so far away. It was idyllic and terribly romantic, a very traditional Italian type of romanticism. I had my guitar with me which I had taught myself how to play since I was about 12 and I sang a few songs accompanied by the guitar. It felt good to have everyone there just for me on that night and I felt that I absolutely wanted to be with Monica. I didn't know how it would work with the issue of distance, but I knew I wanted it to work more than anything.

Somehow Monica managed to persuade her father to allow us to go on holiday together, but with her family. Her family also owned a place in Majorca, so off we went to this apartment. All along I had inadvertently given the impression that I was from a rich background, though in reality I had absolutely nothing. Yet, I had to keep the act going, though it started to unravel once I actually got there. I had flown for the first time in my life on a charter flight from the UK. My overriding memory was of waking up on the first morning down at the beach and in front of my eyes was a large brown nipple. I didn't realise but we were on a topless beach. When I had fallen asleep the beach had been empty but I awoke to a fully packed beach with half naked women strewn across the length and breadth.

I was a naïve Cumbrian boy really and here I was with an exotic woman, in an equally exotic location, all Mediterranean sun, sea and boobs. It was literally an eye opener. I also learned a thing or two about the power of the sun. It was in Majorca where I experienced the devastation of sunstroke. I was extremely ill with it, I'd just overdone it - from Dalton to Majorca was quite a stretch - and I ended up in a dark room for a couple of days to recover. Whether it was the misery from that experience or that fact that Monica was out enjoying herself while I was lying ill I don't know but I decided I wanted to go home.

The problem was I had already stayed longer than I should have after cashing in my flight (something you couldn't do today), so I had to stay on a bit longer. A bit too long as it turned out as I started to feel I had outstayed my welcome a little. I was also completely bereft of money. I'm not sure how but I managed to scrape enough money together to get onto a ferry to Barcelona. It wasn't exactly luxurious accommodation, you had to sleep on the deck, there were no cabins, well, not for the likes of me. I remember very clearly once I was in Barcelona, watching the wedding of Prince Charles and Princess Diana. I spent my day at a café in Barcelona making one bottle of coke last the entire day. I almost overheated again before deciding to lay out under a garden full of sprinklers I managed to find, only to almost be arrested for being a vagrant.

This really wasn't that far from the truth. I had no money to continue my journey and I had to thumb a lift from Barcelona back to England. It took several kind hearted people and multiple journeys over two days but I made it back home. I lost touch with Monica over the course of time but I've often thought about her. It was certainly an advantage to me that through the course of our courtship I became rather good at speaking in Italian. In two years I progressed from the *Teach Yourself Italian* book I bought at the beginning. Ironically, there I was trying to speak Italian to a decent level and using Monica as a sounding board and all she wanted to do was practise her English!

My yearning for travel started to increase more and more and in 1981 I backpacked across Europe. I visited 17 countries on a budget of 50p a day. I'd sleep on park benches or through trains overnight,

I carried a sleeping bag and tent with me. There was still an Iron Curtain then which meant I couldn't go to countries like Czechoslovakia or Hungary but aside from Europe's Iron Curtain I visited everywhere on the continent bar Portugal.

I'd started off travelling with two girls, one of whom was a then girlfriend Elaine Walker, but her friend was pretty much in the way of our time together and eventually she went home.

I had the tightest shorts and long curly hair, very similar to Brian May from Queen, only mine was a bit finer. Considering it was the 1980s many people would have killed for my ready naturally permed hair - all I had to do was wash it, rub it with a towel and the perm was complete. I used to tease my brother-in-law Steve because he had to pay £30 to have his permed, which was a lot of money then. I'd look at him, tease my hair and say, 'Hey man, mine's for free.'

Even though I yearned for complete freedom and a life outdoors, I realised I needed some kind of vocation in life, not to mention a more secure sense of direction. Firstly however I had to go through the ignominy of signing on the dole, the first and only time I had done this in my life. It felt wrong somehow getting money for free, I'd worked all my life and had to work for every penny earned but I couldn't find any work at the time and the dole was the only option.

Standing in the dole queue one day would lead me to a new direction in my life. It was like a scene from *The Full Monty*. There I was stood in line with Robert Qazi and Ian Milburn We were all fed up with the idea of signing on and decided we should be doing something better. Robert was a guitarist like me and suggested we all have a jam with our instruments one day.

The others were, like me, into the folk, progressive rock band Jethro Tull, so we decided to play a few of their songs which I loved - I played rhythm guitar, while Robert played lead, mandolin and sang, with Ian on bass. I was never a virtuoso guitarist though at one stage I did become quite proficient at jazz guitar, which I often played alongside my old tennis playing nemesis Bert Park. We would completely lose ourselves in the riffs, the whole function of jazz musicianship.

After a while of jamming we decided to form a band to hopefully earn a little money from playing. We decided that if we had about 15 songs that people could join in with, traditional folk songs like 'Whisky In The Jar' and so on, then we could get a thing going locally. The band became Jack Snipe, a throwback to my interest in nature, a Jack snipe is a type of wading bird.

We started to develop a confidence and thought, 'we can do this' and we began to approach local pubs to see if they would put us on. We went to one guy at this tiny pub called The Britannia, it's now been turned into a house; a very small one. The room for bands in this place was so small, I've had broom cupboards bigger than that room.

"Can you give us a listen and see what you think?"
"Go on then. I'm not paying you."
Fair enough.
But we played and he liked it - it seemed to work for him, and he'd been involved in the entertainment industry so he knew his stuff.
"Oh...Really good that, right. I'm going to advertise this. What about next week will you do it again?"
"Yeah."
"I'll give you a tenner."
Wow, we'd made it just a few weeks in to our existence! We had barely any equipment; we had just played acoustically and, seemingly, the harmonies worked for him. My experience in the choir probably helped me to hold a tune. Luckily people liked us and eventually we were being paid £20 a week seeing as we were bringing in a lot of extra trade for this pub. On top of our wage we could drink as much as we liked, which seemed to suit Ian and Robert more than myself.

We started to develop a real reputation locally, playing all over the South Cumbria area - we were the band for a night out and a sing-a-long. We became quite friendly with a local rock group, who were doing the rounds at the time. I can't actually remember their name but they were popular in the area back then. They were a really heavy band - much louder and more powerful than we were, but somehow we snagged this support slot opening for them and seemed to go down well with their fans. We played before them quite often after that.

One night when we were due to play a pub in Barrow I spotted one girl who I just couldn't take my eyes off. Rachel, she was just beautiful - gorgeous eyes and hair. There was something about her that I fell for, so I went over and introduced myself. She was shy but I managed to get myself a date with her.

She had a wonderful, friendly family and she herself was a lovely lass. But, by my own stupidity and possessiveness I completely destroyed that relationship. In the end we fell out in a quite argumentative way, she wanted her freedom and I wanted to hold her back so that she wouldn't leave me, I was terrified. Tragically, her mother - who was one of the nicest people you would ever meet - died later of a brain tumour. We'd had some fabulous times, at one point I went off to Europe again with this girl in tow, and we had a fantastic trip. I remember camping on the beach in Greece and going all the up to Finland to Helsinki, Sweden, Norway, everywhere we went, every capital city you can imagine, Rome, Paris, Vienna everywhere.

The possessiveness and jealousy I felt was a real scourge of mine. It was a case of trying to trap this emotion, put it in a box and stop anyone else going anywhere near this because it's mine, you're not looking at it, you're not talking to it because it's mine and then all of a sudden they feel trapped, which they are because you've put them in a box, and they don't want to be in a box because they were enjoying their life before this and you get this resentment and then BANG, all that you wanted is gone and you can't get it back.

Italy, football and romance

Perhaps it goes back to my time at Myerscough College when I went out with a girl called Julie Gray, who had a figure most men would have killed just to hold for a second. We had great fun but it was here that my jealousy and immaturity began. I was still so insecure within myself and desperate for love. I just wanted someone to tell me they loved me and once I had hold of someone I would not let them go. Unfortunately with Julie, she lived above a pub. To make matters worse she also played in a darts team, so there were always a host of eager young men around her. She also would wear very low cut tops, but then I began to realise that other men liked to look too, something I was not fond of. My dislike soon turned to paranoia and after that our relationship was doomed to failure. It took me a long time to realise that not only was I hurting my partners with this behaviour but more importantly, I was hurting myself.

Chapter 7
Music, career beginnings and pregnancy

Being a member of a band with a fair few followers did wonders for my self-esteem. It helped that we were earning enough money for me to sign off from the dole. We were earning beyond our allowance on the dole because we were by now playing five or six nights per week. As had happened to me in the past there were times where other people just couldn't commit and I would be the one left to keep it going. Quite often the other members couldn't make it and it would be left to Robert Qazi and myself to play as a duo - luckily we weren't phased and the crowd still enjoyed it.

All bands go through the proverbial 'musical differences' which luckily was never a problem for Jack Snipe. There were two irritants for me however. The first was that the members started to argue over money - who should get what and whether it should be invested in new equipment or not. What had been enjoyable and straightforward started to become political which didn't impress me. Secondly, we were playing clubs and pubs that were awash with cigarette smoke and it was one thing that I had a real problem with. I hated my clothes smelling of it when I got home, having sore eyes and worst of all, breathing in the horrendous wall of tobacco smoke - it was something I couldn't abide.

It was such a deal breaker for me, even in relationships. I could not maintain a relationship with a smoker. I started a relationship with a beautiful, wonderful lady but because she smoked I had to confront the issue.

"There's only one thing wrong with you," I said, "you're lovely, you're beautiful, you have a great character but I can't stand the smell and taste of you."

"What do you mean?"

"Because you smoke and it's embedded in you - I can't deal with it."

I left her because she couldn't understand that I couldn't put up with it.

Since then it has been a major criteria for me.

I don't care what a woman looks like, what they wear, if they smoked I didn't even go there.

We certainly had fun and a certain amount of prestige with the band. One time we actually played the week after U2 at a venue! It was of course before they hit the stratospheric heights they enjoy today. Whilst playing at Lancaster University at an end of term special gig, it was Jack Snipe who the crowd would not allow to finish. They would not let us get off the stage, we played every song we knew about 5 times over. Our curfew was before midnight but we ended up playing into the wee hours of the morning, they didn't care that they had heard the songs already.

Despite the potential I had had enough of the situation with the band and moved on to playing in a Christian band at local church functions, while Jack Snipe continued with a female singer. The new band I helped form were much more proficient musicians, even though effectively we were playing smaller events. No usable recordings exist today of either band, though I do still have the beginnings of a scrapbook which we started for Jack Snipe. It was an attempt to document all our local reviews and press but the pressures of rock n' roll meant I couldn't keep it up!

It was while playing in the church group that I would meet my first wife Alison, who was only 16 at the time. She attended one of the churches the band played at, an evangelical order that, to me, seemed slightly over the top and a little disturbing. The whole ethos of Christianity to me is one of forgiveness and a lack of judging other people and their behaviour. With the evangelical side of things it was much more judgmental than it should be - a case of if you break the rules you will be punished. That was a bit extreme for me, maybe because I liked to bend the occasional rule.

Though I was 22 at the time the age difference with Alison was never a factor for me, or her as it would turn out. She certainly didn't come across as immature or adolescent. Alison was a petite girl, quiet and well mannered and I felt an attraction to her. She seemed very much like the right type of person for me at that time. I needed to gravitate to the good and proper things in life, especially people. I felt that I needed to change my ways and be grateful for what I had in life; in particular I wanted to rid myself of the pangs of jealousy which would attack me like a cancer.

I'd started to develop more responsibility in my life by the time I met Alison and was gradually starting to find my way career wise. By the time we were married I had been in a steady job with a firm called Dugdales for a year. I had realised from my brief time in the RAF, not to mention my stint in a x ray department and within the smoke filled tombs of the north west, that people and aircraft did not work like animals. So I had decided it was time to return to basics and go back to the farm, once again to work with Keith. It became an ironic decision because on the surface I was being irresponsible to go back to something that paid nothing, I still lived with my parents (when I was actually in the house) and I had no economic future to speak of.

But it was only after a short while of returning to Keith that he told me of a position which had come up with a local company. We used to have feed representatives coming round the farms, from a firm called Dugdales in Lancashire. This particular person who we were used who was friend of Keith's didn't do himself any favours with many because he was a devout Christian and would use his visits regarding animal feed to attempt to convert farmers to Christianity. Fittingly he ended up leaving the job to set up his own church which left an open vacancy. Keith said he would put a word in for me and suggested I would be good at the job, seeing as I knew all about animals and could talk for hours.

The manager of the firm Alan Sayle seemed to be convinced I could do a good job. I knew I could seeing as I knew a lot of the local farmers and these were the people I would be dealing with. The fact I loved both farms and animals was a credible bonus.

Still I was as surprised as anything when he actually decided to give me the job. It was even better when I realised I would get a decent salary as well as a company car. I became the proud owner of a bright red Morris Marina, with an 1800 petrol engine. You'll never see one on the road now because after they built them I think everyone disappeared into rust and disrepair after about five years, they were built not to last and they didn't.

I could not believe my luck because back then you were not taxed on having a company car and it was worth a small fortune. I said to myself,

"You have screwed up the last five years of your life - you have made a mess of things, you didn't know where you were going, this is your chance, do not mess it up. You have got an opportunity here, do it."

Maybe my attitude helped but I finally found something I liked and a job that was rewarding and suited me down to the ground. It was a small family company and they paid attention to their employees. Most importantly, I believed in their product because I had been feeding it to all of our animals for many years. People would know if you were selling a product you didn't believe in, and the opposite was also true, if you personally believed in the product and used it yourself, people had no problem going with it. It was nutritionally sound and I had every confidence in it. I was so convinced about what I was doing the boss said to me I could have sold sand to the Arabs.

It was the hardest I had worked in my life - I was not just selling a product, I was trying to help them expand beyond just the local area. The job was a lot easier when I was trying to sell to people I already knew, as they would often do me a favour and try it out just to see. Cold calling I found much more difficult but I did it regardless and gradually found my stride.

I started to learn that it was pointless to try and sell the product, instead I sold myself.

I realised that if you were a person they wanted to see, someone they wanted to talk to and have a good hour or so with, they were far more likely to show interest in what you were selling. If I could bring something to their lives instead of just trying to flog them something because it was my job, then by the time I asked, in the last five minutes of my visit - 'oh, by the way, how is your feed doing?' - they were more likely to be honest because they had built that rapport with me already. Eventually they might admit they didn't like the other feed they were using, or the person who sold it. And they would give me a try.

I was soon outperforming many of my co-workers, most of whom had been in the job a long time and had lost their enthusiasm. It didn't take long for word to get around that Dugdales had a new salesman and I like to think that most of the farmers had warmed to me and wanted to give the product a try. It helped that I was able to communicate well with the ladies of these farms. I would always be dressed very smartly with a suit or a jacket, tie and always carried a briefcase. If the farmer wasn't there the lady of the house would always invite me in and I would spend time chatting and listening to them which seemed to please them - quite often I built a relationship more so with the farmer's wife than the farmer. It wasn't exactly *Confessions Of A Farm Feed Salesman*, it was all very innocent and friendly but it certainly seemed to help my sales.

Quite often, having made bonds with the women on the farms, they would assist me in my quest for sales, pushing their husband to give me a go, saying, "Come on he's only a young lad and he's trying hard." I made sure I could back up why our feed was better, especially as it was harder to sell than most because it was better quality and therefore more expensive.

But there was a scientific reason why it worked and I made it my job to find that out in order to break it down for whoever I was taking the product to. I realised we had to find any deficiencies in the cow's diet in order to help them perform better. So I presented a scientific argument as to why this feed would work and how it would make the cow perform better.

I made real friendships during the job, so much so that a lot of these families became like additional family for me, I would even have dinner with many of them. Some days I had two dinners in the space of a few hours because they would prepare dinner for me and have it ready when I came in - and I didn't want to be rude so even though I could barely move I would eat a second dinner at the next farm I visited. Then there was tea, cake and lord knows what else, I'm not sure how, but I managed to stay the same weight for years.

I warmed to every aspect of the job and the company, even my manager who had some radical ideas that he had brought in from America. It seemed that I performed best in life when I was around people who thought outside of the box, and these were subtle subconscious influences that were working their way inside my brain. The love for the job and my dedication to selling meant I was soon doubling and trebling the amount of business I was expected to do. For me the products I was selling were exciting and innovative and it truly excited me so I ended up selling many times the amount anyone else did because I was so sold on the products myself.

I even had a degree of flexibility in the job, if I started early enough, quite often it was about 7am, then I could be finished by 3pm and I would take off to play golf with Alison's father. It was beginning to feel like the perfect family life. I'd worked at Dugdales for a year by the time I met Alison and I had already invested in a house, which I had bought from the vicar of Dalton. It cost me just £10,000 but it was much more of an investment property because it needed so much work doing to it.

It needed a new roof, new floors, new ceilings, new everything. Still, it was at the dead end of a quiet road and it was a beautiful stone built house which I called Valley Cottage. Though I owned the house I was still living with Mam and Dad, but I would spend my days working and then most of the rest of my time working at the cottage - knocking walls through and rebuilding or renovating other sections.

It was all well and good having my own house, bricks and mortar. My problem however was my Morris Marina. With this little beauty I was by now used to transporting myself and Alison all over the place, and whispering sweet nothings into her ear on the back seat. But after one particularly amorous trip to the local island of Walney I was set for a rude awakening. Our backseat enjoyment turned into the daunting news. My 17-year-old girlfriend, turned to me and said, "David, I'm carrying your baby."

My first response was, "How on earth did that happen?" Alison looked at me and sneered, "What, you don't know?!" Morally I knew immediately the right thing to do, all the years of Christian ethics certainly came to the fore. The only thing we could do was to get married. It might not seem as if I were on the moral high ground to be in this position with such a young girl but the truth is I never saw Alison as being that much younger than I. Both our parents might have felt differently however so confronting them with the news was daunting. Alison's mother Christine was instantly placated by the fact that I was prepared to do the right thing by her daughter, and she has always been a nice woman to this day, which made our confession fairly straightforward.

My own parents were a different story.

"Mam, Dad, I've got something to tell you."

Their faces instantly changed, they seemed to know exactly what was coming next.

"Alison is pregnant."

"And how did that happen then?" said my mother, proving there were some similarities between us after all.

I knew that the best thing to do was to get married quickly so that by the time our baby was born we would be wed. There was an element of romance in my thinking; we booked February 16th as the date, close to Valentine's Day. It had to be a cheap affair however given we were quite poor at the time, so everything was very basic. It was a small catering firm and our post wedding celebration was in the local church hall. There was no big honeymoon but I had been working flat out on the cottage so that it was in a good enough state for us to move into. I made sure we had the kitchen, living room and bedroom to move into and at least we had a family home. We did have a local excursion just around the lakes after we got married and it was during a winter I will never forget. It was the coldest time I've ever experienced in the United Kingdom. In February 1985 there were icebergs floating down the sea at Greenodd, every lake in the Lake District was frozen solid, every waterfall was frozen solid, it was dreadful. Perhaps the temperatures might not have been record breaking lows but it was the consistency of the cold and freezing temperatures, it must have been freezing for two months and with that consistency the ice just got thicker and thicker.

Alison and I married quickly and I didn't have much time to question whether it was the right thing to do but given my actions at the time I think I knew deep down that it was not the best thing for me. Ironically the build up to the wedding, where I would seek advice from a goat, was the genesis of the South Lakes Wild Animal Park.

Chapter 8
The event that started the "zoo"

One day while working for Dugdales I found myself at Jack Coward's Farm in Kirkby-In-Furness. It was a bizarre mixture at the farm between a very erudite well mannered lady and the man of the farm who could have performed swearing as an Olympic sport. He was a nice enough chap but rough as rocks. I preferred Jack's wife to talk to, he often didn't tend to go with much by way of product and she was far more on my wavelength.

One day I went into their imaculate kitchen and under the table were two beautiful baby goats who had only just been born. They were bleating away.

"Aww aren't they absolutely cute, aren't they lovely, what are you going to do with them then?"

"I'm gonna take them out and kill them," said Jack.

"You're going to do what!?"

"I'm gonna take them out and kill them, they're no good, just brought them in to show the Mrs, I'm taking them straight out, BANG in the head."

"You mean they're not worth anything to you?"

"No they're worth nothing. We have the goats because they produce a lot of milk and when I get orphaned lambs off the sheep, instead of me bottle feeding them and all that work, I just put four or five lambs on a nanny goat and she keeps them happy, job's a good 'un."

"So these poor little things, you're just going to kill them? No you're not...they're worth nothing to you?"

"No they're worth nowt."

"Right, stick them in the back of my car."

"Fair enough."

So I finished my cup of tea and put the two goats in the back of the car. I started to pull away from Jack's drive before I put the brakes on and thought for a second.

'What the hell am I going to do with these, where am I going to put them?' I'd made this totally emotional decision to save their lives with absolutely no thought as to what I was going to do when I got home. At the time, though I had the cottage, I was still living with my parents and the only people I knew with land were Keith and Janet but I didn't think they would let me give them two goats to look after. Still, it seemed my only option.

Onwards I went to the Howson farm. I went inside and said, "Keith, I want to tell you a story. I've just rescued these goats, I have nowhere to take them and would you do me a big favour, could I please just keep them here for a short time?"

Quite predictably Keith wasn't too enamoured. "Oh, I don't want any goats around," he said. "Goats are a nightmare, they're into everything". He didn't stop there, in fact he came up with a number of reasons why he really didn't want these goats on his land.

"Look Keith this will be temporary I promise. What can I do? I can't take them home. Could I put them in the dog shed or something? Don't worry I will look after them and feed them, you won't even know they are there."

"Go on then, but you've got to find somewhere else."

"Okay, thank you."

That was one problem out of the way but goats require a lot of feeding. Four or five times a day, so I had to ask a few favours while I would be at work. Everyone became attached to the goats, who were named Jethro and Ellie May after *The Beverly Hillbillies* television programme. Something I didn't realise about goats is how big they would grow - when I took on the responsibility of the animals they were just small babies but they grew and grew and grew some more. They were eventually tethered in Keith's field - they couldn't really go anywhere else and they did become a part of the farm furniture. Keith got used to them in the end though they remained my responsibility.

With my feelings about captivity however I had to make sure the goats were comfortable and could move up and down freely so I made sure the ropes were long and loose. One day however Keith accidentally ran over one of the goat's legs as he was driving the tractor. I was inconsolable at the time and let Keith know about it, though of course he was distraught himself. Ellie May broke both her pelvis and her legs and, though we tried to put the legs in plaster it was no good, she had to be put to sleep. I know Keith felt bad but at the time, to me the goats were my babies and to lose Ellie May was terrible. I'd only had her for five months.

I became closer to Jethro, he became just like a dog in fact, I would take him for long walks on and around the farm. We would be together in the mornings before work, at night when I'd finished work as well as weekends, he went everywhere with me or me and Alison. If I whistled he would come to me like a dog, I even walked him around with a collar and a lead. A lot of people thought there was something wrong with me, but I didn't care. It wasn't a cry for attention either, I simply walked Jethro around with me because I enjoyed it. I would take the backseat out of my Morris Marina and he just jumped in the back and he would go everywhere, window down, head out the window, just like a dog! We would visit the Lakes, to the forest for walks, he'd go everywhere. One time I even walked him down the promenade at Blackpool, he even traipsed after me when I took his lead off. Jethro even came on our makeshift honeymoon to the Lakes; he was truly part of the family. I have some wonderful photos of Jethro even with Amy once she was born. We would go out on walks, Alison and I pushing the baby with Jethro walking alongside us. Eventually Jethro's legs grew so big they were just too big for his body, his knees failed and he had to be put to sleep. By then I'd had Jethro as my pet goat for many years and I cried my eyes out.

Chapter 9
Goats, wedding and farm tales

During the build up to my wedding there were times when I questioned everything. I didn't question my sanity regarding the following story, but I certainly questioned whether I was doing the right thing in my personal life. As I was becoming closer to becoming the husband of Alison I questioned whether it was the right thing. I knew it was the right thing for Alison and for our unborn child but was it really the best thing for me? It suddenly occurred to me that though I was doing the right thing it was for forever. Forever is a long time.

The morning of the wedding I went down to the farm and saw the goats. I also washed my car and then realised I had a few hours to kill before d-day. As I recall the wedding was at 2pm and by late morning I decided I would walk the goats, Ellie May was still with me then. I went and sat on a hill with my two goats. I spent about an hour talking out loud to them.

Should I go?

Should I not go?

Am I doing the right thing?

Am I not?

Asking goats for definitive answers about the biggest question of my life.

The thing was I felt closer to the goats than I did any person that I knew. And even if I had been tempted to ask someone I knew I would have been putting pressure on them to give me the right answer. If they had advised me to get married and things had gone wrong they might have felt guilty.

There is a part of me, something deep inside, which says I must find a way to do the right thing. The first resort was always to try and find a way out and do the right thing while doing so. It reminds me of a Theodore Roosevelt quote; *"In any moment of decision, the best thing you can do is the right thing, the next best thing is the wrong thing, and the worst thing you can do is nothing."*

So I did what I thought was the right thing and that was to put my unborn child first which meant entering into the sanctity of marriage. I left my goats and headed for the wedding. It was a tough choice all things considered and when I see films like *Runaway Bride* they certainly have more than a touch of irony for me because I could easily have run away that morning, I was going through sheer panic. The realisation that my entire life was going to change that afternoon.

I enjoyed the wedding ceremony and felt like it was the right thing after that - it helped that Alison looked stunning in her wedding dress, something that is a particular admiration of mine, I think most women actually look stunning in a wedding dress. I even realised just how beautiful my sister Alison was when I saw her in a wedding dress, something just clicked and I could understand why she would be attractive to another man. After so many years I have seen a lot of women wear a wedding dress and it certainly does something to each and every one of them, it is like a glorious halo which surrounds them, a golden aura.

I can say with the benefit of hindsight that sometimes doing the thing you believe to be right, when it actually isn't, is one of the worst things you can do. It is akin to setting off on a road trip with a hole in your tyre. If you do that then there is no choice but to fail. Sometimes trying to do things for the right reasons can actually be the ultimate *wrong* reason to do it.

I certainly had a great time in the early years with Alison and it is not something I regret by any means. Something which probably helped to lengthen our marriage is the fact that I had a good career

Goats, wedding and farm tales

where I spent a lot of time working away - it meant that when Alison and I did spend time together it was of quality and we enjoyed each other's company.

As well as my job and my new family life, I had begun to make something of a garden for us. It wasn't quite on the grounds of our house; in fact it belonged to the local verger at the church. It was his private garden but he was essentially using it as a rubbish dump, most of it had never been tidied up and it was rapidly becoming ridiculously overgrown. I cheekily asked if I could take it over and he agreed to rent it to me at a very cheap rate. There were mountains of rubble and litter which I worked like a trojan to clear, it seemed to take forever but it was something I wanted for the family. At the time I also wanted it to be somewhere I could keep Jethro.

I eventually cleared the rubble and made a pathway so we could access it from our house. I managed to construct a small pond as well as a vegetable garden and a proper path. It was an awful lot of work but I wasn't about to let the physical nature of the task stop me, it was something that of course I had always loved to do, to just get stuck in. I even built a hut for Jethro which meant that he was on my land then.

This was where the path of my life diverted somewhat as I met a farmer one day on my rounds in Kirkby, who seemed intrigued when I told him about my little set up with a small plot of land which housed a goat, a distinctly uncommon garden animal!

"Well, if you're going to do that, I've got a bunch of chickens I was going to neck." "Why?"

"We've got too many, they're laying well but I can't afford to keep feeding them, I can't sell the eggs".

"What sort are they?"

There are many different types of hens but many are just ordinary brown hens, these ones were quite fancy and I thought it would be a nice addition to our little set up. As soon as I mentioned the goat and chickens to somebody else, I was then in line for a couple of ducks and eventually I seemed to become a mecca for unwanted ducks, geese and hens. I soon had a large collection of various birds which I had to build huts for. I had Bantams, hens, geese, Muscovy ducks, Aylesbury ducks. I had eggs galore, which I then sold on to mam amongst other people. It became a perfect little treasure chest for my children as they grew up, to be in amongst all these ducks as well as rabbits and guinea pigs just as I had when I was little. Unbeknownst to me as I never really saw it in this manner, I had created my own mini farm while I was still working travelling around to other people's larger farms.

Once Jethro had passed away and I had decided to replace him I realised the only down side with Jethro was his sheer size, he was like a mule. So I found out about a couple of pygmy goats two neutered males, Billy and Gordon, then we eventually got two females and eventually I went on to breed them.

When Amy was a year old we took her on holiday with us, we often went to Austria camping but this particular year we travelled to Switzerland, driving all the way in my diesel Orion car. It was one of the first to come out and it averaged about 60 miles to the gallon. We had a brilliant holiday in Switzerland and I managed to pick up a few bells for my pygmies. Once they were fitted with the bells you could hear them everywhere, we would walk in the forest with the four goats chiming behind us and - just as I had done with Jethro - the goats didn't seem to mind being in the boot of the car. They would often just settle there in the darkness and go to sleep, rarely making a mess.

It was always amusing if we stopped in a public place though. If we stopped at a car park and opened the boot these four goats would jump out and people would wonder what on earth was happening. The goats were wonderful and though I just believed I was being helpful to people at the time, by taking injured or unwanted livestock from them, it was the stepping stone to something much bigger.

It helped that the animals were fairly cheap to look after, their food wasn't a problem given I worked for an animal feed company and received a discount. We started to build a reputation locally given we had so many animals running around the garden. It meant that when I decided to sell the house everyone knew about it, and there was literally a queue of people who wanted to buy it from me. Given I had undertaken so much renovation work the house was a real talking point and it was worth far more than when I had purchased it. The house cost me £10,000 but I sold it on for about £50,000 which was a small fortune and it was all the more surreal as people were bidding against each other to secure this house. To me, that was the benefit with having Margaret Thatcher in power. Those who wanted to build a life for themselves and work hard to do it were afforded opportunity, they were the good old days, unless you wouldn't pay poll tax or were on the dole that is.

It was a time of growth for all of us and life was moving along so nicely that we decided to have another child. Once we had decided that we both agreed that we wanted to have a child as quickly as we could so that they would grow up while we were still young and we could enjoy life with the kids all grown up, it was quite a long term plan but it felt right at the time. I'd hoped that the next child would be a boy and that's how it turned out much to my delight. I didn't realise it at the time but, though I loved Alison, we had more of a brother/sister love. It wasn't until much later in life where I fell deeply in love with another woman that I realised what true, exciting love really was.

Alison fell pregnant again and lo and behold, the baby was a bouncing boy. It took a while before he bounced however, it was actually the worst birth I've ever attended, it was very stressful for me, not to mention Alison. He was actually face down and they just could not get him to come round the right way. This went on for some time, with a lot of stress and a lot of monitoring of both Alison and the baby's heartbeat. In the end they became very worried and they must have panicked because they just cut Alison open with a scalpel, no anaesthetic or any sedative. His whole head was bruised from the ordeal and we were worried that the whole process might have affected him. The poor little soul had a crinkly head and a huge bruise across his bonce. We named him Ben.

The whole build up to the event itself was a time I loved, because suddenly I had to look after Amy all by myself. I was responsible for my little girl and I dressed her and did everything that I hadn't been able to do for a long while because of work. Finally I took some time off to look after her. I remember putting her in a little red dress and she was so pretty and cute, everybody loved her. I was so proud that I was the daddy and I could do this all on my own. Amy was always a daddy's girl and ironically Ben became mammy's boy. Amy would run to me and Ben would run to Alison. With the two children and a wonderful family set up I had everything that I could ever have wanted. I had a great job, which I loved, two beautiful little kids, a settled marriage and we looked forward to our modest camping holiday every year. We would all go out for walks around the lake district at the weekends. Life was settled, life was right. I had no further ambition or wants in life at the time, I was perfectly content.

It was a more poignant feeling of contentment given that as a child I had a very strong fear of death. It might have been brought on by the beer Wilf Rigg had given me when I was only fourteen, but that was the only time in my life where I went through immense panic attacks having realised that we were all destined for death, that it was a glaring inevitability. I am sure everyone has that fear at some point in their life, we start to comprehend death and it is the worst feeling in the world trying to come to terms with it. I can clearly recall sitting on a curb, shaking with panic, realising I was going to die - what can be done? The overriding thought in my mind was that I did not want to die without having children. Another fear of mine was whether I would ever reach 40. There was actually a third and that was wondering whether I would ever live to see the millennium, it seemed like a cut off point. Ironically, I would turn 40 just a year after the turn of the century. Yet the birth of my two children was a massive milestone and it was comforting to realise that nothing bad happened, I didn't instantly die, and I have lived to see my children grow up beyond then.

My ambition was possibly limited in a career sense because I actually loved my work - my only ambition was to be the best within that job. Ultimately the people I dealt with are the ones who made that job a joy to have. These were traditional country folk, homely loving people and their attitudes and humanity begins to rub off on you, how can it not? Their vivaciousness, their love, their caring attitude, their concern, all of those things that you feel coming from them, absorb within you somehow helping you to become a better person. It is certainly true that the people you spend time with are going to have a huge influence on how you become yourself.

There were so many families I loved to spend time with and be around, especially the women of the house. They often became like surrogate mothers. I felt so much love from people which outshone the lack of love I had always perceived within my own family. As much as I loved the interaction with many of these families, there were a number of incidents which will remain indelibly inked in my mind as some of the most humorous yet revolting things to ever happen to me.

I drove to one farm, high on a fell side, which was one of the roughest farms in the vicinity. They had not paid their bills for an eternity and so my company said to me,
"David this time you go and you don't come out until they've paid."
I had only been to the farm a couple of times but the food they had from us had not been paid for and I'd received my orders to stay there until I was paid so I had to.
When I got to the farm I found out the farmer was still out in the fields but his wife told me he wouldn't be long.

"Are you sure, because I've got to wait for him."
"Aye sit down, he won't be so long, have you had anything to eat, have you had something to drink?"
"No, no thank you, I've just had a cuppa, I'm alright thanks."

There was method to my thinking. The kitchen was absolutely filthy and I daren't touch anything that had been made within its putrid confines. There were kids all over the place accompanied by noise and bustle. The wife was carrying a naked baby who was screaming the whole time. She was holding this poor little baby while she was trying to cook wearing a plastic apron. I had to sit down on a stool by the door, whenever I moved on this stool it would stick to my bum. I didn't want to touch anything because everything was so filthy. I was used to country living of course, but there was no excuse for a lack of cleanliness, Keith and Janet's house for instance was always immaculate. To this end, I was convinced enough to be able to eat in their house, curing my fear of eating at other people's houses. This particular farm however was somewhere I couldn't dream of even touching anything, much less eating any food made there. As I was looking around I began to feel sick just thinking of my surroundings. I couldn't escape the farmer's wife however.

"Come on, you'll have to have a cup of coffee, you'll have a coffee won't you?"

"No, I'm alright, you're alright."

"Well I've made you one now, you'll have to have it."

She laid the coffee down on the sideboard and I just looked at it with complete disgust wondering what was in that cup. Just recalling this is bringing some horrific physical reactions to me.

"Would you like some toast?"

"No I'm alright, honestly I'm alright."

"Ah you're just saying that, you'll have some toast, I know you do when you go down to our mothers." (I used to visit her mother's house too).

"I don't really, I don't."

"No you do, I know you do, you'll have some toast."

"No, please don't do it."

"Alright then, I can't force you."

Just minutes after this the screaming baby proceeded to produce a wave of diarrhoea, which went all down her apron and dripped onto the floor. She was holding a big knife and she just put the baby on the sink, before scraping all of the diarrhoea off her apron with the knife. She took a tea towel and wiped the knife 'clean' before using a flannel to wipe the baby's bum in the kitchen sink. Once the baby had been wiped she put it on the floor before using the very same knife which had been covered in runny faeces a minute before, to cut the bread for the toast! She toasted the bread in their aga cooker, spread the butter with the same knife once it was toasted and placed it in front of me.

"There you go! Now you're not leaving until you've eaten that."

Of course I could not even conceive of touching that toast, or the coffee and I had to quickly make my excuses to leave. I had to tell my boss that I didn't have the money but that under no circumstances was I going back to that house. I bumped into the farmer a few weeks later in the great outdoors thankfully and picked the money up then. They were nice people I have to say - it is just that in terms of hygiene they were not in the same stratosphere as most other people.

Another time on my rounds, I visited a farm, which must remain anonymous once again. Some farm families manage to keep a pristine house, I don't know how but they do, if you drop a piece of straw on the floor they would pick it up straight away. Others are completely unaware of what a mess they are in. You often had to fight things in the way of the path walking up to this type of farm, there would be junk and bits of tractors all over the place. If someone dropped anything they just left it. This farm was just one of these, where everything was in a state of disrepair. It was a real dump. Once again I was there to collect money from the farmer. When he offered me a coffee I said 'yes' because it was a friendly way of beginning to build a rapport. As I sat down and turned to look in the kitchen I saw the farmer put his filthy welly boots, covered in cow muck, right on top of the aga stove. This muck was dripping down the side of the boots onto the hot cooker, producing a brown, bubbly mixture.

He caught me looking and said, "Oh I see you're looking at them, I have to go out in a bit, it's cold but I'll have warm feet when I go out!" I thought, 'Yes and your cooker is covered in cow muck.' He could at least have wiped them before putting them on the cooker! This was another farmer who couldn't help himself cursing all the time, every third word was f-this and f-the other. For me, it was actually difficult to translate. His wife started to talk and she was exactly the same. Their son then joined in and he too was possessed of a limited vocabulary. I did actually go to drink the coffee, despite the welly incident, but it tasted too sweet for my liking and so I politely left the drink and it just went cold.

Just a few weeks later I was back there, as there was a food delivery for the farm from our company. It was important for me in my line of work to get on well with the driver who delivered the feed to the farms and luckily I did, Roger Haythornthwaite was a very amicable, friendly fellow.

Out came the wife of the farmer.

"Come on then you two, you'll have a cup of coffee."

"Aye, no worries, get one out here," said Roger.

As the wife brought us the coffee Roger downed his almost all in one go. As he pulled the cup away from his mouth he made the mistake of looking inside. He mumbled something but the farmer's wife was quite close to us.

"What?" I said.

"Nothing, nothing, nothing."

"You were going to say something, what?"

"Ah nothing, nothing at all."

I still hadn't tried any of my coffee at this point. I brought the cup to my mouth and I tipped it but I saw just in the nick of time that this was not something I was about to touch. That cup had never been washed. If that cup had ever been washed it certainly hadn't been washed in water or with a hand or a scrubbing brush. It had fur growing on the side of it which had obviously been noted by Roger but he couldn't say anything. So he had to accidentally throw the remainder of the coffee on the floor and pretend he had spilled it. Quick as a flash the farmer's wife asked, "Do you want another then?" "Ah no no, I'll have to get away, I'll have to get away." It was enough to make you want to vomit. Unfortunately I had to return to this farm and I knew I would likely be offered a coffee again, so I had to develop a strategy so that I would never have to touch anything I was supposed to eat or drink from that house.

I couldn't upset these people and if I had just said 'no' they wouldn't have listened so I needed a reason. 10am one morning I arrived at the farm, unluckily it was coffee time.

"Have a coffee then?"

"No I can't."

"Why can't you, what's the matter?"

"I've been to the doctor last week, and he told me I've got an issue and I'm only allowed to drink so much in a day now. I'm allowed a cup of tea in the morning, a cup of coffee at dinnertime, a cup of coffee at teatime and a cup of tea of an evening and I'm only allowed those four drinks in a day. I must have bottled water but it's got to be special, I can't just have it from anywhere so I can only have these four drinks and they must be at 7 o'clock, 12 o'clock, 4 o'clock and 8 o'clock."

"Oh, boy that's terrible."

"I know! It's a damned nuisance but I'll have to deal with it, I'll get used to it, I know I will, never mind, don't worry about me, I'll be fine, it's nothing serious, just a slight kidney problem."

"Oh you won't be able to have a cup of coffee with us now will you, look, it's 10 o'clock."

"No. Oh dear."

For the next ten months I turned up at this house religiously at ten in the morning every time. I was never ever offered a drink. One day however there was some kind of delay on the road and I didn't arrive at their house until noon. By then I had forgotten all about the furry cup incident. As I walked in the wife said, 'Hey you are just here at the right time so you can have a coffee!' I am sure it was still the same cup and it still hadn't been washed.

Chapter 10
The menagerie grows

I didn't have an asset to my name aside from my house. I had my family and a job I loved. Yet I was very happy. We had next to nothing of any material value in our house at all. The only thing I had were three fish tanks as keeping fish was a hobby of mine. We had no real ambitions, we loved our holidays, we loved camping around Europe and driving around the lakes and mountains. We drove virtually around the whole of the Alps. I loved travelling through the Alps, Swiss, French, Austrian even Slavian Alps. These were precious moments that I truly looked forward to. Something I would also come to learn in my later travels is that the people who have the least and don't expect anything beyond the small amount they do have, are some of the most content people in the world. I believe it is ambition, greed and jealousy of other things and other people that leads to frustration, disappointment and depression in life because you don't achieve it. If you don't set out to achieve or you don't have that in the first instance then how can you possibly get upset about it?

The trouble is with our world, more and more every year we are led to believe by our politicians that we should expect more from everything which is ridiculous. It's a way of life that cannot be sustained or make you happy. We have to change the politicians' talk about life because if they push the expectation of 'more more more more' and can't deliver, we are all going to get extremely disappointed. In my view this is the biggest fault with the system in life that we live in, it pushes far too much expectation on people.

Despite being happy at our relatively limited earnings, it didn't stop me being pursuant of the best budgeting skills in Cumbria. I found a stack of bank statements from that time recently and they read like a bank reconciliation. I was meticulous in the checking of everything that went in and out. If anything could be put to one side for a holiday then that was all well and good, or it might have been a new pair of shoes or a coat for Ben or Amy. This went on for month upon month, year upon year, where I had to be aware of every little penny that went here or there because I had to be sure there were not going to be any shocks.

The arrival of a material gift into my life heralded a very negative memory of my time working for Dugdales. They had rewarded me from my good work for them with a brand new Ford Orion which was the colour and specification I had asked for. This was unusual, to allow an employee that privilege, it showed they were very keen on keeping me happy. I chose a white car with red stripes and a sun roof. The build up to the presentation of the car was gratifying because there was a bonus scheme in place for employees whereby you were rewarded with vouchers depending on the amount of feed you sold.

We started to sell a product by Kodak who were beginning to work a lot on the biological side of things. It might well have been related to photographic materials but they experimented and found a product that, once placed into animal food, stimulated the production of bacteria in the gut which digests the food. Effectively this meant that for everything an animal ate they were far more productive and efficient. Literally, for every pound put in, there was far more made. I was very convinced by the product. Dr. John Allen was working for Kodak who I got on well with, partially because I seemed to grasp the concept behind the product.

Out of our entire company staff it seemed that only I could grasp the nature of the science behind the reason the product worked. It was interesting to me to see how things worked, not just A + B = C but how did you get there? It was an aspect of my childhood of course and I was fully free to pursue it within my job. I managed to sell the hi-tech feed to every single person I visited. It may have worked a dream but the feed itself stank to high heaven. When it was blown into the feed loft the smell was like sweaty socks. Most farmers had an adverse reaction and would say, "Oh my god I can't live with this."

"You'll get used to it," I responded, "a lot of people get used to the smell of cow muck as well, you'll get used to it, just work with it, work with the stuff, see what it does for you."

Luckily I was proved correct and everyone who bought into the product saw an improvement in production - the smell was no longer an issue. Kodak's incentive for each salesman was along the lines of £1 for every tonne that you managed to sell. I sold around 3000 tonnes of this feed. I didn't get a cash bonus but it was the next best thing, a huge return in £5 vouchers, which were valid in the majority of big name shops. There was a ceremony to reward all the salesman for their selling of the product. My colleagues, around nine of them, were coming out with £5 or £10 here and there and suddenly I walked out with three grand.

Someone must have cursed me because I was driving home in my brand new Orion, pleased as punch, with my £3000 of vouchers sitting on the passenger seat. It was August but it was a cold day, despite this I was driving with my sun roof open.

I was still on work duty because I had agreed to drop a few bags of hen feed off at a farm on my way home. It was out of the way really, and I had to go up to Millom to come back. The traffic was slow and there were five or so cars ahead of me which were driving slovenly for what seemed like an eternity. Eventually I knew I was coming up to a new piece of road which was wider and would enable me to overtake. I knew the roads so well that I knew I would have an opportunity any second.

I managed to overtake all but one of the cars; the vehicle at the head of the line was still driving at a snail's pace. I just thought, 'stuff it, I've come this far, I will keep going'. I kept moving past him with plenty of straight empty road in front of me but out of nowhere he decided to turn right, without even signalling. I was driving at 55mph which was fast enough for my car to swing right out as he clipped the back end. It was probably a millisecond in real time but - as many accident victims will describe - it happened in total slow motion in my mind. I could see it happening but could do nothing about it. I completely lost control of the car and somehow flew right in front of all the other cars coming the other way on the road, before I somehow launched the Orion straight down a banking. The banking continued through a mass of trees before leading to a river lying at the bottom. It must have looked like something from *Starsky And Hutch*, my car turned over and over in mid air before I hit the bottom with an almighty crash.

Once I had actually come to my senses I realised I was pinned into my seat, upside down. My seat belt had saved my life but it was now wedging me in so tightly that I couldn't release it. My sun roof was open but it was flat on the ground and there was nowhere for me to go. What seemed like a bad dream suddenly hit me with a wave of panic, this was real and I had no way of getting out. I banged and banged and the belt eventually came off but all that happened was I smacked my head on the inside of the roof.

I couldn't open any of the doors or escape out of the sun roof, even if I could there were branches from trees protruding in every direction which could easily have killed me. I started panicking, then kicking, kicking, kicking.

The whole incident had not escaped unnoticed and eventually there was a procession of other motorists following my route down the banking, towards the beck at the bottom, wondering if I was alive. They soon knew that I was, with the screaming coming from the inside of the car. I was lucky not to be in deeper water, it wasn't enough to drown me. No one could open the doors in the car so I had to wait, panicking, before the ambulance and fire brigade came, which seemed like forever.

Though there were people outside I was still trying to break free all the time I was waiting and I ended up badly damaging my ankle and foot. The reason I was panicking was because I had seen a film just a week before, where it reminded me of the age old movie myth that every time a car overturns and crashes it sets on fire, barbecuing the person inside. My whole mind was taken over with thoughts of being burned alive, one spark or drip in the wrong place and I was a goner.

The feeling of being trapped when you are terrified and cannot see a way out is one of the worst things in the world. The stupidity of people somehow prevailed even in this scene of carnage however. When the fire brigade arrived and realised they would have to cut me out of the car, a young fireman who had seen the brand new registration plate on my motor, came up with the immortal line: "Oh you can't cut that, it's a brand new car!"

This car was smashed to pieces, completely written off yet he was in awe of a registration plate. An elder statesmen in the fire brigade brought reality back and with a retort of "bugger that" he used huge metal cutters to bring me out.

Amazingly I had very little by way of physical damage. I had grazed my neck and part of my arm and that was about it. My foot was damaged and I could do nothing with it, but I had done that myself by trying to escape. My vouchers, which had been beneath the open sun roof had blown all over the place out of the roof - it was like a scene from *Butch Cassidy And The Sundance Kid* where the safe blows the money all over the place. I of course travelled to hospital in an ambulance but once there the fire brigade brought me every single one of my vouchers back, there wasn't one missing. They were crumpled and wet but they were all there. That shows the integrity of the service.

I later found out from the police when they interviewed me that the idiot who pulled out into me had drunk something like eight pints at lunchtime. He had driven off once he caused the accident and by the time the police caught up with him there was no point in breathalysing him as he was no longer over the limit.

Despite the witnesses who confirmed he was indeed drunk when he had left the pub to drive his car, there was not enough evidence to convict him of drunk driving, though he was found guilty of dangerous driving. Amazingly, he didn't even receive a driving ban. He could have killed me yet he was allowed to drive the next day.

I was in hospital for an afternoon and then allowed to go home, which was something of a miracle. As soon as I could bend my leg again to get into a car I asked Alison's dad to drive me up to the scene of the accident - I thought it was a good idea to get into a car again. I relived the whole incident of course but it was the best thing to do, to eradicate it from my system as soon as possible - and it meant that I was not afraid to get into a car again. I've learned from the accident however and the lesson is that I don't need to watch the road, but other drivers. I now watch them like a hawk and whenever I overtake now I always leave as wide a berth as I possibly can.

I couldn't drive myself with my foot completely strapped up, but I went back to work within a few days. Alison drove me around to the farms so that I could get back into work. I loved my job and missed it. The accident had been a frightener but I wasn't going to let it stop me. I went back the moment I could control the pain in my foot.

My dedication to the company and my work paid off as I was being observed by an international company called Colborn Dawes Nutrition. They had a vacancy for an area manager, for all the companies in the north west involved in animal nutrition. I'd been in my job for five years and had learned an awful lot, especially from my manager Alan Sayle. It was a tremendous learning curve, being involved in field work, and not just studying at a college. By my estimation I learned ten times more doing this. I was offered an increase in wages of about 40% as well as a bigger and better car and excellent employment conditions. Colborn Dawes was a British arm of a Swiss pharmaceutical company called Hoffman Le Roche. The company produced different types of medication, such as Rennie indigestion tablets. They were the biggest privately owned pharmaceutical company in the world, and were the biggest producers of Vitamin E in the world for instance. It was a huge step up for me. It was also a difficult decision given I was happy working for the company I was already with. Yet it seemed like too good an opportunity to miss so I took the job. I drove to their UK head office in Derbyshire and attended all the requisite courses, learning more and more about vitamins and minerals and every other aspect of nutrition. I was genuinely enthralled by the fact that I was learning much more about the in-depth aspects of biochemistry and the way that minerals and vitamins actually joined together and worked together to create us: meat, milk, eggs. I wanted to know how it all worked and refine my knowledge to the utmost extent.

Once again I found a wonderful group of people whom I worked with, I was connected to area managers in Scotland, and I literally looked after the whole of the North West of England. Our regional manager George Ritchie was a decent fellow who later lost his job and became a financial advisor. I helped him on by taking out a few policies. The Scottish lads were tremendous people and every few months we would have a regional get together somewhere. We would spend a few days in a hotel and go out and play games of one sort or another. I loved the times in Scotland. There was one occasion where our get together was held in Aviemore in the highlands of Scotland. We went to play curling one night but I underestimated the subtleties of the game. The curling implements were huge granite stones and I presumed you had to throw them quite hard. I gave it my all and proceeded to throw the stone through the back of the wall, wincing as it continued all the way into Loch Ness! Well not quite , but it stopped very quickly and noisily.

I soon learned that the game consisted of using the ice to generate the required power and that you had to slide each stone gently, not at 100 miles an hour. Still, we had fun that night.

Colborn Dawes was a very good employer and I was enjoying my work once again but there was a problem in that the driving was killing me. My area stretched from Staffordshire all the way up to the Scottish border and then eventually all the way over to the east coast because the Yorkshire representative retired and I commandeered his area as well. My drive time to work was sometimes five hours, with a full day of work in the middle. I did have the option to stay overnight whenever I had driven a long way but I didn't like to spend the company's money on hotel stays or anything I deemed unnecessary, I was never one to milk the expenses. To me I was doing the company a favour by driving back home, that way I kept the costs down. But I was clocking up 40,000 miles a year.

Still the company looked after me, within the realms of decency I was given whatever I wanted. I had one of the first 414 Rovers that came out - a racing green model. My most abiding memory of that car was in the French Alps when I decided to take a wild mountain road very high up, it was gravel, rough and obviously not used much, but my adventurous spirit took hold ! Half way down the road it was washed away, I could not turn round because the road was so narrow and the drop on one side breathtaking, so I tried to cross the breach and just like in the film "RV" with Robin Williams, the car beached in the centre, not a wheel touched the ground. With no one within miles the family had to get out and we had to all get on the front and weigh down the car so the drive wheels would touch and eventually after much bouncing and effort the car finally got free and we carried on down the mountain. I can say that the family never were that confident about my choice of road to drive down and it would become even more apparent in future adventures.

I was also one of the first people to have one of the very first mobile phones. They fitted my car with a mobile phone with a handset in the front by the radio. It was wired up to the back and in the boot was a great big box and that was the phone! There were very few masts at the time and there was just one phone company that covered the entire mobile network. It was so poor that if you left the motorway you wouldn't have a signal. I knew there were two places that actually worked for me to use the phone, that was one advantage to being perpetually on the road. I could ring home at the A500 turn off for Stafford on the M6 and from there it would be two hours before I would be home, with my tea ready and waiting for me thanks to Alison. If I was at the Tickled Trout pub in Preston I knew I was an hour away and I would ring and give Alison the ETA.

I wasn't allowed to use the phone for personal calls but I think they would have let those minor indiscretions slide, ten seconds here or there. I could hardly walk around with the phone and use it as you would a mobile today. For starters I would have needed a 12-volt battery and a pack, I might have looked like a ghostbuster.

If you watch *Pretty Woman* Richard Gere uses a phone that looks like a house brick with a huge aerial - that is what they were like. You can laugh now but at the time these contraptions were mightily impressive. Here I was with a brand new car and a portable phone, wearing a nice suit (although unlike some of my colleagues I never owned a filofax) - I had made it in most people's eyes. My starting wage in 1988 was £14,004, which was a very impressive figure at the time, particularly with the extra £4, which I could never understand - what was the significance of that £4?

This increase in my salary enabled me to actually afford to buy a more traditional house, a semi-detached in Dalton. It was in a quiet cul-de-sac in an area which was renowned for being a nice place to live. The house itself was nothing special in fact the owners had not particularly looked after it or renovated it to any decent degree. Yet it was full of potential. The sheer size of the place was enticing to me and unlike most semi-detached houses which would just feature a square garden, this one stretched out at a 45 degree angle, because it was on a corner, and it just seemed to go on and on. It continued all the way down to a hedge which, ironically, bordered Keith Howson's farm. The land went on even further towards St. Helen's valley - it was mighty rough but it was still my land, something I was enormously happy about.

Here I was with my goats and ducks with a glorious plot of land.

Not only that but we also had plum trees, apple trees, pear trees, damsons, a truly stunning natural array of life. I found a space between the trees where I managed to dig out the plot for a pond so that I could create a pond for the ducks. I also built a large shed for the goats. I made friends with the Greenhow family, from my years with Dugdales, who lived up in the Ulpha valley. They were in the middle of nowhere really, and they were as far removed from modern technology as is possible, real true sheep farmers. This aversion to modern life was one of their charms - the man of the farm Tommy Greenhow was extremely old school and traditional, and a thoroughly nice chap, one of the friendliest people I've ever met. He always wore old style clothes without a collar and real clogs. His wife was a younger than he was yet she too was a wonderfully friendly lady, whom I sometimes still see at the Park today. I enjoyed visiting the Greenhow farm, it was long drive up the valley in the middle of the fells, but it was like home when you arrived. Everything was old fashioned because Tommy was averse to change, but it was a beautiful house and there would always be something homemade waiting in the kitchen.

They had five daughters altogether and I made a connection with his youngest, Helen. It was always a platonic relationship as she was in a relationship with a young lad called Glen Fitzwilliam, who was to become instrumental in my next few years. He worked at the local shipyard and also helped out on the farm in his spare time. I started to become good friends with Glen and eventually he and Helen would start coming over to spend Friday nights with Alison and I. We would eat pizza and play monopoly and a host of other board games. Oddly enough, I would always double up with Helen, and Glen would partner Alison - we never stuck to our relationship protocol. I became very close to Helen it was a sisterly type affection.

The shed which I was using for my goats came from Tommy and it was some piece of kit because it also contained the chickens and ducks, with nesting areas and a spot for storing all the food. I had a loft at the top with pure white doves. I also found a use for another of my passions, flower gardening. I'm no pansy but flower gardening was in the family in some respect, it was perhaps one of the more enjoyable influences I took from my father as it was always an interest of his. It was also an interest of Jean and Jeff who were the daughter and son-in-law of my 'aunt' Betty. When I was younger I would be sent to spend time with them and it was here I further cultivated my passion for flowers. I remained friends with them as I grew older, I think I was the only one in the family to do so. This actually helped me to build my garden into something special. Quite often I would pop in to see them as I was coming home from work and they would give me a few cuttings from some of their amazing flowers, or some seeds. With their help I produced one of the most stunningly beautiful gardens with a rockery and a little pond. We had beautiful annual flowers with perennials coming back every year. It wasn't the size but the colour - when it was in colour it was staggering. I also had climbing plants, which came with me to the park, they now sit alongside the tigers. I was incredibly pleased with the garden that was created. Unfortunately today I can't have such delicate flowers because I have free roaming animals, the birds and monkeys in particular would just demolish the lot.

In tandem with the furthering of my flower garden I was also renovating our second house, it was becoming something of a habit for me. I couldn't stop. When I wasn't working I was either social- ising briefly, spending time with Alison and the kids, or quite often, modifying our semi-detached. I built an extension and replaced all the windows which were very poorly constructed, I had to re-carpet and completely redecorate the bathroom. Eventually, after a huge amount of work we ended up with a wonderful house, pretty and bright in all departments, ably complimented by the flowers.

The skills I had picked up around Keith were put to further good use and I could not resist building something else outside. At the foot of the garden I constructed my very own aviary all by my lonesome - everything from cutting the wood to length and constructing the shell before covering it all with mesh. Occasionally with all the work I was doing around the house, I would ask Glen to give me a hand and many a time we worked together all day Saturday, and we would swap our Friday pizza night to the Saturday. I would work in all weathers and there was one time where poor Glen also got a soaking on a horrendous day, helping me move a prefab garage. Generally however, at this stage I did all the work on my own. By now Ben was old enough to help his dad and would often push a mini wheelbarrow copying me and helping to dig the sand and clean out the animals.

Soon I had built a number of aviaries and started to fill them with pheasants and parrots. We called our house Dove Cote because of the fact we had so many white doves, it was something I was known for in the area, no one else had white doves. I never had a problem with my neighbour on one side; it was actually Wilf Rigg's brother Brian next door, a local milkman. Wilf's mother lived next door to them as well. It might all sound terribly inbred to the outsider, but it is just the nature of country living. Brian's wife succumbed to cancer while we were living next door and sadly he followed himself by the same illness a few years later.

I did however experience a little resistance from my other next door neighbour, he was a pleasant enough fellow but he wasn't keen on my little animal kingdom. He had a beautiful garden himself and perhaps felt a little aggrieved that he could see my chickens and ducks - lowering the tone no doubt. I appealed to his private nature and agreed to put a fence up between the garden border. I only asked him for half of the money and I built the whole fence myself, a six-foot high panelled fence. Sadly his wife would also die of cancer. We eventually struck up a friendship over time.

I started to talk with a local RSPCA officer who showed an interest because I had so many small animals myself. The conscientious officer was in part responsible for extending my interest beyond the few animals I kept. He came to me one day to ask if I would know anything about looking after a raccoon. A family in north Wales had bought a baby raccoon on the black market somehow but they needed a license and the council had impounded the animal. The RSPCA were supposed to look after the raccoon but seemed clueless as to what to do. Their presumption was that I was the local animal rescuer and I would know what to do. I had no idea about raccoons but didn't have to think too long before deciding it was something I would like to give my best shot. I presumed it couldn't be that difficult and I already had nesting boxes and pens. What I didn't expect was the feisty nature of the raccoon. She was used to human contact but her previous owners had spoiled her and the animal had been living the high life, filling herself with chocolate and all kinds of sweets. The raccoon had turned quite nasty, an unfortunate trait of the animal and they had then impounded the poor thing themselves in a bedroom.

I put my gift to good use and managed to tame the raccoon quite quickly; in a matter of weeks she was sitting on my shoulder and behaving herself. Ironically, this overweight raccoon was called Twiggy. It got to the point where we could bring her in the house and she would play with the kids without a problem. The only time Twiggy went back to her old ways was when it was bed time. When you said, 'Time to go to bed', she would know exactly what that meant and would hide under the bed, or somewhere else out of view. As you put your hand in to try and pull her out she would bite, drawing blood and hurting like hell. Overall however Twiggy was fun to have around though she had to live outside because she would still happily defecate in the house. Thankfully she would use the toilet in the same place, so you often could catch her before she spoiled the carpet.

My conscience soon caught up with me however and I began to feel for Twiggy that she was on her own. As luck had it the RSPCA soon came across another raccoon, a male known as Ricky. He was far more gentle however. He was older and far more meek which was perfect for the kids. Somehow Ricky and Twiggy managed to get on perfectly, they never bred but they were friends for life. Nevertheless, raccoons were still considered as wild and dangerous animals, so the process of applying for a license to keep them with

Barrow council was fun, they were frightened to death and didn't actually know how to go about producing such a document. It must have been the first they had ever produced, it was a crude looking piece of paper which doubled as my certificate, the original of which I still have.

Soon word had spread and as far as the south of England they seemed to be aware of me. I can't remember the precise details of how I acquired them, but I was soon the proud owner of two coati's and their two babies, a South American animal which is, ironically, very similar to a raccoon. At the time I actually had no idea what a coati was and had to visit the local library to find out. The process of collecting the coatis was quite unpleasant as they were keeping the poor things in a box that would barely have been big enough for a budgerigar. Swiftly I carried them away, drove them all the way home from Hertfordshire, and soon made sure they were in a far larger facility. Once again I managed to tame the babies, I was even on good terms with the male coati.

It was around this time that the local paper produced a piece on me and referred to me as 'Dalton's Doctor Doolittle'. It didn't sound right to me at the time but with hindsight there was a fair degree of truth to the article. Something about it rings true now however because today it sits in a frame in my office.

Chapter 11
The zoo plan develops

The character 'Doctor Doolittle' was a fictional doctor who preferred to treat animals rather than humans as he could speak in the animal's language. In Hugh Lofting's books Doolittle has close friends consisting of a duck, a parrot and a pig. It was certainly not too far removed from my own experiences, even at that time, several years before I have the array of animals surrounding me as I do today. The pseudonym Dr. Doolittle didn't seem to work for me at the time, it just didn't sound right, but I soon got used to it. Like the fictional character, once people learned of my 'talent' they were intrigued and wanted to see what the fuss was all about.

The first to see my mini farm set up were the local cub scouts, the leader had called me and asked if I minded them coming to see. I wasn't at all adverse to that but people began to arrive unannounced on my doorstep asking to see the animals. My first instinct would be, "No! This is my house, not a public free for all." Still, most of the time I let people in to have a look around.

Whether it was the newspaper article or the word of mouth locally I'm not sure but eventually I started to branch out with the animals I kept. The next arrivals were a male and a female wallaby. After this I was called and told a now familiar sob story regarding a Shetland pony who was in distress and, if I didn't take him, would have to be put down. Once again he was a feisty creature, which was one of the downsides to me taking on wild and often neglected animals, they weren't used to friendly human contact. Toby was an incredibly wild pony who bit and kicked, though in the end I managed to calm him down enough to ride. Ultimately I gave Toby away to a family whose little boy learned to ride him and even used to parade him at shows - they later brought some amazing photos to me of the little boy who had completely tamed the once wild pony.

The increase in animals suddenly began to move more into the realms of the more exotic. I secured a few rhea's (a large bird which is the South American cousin of the ostrich) from somewhere in southern England. The rhea can be extremely fierce, more so than even their other cousin, the emu. They can kick with an 800-pound force. I didn't do things easy in the old days!

I managed also to acquire two Mara's from Whipsnade Zoo - the Mara brought me back somewhat to my younger days given they are a larger type of guinea pig. These kinds of animals were, at that time, sold privately as surplus stock to those in the know, though it is something that would not happen today because of regulations. It suited me however because I built connections and managed to ingratiate myself with the zoo fraternity. I often visited Chester Zoo and talked to people who worked there about exotic animals in particular, I was inadvertently building a zoo myself but I knew that if I were to do it I wanted to do it properly and to the best of my ability, armed with all the knowledge I would need.

I went through exactly the same process as I had with Keith Howson all those years before - asking 'why' and 'how' to anyone who would know the information. Reading books is one thing but talking to people who have actually done it is quite another, it will give you so much more. You can read all you want on the Internet, but the majority of what you can find on the Internet is complete rubbish.

My life was moving along at a fair pace what with a full-time job, work on our house, acquiring several different types of animals and looking after them, and even playing golf at the weekends with Alison's father, Peter. I was by far the youngest of those playing the sport but it was a touch of exclusivity to be invited to play with Willie Horne who was a real sporting legend in Barrow-in-Furness. He also always carried a bag of sweets with him and was very generous in sharing them out. I truly enjoyed it and began to play regularly on a Saturday afternoon. It dawned on me after about four times of doing this however, that each time I played golf I had wasted four hours away from my wife and kids when I had barely seen them all week. I didn't like it. I felt guilty that I was leaving my wife and kids on a day that I would normally spend with them so I just stopped. I continued to play golf but it was at a ridiculous time on a Saturday morning, quite often 5am. I would be back for nine or ten o'clock to spend the day with my family. I still enjoyed the golf, even without the banter, the peace and solitude seemed to appeal to me. I played with a handicap of about 23, and was even competent enough to play in a few competitions but eventually I gave up playing sport to spend more time with my family.

Within my job there were changes afoot, my manager was suddenly removed from the company due to streamlining after a takeover by another company. They cut costs but caused complete uproar by sacking several people. I was lucky to keep my job but the downside was they extended my area. It was already too large in all probability, but now it was getting ridiculous. I now had control over an area that extended from Lincolnshire all the way to the Scottish borders. The area looked too big, all too much to handle and I asked myself how I could possibly manage it. At the time this was all I had, to me I had nowhere else to go, this was it, this was my job and my life. What was the alternative?

So many people ask me how I decided to build a zoo. The change in my employment was really the catalyst, made easier by the fact that I had already amassed an impressive private collection of animals. I had a very large collection of parrots for instance, not to mention all of my rescued animals. It was becoming unmanageable in this area of my life as well. For example, if we went on holiday as a family I had to entrust my brother Colin to look after all the animals. Poor Colin had a huge list of things to do and the ins and outs of feeding each animal. He was very good to do this but he had no experience with animals and it would worry me that I was leaving all of my animals in somebody else's hands.

In the spring of 1993 I woke up with a eureka moment and I knew that I did not want to carry on with what I was doing, I had a burning desire to do something else. I loved my animals so much and I was totally engrossed in what I was doing - bringing the exotic animals in and tending to them. I was still being asked whether I could show various groups of children around my selection of animals and it had reached the stage where I had the idea that I could open up the garden to the public and charge something for it.

This was quickly brought into the realms of the practical as I realised that in order to properly open up to the public I would need a zoo licence and special protections of one kind or another. I would have to come under public regulation which meant safety barriers, washing facilities, toilets and many other things.

I returned to my instincts and remembered why it was I loved animals and just what they meant to me. I also thought of the predictable, unpleasant realities of many zoos –that animals were caged or entrapped in some capacity and they were not allowed to follow their own wishes or instincts.

It suddenly occurred to me. I want to bring a message to the world, I want to tell people about animals and about their needs and about the problems they face. They are very rare in the wild and we, as the human race, should be doing something about it. Regarding captive animals I wanted to pass on the information and belief that people should not keep animals if they cannot look after them properly. It had been a familiar theme through my work so far, that I was often taking animals from people who could not look after them, or more to the point, couldn't be bothered to look after them properly.

I woke up with the *urge* to do this, the emotive instinct to do it. I didn't know how, I didn't know when or what. There was nothing I could possibly put my finger on or give me a factual clue, it was just a feeling and I needed to do something. Alison seemed to think I had flipped my lid, though she understood my love for animals and my desire. The timing was perfect with the unsettlement within my job and it gave me the impetus to look into the idea of my own zoo practically and vigorously. I began to look for land where I could expand my rapidly swelling animal collection.

I approached Barrow council first of all, asking if they might have any land for lease or rent that I could possibly use. I was faced with a brick wall, there was nothing available. I began to look of my own accord, at a number of derelict sites, for instance I came across an old quarry. There was also an old farm which may have been partly for sale, it would have been a 50% ownership. Yet nothing seemed right and in fact, the practicalities suddenly manifested and it seemed incredibly difficult to get anywhere, once you truly looked into it. I wasn't about to be dissuaded by this however, everything I had ever achieved in life had been through determination and hard work. It wasn't going to stop me now.

I had spoken with a couple of local councillors who told me about the possibility of reclaimed land, before a man called Jack Dent, who owned Maidenlands Farm, approached me. He was also a Barrow councillor. By now the local people were well versed in who I was and what I was doing, I had been in the paper several times and had been interviewed on Radio Cumbria. Jack Dent told me he had heard I was looking for some land for my animals.

"This bypass has just been approved and it's coming right through my farm," he said, "it's splitting it right in half so it's not viable anymore so I'm going to retire, I'll keep a few cattle but really it doesn't matter where I have them whether it's over here or over there, it won't matter to me. So have a look both sides and you can take your choice, pick your spot and we can have a talk about it if you want, if you're interested."

This peaked my interest, though the landscape was daunting. Where I sit writing this today was split in two sections; an area of old mineshafts and mine workings that was very overgrown and had been for 120 years or so. It was as natural as it could be with all sorts of unique topography. In fact, you couldn't even penetrate into half of it, it was so thick with undergrowth, so dense that you could barely see what should or could be there. Three quarters of the overall land was also one giant, and much clearer, field. This field was more like it. It contained cows at the time and had, a few years earlier, been ploughed for barley.

'Wow this is it,' I thought, 'it's big; it's a lot bigger than I'd been looking at everywhere else. It has formal sides for fields and paddocks and it has a wild side for letting deer go and have a truly wild experience. I told Jack, "This is exactly what I want - space."

Jack was a down to earth bloke who was open and honest, not to mention unselfish. I asked what he wanted for the land.

"Well, I just want agricultural rates. I don't want 'owt more, I'm not being greedy."

He asked me what I wanted to do with the land, when I told him, he said, "Well, good luck to you mate."

Initially the land cost me £32,000 for everything, but there was an additional piece which was supposed to go to another buyer, who pulled out. Jack then offered me the additional land, which I am extremely thankful for, as well as the fact that he only asked for an extra £4,000.

Completely old school, there was no contract, no signatures, Jack went by his word and a handshake. It is called honour, something you rarely see nowadays. We shook hands and that was the deal done. The paperwork was a formality. However I still needed to raise the money to afford the land. My house had cost me £65,000 and the only way I could raise the money was to sell the house I had so lovingly restored. Luckily I made a decent profit on the two houses (including the first house I had sold for £50,000), something in the region of £35,000.

It was a phenomenal amount at the time, and curiously the house would be worth little more today than it was in 1992. At the time the price I received was highly over inflated - way more than other houses on the same street - and the reason was simply that I had put so much effort into the restoration. The house was an Olde World cottage effectively because I had used mock oak beams to furnish it. They were only hollow beams, made by myself in the back yard, then 'aged' and stained but they looked real enough.

This was the beauty of Margaret Thatcher's tenure as prime minister, at that time there was a sudden increase in house inflation and if you were selling yours, you made money. My wife and kids were effectively on the streets, we had no house, but I did have the difference between the price I had sold my house and the cost of the land I had bought. It was the first time in my life I had ever had such a sum of money in the bank.

I had to finance the project as I had not yet sold my house so my natural instinct was to go to Barclays bank and ask them what to do. I had banked with them all through my life, I might have had very little in there, but I was a loyal customer. We had always budgeted perfectly and had never been overdrawn. They told me I needed a business plan. I had no idea what a business plan should consist of.

My whole business life had consisted of following someone else's plan, to do a job which fitted in with someone else's strategy. I was never the person constructing or developing the plan. Luckily, I had at least been very au fait with the accounting side of finance, I was very good with money and knew a fair amount of about borrowing money and interest rates. This was one skill which I had developed through my job at Dugdales, and in fact many of the things I had learned in that job would become useful in building a zoo.

My initial idea was not actually a zoo however; it was more like a wildlife centre to teach people about the animals, it was quite different from the average zoo concept. The image of a zoo would instantly convey the notion of an animal in a cage and that was something I could not abide, I had never in my life wanted to keep an animal in a cage, in fact I had spent most of my life - even at that stage - springing them free from their confines. I had to combine my concept and beliefs with the realism of a business plan. I knew I had to learn very quickly what a business plan should consist of and so I found a guide model. It all seemed very complicated to me at the time: cash flows, forward planning, projections of income, projections of expenditure.

It occurred to me that I had no idea where to even start. What I did know was that my idea to build our house on site seemed to be financially sound. Building materials were much cheaper to buy and build with yourself back then, today it is more on a par. My business plan needed to include the cost of building our house. It is here that I must introduce my longest standing true friend, Stewart Lambert.

Stewart was a dairy farmer at Lupton, near Kirkby Lonsdale and I'd been told about him by another customer of mine, James, a farmer at Lowick. James suggested I talk to Stewart - a friend of his from college - because he had mentioned to him about the feed I was selling and he thought he would be interested. I met Stewart and his dad, Arthur, who has sadly passed away now, and he certainly was interested and began to buy feed from me. But more than that, we developed a very good friendship, he was someone I loved talking to and felt I had much in common with. He is the sort of person who will do anything for his friends.

He is a big, strong farming man but also extremely understanding – a real country character with very strong morals and ethics. He is a committed community man, he sits on a Parish council and has been on the board of school governors. He is a real team player who genuinely cares for his community and people around him. He is also extremely helpful. He could see the passion I had for building a zoo and just wanted to help in any way he could, a habit he continues to this day. He will help me find pieces of machinery I might need. For instance, he found me a second hand motorcycle and also made me a trailer from his home workshop. He is a very busy farmer but has been there from the beginning to help me. In fact, in later years when the zoo was a functioning business, Stewart would help me build the railway line within the Park.

Stewart and his girlfriend Christine, who would later become his wife now 25 years ago, have been there as my friends through every trial and tribulation in my life since 1984.

When I was about to begin my house building journey on my newly acquired land, Stewart was the first person I wanted to speak with. Stewart's dad had just built a bungalow on their land so that they would be able to move out of their farmhouse. I was in awe of their bungalow, I loved it. There was so much to admire, out in the middle of the countryside with a beautiful interior and a little pond just in front of the house.

I asked the Lambert family if they would mind showing me their plans to see what was involved in building a bungalow just like that, because I had no idea of the process, not to mention the cost. Typically they were only too happy to help and let me take the plans away to use as I required. In all honesty I only slightly modified their own plans, though it might be hard to tell. In general I took every inch of their plans and used it to my own advantage for my own house.

Once I had the plans devised I took them to builders for a quote on what this would all cost. It was quite demoralising as I knew the amount I had left from the sale of my house and after buying the land for the new house I knew I would have to borrow money from somewhere.

When I look at my business plan now it is rather amusing, it looks like a primary school kid constructed the whole thing, but at the time I was bursting with pride to have devised such a professional looking plan. I had to work out the very basics - what money did I need to survive, how much would the food for the animals cost, what was the bare minimum I could expect to make from visitors? I had no idea how many people would come and I had no idea how quickly I could make any money back that I had borrowed. I had identified my level where I would break even and that was 10,000 visitors in a year, which would produce £30,000 in visitor fees. I felt that was achievable.

I was still friendly with the staff at Dugdales and used it to my advantage. Being a little cheeky I asked the girls in the office if they would mind typing up my hand written business plan during their breaks, and bind five or six copies for me to make it look more professional. Computers existed but they were like something out of *War Games*, so my plan was going to be relatively crude if I didn't enhance it somehow. The girls were very kind, I had always got on well with them, and they did it all for me. I had a professional looking business plan and I was primed for my first visit to Barclays bank. What I didn't bank on was being laughed out of the place.

Everything was in place, I had my business plan, my formal meeting with the manager of Barclays bank, I was in my suit and I was ready to do this. The first disappointment was that the manager didn't actually read the business plan at all. All that hard work and he had a cursory flick through.

"What are you gonna do?"

"I want to produce a little wildlife park so that people can come and visit, see the animals. Schools can visit and learn all about how to keep animals properly and how rare animals are and it will be an educational thing where they could also have a picnic."

The manager's laughter reverberated around the dank, windowless office.

"Yeah, yeah, yeah, round here? No chance, not a chance."

"Well look, I need to borrow some money to do it, I've been banking with you for…" "No sir, sorry sir, it doesn't capture me."

That was it. My dream seemed to be over. The amount of work and effort that had gone into my preparation plan was extraordinary and I had not even considered this could fail at the last hurdle. I was dreadfully disappointed. I had no idea what to do, I had made up my mind that this is what I was going to do, my head was no longer in my regular job, I was going to have an animal attraction and I was utterly single minded. But without a loan I had no method of doing it. If I couldn't get the money

I couldn't build my house, I couldn't put the fences round, I couldn't do anything - nothing.

Alison had always put her faith in me and she wasn't the type to put her foot down. If I suggested going to the Pyrenees on holiday she wouldn't say, "no I want to go to Italy." She would go with my suggestion. She must have believed in me, even if she didn't believe in the idea wholeheartedly, and I was going to let her and the children down if I could not now go through with my initial idea - the reason I had put the house on the market and agreed to buy a portion of land which for all intents and purposes could now be meaningless. I didn't know what to do but domestically fate intervened. My parent's neighbours were Mr and Mrs Mills. The couple had no relatives and Mam and Dad actually helped to look after them in their old age. When I was a child we would often spend some time there at Christmas. They were old time people but I was a little scared of Mr Mills as he was the sort who wouldn't give you your ball back if it went into his garden, though you might get five back at once one day. They were incredibly old fashioned but their generosity showed through in the end because when they died they left their house to myself and my brothers and sisters.

It came at just the right time too seeing as my own family now suddenly had nowhere to live. I asked my brothers and sisters if they would possibly retain ownership of the house but allow me, Alison and the kids live in it temporarily. Thankfully they agreed that we could. Beggars can't be choosers but even so, the state of the house was a concern. It was built in the 1800s and hadn't been updated very much, though there had been an inside bathroom added which was a relative godsend. The house still had lead piping, there was no real hot water system, there was just a fire in the front room. It was absolutely freezing and falling to pieces, it boggled the mind to think that this poor couple had actually remained in those conditions for so long. Still, if necessary the house would have been something of an asset, even if I only had a fifth of its value.

The entire figure I needed for my plan was £177,000. This covered absolutely everything I needed to do for the whole of the land as well as the house construction. The obvious course of action was to visit another bank and the manager of Lloyds was a different breed from the other guy.

"I think it's a wonderful idea...

but..."

There is always a but.

"Wonderful idea but you know, have you really thought this out properly? I have no asset to lend against."

He had a point. Once I received my mortgage money on our refurbished house I no longer had an asset. The Mills' house was worth no more than £15,000 though the manager suggested it would probably be more like £10,000. At that rate I would only have £2,000 from the sale of that house.

"You have no asset, how can I lend you money with no collateral? That is an issue, you want money but you have nothing. Even though I think it's a great concept, a great idea, I haven't got the ability to lend you the money."

I decided to fulfil my already arranged appointment with yet another bank, and so the next day I met with the manager of NatWest. This chap was more studied and open minded in his outlook.

"David, just leave me the business plan, I'll take it home over the weekend and have a read of it, then come back to see me. I've got a vacancy Tuesday morning at 10 o'clock, come back and see me then and we'll discuss it."

Tuesday morning could not come soon enough.

"Right then, what do you think?"

"You've got fifteen minutes, tell me all about the thing."

"But you've got the plan, you've read it."

"Yes I know I have but I want you to tell me about it."

I told him I wanted to put a load of pens together that would enable people to visit and feed the wallabies, feed a Shetland pony and feed chickens and ducks but also all the pheasants were out in the wild in the trees in the woodlands so they would see them just as they would be in their Asian homeland. I would have parrots flying in the trees overhead. I wanted people to be able to see raccoons and coati's in their natural environment. I added that I wanted to educate people to think about the wider world and potentially change the way they looked after their own animals.

We would have a picnic area and a small souvenir shop - in fact the café, shop and toilets would all be in the same building. I must have spoken for the whole fifteen minutes selling the whole idea of the proposed venture.

"Right. I've had a little think about this before you came and you've got your money." I was shocked because I just couldn't imagine! By now I had cut myself off from the chance of doing it.

"I think we've come up with an idea if you're interested which I could put to you."

First of all I needed to know why. Why did this bank accept my idea when the previous two came up with reasons against it.

"Can I just ask you why? I went to Barclays and he just laughed at me, I went to Lloyds and he just didn't have any way whatsoever that he could finance this even though he thought it was a reasonable idea, so what's different?"

"Well, with your enthusiasm, it cannot fail."

It hadn't been the infallibility of the business plan that had convinced the manager, it had been my enthusiasm, which meant the world to me. I will never forget that feeling – I was suddenly renewed and invigorated with extreme confidence that I could do this. I was given an opportunity once again. The words spoken then have in fact been a consistent motivation throughout my life ever since, I have never forgotten them and have always tried to live up to them.

"Right, now is the difficult bit because we have to find a way of getting you this money. We have rules, just like Lloyds Bank do, and I can only lend to collateral. I've thought about this, you're going to build a house, so what we will do is build that first. How much is it for the house?"

"About £44,000."

"Right, well I'll approve a loan on that house, I will take a charge on that property and we'll release the money as you're building it, and once that house is built and liveable, we can have it re valued as a property, then we'll lend against that value, whatever that estimation is."

We estimated the value would eventually be £170,000 which was an awful lot of money for a bungalow in the middle of nowhere. Effectively the bank would loan against each progressive part of the property. I then built another bungalow on site which I was going to renovate to become the café, shop and toilets. The bank would loan me money against the value of the house which at the time contained everything a residential property would - windows, front/back door, bathrooms, kitchen etc.

I had to remove the middle walls from the plans of the bungalow in order to put the required elements for a public visiting place but if push came to shove all I would have to do is to reinstall the partition walls and I would have a three bedroom bungalow over-looking the lake.

"What we'll do is we'll build that as a bungalow and if worse comes to the worst we have two houses to sell so we'll value that up as a property as well and then we've got two assets. I can then lend one against the other in order to take you into the next stage. It will have to be done in order, with the final piece of the jigsaw being the building of a couple of roads and a children's farm area. That will cover your entire plan - how's that?"

"That's a very clever and feasible plan."

"We'll need papers in place of course and guarantees and have to do this properly but if you're prepared to go along with that, let's get on with it."

Chapter 12
The Zoo is born

"Life is a series of natural and spontaneous changes.
Don't resist them- that only creates sorrow.
Let reality be reality, let things flow naturally forward in whatever way
they like"

I now had to move onto planning permission so I had to construct my plans and send them to Barrow council. At the time there was a Conservative council which was a very positive thinking business development council but also at the time, luckily for me, there was a very short-term loophole in planning law which was designed to stimulate tourism development in this region.

There was a six-month window where green field sites could be considered and it was felt to be a good strategy for the area. It was one of the most unlikely plans they had ever seen and normally it would probably have not been approved - my entire plan went in as one, my residential dwelling, the buildings, the lands, the animals, it was all in one huge plan. The chance of having a house in the middle of a green fields site would have been minimal usually, yet I convinced them I had to live on site because of the animals, and because of the loop hole, the plan passed with flying colours, a unanimous vote. Today the planning process is so much more complicated, not to mention expensive. In 1993 the whole planning process cost me £135, which today you can't even sneeze for. Applications for expansion of the park today run into tens of thousands.

There was another difficulty however - there was no road up to the site of the proposed park. They were building a bypass next to my land at the time and I decided to go and see the foreman in charge of building the bypass. I was straight with him and asked if there was any chance they might help me to put a road in leading up to the park. Conveniently the workers had to put a large amount of top soil near to the top of the hill where my land stood. In order to make the route easier they were going to build an access road. I took my cheek one step further and asked if there was any chance they would tarmac the road at the same time. He wasn't sure they would get permission but seemed willing to help and eventually I did indeed have a road glossed with tarmac all the way up to my site, for free.

There was a small inconvenience for this. The road was approved because it was at the behest of giving farmers good traction access to their cattle pens, so in order to have it approved, they had to build the cattle pens, which I promptly took straight down once the road was built. While the road was being built there were also workmen digging the drains. I went and spoke to the contractor and with more bare faced cheek I managed to get our water main put in the same trench and buried without charge.

When I bought the land there was no road, no water, no electricity, no telephones. In fact there wasn't even a fence around the land as it had only just been cut off from another farm.

I was still working at my job but I was doing the absolute bare minimum in order to keep the job. I had lost all my enthusiasm for the job, all I wanted to do was to get a move on with my project. As soon as it was approved I could not wait to move. My lawyer John Illet from Thomas Butler and Son, in Broughton was able to quickly pass through the legal requirements such as the land and the deed. The moment the deed was transferred he was on the phone telling me I could begin work. John is one of the few old school lawyers left in the world. He behaves with dignity and exhibits honesty as the first priority. The legal profession has deteriorated over time with many people involved merely to make money; thankfully John was never like that.

Even in my haste to start work on my own vision I had the realisation that my job wouldn't last too long if I didn't have enough miles on my clock, I was barely doing the rounds and should really have been driving the length and breadth of the country, so I needed a way to show I was still active in my job.

I had a Lancia Dedra which I placed up onto some wooden blocks. I placed the car in top gear and put a block onto the throttle. If anyone had knocked the car over it would probably have run for about ten miles before it stopped! I ran the wheels incessantly, placing more and more miles onto the clock, it was the only thing I could do to give the impression I was still doing my 'real' job. It makes me laugh now but I don't feel too guilty about it, I believe I made them enough profit to justify the block scandal. Besides, I didn't do it all the time, only the odd day when I was supposed to drive 250 miles and actually did none because I would have to go to meet a guy driving a bulldozer and show him what to do.

Like the impromptu inheritance, another thing which seemed to happen with perfect timing was that Glen Fitzwilliam had been informed that he was going to be made redundant at the shipyard. As an apprentice he was the first to go. I'd told Glen about my project and said to him, "Well, seeing as you will be losing your job, how about coming to help me build an animal park?"

I had set myself a target. It was October and I thought that if we really moved with it we could have the zoo ready for Easter. I was in dream land really but didn't know that at the time! I told Glen, "We have to get roads, we have to get paths in, we have to get fences up, we have to move animals in, we have to get the shop building up and open and ready for go and somehow or other we've got to do this in time."

I knew Glen was a hard worker and he was exactly the type of person I would need. I asked him what he thought. He said he would leave his job before they got rid of him and come and work for me.

"The hours are going to be all God sends us," I said candidly, "from twilight to darkness, this is the only way we'll get this done." Ever the grafter, Glen said, "No worries to me, you can pay me by the hour."

He became self employed, bought himself an old Land Rover and travelled every day to work with me flat out. Just clearing the undergrowth was the most horrendously hard work, you were prickled, impaled by thorns, you had to crawl half the time to get where you were going it was that thick. The only tool we really had that was of any use was a small chainsaw of Glen's. This was real work, it was by far the hardest I had ever worked in my life and the same was true of Glen.

We had a male ego contest going on which somehow seemed to inspire us. It was something of a competition that was ongoing between us, who was the strongest! He was at least ten years younger than myself, though I like to think I might have won the contest! Nevertheless we both had to admit, we thought we were fit, but working like that proved to us just how far we had to go.

As far as my planning methods on the outline of the land, I stood at the back of the entire area, surveying the land. I took several photographs and drew all the natural lines I could see on the land, onto a piece of paper. My neighbour had owned horses for a couple of years and it was clear to me that the horses had found their own path, the easiest way of traversing up and down the land. I realised that the horses weren't stupid, if it was good enough for them it was good enough for me.

I followed the paths for the boundary and for each individual area I followed the same natural lines that I could envisage. I would naturally follow the obvious dictations of where paths and fences should be often using the natural creations of the old mines and railway lines. It was a fairly crude and quick method of devising where I would put the entire contents of my animal park but I knew in my head what the right method was going to be. I could see where each section of animals would go, where the children's farm would go. Somehow the land that I had seemed to fit all my requirements, it was simply that we had to carve out the correct landscape in order to fit everything in the parameters. There must have been an element of destiny at play because my very first plan for the entire park has changed very little over the course of time, it is very much the same today in fact. Obviously many new and different animals have since come into the park compared to the early days but the roads and paths surrounding them are the same as they were the day we first constructed the zoo.

Many people have since commented how clever my layout is and what a quality construction the whole place is. It wasn't clever in the least! It was a natural occurrence, I barely thought about it. Nothing was placed with any great merit or forethought, it had come into its own naturally, and to an extent, fortuitously.

The Zoo is born

One thing which I can perhaps take more credit for is the up and down nature of the land. We used a huge excavator to dig ditches out of the ground. When I first came to the land it was almost completely flat on the lower section. But with the digger we created natural topography by digging out one part of the ground and piling it high on the other side - a large swathe of dips, ditches and mounds. I also bought 5,000 trees to create more of a forest effect. I planted almost every single one of those trees myself and they are all still standing today. It was a ridiculous amount of work, and took me twice as long as I expected.

You would think by this stage that I had avoided all potential difficulties with regards to my proposed zoo but in reality they were just beginning. My next door neighbour was, at the exact same time I had put my plan in, aiming to be approved for a plant hire business in the adjoining land. At the time he had put the application in I had no idea because it was before I myself had been approved, no one had to tell me as I was not the land owner at the time. He did manage to have his application approved and was then able to trade as Marsh Plant Hire next door to me.

He had also, like myself, asked for permission to build a bungalow. He has a son with disablities and knew a bungalow would be more accessible for his son and useful from the point of view of all his equipment that would be around the place - the house, especially a bungalow, was really a necessary requirement. Bizarrely his application was refused, whereas mine passed. Principally the reason must have been the fact that I fell into the planned tourist development whereas his bungalow did not. Disgusting that a council could be so heartless, but nothing unusual there.

The council had asked my opinion on the bungalow being there and I was honest. All I told them was that the owners (who I did not know at the time) must realise that my application had already been passed and that the noise of the chickens, cockerels and monkeys - or anything else that might make a noise - was something they knew about when they built their house, and that they could not then complain at a later date. I didn't say I was against it, I didn't say I was for it, I just said so long as they realise in the future that they chose to live next to a noisy place.

Unfortunately my neighbour Mike Marsh saw my objection as possibly the thing that refused his application, something which today I completely understand. As the Marsh application did not fit council criteria they obviously used my comments as a reason to object to his proposal, despite the fact that I personally did not mind if he built a twelve-storey mansion next door. From the Marsh perspective I became an outlet for their frustration, and they made sure that I was aware they did not like me - they were very unfriendly neighbours.

The problem with the neighbours was not just during the process of constructing the park, it went on for around a decade, with silent hate existing on both sides of the fence. For all that time Mike Marsh seemed to believe I had prevented him building a bungalow which was just nothing like the truth. Bizarrely, ten years later would be the first time we actually met each other, during negotiations for expansion of my park. It was strange because we realised instantly that we were both decent blokes. Once we shook hands and shared a cup of tea it was as if nothing had happened in the preceding years, the slate was wiped clean.

The other difficulties for me in the building of the park were both physical and financial. A lot of the time we couldn't even drive directly to the land, there was no road at the time and we had to park the Land Rover a fair distance away which meant we had to carry all our materials. When we were putting up fences it was extremely difficult to carry all the poles and posts and that was before we even started putting them into the ground.

I will never forget David Troughton, from Broughton Mills, who helped me enormously in this respect. He owned an item worth its weight in gold and it was a fair old weight. The post knocker was a 25 kilogram weight which was made to sit over fence posts, with handles on each side. He had made this himself, welded it together personally. In truth it was far too heavy. At the time I was working on the land he had got himself a modern version and no longer used the heavy one.

He told me this and I asked if I could use it. I was used to begging and borrowing for everything I needed, because financially we were in a mess. We had no money for anything, it was so bad in

REPORT 1969.

NAME **David Gill**   FORM **One**   NO. IN FORM **38**

AGE **8** yrs. **2** mths.   AVERAGE AGE **8** Yrs. **6** mths.

	ASSESSMENTS		REMARKS
	Year's Work	Annual Examinations	
Reading	A+		David takes a lively and intelligent interest in all Class activities.
English, Oral Spelling.	A+	A	
" Written		A-	
" Comprehension		B+	
Mathematics			
Number Problems	A	A	He has developed a sense of responsibility which is very pleasing and which appeared to be rather lacking at the beginning of the year.
General "			
Topics & Project work			
History ..	A-	B+	
Geography ..			
N/S Science			
Handwork & Manipulative Skill	A-		
Music	A-		
Art	A-		He has done some very good work and I hope that he will maintain his enthusiasm for work next year.
Drama			
French			
Muscular Co-ordination, General P.E., Games.	A		

Willingness to work......**A**..........

Conduct........................**A-**..........

Attendance....................**A**..........   Signed.....*Carol J. Whiteley.* (Mrs.
                                                            Form Master/Mistress

A pleasing start David.

Signed.....*R. Murray*..........
                ~~Headmaster~~

Signature of Parent/......*G. J. Gill*..........
            ~~Guardian.~~

A represents Excellent, B Good, C Average, D Poor, E Very Poor.

1969 School Report

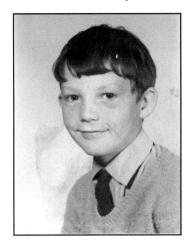

No. 3

DANGEROUS WILD ANIMALS ACT 1976

LICENCE TO KEEP DANGEROUS WILD ANIMAL(S)

THE Borough Of Barrow In Furness
being the local authority for the purposes of the above Act HEREBY LICENSE
. Mr. D. Gill
of 3 Romney Avenue Dalton In Furness Cumbria
being the [proposed] owner and keeper of the animal(s) specified in the Schedule
hereto TO KEEP such DANGEROUS WILD ANIMAL(S) at
. 3 Romney Avenue Dalton In Furness
subject to the conditions endorsed hereon.

A fee of £ 72 has been paid for this Licence.

This Licence shall remain in force from the 21st August 1992
until and including 31st December 19 92.

GRANTED at the Office of the said Council at Town Hall Barrow

on the Twenty First day of August 19 92.

D Hodson

Chief Environmental Health Officer †

† Insert title of proper officer.   (The officer appointed for this purpose.)

SCHEDULE

4 Nasua Nasua (Coatimundi)

6 Rhea Americana (Common Rhea)

CONDITIONS SUBJECT TO WHICH THE ABOVE LICENCE IS GRANTED

1. While any animal is being kept under the authority of the Licence:—
   (i) the animal shall be kept by no person other than the person or persons specified above;
   (ii) the animal shall normally be held at such premises as are specified above;
   (iii) the animal shall not be moved from those premises [except in the following circumstances, namely, For Purposes Of Transporting For Veterinary Treatment Or Removal In Case Of Fire Or Like Emergency, At Which Times The Animal/s Shall Be Confined In A Suitable Container];
   (iv) the person to whom the Licence is granted shall hold a current insurance policy which insures him and any other person entitled to keep the animal under the authority of the Licence against liability for any damage which may be caused by the animal, the terms of such policy being satisfactory in the opinion of the authority.
2. The species and number of animals of each species which may be kept under the authority of the Licence shall be restricted to those specified in the Schedule above.
3. The person to whom the Licence is granted shall at all reasonable times make available a copy of the Licence to any person entitled to keep any animal under the authority of the Licence.
4. Removal Of Barbed Wire Stand From Fence Of Rhea Compound.
5. Adapt Floor Of Coatimundi Enclosure For Soil /Peat In One Area.
6. Additional Fencing At Rear Of Animal Enclosures
7. Two Fire Extinguishers Placed Near Animal Accommodation.

* Insert additional conditions, if any.

Cat. No. DWA 4.   SHAW & SONS LTD., Shaway House, London, SE26 5AE   W246 (M) ☐

My first Dangerous Wild Animal Licence

Me and my sister Alison, 1962

Alison, Karen and myself posing for a family photo in 1963. I'm the cute one in the middle

Looking dapper at comprehensive school, 1975

In Venice, Italy whilst backpacking
round Europe, age 18

Janet and Keith Howson circa 1970, they changed my life

The Howson farm, 1975. Sam the Cow Dog looking on

My very first car, a Ford Escort 1100

My folk rock band Jack Snipe who played
professionally in venues around the region

Looking trim for the RAF
in Swinderby.

Rachel Howson on the farm having fun in the snow. The two of us became very close

The Gill family in 1985. Right to left - Karen, Alison, Mam, Colin, Dad, Me, Michael

The day it all began, bringing the goats home to the farm in 1982

Me, Amy and Jethro on the beach. I used to walk him everywhere. 1986

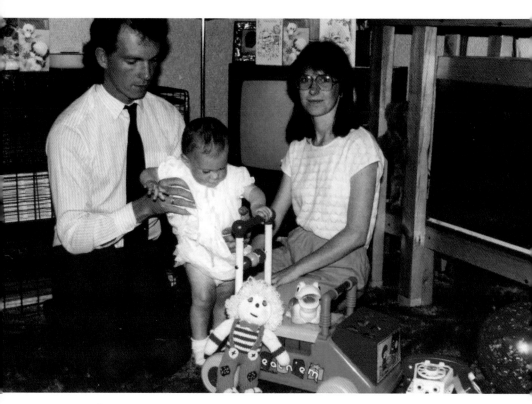

Amy's 1st birthday, in Valley Cottage, Ann Street with me dressed for work at Dugdales. 1986

The garden I created at Ann Street for the first ever Gill menagerie. 1989

A walk through High Dam, with the family and four pet goats. 1990

Glen and Helen Fitzwilliam's wedding. Amy is the flower girl.
I took all the official photos

First earth broken when building my house on the new zoo site in 1993. Ben and Amy helping

In the Pyrenees with Alison, Amy, Ben and Claudia Ullman on the far left. 1993

The view looking down toward what is now the restaurant and entrance
at South Lakes, before I started work. 1993

Just 8 weeks before opening the park...not much to do! 1994

The same view of the entrance road in 2006

The official opening ceremony for the park, with 4X the emu. 1994

4X walks through the ribbon

May 29th, 1994, the first weekend South Lakes Wild Animal Park opened

The show must go on. Giving an owl talk with leg strapped after being attacked by an emu

Close up with ringtailed lemurs whilst filming for the BBC in 1995

The Babirusa that made a meal of me, but his tusks were much larger than this at the time he bit me.

Padang, a male Sumatran tiger testing a new satellite tracking collar in the park

Still the most popular event every day. Toba in 1997

fact that we could hardly afford food for the kids. I had given up my job and there was literally no money coming in. At the time we simply lived day to day.

Though I had bought the land for the precise purpose of having a clear public animal park I couldn't see through the sheer thickness of the undergrowth in order to penetrate - it was something we couldn't give up doing but it seemed never ending. The immense density of the briars and thorns was just unbelievable, most of it was very nasty - black thorn bushes and so on, we would always be going home with holes all over us. It was during one of these thorny encounters that I almost blinded myself, an incident which reveals both my determination and stupidity in equal measure.

I was laying hedges the way I had been shown by Keith. I was pushing a hawthorn branch back and it fell out my grip and snapped back into my face. It hurt like hell, my eyes were watering but I just got on with it and worked the rest of the day. I got home about 6pm that day, it was completely dark outside and there weren't too many mirrors where we were working!

As I walked through the door Alison looked at me with horror.

"What is wrong with your eye?"

"Oh I got smacked in the eye with a thorn bush this morning, it's been giving me hell all day, I've got a real headache now, actually I'm going to go to bed."

"Something's not right with it, something's not right."

"What do you mean?"

"It looks odd, get down the doctor's now."

"No, I'm going to go to bed, it will be alright in the morning."

"No, I'm not allowing that, I'm phoning the doctor now and you're going to go down."

We caught the doctor just before she was about to leave for the day and she agreed to see me. I went straight down to see her.

"David, you're going straight to hospital now, can you find someone who can take you down?"

"Probably, why?"

"You've got a hole in your eye and your eye is leaking, that's not tears, that's the inside of your eye coming out. If you don't get somebody to operate on that, in a few hours you'll be blind."

I was terrified. I believed I had been suffering with tears from a branch scratching my eye when in actual fact my eye was leaking all over my face. Alison rushed me to hospital and within half an hour I was in the operating theatre. I woke up with an eye patch but didn't realise straight away that they had actually taken my eye out of its socket to operate. The way it was described to me was that they removed skin from the back of my eye and grafted it onto the front, filling the hole. Given it was a new layer of skin they had to sew the inside of my eye with stitches. When you think of a grain of sand in your eye, you can just imagine what it was like to have two stitches with the end of the thread stroking the inside of your eye lid for week after week. Every time I moved my eye in any way it scratched, it drove me insane.

The specialist told me I was allowed to go home after a day or so but I was told not to bend, lift or do anything remotely strenuous for a month. On the way home we went to B&Q and bought a set of goggles so that I could go straight back to work in the afternoon. What did the doctors know? I couldn't do nothing for four weeks, I would have trouble doing nothing for four hours. Alison couldn't believe my stubbornness and played hell with me but I didn't listen. To me I was still being sensible, I did think twice before bending or lifting and I tried to manage other people instead of doing everything I would normally, but for all intents and purposes I still worked.

The stitches came out naturally after a while and when I went back to see the specialist I was expecting that at the very least I would need to wear glasses, but amazingly, there was no damage to my eye at all. Only recently have I needed to invest in a pair of glasses and that is just for reading small print. At the time however my eye was perfect, though it still bears the scar, which is just remotely visible. In fact the specialist has come back to my zoo for years afterwards and always was proud of the work she did on my eye and so she should be - she saved my life.

Another issue with building the zoo was the fact that the pond which was now on my land, had been used for many years by fishermen who could not understand why there was now a fence around the pond and they were no longer able to fish there.

I couldn't afford to have people fishing within the grounds of my own private business, not to mention my future home. So I banned it. But the fisherman's legacy had been left, they must be some of the most untidy folks in existence. The rubbish they left behind was atrocious: empty bread bags with old sandwiches, tin cans and bottles, broken bottles and then the worst thing of all: fishing line with and without hooks still attached, lead weights, floats, every tree was decorated with fishing line and various adornments.

I had to find a dinghy in order to travel out into the pond and cut off branches with hazardous material hanging from them - the boat would be full to the brim with wires and all sorts of other problematic material. There was a staggering amount of litter - everything from old car tyres to washing machines. Glen and I could never understand how someone would want to take a washing machine all the way up there, much less how they managed it, it was inaccessible to say the least.

I was particularly worried about the amount of lead that must have been lying at the foot of the pond, it could have been fatal to the birds who I intended to house there. There were also regular shooting gatherings in and around the land I now owned so there were hundreds of cartridges from guns lying around, lead from the shot and lead from fishing lead weights. Sure enough, over time I lost five black swans through lead poisoning from lead weights lying around in the water. Luckily today a lot of silt has buried the majority of the nastiness but for a long time it was a serious problem.

The land which I had marked out for my very first car park was another staggering mess. It was an official council waste ground - a huge hole which was used for all sorts of excess tarmac and other solid, awkward material. I had no idea how I was going to clear the stuff, it was a complete tip. Somehow I managed to afford to hire a bulldozer for a day and luckily it made an enormous impact on the mess, it was quite incredible.

Apart from the cows in my one clear field the whole site was a mass of rubbish, we removed trailer after trailer of complete trash - bag after bag of general waste. The sheer volume of litter just from the pond was staggering. It was a thankless task and for many months there was seemingly no end to the carnage, it was demoralising to be working at full force but to return the next day to see the same pile of rubbish staring back at you. Eventually however we did make head way into it, it took a solid two months of work but there were soon days where just the odd strand of rubbish got in our way.

My time was completely taken up with the work there, I even went up on New Years Day. Sure I spent Christmas with the kids opening presents and we had Christmas dinner together but on New Years Day I was back in the afternoon. My reasoning was I was worried about people stealing the posts and wire we had left out around the land.

Just before Christmas I had also begun the work on our future home and hired a contractor for the digging work. It was ironic that there was a plant hire firm next door who could have helped, and surely would have been grateful for the work. But seeing as we were at odds I went to another firm, Cliff Hindle Plant Hire.

Once again I had my own ideas of the way the park was going to be and I had a crude drawing to present to the foreman. It was a basic drawing, not technical in the least. I said to the digger driver, "I'll put posts in the ground, I want you to follow it until you knock them all down with the middle of your digger and as you're digging it, dig out that side and pile it up on the other side."

And so it went. I placed posts on either side of the road, and the bulldozer would follow the line taking the top soil out. It was certainly interesting and eventually, fulfilling but I was now running around twice as much because I suddenly had other people to keep busy. It was a crash course in managing others. I had to stop my own tasks and worry about how others were performing and what they were or weren't doing. I was paying by the hour for the labour as well as the machines so I had to be convinced they were doing everything I needed. It was an expensive job to get them to work with all the necessary machinery, but if used effectively labour plus machinery can accomplish an awful lot per hour.

The footings were soon laid out for the house, an interesting process given I had never built a house before in my life. It was one thing renovating an existing building, but to build one from scratch was quite a task. I brought in a contractor and he was probably closely related to O'Reilly, the builder from *Fawlty Towers*. His company is now referred to - by all other contractors I now use, as the Wobbly Wall Company. The reason for this is that there was not a single wall in any building that they built for me that was straight - not one. Their spirit level must have had a nail in it!

It has caused problems ever since for any building on the park. Whenever new doors or windows are added we have to fill in the gap to make a straight line. The café was one of the worst buildings, frighteningly bad. The new contractor who came to put a new roof on the building said, "Who built this?" As soon as I told him he said, "Ah no, I'll have to measure every single one then."

They were well known for this and they could not even go through the normal process which would involve measuring one end and replicating it throughout the building. They couldn't risk it because they knew it would not be accurate. I never used them again, though he worked hard, the house is still standing and I am very happy with it.

We had to prove that there were no mineshafts underneath where we were building to which end I hired a company in Ulverston to carry out some historical research. They had to look back 160 years ago to see what had taken place when the site was active. Back then, as we discovered, they were working to extract the purest iron ore imaginable and they worked from the bottom to remove it. The voids in which the iron ore was extracted were never connected and we managed to prove this. Because there were no linkages between the sites we were able to build anywhere.

There was also found to be a fault line running through the land and mines were never built near to a fault line so it was double proof that there would be no mineshafts beneath. Any major earthquake and I might be in trouble though. It was amazing to try and imagine the hive of activity the site must have witnessed back then with steam trains and mine lifts all working round the clock to extract the iron by hand. The site where the house was built was an old marshalling yard for the railway.

In general the reason Glen and I accomplished the building of the park as it is today is precisely because we did not use contractors for the majority of the time. Contractors cost money and if we had hired outside people to do the jobs it would have been a small fortune, money I simply could not produce. My time was for free, and I only paid contractors for the job, by the hour. There was then no danger of quotes which would run way over their estimate. I would have had no chance of doing what I did were it not for the time I had spent as a boy with Keith Howson. If I had not learned the physical aspects of working on the farm that I had–how to build fences, how to lay a hedge, digging and putting posts in the ground, I would have fallen at the first hurdle. In fact I probably would not have believed I could even attempt to build a zoo myself.

Those specialists I did use - electricians, joiners and plumbers - are still the same people I use today, they have been very loyal and always given me perfect service.

But only Glen and I could perform the basic grind that was needed to bring the main site up to scratch. So there I was on New Years Day 1994 chopping trees and bushes down in the field because it was still overgrown. I felt I had to. To me those hours were vital and they weren't any less vital just because it was a public holiday or a day that traditionally I would have been spending slumped in front of the television.

There was some driving force within me, call it personal will or perhaps something undefined. I had to keep going and going and going. I didn't take a day off because there was no time to do so. It was a work ethic that may well have been something I can give credit to my dad for. In 40 years of work he had one day off and that was when he collapsed with the flu. Even today my dad never stops doing anything because he is sick and it is something that influenced me positively. In the first phase of the zoo I would eventually take a little time off after spending four-and-a-half years working every day. Regardless of what minor incident irritated me I had to keep going because it was a financial necessity.

It started to pay off when an area was finished and I was able to bring in my first animals. The first to come were the pheasants. I actually had to make an agreement with the person who had bought my house from me, he kindly allowed the pheasants to stay for a few extra weeks while I built their enclosure. He allowed us to keep a fair amount of equipment there as well and he let me come to feed the animals, it was extremely decent of him.

The pressure I felt was immense, I had to rush. The people who had bought my house obviously wanted to move in but my own family had no house! And the animals were still in limbo while the zoo was being constructed. I had to make priorities but even trying to choose what was a priority brought the most incredible pressure.

During January 1994 we had a further difficulty - a particularly harsh winter. Like many parts of England the north west can endure some especially difficult winter periods and the Lake District often experiences a further set of difficulties given it is not the easiest of terrain. Once some roads are attacked by snow or ice they are often impassable. This particular January was a nasty one, and it was snow that caused the problems. For a three week spell the road leading up to the site, that had just been completed, was completely blocked given it was laden with six feet of snow.

You couldn't move, the entire place was frozen solid, even the lake was frozen solid. We tried to get to the site on foot but even that proved impossible, it was simply too deep. I couldn't slow down now but there seemed little we could do if we couldn't get on site. Then I had an idea to ask Jack Dent, the chap who had sold me the land in the first place, whether he had any suggestions. He told us of a few large barns he had that were now empty of cattle and said he wouldn't mind us working in there. Luckily we had easy access to the land and I decided we could build the aviaries for the birds. For three weeks we worked on the enclosures that would eventually house the parrots and all manner of exotic birds. I planned the whole thing to work like a jigsaw where we would build each part at a time and then fit it together at the end. There were wooden frames and mesh all over the place but it would come together when everything was ready. Whether by skill or a touch of luck, the aviaries were perfect when it came time to put them all together, once the snow had gone we were able to put them on site. Those aviaries don't feature on the park today but I still have the photographs, it's a real mark of South Lakes Wild Animal Park history.

In a way it is quite a shame the aviaries are no longer there because the work had not finished just by building the basic shells. The laying of the aviaries was to be one of the most difficult jobs I have ever endured. Where we were laying the base was still saturated with mounds of pure iron ore clay, the stickiest material I can think of. When iron ore clay hardens you can't penetrate it and when it is wet it sticks to you like glue. It gave me an immense admiration for miners who had worked in amongst the stuff. As soon as it goes onto your shovel it sticks to the shovel. So you push it off with your boot and it sticks to your boot. Then you have to use the other boot to get it off and you look like you are in a *Carry On* film. It was like trying to dig through bubblegum. When we decided to bulldoze it out of the way we actually made it worse as water then seeped in and made it even more sticky and swamp like. We could not lift our feet up to move.

It was the worst possible time of year we could have done it but we had no choice. Come summer the ground would have been harder but with it constantly being wet the stickiness just got worse and worse. We had to clear all the iron ore clay out in order to put the blocks in for the foundation, which had to be plumb level. All the years I have now worked at the park, I can honestly say that was the most difficult and unpleasant job I have ever done. It was, again, something where I didn't have a choice, the poor fellow who had bought my house had all my birds in his house waiting for their new home! During this period I was still feeding the birds twice a day and once a week I would also have to clean them out. By the time the pheasants were in their new enclosure they were swamped with snow, not that they let that stop them. Somewhere through all the snow the pheasants managed to find their food.

Some people might think I would have been given a grant for the zoo considering it was given the go ahead for potential tourism but I have only ever been given one grant and it came at the beginning, very useful as that was when I needed it most. It was £5000 which came from the Rural Development Commission. I received a plaque and a cheque courtesy of one of their representatives. I was not allowed to spend it on infrastructure or materials however, it had to be used for employment. Considering I had no staff it seemed a little strange, but I realised I could pay Glen from the money.

The time was getting nearer to opening but things were no less frenetic or difficult. The extreme frost delayed us in many respects. We were days behind with the entrance building, the paths were laid but they were extremely rough - it was a white knuckle ride for anything with wheels during the first few months of the park's existence, prams or wheelchairs were in for a ride when they first navigated the path.

I was asked by the leader of a group of adults with disabilities whether I needed anything that they might be able to help with. I was only too happy to give them something to do and it certainly assisted me as well. They were in need of some fresh air and something physical to do. I had just the thing! I needed 100 posts moving from one side of the field to the other and they were terrific in shifting them. They were mentally disabled to a fairly extreme level but they were able to perform any physical labour. They came for several weeks, two or three hours at a time and helped with an awful lot of odd jobs, from moving posts, to rolls of wire and even some digging and planting of extra trees. They were a pleasure to have around and extremely useful. It was unfortunate that, at the time, we had no shelter for them, so if it was wet or cold in any way they couldn't stay for long.

The times where Glen and I did actually stop to have a drink or a bite to eat we were cooped up in the Land Rover together as it was the only place we could sit out of the wind and rain. Looking back it was quite staggering that we worked every single day in the wind, rain and snow from morning to night. You might expect it affected me physically and it did - I got much stronger! I had a rather impressive sculpted body after all the physical work and for me being a skinny chap, my muscles were something else. Suddenly my previously thin body filled out but it wasn't fat, it was muscle. I could feel it tighten and harden, my shoulders spread out, my arms filled out. I was as strong as an ox, I could lift anything regardless of the weight, I could lift something four times the weight of most men my size because I was doing it every day. The down side to all this lifting, and a hangover from my childhood was an increasingly bad back.

It had started when I was twelve-years-old. Keith used to take me to a farm in Ulverston where, every Christmas, we had to go up to kill the turkeys and pluck them all. I had been going with him for a year or two before my back gave way. My job was to hold the wings of the turkey, as if hugging it, while it was hung up on its back legs. I had to hug the turkey and hold his wings tight while someone else took a penknife and slit the turkey's throat and then held its head so that the blood dripped out.

If I let go the blood would go everywhere so I had to hang on for dear life. Some of them were so big they would lift my feet off the ground. All the time the turkey would be thrashing around. Every time I came out of there I would be covered in blood and white feathers. I hated every second of seeing the turkeys killed before my eyes. I had never seen death like it.

We would go to the same farm for potato harvesting. The health and safety officials of today would have a grand old time indicting those farmers because I was only small yet I was asked to carry huge bags of potatoes. When I was twelve, some kind soul gave me a bag of potatoes which I was supposed to carry on my shoulder. My entire body just gave way beneath me, I ripped all the muscles in my back, I couldn't breathe. Ever since then my back had given me trouble. I have learned later that it is compression in my spine which causes a trapped nerve, leading to the legs giving way. I now know how to deal with it but back then my legs could just give way as I was walking along.

After the potato incident I often had to lie on the floor at home, barely able to breathe. I would be so tense, out of fear and the lack of breath. Ironically, as I have since found, the secret is to relax. The more relaxed you are the more your back can expand and eventually it pops out and there is no longer a problem.

Still when it does go it can be a real problem. I have the strength to lift a ludicrous weight but if the back goes I can't lift a loaf of bread. If I lean the wrong way it is usually the catalyst, whereas if I keep the back straight I can usually keep going.

For many years I actually went to hospital for scans and discussions about keyhole surgery in order to find out what was wrong yet they could never find an explanation, all they would tell me is that they could not operate because it was too close to my

The Zoo is born

spine. As it happens they didn't need to operate, I just need to manage it.

Also at the time I was building the park, I had a visit from the police. They knew I rescued wild animals and had brought me a bag with tiny fox cubs thrashing around, five altogether. Someone had thrown the bag out of a truck while driving along the A590. I had no idea what to do with them, I had never taken care of foxes before but there was no doubt in my mind that I had to take them. I couldn't have been busier but I knew I had to look after them.

We reared the foxes in the backyard of the old house in Cleator Street, where we lived temporarily, and bottle fed them regularly, Alison much more often than myself because I was hardly ever there. The worst thing was their teeth became like needles very quickly. We might have saved them but we didn't want them to become domesticated, it was the worst thing for them. The foxes were getting bigger and eating more and more, more than we were able to provide. The smell was also a concern. I spoke to a pheasant enthusiast I knew, a great bloke who had provided me with a few pheasants.

"Look I've got a problem, I've picked up five foxes and I don't know what to do with them, I don't want to have them killed or anything but they are becoming hard to keep and they are getting big. Any ideas about how I could go about letting them go?"

"Yeah, we could sort that out," he said, "we've got somewhere where we could keep them a bit longer until they're a bit bigger, and then we'll probably take them up on top of the moors in Lancashire and just let them go up there."

It seemed like the perfect solution, I didn't have the time or the facilities for the foxes. We had raised the foxes from little cubs and it seemed the best thing for their development to be sent into the wild. The pheasant breeder came to pick them up, reared them for a while longer and then released them on the moors. We have no idea what happened to them but we gave them the best possible chance we could. It might not please some people to know that we unleashed several foxes into the countryside but my view is they are beautiful creatures and they deserve their place in the wild.

My love for foxes is the reason I ended up parting company as friends with Glen Fitzwilliam. Glen was a shooting man. All he lived for was killing foxes, it's all he talked about, he bought guns, it was all he could think about. It had long been a bone of contention when we were friends. Though I was totally serious, it was initially more of a game, light banter. I would say I wasn't happy with him shooting foxes and he would retort saying that if he didn't they would kill chickens, my chickens most probably. My view was if you had any livestock in an area where foxes roamed you should provide adequate fencing to keep the foxes out, not shoot them. If there is truly a vicious rogue fox causing havoc then it might be justified but in all honesty, most people who shoot foxes come up with justification that is simply not warranted.

Unfortunately Glen belonged to this camp and it became something I could no longer tolerate, my conscience couldn't deal with it any more. How could I be best mates with someone who went against everything I believed? He could not understand why I would rear foxes and let them go again.

Glen was not a conservationist, he was a killer, and I found it impossible to accept - he couldn't change the way he was and we moved apart. This came to a head about a year into running the park, he had been working for me but ended up moving up the road to be a farm contract worker. Perhaps our friendship would have ended sooner given this major discrepancy in our beliefs, but Glen was an extremely hard worker and helped me build the park - we got on and worked well together. The fox issue was the only problem we ever encountered with each other.

We were running perilously close to not being finished in time for our grand opening which was to be May 28, 1994. I had contacted the *Evening Mail* and they were excited enough to put a double page spread on the big unveiling, yet I couldn't keep up with everything that still needed to be done, nobody could.

We weren't ready. We were supposed to plaster out all the walls of the entrance building, café and toilets, but it would have taken weeks to dry, time we didn't have. Instead we used sand and cement which made an unbelievably hard internal wall, but it dried in two days. It might have worked at the time, but try to put a picture up today and you are faced with solid masonry.

At the very last second before our grand opening the carpet was just being laid and people were still painting the inside of the building. There was wet paint on the walls minutes before the dignitaries, including the mayor of Barrow, arrived. The poor souls, so used to perfectly smooth tarmac everywhere they went, were strolling across uneven paths in their perfectly polished loafers.

We were treated to a lot of helpful local press courtesy of a young man named Tim Rodgers who had just become the new local tourism partnership chief. He was to further tourism and our little project was a godsend for him. There was nothing in the area and he really had nothing to work with except us. He had a focus with the park and it helped us too with the attention his help brought to the zoo.

We opened on a day which wasn't the best of weather, but there was a fair amount of attention. The entire land had been shut off for months and many people were intrigued to see what was behind the barriers. I had a figure of 10,000 people in mind for a whole year when I had first constructed my business plan. Our first weekend saw 1500 people come through the gates. It was a £2 entry fee, which produced a fair return in just two days.

We had a wonderful animal representative who opened the park for us - 4X the emu. It was perhaps a little crass but the only Australian association I could think of was Castlemaine XXXX lager, so the Australian native was represented crudely but appropriately. 4X walked through the ribbon to open the park. We had been given 4X by Blackpool Zoo and had raised her from being a tiny chick. It took a while to realise it was a female emu, when she laid eggs it was a clue! 4X lasted many years before she passed away.

It is ironic too to look back and see that the initial version of the park was just a showground for various types of animals, it wasn't like today where visitors can feed the animals directly. People were encouraged to buy wheat to feed the pheasants but that was about the extent of it. The idea of the public feeding the animals came much later. The basis of the park was simply about seeing the animals roaming freely and to take photographs and have a picnic, pretty much the conclusion of my initial idea in fact. I was astounded by our immediate success and quickly realised my forecasts were way off the mark, we ran out of everything. We were grossly unprepared in fact, the sandwiches and even tea ran out.

Our success then improved because word of mouth started to work its magic. All the things I never imagined I would be able to do I suddenly could. I soon ran out of the money provided by the bank, but I had a cash return from visitors' fees. The bank were very helpful in that they gave me a year's capital holiday, so all I had to pay was the interest on the loan. I then had a pile of cash to invest. I knew I wanted to expand and joined the British and Irish Association of Zoos and Aquaria, it was called the British Zoo Federation at the time. Through a man named Tony Warburton, who was involved with the World Owl Trust in Muncaster, I was put in touch with the federation, which he assured me was the path to new people and expansion. Every major zoo in the country had representatives or owners who belonged to the zoo federation. Tony told me, "Once you're in with that you'll meet a lot of people: Chester Zoo, London Zoo, Dudley Zoo, Edinburgh Zoo. If you get contacts for people, you'll build your knowledge and that will help you a lot. They're friendly people."

I took his advice and got in touch, admitting I didn't have a huge array of exotic animals but asking if I could join. By now I was officially a zoo owner. I had to apply for a license because the law in England states you are only allowed to show a private collection of animals for 30 days a year, but we were acceptable as a zoo because of our collection of animals such as raccoons, coatis and wallabies. My goals were still relatively humble, for example I did not list our organisation as a company, it was merely a partnership between Alison and I.

The British Association of Zoos accepted my application. I attended every meeting I could, meeting a vast amount of new people, learning all the while. May of the people who would attend meetings and gatherings became friends. The biggest connection I made was with the good people at Chester Zoo. I began to discuss the possibilities of taking their surplus animals at the end of each summer, a crucial time as many zoos do not want to retain animals they don't intend to keep, especially through the winter when they need greater care. By September of the first year in business, Chester Zoo supplied our park with blackbuck (an Indian antelope) males and the large Indian antelope known as Nilgai. We also acquired five guanaco males, which belong to the llama family, along with a group of Chital deer.

We had the correct fences and I simply had to build a few wooden shelters for them - they didn't require any special care or attention, they were grazing animals who looked pretty. At the time I had to take any type of animal I was offered because I did not qualify to display any rare animals, nor was I involved in any breeding programmes, I knew nothing of that as they were only just starting to take off at the time. They might well have been cast offs but it was fantastic to feature animals from all around the world.

I had accrued a fair degree of credibility within the zoo fraternity; I wasn't just a chap who decided one day that he wanted a zoo with no formal experience. I had worked on farms all my life and, crucially, I had worked within animal nutrition, which afforded me an enormous amount of respect and approval. I had also thought carefully about the name of my 'zoo'.

I had, in some respects, chosen a bad period to build a zoo. There was a lot of campaigning by the likes of Born Free and many other animal rights activists and groups. Quite often there were many demonstrations outside zoos - Blackpool Zoo and Southport Zoo in particular was targeted in the North West - complaining of poor conditions and their distaste with captivity. Zoos were chided as a bad thing and the zoos themselves were being given a bad reputation.

I had to avoid this given I was only just starting so the very last thing I wanted in the name of my park was the word 'zoo'. Zoo creates an instant image of cages and animals pacing back and forth in often squalid conditions. Quite often people were telling me that because I didn't have any cages for my animals that I couldn't be a zoo - to most people a zoo equalled a cage, a trap.

I realised the irony that I couldn't tell people exactly where we were because no one knew where Dalton-In-Furness was, unless they were close by. Barrow was the nearest big town but it has a terrible bleak, industrial image, something which hardly complimented an open animal space. Besides, the comedian Mike Harding once described Barrow as, "The longest cul-de-sac in the world." I personally have nothing against Barrow and don't actually think it as bad as others do, but Dalton locals in particular tend to look at the place negatively. Ulverston, a town also near to Dalton, is far prettier but again it is barely known outside of the local area.

I realised I needed to reference the Lake District, a beautiful area with a positive reputation. I had to be more specific and describe the area as South Lakes so that people would know if they were driving up (or down) where we were likely to be.

It's not quite part of the lakes but near enough!

I still needed something which would describe my land without mentioning the word zoo. At the time London Zoo had built an additional country area for animals which they had called Whipsnade Wild Animal Park (interestingly this was recently renamed Whipsnade Zoo).

I liked the idea of this given the instant connotations between a park and the outdoors, green belt, countryside. No cages. Likewise there was no mention of farm animals, these animals were completely different, they came from all over the world, these are truly wild animals. That is how I came up with the name South Lakes Wild Animal Park. It is a description of where we are, what we are and the type of place it is. Unbelievably I did receive criticism from certain sectors, people who thought I was disassociating from what kind of place I really had, why was I so afraid of the word 'zoo'? It was quite simple, I didn't want animal rights protesters damaging the reputation of the place before we had even truly started, and I don't particularly like the idea of traditional zoos myself. We don't have a typical zoo and I have never worked in one myself - this was something completely unique and it needed to be termed as such.

With the greater numbers of visitors than I had perceived we were able to expand a little, gradually we acquired different animals and a reputation. Personally I could not believe how many people actually came through the gates. We then managed to agree to bring in a tapir, named Paddy, from the Welsh Mountain Zoo near Colwyn Bay.

We went down with a cattle trailer and brought Paddy back in the right type of box. For some reason it daunted me however, I had no experience or knowledge of tapirs and I didn't know what to expect. He wasn't particularly big but I was extremely wary of him - he could have bitten me or chased me, anything!

He turned out to be the softest creature imaginable; he would lie on his back and let you tickle his tummy. It was all a learning curve for me, a type of animal I would not be wary of at all nowadays, but back then it was a grand initiation. Initially I wouldn't dare go too close to Paddy. He was certainly happy when he found the huge area he had to run around and it would be a long time before we would bring him some female company. We managed to acquire a female from Curraghs Wild Life Park in the Isle of Man. She is still in the park today. She and Paddy even had a baby together.

I had to make sure that the park passed the correct inspections, one of which would become crucial to the development of my overall, innovative idea. If the animals were not allowed to roam freely then it defeated the entire object of what I was setting out to achieve.

The park was inspected by government inspectors as well as the local council for health, safety and hygiene – an unbelievable audit of the premises, especially when it came to the exotic animals.

My inspector, Michael Fielding, was a well known zoo vet with his own practice, and he was particularly a detailed fellow to say the least. I felt, in fact, he was a bit OTT. When I told him about kangaroos being on the loose as they would be in an Australian zoo for instance he freaked out a little, saying this couldn't happen as they are a dangerous animal – Category One. "I know," I said, "but the truth is they are quite safe with people as long as there is space and time for them to get away there isn't a problem. They would be dangerous if cornered, but so too would a cat or a hamster."

He told me I had to put a six-foot fence around the kangaroo. I replied that this defeated the object – "if I do that then that's just an enclosure."

I was told I had to.

"No," I replied, feeling I could push this now the zoo was well underway. "My whole idea is freedom. You will have to accept this because I am going to do this and prove it is going to work."

Luckily, common sense prevailed, and Michael Fielding decided on a compromise. I was allowed to proceed with having free roaming 'dangerous' animals such as kangaroos but it had to be monitored and if there were any issues at all I would have to enclose the animals immediately and we would go back to square one.

Fielding's trust in me would end up working. Looking back in 2011 I have had up to 35 kangaroos in that area and never had a problem, they go up to members of the public for food but the great thing is, with the way their area was designed, they can go anytime they like into the privacy of their own area without anyone bothering them.

I had the same potential problems with both emus and lemurs. When viewed with objectivity, an emu is a very large, imposing bird that can be extremely dangerous. Again, these are Category One dangerous animals. I brought the birds in when they were babies and brought them up myself, training them to be used to human contact. They still caused a stir with inspectors as they could be so frightening to children, and even adults but my argument was always that I trusted them and they wouldn't be in there if they were going to cause trouble.

One thing I cannot stand is working with a shirker, they don't last five minutes with me because I can't deal with it. I need people to put effort in because that's what I have done my whole life. To see people who don't put effort in is difficult for me, I just can't understand why because even when I didn't own my own business, when I worked for somebody else, I worked to the very best ability I had.

In every job I have ever done I have worked my socks off for my employers, every one of them. I know they can't criticise me because I did the job to the best of my abilities, I pushed myself to achieve because I wanted to achieve and I wanted recognition, constantly looking for a pat on the back. Every employer I had, regardless of which one, I wanted to be the best, to receive the recognition. It's what drove me, constantly looking for the praise. I might be the owner of a wild animal park now but even today I seek approval from those above me, and there is always someone above you. Today it would be my peers in the zoo or the conservation world. There is always something driving me, and always someone who will give you the recognition if you deserve it. The only one who has no one above them is God.

Chapter 13
Tigers, me falling through ice and conservation

No heat and no meat.

That was my phrase for the future. It was also a phrase which had partly made the present so successful. I was regularly being interviewed, sometimes for television, but mostly for radio, and in one BBC interview I had been asked what my plans for the future were. "No heat and no meat," I had replied. It was a saying of mine which referred to costs. I meant that I had no animals which needed external heating to keep them warm, nor did I have any animals eating meat. Heat and meat were both high cost luxuries and I had had to budget according to receiving a low turnout for the first year. Consequently I needed to design my animal dwellings accordingly.

We built concrete block buildings with boxes within them that were filled with straw. They were extremely cosy and meant no heating was needed. I was desperately trying to keep costs down, it was key to my business strategy and has remained in place ever since. Despite now making far more I am always wary of overspending or needlessly splurging money.

My theory didn't last for long with regards to not heating the animals but that was simply because of the overwhelming success which I certainly had not expected - it allowed me to soon bring in animals that would require external heating. During our first twelve months of opening we welcomed 55,000 people to the park. Our takings were £150,000, which was £120,000 more than my most ambitious projections.

This phenomenal return enabled me to start putting extra facilities in place as well as bring more animals to the park. I decided that I would really need to bring in tigers and lions if we were to really extend the reputation of the park, though these would come later. At the time it was exciting enough to feature a South American tapir. Today that animal might blend into the background a little more but at the time they were unusual, exciting and to have them running around was fantastic. I gradually started to build some small cat enclosures, it was a fairly crude facility, essentially an aviary-come-cage for small cats. I also planted even more trees in a bid to make the park look as natural as possible.

I realised than in order to fulfil the plans I had for the park I would need to increase and improve the facilities, that was the bottom line. With greater facilities we could also introduce the 'wow factor' of animals brought in. During our first year we were perfunctory in our system, it worked but it was extremely basic. The kitchen where we kept all the food for the animals was operated from my garage which was attached to my house. There was a sink, toilet and cupboards built for those who had to work with the animal feed.

Another way I kept costs down was to employ a small number of staff and pay them a fairly low wage, the easiest way to do this was to employ mostly sixteen-year-old girls and boys. The few lads I did employ didn't last too long however as they were lazy, all they wanted to do was stand around chatting. In the beginning I was extremely angry with their work ethic and became quickly very intolerant of their apathy to work. Luckily the girls were a different matter and there was a terrific balance that I managed to strike alongside the girls. While I worked on the physical aspect of improving the park facilities, the girls would deal with the public and the animals. I had three especially good workers who were all very keen to learn: Belinda Porter, Helen Hazelhurst and Shelley Goodwin.

It was all well and good making simple, fairly minor changes in terms of the park but in order to go to the next level I would have to think seriously about changing the layout of the place, better facilities, flagship attractions - instead of no heat, no meat, I would need to turbo boost my input to the park. I said to myself, "I'm ready for this."

I was also by now, alone - there were no other males to take the mantle of the physical hardship that was needed to constantly go at working on the park personally. In order to keep costs low I would still need to be working on everything myself as far as possible. But the man who had been there every step of the way helping me enormously in all the physical aspects, was no longer by my side. Our split had not been acrimonious and I remained good friends with Glen's wife Helen, but regardless, I was the last man standing.

Nevertheless this was not a prospect that daunted me. I knew I had tremendous physical capability. I had the ability to do it, I had the work ethic to do it, I was as strong as a horse by then, I was sheer muscle and bone. I was a powerhouse, with a frame on me that could just do anything, lift anything and take anything on. If I knew I had to knock in a hundred posts that day I would do it, I'd bang them in like you wouldn't believe. I was confident about my ability.

I also had the help from my newest recruits, the young girls who helped me a great deal, their effort and dedication was a touching aspect of the early days at the park. In all honesty I am not sure how they coped with the work load, I think it unlikely that girls of that age would work the same today. Nothing seemed too much for them to do, they were bursting with enthusiasm.

After the first year of the park being open I was also helped by a very welcome outside source, both Asda and Marks & Spencer have made huge difference to the animals in the park from the outset by suplying out of date foods.

I received a visit one day from an Asda representative from the store in Barrow. He told me that they were aware of what I was doing and thought it was a wonderful thing. He also said that they often had a lot of unsold food which they were reluctant to throw away. Would I be able to use it at all?

I couldn't answer yes quick enough. It was an absolute godsend for the park. The food was free and there was a great variety in the ingredients we would receive, in huge crates packed to the brim. It was a great help to suddenly have a job lot of free food and it fit in perfectly with my urge to keep costs down. It enabled us to free up a lot of money to help with extending and improving facilities.

To this day Asda are our loyalist supporters and we are loyal to them. I don't buy my groceries anywhere else because they have been so good to us as an ongoing business. Marks and Spencer followed soon after and we have had an excellent relationship ever since.

It was just another link in the chain and it was around this time that I came to the conclusion that in order to improve visitor figures even further I would need an iconic species on display. They don't come much more iconic than the tiger. Through the British Federation of Zoos I approached the tiger breeding programme to see if I would be able to get on board with the conservation work. If we had tigers we would be able to develop exponentially.

A positive development came in the shape of Marwell Zoo in Winchester. Peter Bircher, the curator of the zoo, had been born in Barrow and he often came to visit his step-dad who still lived in the town. Given I was building an animal park near Peter's hometown he was very interested in my plans. He showed a lot of enthusiasm and started to help me out - assistance which gave me a huge step up. With Peter's assistance we were given a pair of male babirusa from Marwell Zoo. The babirusa is one of the rarest pig species in the world and we were honoured and blessed to suddenly feature the animal. It might not have been a huge thing to the majority of people but at the time, only Marwell had bred Babirusa. For my park to have two of them before any other zoo in the country was a real coup.

Sadly both of the Babirusa's have now died, but one has fathered a number of babies, to the point that today we are the most successful breeder of Babirusa's in Europe. Peter Bircher helped us enormously in this regard and he also helped improve our general standing amongst the zoo fraternity. It was my connection with Peter Bircher as well as the likes of Nick Ellerton, from Chester Zoo, which granted me the respect and approval of the wider zoo society. With this I could house a rare or unusual species. It was a huge leap from the kinds of animals I currently featured but they showed belief in me and I had the belief in myself. The powerful people in the zoo world knew my head and heart were in the right place to be able to house such delicate creatures. They knew I was heading in the right direction and they also knew I needed their help and support, there was a mutual respect and I was thankfully helped by them.

We brought in a group of Axis Deer, Blackbuck and Nilgai antelopes, all Asian species and they made a wonderful sight on our large grassed paddock, later to become the rhino area. We had great success with them all breeding, the Axis deer and Nilgai regularly; we had an all male group of Blackbuck. My first experience of the natural instincts of a large wild animal in protecting its new born took place in 1995, I knew all about the way dairy cows can protect their calves and change character in seconds from all my years working on the farm but Nilgai were a new experience and this turned out to be a very lucky escape. I saw that a young Nilgai had been born at the far end of the paddock, the mother had left it alone and it didn't look like it was alive so I decided to go and check it out. I walked quietly down the field and approached the calf with care, the small animal was doing what it was naturally supposed to do lie totally still to avoid attracting a predator and playing dead. As I tried to lift it up to check its sex it let out a short but piercing scream. Within a second the mother set off towards me with a start and sprint that Usain Bolt would never have kept up with, before I was totally aware of what was going on the antelope that stood as high as myself was upon me and I side stepped to avoid its head that was aimed directly at me. Without slowing at all, the full weight and force of the animal intended to hit me and protect her new bundle of joy. I then decided to get out of the field as fast as possible and mother just set off chasing me after a quick few seconds checking out junior. It is a fact that if that female antelope had possessed horns I would have suffered a goring and serious injury but as she didn't have them, only male Nilgai posses short but strong horns, I managed to get out with only a bruising after running the length of the paddock in fear of my life. Another lesson learned and logged and a lucky escape.

It was with the support of my new relationships with zoo professionals that I was approved to hold Sumatran tigers. The Sumatran tiger is utterly unique. The smallest of tiger sub-species, it is only found on the Western Indonesian island of Sumatra. They are perilously close to extinction.

You are a given a position within a breeding programme, depending on your status and approval and they did take a relative risk to approve me to the extent of being allocated rank three in the breeding programme. We were able to secure Toba, a female Sumatran. This was an incredible honour and opportunity. The ranking relates to the genetic importance - the further away the animals are as relations means the higher they are ranked. A brother and sister pair would have the highest mean kinship because of their genetic equality, so the programmes try to pair animals with the lowest mean kinships and by that the most unrelatedness.

We were almost stopped before we could start keeping tigers however. There was uproar locally as the National Farmers Union made an appeal to Barrow Council to prevent us from bringing tigers into Dalton and Cumbria. According to their complaint the reason was the smell of tigers was so unbearable, and additionally the noise of a tiger would make a cow abort up to five miles away. I could not believe the rubbish I heard, it was frightening in its ignorance. My initial reaction was, how on earth could that happen? In the wild tigers sneak up on animals, so deftly that the prey does not even realise they are being hunted. They will sneak up on deer who might be pregnant but they will not abort babies or drop dead themselves just because they think there is a tiger in the same forest as them.

Yet the NFU contacted the press and created a scare mongering tactic to frighten everyone about us keeping tigers. Thankfully sanity prevailed and their complaint was dismissed but the scare mongering was forceful and potentially very damaging - it was an extremely serious threat to the park. The objections were vociferous and I had to take them seriously though now we can look back and laugh at such ignorance.

This leap in our standing after we were able to keep tigers was the most significant change within the history of the park. It turned us into an internationally renowned zoo as opposed to a mere wildlife park. It was a combination of hard work, determination and a fair spot of luck and help from others.

I was in readiness to receive Toba the tiger from Augsburg in Germany. The entire winter of 1995/96 I spent my time building the facility for Toba. It will forever remain the hardest winter of my life, and the time where I had to learn my harshest lessons yet.

During the time where I was building and developing the tiger facility we managed to acquire a group of ringtail lemurs thanks to Chester Zoo. Every one of the lemurs came with a little silver necklace with their ID tags attached. They were ultimately superfluous given the lemurs were instantly recognisable, and these days animals are not sent with ID tags.

The caged facility I had built towards featuring cats was initially used for the lemurs, along with the raccoons. It became a holding area for new species. My whole belief system with animals encompassed the need to keep them free. I wanted them to roam, to have their own fun and not realise they were being 'kept'. To this end I had to find a way of maintaining their safety as well as their natural creativeness and cheekiness. With lemurs this task was somewhat more difficult given they like to roam, they are not huge animals, and there were many of them. I tried putting electric fences up to keep the lemurs in - hoping they would stay in and around the trees within the boundary. Yet, no matter how we tried the lemurs would not stay within the fence boundaries!

It became a humorous issue in the end, and luckily they did stay within the perimeters of the zoo itself, so ultimately I had to admit defeat and let the lemurs run freely. This has become a unique feature of the park, no other zoo features free running ring-tailed lemurs. Many zoos have walk through areas where you can observe the lemurs, but you will be on a bridge or footpath. My park was one of the first to do this after I copied the idea from a zoo in Holland. We were experimenting and other zoos and parks watched us, if it was a success they sometimes followed.

The idea of free roaming lemurs was one of the biggest hurdles to overcome with regards to public interaction. Most people see lemurs as cute and cuddly and don't realise just how sharp their teeth can be. I had to find some separation between allowing the lemurs to run free but not cause a danger to humans. If I allowed them to be fed by visitors then it would be game over – the lemurs would want to jump on people and bite and the public would doubtless have a few complaints to present to me. My whole level of thinking with regards to primates was to instil in them a sense that visitors are not a source of food. The park had to be policed hard to ensure visitors do not touch or feed the lemurs.

We trained the lemurs to expect to be fed in one specific place at a specific time. They had to sit on a specific fence line; they cannot be touched or fed on the floor. It builds into them a routine, so they realised they only go near humans for that particular time of day. Beyond that they can look past, and sometimes even through visitors!

They've been brought up to see humans as part of the experience, but they don't actually expect interaction. Later on in the park we would put posters up to constantly remind people not to go near them; in fact we will remove anyone from the park who actually touches a lemur. Visitors are told in no uncertain terms that it is down to them to keep the animals free, because the inspectorate would lock up animals if they were all over people.

Tragedy would strike with the lemurs in 1996. It was while I was working on the building the tiger facility. The winter had been extremely wet and mild so far. The girls were working with me but effectively I was doing all the hard graft alone. I dug holes, mixed concrete by hand using a hand mixer - I had to put a meter cube of concrete into every post hole. The inside of the tiger house was built by apprentices from a college in Barrow, they were being observed by a teacher and managed to build all the concrete block walls I needed, with the labour all for free. It was a wonderful help to the project.

I had to build the outside on my own and I'll never forget how hard it was. It seemed from morning until night all I was doing was mixing concrete. I was trundling backwards and forwards with a wheelbarrow. It was muddy and extremely hard to push. The holes were actually too big, something I did not know at the time. I was making it harder on myself but I had no awareness as I was learning on the job. I was so excited to have a tiger on the way that I went a little over the top, I put three times more concrete in the holes than I needed. I probably built the poles and the mesh a lot stronger and thicker than I needed but I wanted to make the perfect facility. I had a lot of press regarding the arrival of the tiger, it was front page news in Barrow and everyone knew the tiger would arrive in Easter of 1996.

It turned freezing cold while I was building the facility. I had to sandwich large mesh panels in between metal bars and bolt them together. I slipped with the spanner I was using and smashed my knuckles against the mesh, they were bleeding all over the place but I couldn't feel a thing because it was so cold that they were numb. I couldn't have worn gloves because I couldn't then fix the nuts to the bolts so it had to be bare handed. I just kept going; I couldn't feel the pain anyway. Shelley was working alongside me, freezing cold but not once did she complain, she was helping pushing large mesh sheets to me at the top of the ladder. With healthy and safety in the current age, there is no way I would be allowed to have a worker do the same, they were probably much heavier than she should have lifted, but she was eager to help and just got on with the job with a smile and unquenchable enthusiasm.

One day, though the forecast said it was to continue being bitterly cold, we didn't expect snow. The sun was shining and it was down into minus figures but no snow. Suddenly the flurries started and it gradually worsened until it became a blizzard. We continued to work on the fence but eventually I realised we would have to get the lemurs in. It had been so dry that by the time we stopped the ground was covered with a fairly thick layer of snow.

The lemurs wouldn't come down out of the trees, we were struggling to get them but whatever we tried we could not get them down. The majority of the lemurs were brought in eventually but there were six who were defiant. All the while the snow continued. When the weather was bad the lemurs went into small wooden huts but no matter how we tried they would not come in. By the time it was dark there was nothing more we could do.

The next day we found one ringtail lemur dead. It had fallen out of the top of the tree. He had eventually fallen from the tree, hit the ice and died on impact. In the end four white fronted brown lemurs had completely disappeared, they were nowhere to be seen. We searched high and low for the others but could find nothing, no wonder given we had the heaviest snowfall for some time - around ten inches of snow.

Eventually we managed to find two of the lemurs but by then they were so cold that even when they were inside they developed frostbite and lost their fingers and toes. One lost a hand, their tails had snapped off. They survived but they must have been suffering, it was terrible. We didn't find the bodies of the other lemurs for weeks because of the snow, but eventually we found them under a snowdrift and they were dead. I learned a huge lesson that day about watching the weather, especially with regards to lemurs in that type of situation. It was a lesson I desperately wish I had never had to learn. Yet I learned that the second it starts to snow we were to bring the lemurs in, in fact the same applies to all small monkeys. Most of them don't like the snow or ice and if they feel as if they are stuck they will stay where they are, because they don't like to walk on snow or ice. The other, more instantaneous problem is frostbite. Lemurs have extremely thin tails and virtually one blood vessel up, and one blood vessel back down. If they suffer frostbite on that one blood vessel the tail will drop off within weeks. In winter it is absolutely imperative that these types of animals are in every night, especially when the weather forecast is proved wrong. The following winter, it was so cold the ponds were frozen over. The animals that were still free roaming and curious, did not realise they were risking their lives by exploring and they started to tentatively crawl across the ice. Eventually two large red kangaroo males explored too far, across the ice into the centre of the pond. They were sitting on top of one of the old iron ore mineshafts, which were extremely deep.

I was watching with horror as their weight finally took them both through the ice into the perilous cold water below. The kangaroos were paddling desperately, trying to keep their heads above water. I knew I had to do something to try and rescue them. As many people often experience when they try to save their dogs during times like this, logic completely leaves your thoughts and you only concentrate on trying to save the animal. I shouted to my staff to grab me a long ladder and a rope. They duly rushed and with items in hand I made my bid to rescue the 'roos.

I laid the ladder across the ice and tied the rope around my waist, telling my staff to keep hold of the rope, come what may. I crawled across the ladder out to where the poor kangaroos were still scuttling in the icy water. There was nothing I could grab hold of, the 'roos were slippy and wet, not to mention confused, they didn't know I was trying to help them. The more I tried the less I could do, and with my hands getting colder and colder it was even more difficult to find purchase to grip the 'roos.

As I was panicking wondering how on earth I could get to them, the ice beneath me gave way and I plummeted into the freezing water below. I had never experienced cold like it, and never have since. It was just like in a film when someone falls into water and drowns – all I could see were bubbles and the vague outline of the sky above. My arms were flailing and I was looking vainly up in the hope of seeing the outside world again. I could feel the rope being tugged against my body but I was underneath ice by now. With a great pull on the other end and a thrust upwards I managed to break out of the ice. Breathless and panicky I had to clamber back onto dry land. I knew I was in trouble. I must have only been under the water for 90 seconds but it was a traumatic 90 seconds.

I ran the 150 metres up towards my house and flew into the bathroom, turning the taps to run a bath. I couldn't feel any part of my body but I managed to remove my clothes and jump into the water. It was like a hundred knives being thrown into every part of my body. I screamed in pain, shouting at the top of my lungs – "I've broken my legs, argh, my legs are broken! Help! Help!" I was in tremendous fear and excruciating pain. This was a kind of pain I had never known and have never experienced since. Logic entered my brain for the first time and I wondered how, with broken legs, I could have run all the way up the hill to my house. Clearly I had not broken them, it was merely the feeling and circulation returning to my deadened body.

It must have been ten minutes before I realised I was still alive and intact as the feeling slowly flowed through my veins once more. Gradually the pain subsided and a normal body temperature returned. I actually scolded myself in the bath because I had no sense of heat at all when filling the bath.

The kangaroos were not so lucky. Both of them died that day. There was nothing I could have done and in fact it was a huge lesson to not even attempt something so stupid ever again. If anything ever happened like that again I would just have to say goodbye. I would never put a member of my staff in that position so why was it acceptable for me to risk my own life? The kangaroo's deaths were inevitable. Their bodies which had no doubt plummeted to the very depths of the old mineshaft, took many months to float to the surface, as the weather warmed and the bodies filled with gas. Extracting the lifeless bodies from the water was a sombre occasion. It was also a reminder that I was only still able to recover their bodies because I had had a rope tied around my waist.

We continued with the tiger facility and the good press inspired the local Army Cadets to offer their help. I managed to pick a few logs up locally and the cadets helped with carrying and placing all the logs. I had managed to learn a great deal about just how to build a tiger enclosure - I visited a number of zoos to observe how their tigers were kept and what was needed to build the same myself. In particular I went behind the scenes at Chester Zoo. I recall they locked the tigers outside while they showed me into the tiger house itself. It was one of the most frightening things I had yet experienced, I had a sudden panic - what if they had not locked that door properly? I was a novice at dealing with lions and tigers and I knew that I would have seconds to live if a tiger had followed me into a room with no escape. I had an immense fear of their power.

By the time Toba arrived anticipation was rife, the first ever tiger in Cumbria. I was still staggered by the sheer number of people who came to see her. Even with Toba placed in quarantine the volume of visitors was incredible, queue after queue of people all eager to observe the tiger through a pane of glass.

I didn't want to stop at one tiger, given my passion which was to have a breeding pair. I was now a part of the conservation process and was allocated a young male, called Hari, who came from London Zoo. The tiger had become something of a celebrity as he had a very unique story. When he was born his mother had bitten his tail and part of his foot off. This is an unfortunately familiar occurrence with tigers, the mother rejecting the baby. Hari had therefore been hand reared and followed through the course of a TV documentary. We were blessed with Toba in April and Hari came just a month or so later.

But it was with Toba that my love for tigers increased, not to mention the profile of the park. We got on extremely well from day one, I had a superb relationship with her. I loved every muscle in her body.

Perhaps because of this my relationship with Hari was never quite on par, he was far more mischievous and problematic. He would regularly run at me and try to attack me. One of the main things we wanted to achieve at South Lakes was to successfully breed tigers. When we first had Toba she was prime for breeding and equally, with Hari, at the age he was he should have been perfect for breeding within a couple of years. Nothing happened, we couldn't get anything going at all. We asked researchers from Cambridge University to take sperm counts and to check the ovaries and the hormones of the tigers – we wanted to identify what the problem was, whether it be the male of female. It was here I met Philippa Forrester when she came to the park to film the investigation process for a programme called 'Making Animal Babies', a spin off from *Tomorrow's World*. It was a fun event.

In the end the results proved that there was nothing wrong with either male or female tiger. There was no conclusive evidence and we were still none the wiser. We tried changing the males and that didn't make any difference. We brought the male back and that didn't make any difference and, as time went on, we thought that our female was pregnant. In 2002 seven years after Toba arrived to such acclaim, we didn't witness any mating, but she started to carry a swollen belly and her teats started to swell and increase in size – we were very excited at the prospect of a pregnant tiger. We made sure her den was fully bedded in preparation for the cubs but she continued to swell in size with no appearance. We were worried and put her in for an ultrasound scan. It became one of the most upsetting days of my life. We were curious to see the appearance of tiny tiger cubs but all that was found was a very large tumour inside Toba's belly. She was asleep for the ultrasound scan and I had to make the decision. Now we knew this terrible affliction had grabbed hold of Toba, should we even let her awake? It was clear that the humane thing to do was to put her to sleep permanently. She was administered a lethal drug and never woke again. She died in my arms. Tears were streaming down my face and I couldn't move for many hours, cradling Toba's heavy head in my arms.

When I finally left Toba in peace and thought about her impact, I had the realisation that her death was the end of an era in many ways. I will always remember her and am forever grateful to her and the impact she had. Ever since that day she has remained prominent in the park, her image decorates the Guide Book and website. It advertises the Sumatran Tiger Trust and appears on almost everything we sell in the Gift Shop. I also have many pictures of her which adorn my own living room walls.

Toba made the South Lakes Wild Animal Park. She made me, she changed my whole life, she got me involved in things I never dreamed I'd be involved with. Her impact was immeasurable and to think of her not being with us anymore still fills me with hurt. Toba was, without a shadow of doubt, the key to the success of what happened at the park – she was the stepping stone that made it all happen. Without her my zoo could not have been as successful as it has been and I would not be the person I am today.

Through having Toba and Hari I gradually developed a true realisation and respect for the place tigers have in our world. I will be the first to admit that I did not quite understand the yearning people have for tigers at first. You see tigers everywhere, on petrol tanks on, Frosties cornflakes; they are used as iconic pictures for a variety of products. Tigers are everywhere in your life and the tiger is one of the first animals a child will ever identify. Yet, they are one of the rarest animals on the planet. I quickly realised I did not just have a need to display them, but to help conserve their existence. In 1996 I made my mind up immediately that I was going to do something to save Sumatran tigers from their fate.

I had been to a conference all about tigers in London the year before and I had watched a speech by Ronald Tilson, a world-renowned authority on tigers. His talk had been all about a research project he was starting on Sumatran tigers - they had very little funding and were looking for people to help. The Zoological Society of London had promised they would step in and help him so I got in touch with them and said, "We want to get involved, we have got these tigers now, we want to get involved and we got one tiger from yourselves." I told them I wanted to do something, and to find out more. I was given the contact details for Ron Tilson. I e-mailed him in Minnesota where he was based.

"Ron, we are a zoo in England, and we have tigers, what can we do to help tigers?" I said.

"Well, we've got a big project."

"Yes but I don't want to just give money, I want to *do* something, I want to aim for something, I want to have focus because I think if we have a target we might achieve it. What items do you need?"

"Oh, socks, uniforms, backpacks, a boat..."

"A boat? How much will a boat cost?"

He told me it would be around $4,000. I was a little taken aback but I said I thought it was achievable.

In May 1996 we organised a Tiger Awareness week where we did everything we could think of to raise money. We were blessed with the support of a couple of families who were regular visitors to the park and they had befriended myself and Alison, they offered to help us organise the week.

We had a marquee set up, one family organised a raffle, one set up a tombola, there were various little events going on, with several young couples and their kids all helping out.

Somehow Coca Cola heard of our fund raising attempts and got in touch with me. There had been a manufacturing error in the production of a new fruit drink they were bringing out. The labels were illegal and they couldn't sell them officially, there was no ability to sell them through retail but we were able to sell them on behalf of a charity. Naturally I was eager to accept their donation but had underestimated how many bottles there would be. We were inundated with pallet after pallet of the drink, and we had nowhere to put it. Every donation was welcome of course and we sold the drink at a cut price, something like twenty pence a bottle.

With the help of people and companies, that week we managed

to raised £5,000. Amazingly, the British Federation of Zoos was also holding a Tiger Awareness week and it was the exact same time as ours. We were lucky as we managed to glean some of their focus as it was obviously a time where people were focusing on the situation with tiger conservation. Yet, as I would soon see, it was clear that most zoos were not passionate about conservation, they paid lip service to it, but it was no huge commitment. The other zoos who contributed fund raisers for Tiger Awareness week did not raise as much as we did on our own. In fact when you combined all the figures from each of the other zoos it still did not amount to £5,000.

I realised most zoos partake in conservation but it is with passivity, they don't actually get involved and excited about it. From that moment I said to myself, 'we are doing something special here.'

I was immensely proud to send off our money for the boat, we managed to buy this and many other essential items for Ron Tilson's endeavour. It became something of an obsession of mine to learn more about the Sumatran tiger and how to protect it. I didn't have a history of exotic animals and had, to some extent, entered into the world of tiger conservation completely cold, but it had now become a passionate endeavour.

I could only learn so much from other people and from reading. In my experience, the image you have of a country is never accurate. People might have an image of the Sumatran tiger, or of Sumatra itself but unless you actually visit the place it will only ever be an image. I had personally never vacated civilisation and been out to such a remote part of the world. I had no real idea of Sumatra but I wanted to build my knowledge from those who did know. What was for certain is I was completely passionate and enthused for Sumatra and Sumatran tigers.

Before I visited Sumatra I had the urge to feature both the smallest and the largest tiger in the world at South Lakes. Perhaps it was a throwback to my youth where I yearned to stand out, to be unique and hopefully receive recognition. I already had the smallest tiger in the world but in order to house the largest I would need to acquire an Amur tiger, formerly known as the Siberian tiger. The term Siberian tiger is inaccurate as the Amur actually lives in far east Russia in the Amur-Ussuri region. There are also some found across the border of Northern China and Korea but their numbers are extremely low in the wild. These tigers are woolly, lighter orange coloured creatures built to subsist in the harsh weather of this freezing cold part of the world where temperatures often drop to minus 30 degrees.

My desire was for people to be able to visit and compare the two tigers, in as close to a natural habitat as possible, to see the variations between the vastly different types.

The difference is indeed astounding; their size, the different coarseness of the fur, the colour. Tigers live in Asia but also all the way down to the equator. Therefore there is a great difference between the way that they have formed their bodies, their agility, their weight, how they must cope with the prey that they eat and the weather they deal with. Amur tigers were also extremely rare. They were the second rarest of them all at the time. There had not been a wild South China Tiger seen for many years although a few exist in Chinese Zoos. There have been claims of a Caspian Tiger sighting in the past years but no real evidence of these tigers in the wild.

Everything with these types of tigers, in fact, is opposing, yet the majority of people perceive all tigers to be the same, one size with an orange and black striped coat.

Four months after the arrival of the Sumatrans I managed to bring two Amur tigers into the park. I certainly didn't regret it, but I did nearly lose my life at the hands of a tiger.

PART TWO

Chapter 14
Tiger catastrophe and a Divorce

Things were never smooth in the company of certain animals. I would never have the confidence, or stupidity, to feature ostriches free roaming in the park – they are just too big and dangerous to have roaming amongst visitors. Emus however, their smaller cousins, seemed to be a safe proposition. In 1995 we had a group of six emus which on this particular day we allowed to run in the big open field, which today houses the rhinos. After they had enjoyed this area for a few weeks it was time to bring them back into their enclosure. Five of the six emus came in without a problem. One of the emus, Lucy, was not interested in coming back inside however. She would come towards the gate, teasing us, and then turn around as if to say, 'No thanks, I don't think I will after all.' A day passed, and then another, and another. Lucy would not come into the enclosure. By the fourth day I had had enough and I told Lucy from a distance – "Today is the day you are coming out, I am going to make sure of it!" I had a plan.

I would walk into the field and wrestle the hapless emu to the ground. I would tie her legs up and carry her out, just like a chicken. Unfortunately it's an Australian chicken, and the biggest chicken in the world. I sneaked up to Lucy, ready to pounce. When I felt the time was right I grabbed her and held on for dear life. She started to thrash around and tried to run away.

"No, look, you're coming out and you're going to do as I tell you."

Suddenly I had a big part of the bird in my hands – a clump of feathers. Lucy had escaped and run away again. There were feathers all over the place, flying in the wind. Lucy however seemed to be hell-bent on revenge, she was not too keen on my removal of her insulation. She stopped in her tracks and turned back to look at me. Revenge was hers. She walked up to me as I was laying on the ground still covered in her feathers, and she kicked my leg. With her powerful front toe she kicked the back of the muscle connecting my upper and lower leg. She had, I later learned, torn a hole in the tendons and so I lay in agony with stringy muscles hanging out of the back of my leg. The pain was immense – I thought at the time she had broken my leg. I couldn't move at all.

Lucy ran away and must have been 35 metres away when she turned back to look at me. I can just imagine she was saying to herself, 'Hold on, he isn't dead yet.' She ran back towards me and I must have stared in abject fear as I watched the emu gallop towards me as I lay motionless on the ground. She must have believed we were playing football and clearly she did not know the rules of modern football because Lucy lunged at me two footed and used my head as a ball. Thankfully the one thing I could move was my arms and I had covered my head over before the beast had drilled into me. My arms and elbows were covered in cuts and scratches. After my heroic escapade we did eventually remove Lucy from the field and urge her back into her enclosure. No wonder she was called Lucy, it was patently short for Lucifer.

She was a feisty emu to say the least. Whenever there were any problems with the emus they were always caused by Lucy. Most of the time she was as good as the others but there were times where she would turn and she would have to go into solitary confinement just to calm down. As sometimes happens with certain animals, she was beset with hormone problems which would occasionally catapult and cause mere mortals a problem. I traipsed to the hospital to get my wound cleaned and had to wear an attractive white legging/stocking to keep the muscle from being further damaged. There exists a photograph of me wearing the stocking as I had to come back to the park to give an owl talk in the picnic area. I was in absolute agony with the leg throbbing like hell but there was no one else who could give the talk. The photo clearly reveals my anguish although I doubt the members of the public knew anything of the details behind my emu assault.

In August of 1996, thanks to Peter Bircher, we were all set to receive a pair of Amur tigers. Peter came up with the tigers himself in two huge wooden boxes. The boxes were so heavy and large that we weren't able to get them inside the tiger house to let them out, which would have made it much easier. Instead we had to take the boxes to the outside enclosure - the boxes were pushed up against one of the holes in the wall leading into the tiger house in the outside space. Because of this someone had to stand on top of the box inside the enclosure to remove the slide and let the tiger out. It was very risky because we could not securely fasten the crate to the wall and so we had to pin the crate with rocks. I would be the one to undertake the mission.

From indoors Peter and the girls were at some distance waiting to pull the internal slide to let the tigers out. The first, Nina, was a dream. The slide was lifted and out she walked into the house she was supposed to go to. We moved the box to one side and then with supreme strength we had to bring the box in which contained her brother Egor. He was heavier and larger than his sister so this was some task but we finally got the box in place, ready to remove the slide.

Ping! The slide went up.

Egor didn't budge.

He just sat at the back of the box, growling.

We tried everything, we could, "Oh come on, come on, move, move, move" – no, he wouldn't move. We were there all afternoon, Egor wouldn't move. We started banging on the box, put some meat in, everything that we could think of to try and get him out.

Peter was a real expert; he had been doing this sort of thing for many years. I was no expert but even Peter could think of nothing further to bring Egor from the box.

I might not have been proficient in the methods of tiger extraction, nor would I ever have suggested I was an expert, but I had been through similar situations with animals in the past. I had grown up working on the farm and every now and then we would have to bring a bull in. These bulls were tremendously large and dangerous and I had to get used to dealing with animals such as this who could seriously injure or kill a human. I had also, when I was younger, had a fair amount of experience at horse riding. I got to a point where I was extremely confident around horses but eventually I had a very bad accident where I was thrown and dragged a long way. This damaged my leg badly and it also gave me a slight phobia of horses, which eventually I managed to overcome. Still, this kind of grounding with large and potentially vicious animals gave me a certain confidence when attempting to deal with tigers.

I felt that I would be able to communicate with a tiger, as I had with many animals before. I wasn't frightened of the tiger. I had seriously healthy respect for it but I was not scared. Regardless of this however my lack of experience was to teach me a very big lesson.

We were there all day trying to extricate Egor from the box. It went dark, still he would not move. I used a hosepipe and sprayed a little water at him but he still didn't move.

We didn't want to hurt him but we had to get him out. You might have thought he would want to come out and be with his sister but it was fear of the unknown keeping him in the box. They had both been taken from their parents, to a strange place, they had no idea what was outside awaiting them, it was no wonder he stayed in there.

Peter was saying to me, "I've got to get this box back, I need it, otherwise I would leave you but I need the box." Eventually he said, "I'll go to my step-dad's, stop overnight and be back in the morning. Hopefully he will have come out by then and we'll be alright."

Peter went to his step-dads and everyone else went home. I was inside my house and just could not settle, I knew the tiger was out there in a box and I wanted to get him out. I had tried to sleep but by 11pm I realised it was fruitless, I needed to go down to the box again. It was pitch black. I decided that if I completely shocked Egor he would have to come out. I found a large broom with a big handle and quietly walked into the tiger enclosure, cloaked in darkness.

Now I look back and realise how stupid I was, there was no method of communication for me had something gone wrong, no phones, no radios, nothing. No one even knew I was doing this. I was on my own.

I thought to myself that if I could just lift the back slide of the box ever so slightly and push his backside with the broom then he would be shocked and run out of the box. I took a deep breath and thought to myself, 'I know how to do this, I can do it.'

I very carefully and quietly lifted up the slide and Egor didn't seem to move. I saw his bum and I saw his tail. I took the broom handle and shoved it straight into his back. My plan to make him jump worked, he jumped alright.

He flew to the front of the box, before turning round and coming right at me. He seized the bottom of the broom with his teeth and as he grabbed it with his mouth the broom lifted the back slide up, leaving me staring a male Amur tiger right in the face. He had spent all day in a box and I had just stuffed a large broom right up his jacksie, he was a little peeved to say the least.

He looked at me. I looked at him.

I felt extreme shock and panic.

The only thought in my mind was to run which meant flinging myself onto the fence to try and climb up and over it. The fence had three inch square holes which meant I managed to get a strong foothold on the fence.

I managed to hurl myself right up to the overhang, I was hanging there for dear life but I couldn't actually get myself over the fence. I was breathlessly thinking to myself,

'Oh God, oh God, oh God, if he finds me he'll kill me.'

Yet Egor must have moved in the box and the slide very gradually began to drop down until it fell right back into place. I had no idea what to do, should I get back down? Laugh? Cry? I had no idea.

I hung on the fence for an eternity, I was still terrified. Additionally I could still see the end of the broom sticking out, so if he had decided to lift it up again the chances were he could run right at me.

Eventually I decided I just had to go for it so I dropped down, yanked the broom out and ran straight home, to a cosy bed and nightmares of the reality that I had just been through.

The tiger was still in the box the next day and Peter Bircher arrived fresh as a daisy ready to utilise the daylight and bring Egor into his new surroundings. First of all I had to tell him about my escapade through the night. "You crazy idiot!" he said helpfully. He told me the seriousness of the mistake I made, and also imparted a lecture on the rules regarding animals. I should have waited until someone was with me, the rules are that you never engage yourself with a dangerous animal unless someone is there to help you, or you can reach the outside world somehow. In one way I completely understood, though the thought did cross my mind that, in a tiger enclosure, even with someone else there it would not stop a tiger eating me if that is what the tiger decided to do.

It only takes two seconds for a tiger to kill a human, which doesn't exactly leave time to grab a gun, much less use it. With their immense incisors, one bite at the back of a human neck goes in one side and out the other - instant death because they sever your spinal cord as well as your jugular.

As soon as we tried to release Egor he still did not want to know. We were desperate to get him out, he still hadn't eaten and in our desperation we even sprayed him with a hosepipe for a bit longer which seemed so unfair, he was soaking, but still he wouldn't leave the box.

One of us decided, I think it was probably me in my still reckless thinking process, that if we got a bamboo cane and prodded Egor with it we would get him angry enough to spring out of the box. Peter was on the door, he held the door open slightly, everybody else got out and locked the door and I went into the cage area. I could see Egor in the back of the box. I took the bamboo cane and slapped it on the floor – "Come on, come and get it, come on, out here, come on Egor, come on. Come on out."

Still he wouldn't move. This continued for some time and after a while with Egor still static in the box we had a break. When we returned it was the same old situation. I was starting to get fed up of the whole process.

"I have to get going," Peter remarked, "it's a seven hour drive back down to Winchester and I've got to go. I need that box and I don't want to leave it because it will be such a job to get it back. We need it for another transfer."

Peter by now was becoming animated and rather angry and frustrated with Egor. Two days he had been in the box. I decided that we had to take action. I said to Peter, "Ok, we have to do something, give me just one last chance."

I went back in, this time going just one step further so I was closer to Egor. I could just about reach his nose with the bamboo cane, which was still some distance as the cane was around seven feet long. "Come on!" I shouted as I rapped the cane on the floor just in front of Egor's nose. I certainly didn't anticipate he would move, he had been like a statue all day. All of a sudden Egor leaped right for me at the speed of light. I jumped backwards in amazement and Peter pulled the gate shut ferociously, snapping the bamboo cane in half. Egor slammed into the gate. The sound was like a meteor crashing into a barn door, he almost broke his neck trying to reach me. If Peter had pulled the gate one millisecond later I would have been on the wrong side of it.

Everyone was shocked, we had become so blasé that Egor was not going to move, it was a complete surprise when he galloped like a steam train into the gate. It was unnerving to say the least. It was certainly the closest I have ever come to death by tiger. Peter then went home and we had two new tigers in the park. Egor did not forget me after that, he seemed to hold a grudge for a while and he didn't like being away from his parents, but eventually we became very close friends. Yet he showed me who was boss for a very long time after our stand off, he wanted to prove he could dominate me. I was convinced! Every time I went near the fence he would just smack into it and sometimes he would bang his nose, trying to kill me.

A few months after the initial Egor incident I went into the park one night to check on some new animals which had arrived. I would often have the urge to go down and check on things, an instinctive pull. It is not a job, it's my life and it never seems to stop. I was walking towards the new animals, without a torch, in the pitch black and I knew I was walking past the tiger enclosure. So did Egor. There was an almighty crash as Egor ran into the fence, sensing I was there. I couldn't see him but he could see me. It was the only time in my life I have panicked in that area and it was because I had no torch. I suddenly thought, he hit the fence so hard, what if he had broken it and was now prowling around the park ready to attack me?

I didn't know where he was, it went quiet, I ran to the nearest building with a door and locked myself inside. I didn't know where Egor was and I certainly didn't want to go out and look. Eventually I had to leave but I still didn't know if Egor was hunting me.

The next day I very tentatively walked towards the tiger enclosure, still not knowing if I would find a hole in the fence and a tiger on the loose. There wasn't even a mark on the fence. Yet he had hit the fence with such force, it was unbelievable. I knew the power he had. He was a monster. His feet were twice the size of the Sumatran tiger and ultimately, Egor would grow into a beast of a tiger.

Eventually he would last for thirteen years before dying of kidney failure, though his twin sister is still at the park. The arrival of those tigers was a great lesson for me in many respects, it was a frightening introduction and showed to some extent I was still naïve, yet I learned quickly. Everything has to be based on safety first and minimising risk. Today I would never demonstrate the same immaturity in front of my staff - there are far better ways to do things now. Still, we had some test with Egor, it is extremely unusual for an animal to stay in a box for so long, most of the time they are out immediately. We once had a lion who stayed in the box for a while but it was nothing like two days. Egor was a law unto himself.

1996 was a wonderful time for the initiation of the park. We began to receive regular customers and as a thank you we would often host a barbecue night on a Saturday for those loyal animal lovers. We didn't actually have a proper barbeque at the time however so I built one myself out of a few plastic food crates. On top of that I placed an asbestos sheet and then a piece of metal, my thinking being that asbestos prevents heat escaping.

I had a self made barbecue and everything was going fine until suddenly, one side of the barbecue started to slide down, before leaning towards me. It looked like a surrealist painting! The plastic

Tiger catastrophe and a Divorce

crate had, naturally, melted so everything collapsed. The moral of the story is that the heat from a barbecue penetrates a quarter inch sheet of asbestos a lot more than one might imagine. It was rather amusing and I was bombarded with a lot of teasing for many years because everyone remembered my stupidity. Still, it was a bonding experience; everyone would bring their own meat for a family picnic night in the summer. There were some wonderful people who liked to help out and become part of the park's family.

It was around this time that I became unsettled in my personal life with Alison however. My marriage was failing, to me at least. The reason was that Alison had been there on my journey but she had been a mere passenger. She wasn't driving or pushing me, which at the time was something I could have done with. I was driven within myself and this seemed to unnerve her. She couldn't keep up. The way the business was progressing and the manner in which I was improving within my working life was a dynamic she could not grasp. It had grown so far beyond my initial plan.

By the time we featured tigers we had seen 110,000 people pass through the gates, which was eleven times more than my original estimate. Resources were still stretched to the limit. The biggest factor was my lack of time with the family - they might have been sat at home with a quiet night in front of the telly and I would still be working. By the time I got in I wouldn't see much of the kids, who were eleven and nine-years-old at this time, and would barely have enough energy for a quick conversation with Alison. My mind and voice were also saturated with tales of the park and the work I was doing - I couldn't be the family man I once had been. My work life became overpowering.

Our married life suffered because I had no energy left at the end of a long day. Perhaps this might have influenced Alison in some way but whatever the reason she began to speak with a negative tone towards me, and about the park. She was working in the park herself, in the café and she had her own friends and life based around that but with me on a personal level, there was little affection or understanding.

I was doing everything with passion and becoming excited about life, I could see things I had never previously seen. It was as if a window to a new world was opening up but Alison wasn't involved. She wasn't excited about Sumatran tigers, nor was she enthused about where I could go next. To me, the sky was the limit and I could not just rest on my laurels. It was not enough just to have the four tigers now; I wondered where else I could take my vision? I wanted to do more, I wanted to help more, I wanted to become more involved with conservation, none of which interested Alison.

My mind was overrun with ideas about animals and conservation. To this end I joined the European Association of Zoos in 1995, it was big back then but not as powerful an organisation as it is today. Our zoo was one of the first hundred to join, whereas today there are almost four hundred. As soon as I was part of the European Association of Zoos I began to see far beyond the animals I had initially envisioned. The first conference I attended was in Holland and I was blown away by the amount I learned from a vast array of European experts. There were specialist meetings where a great swathe of expertise was shared among those fortunate enough to belong. I learned exactly what was needed from a zoo, which animals were surplus, which programmes were in need of assistance. It took me down a different route where I suddenly considered the possibility of other animals which beforehand might have seemed unusual or unlikely to come my way. I became excited about the idea of featuring rhinos and monkeys. I was already enjoying the fact that the park featured free range lemurs but I wanted to progress with our collection of primate species. I also had a yearning to harbour the best collection of kangaroos.

It helped that when I attended the marsupial meeting I found out there was not a lot going on with marsupials and they were short of enthusiastic contributors. That was perfect for me. Within the next few years I was given responsibility within the organisation, I became a studbook keeper and then a breeding programme manager.

Parallel with my enthusiasm for animals, I started to develop enthusiasm for Shelley Goodwin, who was working her socks off alongside me at the park. Perhaps it was the like minded passion for animals which attracted me. Maybe it was her being thin, blonde and beautiful. As she turned sixteen she started to blossom and I suddenly found her extremely attractive. Shelley always made sure she looked her best, wearing make up and looking great. Before then it had never even crossed my mind to be unfaithful to my wife, but I began to have those thoughts which were troubling and signalled the problems to come.

The combination of my attraction to Shelley and my progression with the zoo world was something pulling me further and further apart from Alison. My wife didn't help matters with some of her comments to me. I had started the park with a vision to change the world, even on a small level. Yet after two years of ongoing success my mind had entered another plane entirely and I saw the world as much larger, with me and my park having the possibility to make even greater changes. I wanted bigger and better. I wanted to make a mark, be recognised and be remembered. It took hold of every one of my senses. Alison however, just wanted to remain Alison.

"Can't we just stay like this?" she would say, "can't we just keep it down, you know, goats and guinea pigs are good for me. Please I don't want to go any further, it's getting too big…"

I would respond by saying this was the way I was heading, unfortunately whether she liked it or not.

Alison, myself and the kids still lived together but, mentally, if nothing else we were living apart. It was therefore a real pull to have attractive girls working with me day in day out. Aside from the odd person who I would interact with in the zoo world and members of the public, the only contact I had was with the girls who worked alongside me. I recall being extremely attracted to a few of them, but I was telling myself that I could not do anything, I was married. I had remained faithful through eleven years of marriage and did not want to fall off the wagon as it were.

Another way Alison and I were different was in our music tastes. I had developed an interest in country music just after we were married. We got a few satellite channels for free and our whole TV package was something like 50p a week. There wasn't much on the free channels but I did find CMT, Country Music Television and for some reason it clicked with me. Each morning I would switch it on. I wouldn't watch the news or a Breakfast Programme, I'd just listen to CMT. When I came home, I would put CMT on and listen to it in the background. I loved that music and that was the start of the era of modern country versus the old style country. It was around then that artists who are immensely popular today were just coming out into the world – the likes of Vince Gill, Faith Hill, Shania Twain, Tim McGraw and Tracy Lawrence. I loved the sound, I loved the feel of it, I loved the melody. Melody in music is very important to me and I also liked the way, in country songs, they always told a story and often it is something you can relate to from your own life. CMT changed my whole music taste but Alison was not keen, completely uninterested in fact.

I certainly liked Shelley and the funny thing is - despite the fact that there was a huge gap of some nineteen years; I didn't see her in that way. She excited me. I loved the way she looked, I loved her smile, I loved the way she talked to me. If there was a work gathering I would want Shelley with me, I could rely on her and I admired her passion for animals, not to mention her work ethic. There was a yearly event in a local town called Flookburgh, the Flookburgh Steam Gathering and I was asked by the organisers to come along, with a promise I could advertise the park. They suggested I bring a few goats and ponies for people to see and pet, at the same I would be able to organise a fund raiser for the tigers. It appealed to me to reach thousands of people in the course of a weekend.

Shelley and I took the animals along, and people had to pay a little to stroke or feed the goats, we had a large barrel which was filled with money by the end of the day. We had a wonderful day but had to leave at tea time to get back to the park for a barbecue. When we got back there, suddenly it didn't feel right that Alison was there, I had enjoyed my day with Shelley. After a while I said I had to go and check on the goats and ponies to feed them as they had been left back in Flookburgh. I asked Shelley if she wanted to come. She said yes but as we were about to drive off one of the regular park visitors shouted, "Oh and where are you two off to - for a bit of nookie?"

I didn't know at the time but Alison had heard this comment and it had made her cry. She had obviously seen the way I looked at Shelley. I must admit it was not a conscious physical urge I emitted, if anything I believed it was merely in my head, and I tried everything I could to keep my thoughts and feelings to myself. In fact I hadn't actually thought to come onto Shelley.

Yet that one comment had an effect on me. It was a twenty minute drive to Flookburgh and all I could think about was that if someone else had noticed we were potentially attracted to each other, then maybe I could actually try it on and my affection be reciprocated. We fed the animals and sat down for a while together. It was getting late. We got closer to each other and started to cuddle. It was then that we enjoyed our very first kiss. I felt like I was sixteen again. I didn't know what to do with myself. I couldn't believe that I could do this after eleven years with Alison. I felt no guilt strangely.

The strange thing is that I had three women in my life at this time. There was Alison, Shelley and Claudia Ullman. I had met this beautiful East German girl back in 1993. Me, Alison and the kids had gone to the Pyrenees for a two week camping holiday, knowing we would likely not have one for a while as it was just before I began to build the park. Here we met the then nineteen-year-old Claudia and her friend Neil. We all became very friendly with each other and as Claudia and Neil did not have a vehicle to get around we invited them to come with us for day trips, which became a regular thing. We all had great fun - the kids loved the two of them. Alison however, did not like Claudia very much.

Part of the reason was that when we would start walking, it always seemed that Claudia and I would plough on ahead, Alison couldn't keep up. It was not a deliberate separation. I can't pretend that I wasn't attracted to Claudia but at the time I had no thoughts about cheating on my wife and it was simply a fun thing to do to walk briskly through the mountains. I swapped contact details with Claudia, I liked her a lot and importantly, so did the kids. I told her all about my plans for the zoo and invited her over for the summer of 1995 and 1996. Claudia was keen; she paid for her own fare which hadn't been easy. Yet, we offered her a place to stay – our house had five bedrooms – as well as work in the zoo and free food. This way she could save up money for university. She came from the recently liberated East Germany and her family was very poor.

Claudia was staying in our house. It struck me that I could be attractive to another woman, specifically a much younger woman than I could have imagined. I also felt that Claudia looked up to me in some way though I had initially felt that this was because I was so much older. It was also attractive to me that both Shelley and Claudia were interested in my life and where I was taking the park and my involvement with animals.

One night Alison went out, leaving Claudia and I alone in the house. We were quietly watching television when Claudia leaned over and clasped my hand.

"You know why I am here?" she said in the most erotic German overtone.

"Because I always like you."

"Yes, it sounds like it," I said somewhat sheepishly.

She kissed me and she told me, "I cannot believe this, this is my dream."

I do wonder today whether she truly liked me or just wanted to escape East Germany!

Yet she told me candidly, "I've been thinking about this for one year, virtually since we have been in the campsite."

"I can't believe you are saying that," I remarked, still taken aback.

In exquisite broken English she told me that from the moment she first saw me she had wanted me. She told me we could have something special and it was her dream for us to be living together, even though Alison was also there. For the remainder of her time in our house Claudia was something like an au pair.

I wanted to keep her there, she had brought an element into my life that I had forgotten all about. Once again I felt no guilt, I can look back and feel remorse because Claudia and I would stare at each other across the dining table knowing and Alison had no idea.

Shelley completed the bizarre love triangle that I had inadvertently created. I didn't have a relationship with either Shelley or Claudia but I was in a pickle because of the presence of both of them. It wasn't love with either I must confess but the lights were turned on in my mind, there was a whole side of life out there that I was missing. By this time with my work I had not had a day off since the camping holiday in the Pyrenees and I was whisked along by the happy times I could spend with other people, it was like a holiday being in the presence of my staff members.

Claudia returned to Germany but in all honesty I was more attracted to Shelley all the while. It was then that we began a relationship with each other. It was poor timing as Shelley had a prior arrangement to go to Australia and spend some time with her auntie. By the time we started to see each other she didn't want to go. Her mother couldn't understand this sudden change of heart when she had apparently been looking forward to the trip for two years. In fact her mother forced her to go in the end.

It became suspicious to Shelley's family however when she would phone me from Australia, claiming the only reason was to check on the animals in the UK. Later on, I would stay at her auntie's house myself and she said, "I knew something was going on between you two just by the way she would speak about you."

When Shelley returned to the UK I could not wait to see her. I went to meet her in town and she ran towards me like a scene from a romantic film. We embraced and kissed. I still did not see any difference between us despite the age gap. She might not have quite been on my level given the vast difference in life experience and knowledge, but we often had deep, meaningful, enjoyable conversations - quite often we would speak about her life and her family, I was emotionally invested in Shelley, I cared a great deal about her. Something I found out later was that her mother was twenty years younger than her father - it had obviously happened in the family before. A few times I went to pick Shelley up at her parent's house - no doubt they picked up on the relationship we were having. Her mother later revealed to me that she always knew there was something going on.

I was naïve to think that Alison had not noticed our attraction, but at the time I truly did not think she knew. Even if she had not initially realised it would not take long before tongues were wagging. I used to give Shelley a lift home to Walney every night as it was impossible to get public transport there. Someone tipped Alison off and she 'hired' her father Peter to become a private investigator. Shelley and I were in my car one night and stopped off on the way to her home by the beach in Barrow.

The windows were steaming up as it was cold outside when I thought I heard something. I turned to look behind me and caught a man staring into the window. He then walked away, I was puzzled as to who it might have been. And then I saw his car and realised it was Alison's dad.

As I drove away afterwards I didn't realise but Peter had followed me and cornered me at a pub where I had driven to watch a band. He jumped out of his car and came over to me.

"Caught you. What the hell are you up to? Your wife's at home worried sick, wondering what the hell you have been doing going out all this time and she asked me to follow you."

I was obviously taken aback. I felt a thunderbolt of guilt.

"Sort yourself out, sort yourself out."

"Will you tell her?"

"I don't know."

"Please don't tell her, please I'll...I'll sort it out. I'll stop it, I will but don't tell her, please don't tell her."

I think Peter would have been decent enough to keep his word in ordinary circumstances but understandably, Alison pressured him to tell all that he had found out and he couldn't keep it to himself. Unfortunately for me this all occurred before I got home. I walked straight into a woman who was absolutely hysterical. Crying her eyes out.

I had a history with Peter too which lent an extra pang of guilt to the whole situation. When I had first met Alison she hadn't seen her dad for about twelve years because her mother had thought it was the best thing to keep him away from the family. The impression Alison had been given was that he was a terrible person. I had a hand in getting the two of them to speak again and form a relationship. I felt that I had let him down with my behaviour.

I had let everyone down, even myself. Despite this admission I could not let go of Shelley and even though I felt like I should stay with Alison I couldn't. I couldn't do it so I decided that I would talk to my children. I didn't expect to move in with Shelley but I knew I couldn't live in this scenario with Alison, it had been a relationship without passion for a long while and she was always pulling in the opposite direction from me. The bond just had to break sometime.

Alison would soon be the one to move out, there weren't many other options given I had to be in the house to work at the park. I was excited by Shelley but I had to admit that it was somewhat crazy to consider settling down with a sixteen-year-old girl - I didn't know what I could do. When Shelley's dad found out he went absolutely berserk. Shelley told her dad she wouldn't stay at home if he was going to be so against the idea of us being together. I told her she could stay with me for the time being if she needed to. Her father's initial reaction wasn't great but the reality was, though Shelley was young, she was old enough to make her own decisions.

Shelley stayed with me but it was an extremely awkward, difficult time, I didn't want the controversy or the bitterness, despite knowing that I was the one to blame for the whole mess. Eventually I believe Shelley's mother spoke to her father, suggesting that he was being somewhat hypocritical to lambaste me for having a relationship with his daughter because I was so much older. After all, he had done the same thing with her himself.

"Look what happened with us," she probably said to her husband. "We got married, we had our two children, we have been happy. You don't have to be like this. Let it go, see what happens."

We were never best friends but Mal Goodwin and I did shake hands and talked a little. After that there was never an issue with Shelley and I being together. We were very different but he accepted me - it was hard not to given he had married a much younger woman.

Suddenly Shelley and I were living together. It was doubly difficult because I still wanted to see my kids and they wanted to see me. I clearly recall Ben telling myself and Alison that he would spend three-and-a-half days with his mother and the same with me. He was not going to give one second more to me or his mum. Amy was slightly different; she decided she would only see me every weekend. It was highly important to me to spend time with the children despite my break up from Alison and for a while it seemed to work. As I outlined earlier I had married Alison for the wrong reasons in the first place, it could never last. It lasted as long as it did purely because she had become pregnant and I did the right thing by her and my children. We were never insatiable or passionate in our connection together; it was more like a brotherly / sisterly love.

During the period of my relationship breakdown with Alison work didn't ease. My next big project was to bring rhinos into the park. I managed to gain approval from the Rhino Breeding Programme and was given permission to take two adult male rhinos which unbelievably were going spare. It was to be a learning curve for me, starting with two mature adults to learn the ropes as to how to handle these magnificent creatures. I travelled to various locations in Europe to observe the design of the buildings and the materials which would be required to build a rhino facility and to train on the management of them.

Chapter 15
The Rhino disaster

In May 1997 South Lakes Wild Animal Park welcomed our very first rhino. We should have had two arrive together so that they could get used to each other straight away - one rhino from Marwell and another from Paignton.

We were then in a unique position, something I didn't know at the time. I presumed that two males together was a perfectly normal thing to do. To my mind, as long as there were no females to fight over the males would get along just fine - it is females which cause the tension! To do this was unprecedented however, and I had to have my facilities rigorously checked by rhino experts.

Fifteen-year-old Zimba came from Marwell Zoo, though his same-aged companion Dale from Paignton was delayed for some reason - it was going to be a few weeks before Zimba could meet his new companion. When Zimba came out of the box we saw he was a monster - absolutely enormous. We managed to attract media publicity, including television and newspapers - to bring rhinos into this small part of Cumbria was completely unique.

Although he was a gargantuan creature I found Zimba to be quiet and gentle, he walked into his stall with the minimum of fuss. He ate well and I soon found that he enjoyed being tickled on his back; I could just about lean on his back and tickle his ear. Zimba seemed to be settling in very well and I could imagine we could develop our relationship a lot further. Soon however, tragedy was to strike Zimba down in his prime.

Once Zimba was settled inside his new enclosure we decided it might be good for him to have a walk around the small outside yard. The experts who had checked his confines had confirmed that the outside area was sufficient to keep Zimba in - there were piles of stones and rocks as a perimeter and, though we were still not 100% finished with the rhino facilities, we knew there was no way he could escape into the adjoining field. Or so we thought.

Perhaps the following story was borne of Zimba's removal from female company. He had been with the same two female rhinos for fifteen years and was very comfortable with the other rhinos around him. The zoo however, for the purposes of conservation, needed to remove Zimba from his environment, as he wasn't breeding. Usually when rhinos are not breeding it only takes a change of male to stimulate ovulation, and this was what they were attempting when they introduced a new male rhino from Knowsley. The plan worked as well, a rhino did give birth to a young male sometime later.

When Zimba was first let out into his outside pen he seemed to enjoy the feeling of freedom, trotting around as if very content. Shelley and I sat on the banking at the edge of the yard and watched him strolling around. All of a sudden without warning, he lifted his head, his ears came up and he charged for the wall.

The yard was situated on a hillside but Zimba couldn't have known this. To him it would have looked as if the ground continued in one straight line. There was a barrier but he decided he would look beyond the barrier to see what lay beyond. We saw him begin to run towards the rocks which lay as a deterrent, but as he ran, flat out, the ground dropped away, and he bashed his head into the rocks.

It was the first and only time I have ever seen an animal do this. He hit the rocks with such a thud. Though I will never know for sure I am convinced he did this by accident, I cannot imagine it was on purpose. The force with which he hit the rocks was enough to separate Zimba from his horn - it flew clean off. A rhino's horn is only kept on the nose by a membrane, it is like a fingernail which sits on the skin and grows off the skin so they can be torn off with trauma such as this.

He smashed his jaw badly, and the momentum of hitting the wall threw him over the pile of rocks. It seems unbelievable, because the rocks were five feet high. Given I had researched the rhino facilities all over the country I had confidence the wall was strong and high enough to contain not just one, but two rhinos. I had seen many enclosures which were nowhere near as substantial as ours, yet given Zimba's desire to run at the wall he now lay on the other side. The gate had been left open in the field opposite given we didn't expect there would be a reason to keep it closed.

The field was some size yet Zimba kept on running and somehow found the open gate. It was obviously through panic by this point which didn't help Zimba to steady himself and calm down. He kept running. Up a small road into another enclosure and bang! He ran into a building, right through a tin sheet wall. Still, he kept going. He ran further up the hill, to where our car park sits today. At the time it had just been bulldozed however and there was a huge dip that was the original mineshaft. Zimba went straight over the edge and fell into the deep hole. His jaw was broken, he was squealing, bleeding, his jaw bent right back. It was horrendous, he was in so much pain, and there was no chance he could survive his injuries or come out of that hole alive.

Before he had fallen into the hole I had grabbed my gun, more out of instinct than anything. As I looked over the hole I knew there was no way he could get out of there by himself. I called the police and everyone else I could think to involve. How could I get this rhino out of the hole he had fallen into? He was so badly injured that I just could not see a way. When the police arrived the first question they asked was, "Can we get anyone here to dart him?"

"Even if you could get a crane, you would never get the straps under him without killing him or a person, it is impossible."

Look everybody there is no way that this is going to happen, this animal is in serious pain, he is suffering, there is no way his injuries were reparable, what are we going to do? I know what I have to do, I do not have an alternative. I have got to shoot him."

"Are you sure, are you sure?"

"Look, even if we rang the guy to sedate him, he is an hour and a half away from here even if he could come *right* now."

"Yeah, yeah."

"I am sorry but this is my choice, this is my rhino, he is on my land and I am making the decision. I am saying I am sorry but I have to shoot this rhino because he has to be put out of his misery."

I was crying my eyes out the entire time.

I stood there and loaded the rifle up with three bullets and shot them straight into his head, bang!

Then I loaded up with three more bullets and went bang, bang, bang into his head.

The first one would have killed him, no doubt about it, but I just wanted to make absolutely sure.

He laid there and I just looked at him.

It had all happened in minutes.

I moved to sit on a bank, in complete and utter shock, still holding my rifle. A policeman came over to me and quietly and carefully pulled the rifle from my hand.

It didn't cross my mind at the time, but I now know he wanted to protect me in case I was going to shoot myself.

I was absolutely distraught. I have never experienced anything similar to that feeling in my life, before or since. It was as if one of my children had died. I chased after him and had to perform a task I could not wish on my worst enemy.

Immediately after the horrific situation unfolded there were reports on BBC Radio 1 which said a rhino had escaped from a zoo and was running around the streets of Dalton. The general public were panicked into believing a huge rhino was on the loose when he was lying dead on my land. Soon it became national news, even though it wasn't true. There had never been a danger to the public. Had Zimba not fallen into the shaft I would have had to kill him to *prevent* him from escaping, but it never came to that.

There was rightly an investigation into the incident afterwards and it was found, by the rhino breeding programme, that I was at no fault whatsoever. According to them it was a one off tragic accident, which will remain unexplained. Their presumption was that Zimba had a panic attack, believing that the female rhinos he had spent fifteen years alongside, might be in the next field. He had never been on his own before and it brought further absurdity to the fact that he had been briefly allowed to come in alone. Had that not happened and he had another rhino with him, it might never have happened.

It was a painful lesson for everyone involved with rhinos to learn but from then on it was established - a rhino should never be moved alone. If there is a delay of any kind then they keep the other rhino behind as well. With male rhinos the conclusion was that they were better off being moved into a group, rather than just two males. It was exceedingly unfortunate that I had to be the person who experienced a tragedy which all other zoos were able to learn from, though at least a lesson was derived. This can be Zimba's legacy. The fact that Zimba's horn had been ripped off brought to mind the horrifying fact that rhino horn is so sought after the world over. It is sadly the main reason for their demise from this planet.

It is folklore that kills animals off, not necessarily anything that is true. People kill spiders and bats because of what they believe from folklore or they kill wolves because of it. They kill all sorts of things because of folklore and the reality is that half the time the truth does not live up to the folklore. Rhino horn does nothing to your body. I have been biting my nails for years and it hasn't helped me.

This was something I integrated into my talks at the zoo. Every day I would give a talk on the rhinos. I would be in the rhino enclosure stroking them, which was a sight in itself. I would tell the people that the folklore belief is that the horn of a rhino is supposed to make a man into some kind of superhuman. They would laugh when I made the fingernail joke but it was a serious message. People believe these ridiculous things about the powers within certain parts of certain animals – a tiger, for example, is valuable from front to back, any part can be used for something, yet it is folklore.

The rhino is my favourite animal. I believe they are very misinterpreted. Most people think that rhinos are dangerous and violent, charging, snorting horrible beasts and yet this couldn't be further from the truth, they are, in fact, the exact opposite of that.

Rhinos are gentle, they're caring. With their enormous head, that can weigh up to half a ton, and their very small eyes, I believe display a certain fragility. Often animals look far more vicious or aggressive when they have large eyes. Yet the rhino has such small eyes within its huge frame. I feel as if I can communicate with them just by looking into their eyes. Yet every time when I walk in with the rhinos at the park people are astounded, they cannot believe I am in there with a vicious beast which they presume to be on a par with a tiger.

Obviously they are dangerous but so is a car, so is a bus, so is a big dog, lots of things. Horses are dangerous in the wrong hands, in the wrong place, at the wrong time they can kill you. It's all about knowing what you are doing and treating them with respect and not being frightened either for yourself or for them.

I've had one or two bumps on my legs from dealing with rhinos but nothing majorly significant. Instead, working with them is the most fulfilling thing that I do. To share time, share space and share thoughts with them. I don't spend as much time as I once did at the park but I always make time to come into the rhino enclosure and spend time with them, I view them as my family. I can always go and visit the rhinos, and the giraffes, quite early on after closing time. They are locked away for a 5:30 bedtime because I am most paranoid about their safety, there is so much more potential for an accident with rhinos and giraffes.

I was flattered by the confidence those in charge of the breeding programme showed in me. I was immediately allocated two young male rhinos for the park. It took a year to actually receive the rhinos, though it was worth the wait. This time one rhino came over from Beekesbergen, Holland, and the other from Whipsnade in the UK. The facilities were checked over again but essentially nothing changed except the internal fences were made even higher and the yard walls lifted. Both rhinos set off at different times but they landed in our car park within half an hour of each other. This time everything went to plan. They came down to the park together; they went out into the pen together. Luckily these rhinos were smaller and younger, attaching to each other immediately for comfort. Even better, they got on well together. It was such a relief.

It had been a remarkable show of faith by my peers in the zoo world, yet Barrow council did not show the same understanding. They felt they had to punish me. It wasn't enough that I had been through the tragedy and torment of having to shoot one of my own animals, they had a burning desire to find fault with me. It was as if they reacted to the news stories rather than the reality. They found the loophole they were looking for which related to an animal escaping from its enclosure. This was enough to prosecute me under Health and Safety regulations.

Given I felt aggrieved at the whole notion of punishment after a clearly unavoidable disaster, I decided I would fight the charge and defend myself in court. This was in hindsight a pointless exercise given the rules of health and safety are incorrigible. If I had broken these rules then there was no argument as to my own case. Perry Mason couldn't have argued his way out of the charge. I was also charged with a couple of minor additions, such as 'irresponsible actions', though the judge threw these out.

I told them I had done everything I possibly could. I even brought along two eminent experts who confirmed I had done everything correctly and I couldn't have done any more. These two men, Nick Ellerton and Peter Bircher fought my case for which I will forever be grateful. In the end I was fined £1500 on the technicality of the rhino escaping its enclosure.

After the whole debacle some of those who work for the council, who remain there to this day, took me to one side and apologised to me for the situation. They told me they didn't see the need to take me through that but they had been pressed by councillors - it was a political witch hunt. Though they had told me this in private, due to their apathy towards prosecuting me, the trial almost collapsed and they nearly lost their jobs. By the time of the conclusion of the court case, by late 1997, I had worked almost four-and-a-half years without a single day off. People who knew me and had been by my side, especially given the high emotions surrounding the Zimba tragedy, told me that if I didn't take some time away from everything I would explode.

I'm sure they were right, though if I'd not been coerced into taking a break I probably wouldn't have done so. There had been coverage of the rhino situation in the press and the court case too had created a further ruckus. It didn't help my reputation within Cumbria that by the mere assertion I should be fined for my part in Zimba's tragic accident, I was therefore to blame. I didn't want the continuing publicity which seemed to stretch far beyond Cumbria.

I decided I would take a trip as far away as possible. Little did I know that in taking time away from one set of stressful circumstances I would be letting myself in for another and that in the process I was going to have to fight for my own life.

The Rhino disaster

Chapter 16
Australia, Leeches and
near death experience

When considering where I would travel for my break from the park it was clear I had to go abroad. I thought of somewhere I had always wanted to go: Australia. Quite decently Alison agreed that I could take Amy and Ben away with myself and Shelley for a month. We flew into Perth, hired an RV and embarked on what would become the most adventurous trip of my life. Amazingly Western Australia was completely different then than it is today, although just thirteen years ago, the roads had not even been fully hard surfaced - that part of Australia was also particularly hard to get to and there was little tourism compared to today. There were no major airports and in order to get anywhere you needed to drive incredible distances. Everywhere we would go seemed to contain a very small population. I was immensely excited.

We had little idea where we were going from Perth other than knowing that our return journey in four weeks time was going to be from Darwin - the distance between the two is over 4000km and that would be the shortest route. Driving all along the west coast and around the top of Australia we had some amazing, privileged experiences. One of these included seeing hundreds of turtles emerging from the ocean when we were on a beach which must have stretched for a hundred miles. The turtles were digging holes and laying eggs, the sort of thing you would only ever see in a David Attenborough film. We watched the natural process all night; it was a staggeringly beautiful thing to see.

We saw huge flocks of colourful birds which I had never seen in my life. We saw huge rivers that were totally dry as it was the dry season while we were there. One night I experienced the most unique vision of the night sky I had ever seen, or have ever seen since. Shelley and I were lying on our backs on the coastline, near the desert. There was zero light pollution, no people and no air pollution. We looked up at the sky, it wasn't black, it was white because there were more stars than space. I felt as if I had been lifted to another dimension.

I started to feel an immense release of all the stress and tension from the past four years. All the negatives I had dealt with came flooding out of me, the rhino shooting, the break up of my marriage, all the problems with building the park. I felt the release valve open, just by being in the most beautiful natural environment; it was exactly what I needed. It was a celestial experience; I was reminded I was a mere grain of sand within millions and billions of other grains. The sobering realisation that the natural world was so much greater and all encompassing.

I would drive every day (Shelley was ineligible to drive at the time) in our huge vehicle, navigating Western Australia, listening to Amy's accounts of parts of the truck which had fallen off that day. Both children were keeping diaries and logging everything they saw and did, for their school work. My children learn more on trips with me around the world than they ever could in a classroom. Amy kept a diary and there were many entries as we were constantly going off the beaten track, we were extremely adventurous. The table in the truck broke once, the water tank broke, something fell off, a wing mirror got broken off and on it continued.

One day we hired a small tin boat from a chap at the side of the Victoria River. We were well out of the tourist area but I wanted to look for crocodiles. The man with the boat said, "There are plenty of crocs down there." As soon as we were off down the river we hit something very hard, it was such a bash that Amy almost fell out of the boat. We suddenly realised we were on a tidal river yet an amazing distance inland, one which had rocks throughout its trail. It was a little unnerving.

We didn't see any crocs either, though we did witness dead cattle by the side of the river. They all had their heads torn off, the reason for which escaped me but clearly there was something sinister going on in the area. We managed to spend all day on the river, even the kids had a go at driving the boat, all in all we had a great day out.

When we returned the man asked us if we had a good time.

"Yeah, fantastic but we didn't see any crocs."

"Oh you are lucky."

"I don't think we are lucky, we wanted to see crocs."

"No you don't want to see crocs, why would you want to see crocs?"

"Because that's what we are here for, to see wildlife and everything."

"Yeah, but these crocs are three times longer than this boat and if they had come up they would have taken the boat and you and everybody."

"Why didn't you tell us that before we set off?"

He laughed to himself and said, "Well, I thought you would know."

The river we were on was renowned for featuring the biggest crocs in all of Australia – Saltwater Crocs supposedly up to six metres long. Later we managed to see freshwater crocodiles hatching, with tiny little crocs emerging. It was rewarding to be on our own little adventure, we didn't once have a guide, yet we saw the most exquisite natural life.

It was a touch ironic that in constantly being on the move - as I had been for four-and –a-half years - that I managed to enjoy myself and relax. It was never going to be a two-week holiday by the beach for me where I sat and did nothing. The idea of an all-inclusive package sitting by the bar all day is my idea of hell. It was one of the differences between Alison and I in fact, I have an active mind and body and want to get out there doing things, whereas she was happy to have two weeks sitting on the beach soaking up the sun.

We moved on to the Northern Territory. It was here that I saw something astounding - a massive bat roost, it is one of the biggest in Australia. We waited until dusk to witness the immense gathering of bats. While we were waiting we went into the river to cool off. We were having a wonderful time swimming and playing around before suddenly realising that every single one of us was covered in black leeches. You couldn't feel them attach themselves to your body so we hadn't noticed, but we were all laced with thick leeches. It occurred to me that there were so many because they had the bat faeces, which was dropping from the roost into the Katherine River, to feed on. We were a nice accompaniment to their meal. They were immensely difficult to remove, it seemed never ending - there were hundreds and hundreds of the things. We were helping each other, picking at each body like a monkey. We didn't do much swimming after this! It has been a downside to my travels, but I have often encountered leeches. In my experience water leeches are not as bad as land leeches.

In 2000 on my visit to Sumatra and our Tiger Protection Programme, I asked the team to give me a real taste of the difficulties facing them when on tiger protection patrols. The team in Way Kambas arranged to take me out for a three-day patrol – this could have been much longer as they often undertake twelve-day patrols. It was extremely hot and humid and we would sleep in the open forest at night. Some might be frightened but I found it quite exciting to be surrounded by tigers without any barriers. There were also elephants and clouded leopards amongst many other animals in the forest that night. I woke in the middle of the night with the urge to empty my bladder. It was an adrenalin rush just going to the toilet in the complete darkness, with the sound of rustling and movements in the distance in the forest.

The biggest danger in a forest such as this is mosquitoes and the possibility of malaria which thankfully I have never succumbed to. Second to the parasitic fly is the forest leech. It is perhaps the only animal which really gives me the creeps. They are shaped just like a worm with a mouth at one end and a foot at the other. They have an admirable sense for seeking out living creatures in the forest and feeding on them. They only need to feed once a year but when they do they make sure to have a full five-course meal. They are small and silent, locking themselves to your boots – it is quite simple, if you don't see them on you, you don't even know they are there. They bite into the skin injecting a painkiller to hide the bite sensation and then an anti-coagulant to keep the blood flowing until they are so full the weight of the blood makes them fall off.

I had not come across a single leech in the three days we were in the forest until the last 500m of the forest before the river where we waited for our boats to take us back to Way Kanan base camp. As we climbed into the small boat we removed our wet boots to find hundreds of blood sucking leeches on and under our socks.

There was blood everywhere, filling my boots, which I emptied into the river, making the water reminiscent of a scene from *Jaws*. The others were in the same predicament, with six pairs of feet dripping blood and water into the bottom of the boat. The problem doesn't end there with forest leeches as removing them from your skin is a skill in itself. Should you leave their jaws in your skin, it can turn septic. I have a terrible recollection of the boat full of blood – it is a sight I wish to avoid ever seeing again. I still bear the scars.

In Australia, when the water leeches had finally been extricated we had the perfect view to see millions of bats fly off in unison. I say millions with no exaggeration - the sky turned completely black. It was black as far as the eye could see to the horizon, swamped with flying bats. It was the biggest moving event of animals I have ever seen and I am sure it will remain so. Strangely, though they were flying very close to us they never once touched us. It was a touch scary but given they seemed to know we were there it didn't seem likely that we were going to come to any harm. Besides I was too busy wondering where they all found their food, and marvelling at the fact that Australia must provide a wealth of natural goodness for the bats. The expanse and quality of the food that must have been available for the bats amazed me.

Moving further north in the Northern Territory we saw a road signed off from the main road. Whenever we saw something like this we were always tempted and had to drive up and see what was there. We came across a famous part of Australia, the Bungles Bungles which features bizarre shaped rocks which have eroded. It is bizarre but they have the appearance of multiple beehives. It is quite stunning.

We weren't in a four-wheel drive and many of the off track natural attractions required a 4WD. When we came to the sign for Bungles Bungles it naturally warned, 'Four-Wheel Drive Vehicles Only'.

The kids said I was an idiot to do it but I decided I would take my vehicle and drive the 27km to the famous site. Unfortunately we were only two kilometres away when we realised we could get no further - the river was completely washed out and there was a huge drop which we couldn't traverse. If we had been in a 4WD we might have made it but even I wasn't crazy enough to attempt it in an RV. It was a pain but I had to reverse the truck back for many kilometres before I could turn around and drive all the way back again. The kids teased me for ages afterwards – I had been warned not to go down the road without a 4WD but then I would be surprised when our humble RV couldn't make it.

It was further on from this hiccup that I almost met my maker.

We came to a junction that was signposted Umbrawarra Gorge. It occurred to me we could drive down here looking for rock wallabies. I was a huge lover of kangaroos and I knew that wallabies were likely to be found in the area we were in. We followed the road for mile after mile, mile after mile of nothingness. We didn't see a single soul yet the drive seemed never ending. It was no surprise given that even on the main roads you rarely saw another human being. It was so rare in fact that when you did come across another person there would always be a courteous wave of acknowledgement.

We continued on the side track road for what seemed like an eternity. We started to go into what the locals call flood ways. In Australia they don't have bridges because they get washed away so they have flood ways. In the dry season, which is virtually ten months of the year, you can drive right through them and up and out the other side - this happens quite often on those sort of roads. The problem is in the wet season in Australia in the north, once it does rain you can get trapped for months because the flood waters and the rivers rise up. It happens in the Northern Territory every year without fail.

We were driving through endless blue sky and complete barren dryness, and we finally made it to Umbrawarra Gorge. It was immensely beautiful, like an oasis in the dry heat. We walked around the gorge and discovered aboriginal cave paintings on the walls. This was a rare privilege. We were enjoying our unique discovery - something the average tourist would never get to see - when all of a sudden the sky turned completely black. From nowhere, the heavens opened before rain fell like nothing I had ever seen before.

At the time we were sat in one of the caves and we stayed in there to keep dry. I could not believe the change in the weather but decided we better get going, despite the heavy rain, as the roads would be turned into clay coated slip tracks. Once again the fact that we didn't have a 4WD was a problem, we would struggle with any problems on the road where a 4WD would override almost anything. We made our way through the rain lashing and got in the truck. I pressed my foot down like I was making a bank robbery escape - I just thought that the sooner we got out of there the better. The landscape looked completely different and not a little scary. In my mind if we slowed down too much we might get stuck in the mud.

We were after a while quite a way from the gorge and had already navigated two flood ways without a problem as they were still dry. By the time we came to a third flood way I noticed there was some water in there but decided we would be fine, even in our humble RV. By now it had stopped raining. I stopped the truck, braced myself and put it into first gear.

"Right, come on then, we are going!"

"No Dad don't!" the kids said with an air of foresight.

"No, we'll be alright," I responded.

In my view we had to get through there or we could be stuck behind the flood way for months if the rain came back.

"We've got to get through," I said, putting my foot down. Then, all of a sudden, it was like a dream.

A wall of water smashed into the vehicle and in a blink of an eye the vehicle was floating on top of a flurry of water. I couldn't move it at all, we were spinning around. I couldn't grasp the surrealism and smacked myself in the face wondering if this really was a dream, or a nightmare. I soon saw that it was real and it was happening right now. Soon we were floating down the river - smashing into rocks and logs with water splashing all over the side of the vehicle.

Then the vehicle came to a sudden halt - we were trapped with cab in the water and the other end poking out from the river. Shelley and I sat there transfixed and completely terrified. Water was violently splashing into the vehicle; we were in the middle of the river. The obvious answer was to get out of the RV. I managed to open the window but as I put my arm out I almost lost it - the current was so powerful. It occurred to me very quickly that if I were to leave the vehicle I would drown instantly. Yet we had a real problem as the water was visibly rising. We could see the height increasing as it pushed its way up the windscreen.

"Come on we have to get up and out of our seatbelts and sit on the dashboard," I said, the panic in my mind clouded by my protective mechanism for Shelley and the kids. "You two kids get into the back, get as high up on the beds at the back as you can." I had already experienced the wrath of the water and despite the immense heat in the atmosphere the water was stone cold, I was worried any one of us could succumb to hypothermia. I kept my calm assuring everyone not to worry, that the water would go down, it had to. We were trapped between the rising water and the roof of the vehicle with a gap just big enough to keep our heads above the water and still breathe.

Only it didn't go down and everyone could see I was merely placating them - the water level just kept rising. It kept coming up and we were completely and utterly trapped, surrounded by a vast cloak of water. I called to the kids to come down to join us and we all held hands - I truly believed this was the end and we were going to die like this. I felt abominable; I knew I had just signed my children's death warrant. Logically I knew that it was an accident I couldn't have foreseen but still, I knew I had been the idiot who wanted to do this drive and the one who had gone ahead into the flood way when everyone told me not to. We started to cry in unison and then it turned dark. It was late afternoon. The electrics in the car had suddenly failed, leaving just a very small emergency light on. Soon that too failed and we were sat in absolute darkness. If you want to know what it was like you should watch the movie *Dante's Peak*. Pierce Brosnan is trapped under a cave with piles of rocks on the top of the car after a volcano explodes. The sheer feeling of helplessness, the immense darkness - the film illustrates exactly what we were all going through.

We were still in survival mode, reasoning that if we stayed still we might be alright. If we moved, we concurred, the vehicle could float away, and could well move into the avid crocodile territory. Every noise, every log, every bang that hit the truck was a reminder that at any time the windows could smash and we would all drown instantly.

I had my eye on the windscreen and after a while the tide mark I was watching seemed to drop a millimetre lower. At first it was surreal in itself - I wondered if my eyes were playing tricks. But it was gradually moving - it was dropping slowly. 'Thank God!' we were saying to ourselves.

And then we heard raindrops on the roof.

It has to rank as one of the most terrifying noises I have ever heard in my life. Those quiet little raindrops signalled that the water could start to rise again and once more, we would never get out. Suddenly there was a clap of booming thunder. My heart sank. It seemed probable there was a storm that was heading our way, an absolute assurance of death. We were freezing cold, huddling together, we could just as easily have died of hypothermia.

This feeling of terror and closeness to death had been going on for ten hours. By now it was 5am, though this meant the light returned. The storm we so feared did not appear - it was dry, it was light and I said to Shelley, "I'm going to try and get out of here." I opened the door, put my foot slowly into the water to assess the depth - it wasn't too bad, I managed to get myself over to the bank. So I said, "One at a time, I'll carry you all over."

We managed this without a hitch and I also went back to the RV to grab as much as I could that we might need. Virtually everything in there was ruined. The only thing that came out of it alive without too much damage was a didgeridoo that I had bought and had stored in the top cupboard at the back out of the way. It was one thing to get everyone out of the vehicle but we then had to walk back to the gravel road we had been washed away from, which was about half a mile upstream. All we had was five litres of water, which was not a lot in such intense heat. As we would see after our escape, the vehicle was completely buried in silt - you could not even see the wheels.

We had a decision to make. With that small amount of water in the bush, with the heat of the day just an hour or so away, we would never all survive. I had also heard horror stories about people who would go off the road or path and get completely lost - they would go around in circles for weeks, sometimes just hours, before they perished. I decided I would leave the girls behind and Ben and I would search for help. We took the majority of the water and set off. We seemed to walk for hours but eventually we found an aboriginal settlement that was just off the side of the road. We thought we had found salvation but as we walked towards the settlement a pack of vicious dingo dogs came out of a group of huts and ran straight for us. They almost ripped us to pieces but we managed to fight them off. With all the hubbub the chief of the village, a very old aboriginal man, came out and called the dogs off. He listened to my tale of what had happened. He seemed very, very concerned about us. I asked him, "Is there any chance you could get us back to Pine Creek? We have to tell the police or somebody." He said, "No problem."

They drove us all the way into Pine Creek in a very old, battered minibus. It seemed such a long way; they were extremely generous to help us to such a degree. They were such wonderful people. They took us straight to the police station but on the way down we had to pass a box hedge. The biggest two wasps I have ever seen in my life flew out of the hedge - one stung me and one stung Ben. I could not believe after all we had been through we had to endure that as well, it was as if we were cursed. The stings were intensely painful.

Luckily we met with more great people in the shape of the police. Rather than admonishing us for being so stupid as to attempt to traverse their harsh landscape, they understood. In fact they revealed we had been extremely lucky. According to the police, the last two people who had encountered the elements to that extent had both drowned. I presumed they were tourists but the police revealed that tourists don't even go down there, these two had been locals. They knew the potential and yet they still drowned.

He said, "If you look carefully down there, there is a huge truck and there is only a part of its bonnet sticking out of the ground because a big trucker went down there one day and he got the same, it was a huge truck and it got washed away so you are no different to anybody else." He told me the power of the water was unbelievable - they were very understanding. One of the policemen went straight to where I had left Shelley and Amy, bringing them back with all the remainder of our equipment. Still, we had nothing of any consequence and we had no money, it had been lost in the rush to escape. Once again we were saved by someone else's generosity. The motel owner gave us a room for free and let us sleep as by now we had gone around 30 hours with no rest.

When we woke and I walked outside they presented us with all our clothes which had been filthy but that they had washed for us while we slept. They sent us over to the service station across the road, promising that they would take care of us. Indeed they did, giving us free food. It was such a tremendous touch of humanity and it felt wonderful to know these people actually cared for us, complete strangers and hapless tourists. We actually had to wait two days in Pine Creek so it was a good job that they were pleasant and helpful.

The man from the local garage thought he might be able to salvage our vehicle but we still had to wait while a new vehicle was brought down to us from Darwin. He did manage to remove the vehicle (the bush people who work in such intense conditions are nothing short of amazing) but the engine was awash with all kinds of rubbish and particularly, silt. Still, we were blessed with the return of a lot of our possessions, which we thought had been lost forever. Much of it was water damaged or messy but we rescued everything regardless. I even salvaged an Australian guidebook which I still have to this day, a waterlogged, morbid reminder if nothing else.

We continued our holiday and were fortunate to not experience any further problems after that hellish experience. I still don't wish I had been on a beach holiday! I was determined in fact afterwards to continue to enjoy the experience of Australia, a truly fabulous country. I must admit however I was at pains to check the depth of every puddle or ditch before I drove the RV through it.

We flew home but there was still some unfinished business, something in my mind which said I did not want to be beaten by the river. Less than a year later we returned. I had had such a rewarding experience within Australia, despite the problems encountered on our travels. I was also at the time fed up with England and my issues with the park - it even seemed to me to be an option to sell up and move to Australia. In 1998 I would indeed travel to the same location where we had almost lost our lives.

I am not crazy enough to say I had a relaxing holiday by any means but I certainly had a break from the usual pressures of the park and my dissolving marriage. It certainly took me a million miles from my zoo. I didn't think about it. I had left the girls behind and my friend Stewart overseeing things but there wasn't, in truth, a great deal to do. Regardless they performed well.

I still look back at that adventure with fondness and we had a lot of laughs when we weren't struggling to breathe! Perhaps one of the overriding memories of the trip was when we were staying at an area known as The Pinnacles on the west coast. I was cooking noodles and for some reason the kids were teasing me and - irritating me - really. They were talking about my cooking or something. I turned to them, intending to tell them to 'give it a rest.' Instead, I said, "Give it a breast!" They couldn't stop laughing and it's something I will never forget either. They would bring it up for years afterwards. It was a case of, 'Dad's got one thing on his mind!'

Chapter 17
Innovations, Australia again
and a hand reared joey

I returned from Australia invigorated and ready to continue with my endeavours in the park. The experience had also helped Shelley and I to bond even further - there is nothing like almost dying together to fuse you even closer. We knew we were very close but almost everyone we knew said it would never last and it could not work long term. Even in Australia people would ask me about my son and two daughters, they couldn't imagine Shelley and I could be together romantically. I just laughed it off.

Our parents thought we were completely mad. My dad and I had never been close certainly but once I split from Alison he completely cut himself off from me, he never forgave me. He liked Alison and he thought I was being irresponsible. His generation is one of sticking to your guns, once the marriage is there you stick with it and try and make it work regardless of your feelings or desires.

Nevertheless Alison and I divorced. Alison was very good to me as she didn't ask for anything - I bought her a car and a house and that was the end of it. In her eyes it was far better for the children that they have their legacy available with me through the park, rather than me and my ex-wife battling it out. It was an important point in the zoo because if Alison had decided to play hardball I might have been left with very little of my own.

At the park we were starting to develop separate areas for animals from different parts of the world. We already had an Australia section with the kangaroos and wallabies. By 1998 we started our African section with the arrival of the rhinos. In 1999, considering we now featured both tigers and rhinos, we received 200,000 visitors. It was such an unbelievable increase. Our average today hovers around the quarter of a million mark up to and including 2010/11 when we had over 300,000 attending the park.

We furthered our African experience by placing zebras in with the rhinos. We brought in the Hartmann Mountain Zebra, which is one of the rarest. Suddenly there was greater colour to the park. We had earlier added Gemsbok Oryx and a type of antelope known as the Sitatunga. Unfortunately the potential of a clash between the oryx and the rhinos was too high and we had to move all the oryx out. We kept the zebras in with the rhino but the horns of the oryx were lethal killing tools and they were too high a risk in a mixed paddock.

1998 was something of a lost year in terms of the park as we were mostly improving the facilities - once people are in the park the income generated is going to come from the café and the shop. We expanded to separate the café and shop; suddenly the park was much better equipped to deal with large visitor numbers.

It was towards the end of that year that we decided to return to Australia. This time we flew into Darwin and learned the overwhelming lesson from before - we hired a four-wheel drive! There was only room for two people to sleep, so once again with Ben and Amy in tow, we returned - two could sleep in the car and two could pitch a tent outdoors. We made a deal with the kids; myself and Shelley were inside one night, and outside the next night.

It was a brilliant trip. We set off from Darwin this time and decided we would head towards the east coast. We visited Kakadu National Park and walked all over the place, in the hills and beyond. We also travelled down the river in Kakadu in canoes. It produced one of my most bizarre, yet humorous memories. We came to a waterfall and knew - even with all the intrepid will in the world - that we could not sail down the waterfall, so we had to get out of the canoes and carry them down - there were two between the four of us. We started to carry the canoes when all of a sudden I had a frightening realisation - I needed a sit down toilet immediately. I knew it was coming, it was one of those inevitable things in life when there is no escape ! I screamed at the kids, dropped the canoe and started to run. While I was running I was already pulling my pants down in readiness for hopefully finding a dunny of sorts.

My kids had never seen their dad's bum moving so fast - not that I could get a clear run. Now that was the first time I had experienced such a frighteningly fast and furious stomach upset but believe you me, I have had my money's worth since then and worse ! The kids did not stop laughing for hours, well days actually.

We returned to Pine Creek to thank people for the previous year's generosity – it was something I felt I had to do. We drove through Umbrawarra Gorge and Dead Horse Creek once again. This time it was bone dry without a cloud in the sky. We saw feral camel footprints in the sand.

During our journeys we came into contact, inevitably, with the flood ways which had so nearly ruined us the year before. This time, whenever we reached even the slightest collection of water I stopped the truck and checked it before driving through it. I was absolutely paranoid about water. It is a habit which would accompany me on any trip such as that - I am now resolute about safety and believe any pothole could see a vehicle trapped.

Still, we couldn't avoid every potential problem. We drove all across the Northern Territory, before entering Queensland. The road was absolutely appalling, it seemed to be falling to pieces, for some reason there was a big difference in the quality of the surfaces once we were in Queensland. We came upon a service station which makes me think of the film *Australia*. The trucks were just as they are in the movie, very old fashioned. The petrol dials were manual and they went round like the hand on a clock, it was like something out of an ancient museum. Still although the cost of fuel was far higher than the larger towns, it was still far cheaper than British fuel.

We were in the middle of nowhere as usual, and decided, having already driven some 3500 miles in Australia, to drive up to the Cape York Peninsula. I clearly recall driving up there with a terrible headache caused by a blocked sinus, I didn't have my usual treatment for this problem with me, not a prescription drug but a simple chewing gum that just clears my head and sinus in seconds and the headache goes, Airwaves are an essential for me on any trip. The vehicle was falling and shaking to pieces everywhere on the corrugations. Yet, once we reached the Cape York Peninsula I managed to use my sound recorder to record some of the most wonderful natural noises, which are still used in the park to this day. Recordings which were made courtesy of thousands of cockatoos, amazing evening birds and whilst being surrounded by hundreds of Agile Wallabies, I even recorded a great thunderstorm. We travelled through Cairns and various rainforest areas (the rainforest hugs the coast) as well as Cape Tribulation. Little did I know that I would be moving there and buying a property in just a few years time but from the very first moment I loved the region and spent quite a bit of time there. We drove two-and-a-half thousand miles altogether before reaching Brisbane. In Brisbane we stayed with Shelley's auntie, uncle and cousins and it was then that I felt a little bit odd seeing as I was virtually the same age as her auntie. It felt somewhat awkward that she had set a bed up for Shelley and I. Fortunately they were lovely people. Travelling with Shelley's family we managed to see koalas in their natural habitat. We also went to a theme park on the Gold Coast known as Dreamworld. We also visited Steve Irwin's zoo which was at that time very small - tiny in fact, and it was owned by his father at that point.

Overall I loved Australia and had a real urge to move there. I was also looking at it from a business perspective. I considered Broom in Western Australia but soon realised that it is so small, with barely enough of a population to keep you going, a zoo would barely break even. There was a crocodile park there at the time and it wasn't doing well at all. Cairns seemed to be the right place for me to build a zoo, there were a few Australian fauna parks but no zoos, yet they have two million visitors a year flying in. Cairns isn't exactly a major city and only had 120,000 residents, but it was the best known place in tropical Queensland and a very famous tourist destination. I said to myself, this is the place to do it. Still, I thought no more of it. It had been another refreshing trip to spend such quality time in Australia and with an air of what seemed like unfinished business, we returned to the UK.

In 1999 the South Lakes Wild Animal Park won the 'Top Attraction in the Lake District' accolade. Considering there are many famous attractions in the Lake District and taking into account our relative youth as a visitor attraction, it was a major coup for the park and immensely satisfying.

It was a real honour. One of the reasons seemed to have been our innovation regarding electric fences. For any zoo which actually featured electric fences – and there weren't many – they were over the top and quite obtrusive looking contraptions.

I thought I could design things that were much better, using my knowledge from my farm days. I had many an argument about designing fences, especially in order to find the right height for the animals. Essentially I was looking to find the bare minimum that would keep the animal safe but allow it to feel as free as possible, and to *appear* to be as free as in the wild as far as possible.

There were also the logistics behind the fence itself. Of course an animal isn't to know that if they touch the fence they will be shocked. Until they do. We tried the fence around the gibbon enclosure and the female gibbon Gail managed to navigate the fence and climb onto a hedge in the next area along. It took a while but we did manage to bring her back in to the correct area. It was only after this that I realised the basic principle of physics were being broken. I learned a lot in a very short period of time - we had to earth the wires directly. I redesigned the fence very quickly and thankfully perfected it. Now when an animal tried to climb over the fence they got hold of a live wire and an earth wire, directly earthed. They would get a real zap. We started to experiment with other animals and started to fence spider monkeys and macaques. They were fenced in but the barriers were much lower and obtrusive than any other zoo had ever managed before. From the smallest to the largest animal, they are not stupid. Once they are given a short sharp shock they don't do it again.

It seems quite trivial and commonplace now but there was a degree of uncertainty amongst people, particularly in the belief that the animals might escape. This is what made our primate facility so unusual and special for people to walk around, the monkeys were able to run freely. There was no cage; we actually had open spaces with high poles for them to swing on - it was completely unique. Electric fences bring animals closer to the public. Instead of having an eight or twelve foot moat and then the animals, there is a small safety barrier and then the animal right in front of you. The year we added the fences we were able to expand the monkeys and apes we had in the park, bringing greater diversity.

We already featured free flying parrots which had been there from the beginning - there were twelve Patagonian Conures that used to fly all around the park. There was no danger of them flying away - they were smart enough to realise where the food was!

We also had a number of macaws. It is an amazing sight to see huge parrots flying freely around with no barriers, I had been free flying parrots since 1991 when I had my private house and have continued with this amazing sight ever since. I was "taught" how to train parrots to fly free and return by a gentleman called John Strutt from Kirkby Stephen who had done this for many years. I visited him a number of times and he was always welcoming and helpful to me giving me two macaws at one stage. One of the first two macaws to arrive was "Mills" she is a Military Macaw, all green with a red flash on the head. Mills had been flying free before she came to me but the previous owner could not keep it up. Mills and Buster , her mate were firm favourites for many years and Mills still feeds at our home every day with many of her "friends" fifteen years after she first arrived at South Lakes Wild Animal Park. It is a dramatic feature that once again is I understand unique that we totally free fly our macaws around the park. This is a wonderful, colourful and spectacular sight any day but has its drawbacks as when the Christmas lights are put up the Macaws just love picking the bulbs off one by one costing us a fortune each year in new lights. The sight of huge brightly coloured parrot like birds soaring over head is worth the little negatives though as any one will testify. It isn't just Macaws we are famous for flying, we have White Storks soaring above on the thermals in the summer that were born and bred at the zoo and make a dramatic feature coming into land at any time of day. It is a great feeling to give animals freedom and expression and unrestricted flight is limited to the few but all the same gives a quality of life that is unsurpassed in any other park.

There are times when being an innovator can be a curse however.

Sometimes when innovating in zoo and enclosure design I will try to do something that had never been done and halfway through doing it I realise why no one has done it before! I do always put a lot of thought into what I am doing, mainly because it could be dangerous if I get things really wrong. I will really think something through, develop a good strategy and put preventative measures in place. You have to really plan if you are going to risk something that's potentially not going to work.

Something that has always plagued South Lakes is difficulties with the ringtail lemurs. We have become famous for featuring free roaming lemurs but it was never my decision to give them such freedom, they have made that decision themselves. We still had to make sure the lemurs were safe and could not escape the zoo itself. I soon found out that Ruffed lemurs would stay behind a two metre high fence that surrounded their enclosure.

Ringtail lemurs were very, very different. They decided they could leap over virtually anything I put in front of them and they proved a point to me because indeed they could! It didn't seem to matter how much I modified the fence. Every modification I made to the fence, they would beat it. Eventually I asked myself, when they do get out, how far do they go?

They weren't exactly escaping, staying within a four or five acre area, and they would always come back in. I decided I would leave them to it and monitor the situation. I have sponsored a couple of studies on ringtail lemurs from the wilds of Madagascar. The studies have discovered that there is a territory of around the same four or five acre area which the lemurs never move beyond. To them, beyond that territory becomes an area in which they might be killed. They stay with their family group and if they are finding food there is not a problem for them.

I started to learn more and more about ringtails. Twice each year – in spring and autumn – young males group together and say, 'We need to go and find ourselves some new ringtail lemurs and we think they must live over that way' and they look at the Lake District mountains in the far distance and think, 'I wonder if there are any ringtails on the top of that mountain?' They then decide to leave the perimeter. I was suddenly faced with a unique situation where six of my male lemurs were jumping over the fence to see if they could find females. It's a long, long journey to find another ringtail lemur in the wild in Cumbria but they didn't know that.

There were many questions asked about how we could stop them but before we found an answer, one beautiful sunny night around fifteen ringtail lemurs leapt from their sanctuary. It was like something from *The Great Escape*. I could just imagine the music as they all went. They had learned from their past indiscretions where everything was, and one by one they had built up a posse who were all going to go at the same time – over the hill in search of pastures new. We saw them leap but that was the last time we would see them for a while, they fled like wildfire.

I sent keepers out after them immediately. Outside of the park barriers is a great swathe of woodland and scrubland which the lemurs just blended into.

I received a call at the park. It was a member of the public. "I've just seen a bunch of your monkeys crossing the road over at Black Dog." This was quite some distance away. We all jumped in the van with our nets, ready for action. Every time we reached wherever they had been spotted they had already moved on. We were on a wild goose chase.

Members of the public were telling us, "Yes, they went that way." We were following them like a *Benny Hill* scene. We didn't actually see the lemurs ourselves, yet we were constantly being told that they had gone one way or another. They were moving so fast there was no chance we could keep up. They had travelled around five miles before we eventually caught up with them. They had disappeared beyond a reservoir and almost as high up as they could. We could see them sitting on a dry stonewall as if to say, 'Yeah, well, no women up here. Not much to report.'

Despite this realisation they didn't actually want to come home. Eventually we started to pick up a few of them and bring them into the van. Some of the others then became wise to this netting attempt and wandered off again. They soon ended up in someone's garden which meant knocking on the door and explaining to the bewildered home owner what we were doing. We managed to back the van into the person's garden and left the door wide open with a pile of food to entice the ringtails. It worked. They all came into the van one after another. It was still one of the most ridiculous chases I have ever been involved in – chasing the elusive lemurs who were only ever observed by other people.

The lemurs were curtailed somewhat after their little escapade so that we could keep an eye on them but it was quite understandable to think that all they wanted was to find other females to mate with because they didn't want to keep it in the family with their mother and sisters. It is one of the things humans have in common with animals – that males do not tend to stay in the family group in the same way as females do.

Another aspect I included in the zoo was the authentic sounds of wild jungles in tropical parts of the world. It is something that links me with Pierre Gay and his Doue La Fontaine zoo. I was always thinking about creating the same environment as the animals would have in the wild and I thought long and hard about the types of things which could provide this for them. Humans rely almost exclusively on their eyes whereas animals tend to use their hearing a lot more. Especially animals that live in forest areas for instance. They cannot rely on their eyes because all they can see is trees. Therefore, their hearing is a massive strength and with most animals hearing is just as important as, if not more important, than their eyes. A lot of animals, foxes for example, locate their food with their ears. In North America when it's snowing they can't see the mice, but the mice are under the snow and they locate them by listening intently. They can't see a thing but can listen for them before pouncing. I wondered what I could do within the zoo to enhance the experience for animals who are used to hearing in order to detect prey. In most zoos the idea of stimulation comes down to physical activities such as playing with balls and jumping at ropes.

I decided we would provide an audio soundtrack for the animals. Whenever I went to Sumatra I would take a digital recorder. The first time was just as Sony had introduced their mini disc recorders and these machines had a very good microphone which was perfect for picking up separate jungle sounds. I would leave it out in the forest for hours on end. In Australia I would do exactly the same thing. When I returned I would put them onto discs, editing them all together, and set up a sound system with speakers in hand picked locations around the park.

Within the park are separate sections for each part of the world, with Australia, Africa, South America and so on. In the Australia section, which features kangaroos, wallabies and emus, there would be genuine sounds from the Australia forest and bush. Within the Indonesian section were actual sounds from the Sumatran forest for the tigers and other animals to enjoy. The discs would be played on a loop so that the sounds were never ending. The additional beauty of this was that each section had a different feel to the previous one, and was especially authentic. If you couldn't actually see something you could hear it. It provided tremendous stimulation for the animals. When the gibbons in the Indonesian section heard gibbons calling on the sound system they would call back. It might have produced an element of fear or a reaction to defend their territory but this is exactly what I wanted.

In my opinion most zoos tend to treat animals as if they need to protect them from absolutely everything. They believe it is necessary to take away any risk, any fear, any danger from them. To me that is asinine because in the wild every animal lives with the fear of being killed every second of its life. An animal's body is naturally constructed to absorb adrenalin – they live an adrenalin filled life. It doesn't have to cost the earth to bring them an authentic environment; we didn't need to go to the extent of bringing in prey for them to kill.

But I wanted to give them a sense that there were threats. Another gibbon in their territory or near their territory is a threat, it stimulates them, it gets them excited. They jump up as high as they can to start looking and shouting. It's a stimulus. It changes their boring life that they would have had in a zoo. Their natural environment just grows and expands as it would in the wild. I had never seen another zoo do the same thing, until I saw Pierre's zoo in France.

"That sounds very wild," I remarked to Pierre. "Yes we have a sound system and I play the sounds," he said. They were doing it in just one area but I was astounded at the way we both thought, on a very similar trajectory despite the fact we had never mentioned it to each other. And, even more revealing was the fact that neither of us had ever been to another zoo with the same feature.

Australia was still on my mind despite the expansion at home. By the end of 1999 I was beginning to think seriously about the idea of building a zoo there. I started to research the concept. I then moved on to contacting a few people in the know. I found a small park that was for sale in Queensland but it had been active before and had to close so I decided there must have been a good reason for that. In early 2000 I decided to return to Australia, alone this time, in order to research the idea a little more.

I found a zoo consultant out there who I paid a fee to accompany and advise me on prospective sites for a zoo in far north Queensland. I did indeed visit quite a few of them but not one had the 'wow factor' and nothing seemed to be right. Ideally I was searching for a farm that had the infrastructure already in place so I would not have the same major problems to resolve as with South Lakes. All I would really need to do then would be put a few fences up and perhaps build an extra building or two.

In looking further afield I came upon a lady who I still consider a good friend to this day, Maureen Lane. She was a real estate agent who helped enormously and completely understood my vision and desire. She showed me a property half way between Kuranda and Mareeba that had been used by hippies as a commune, or that had been the idea. They had started to build and then run out of money. It was a strange site when viewed objectively. The main building was a huge community centre that was octagonal and steel framed. There were palm trees all over the place so there was a part tropical feel, but there was also bush land - in which were two major valleys. All in all there were 100 acres of potential. The hippies were desperate to sell, they had gone into warring factions, fighting over money. Even their next door neighbour seemed to be part of the fallout. According to Maureen she was looking to sell her house, which was perfect given there was no house on the main land and I would have to live there at some point.

Following Maureen's advice we visited the lady next door. She told me she was indeed ready to sell with the right offer. Unexpectedly she showed me around the property on horseback.

Her property was idyllic, exactly what I wanted. There were many termite mounds and there were also millions and millions of ancient grass trees, which looked like something out of *Jurassic Park*. The combination of this property and its surrounding land, as well as the potential of the hippie site spurred me into making a decision. I'm not one for dwelling on an issue, if I want to do something I will. I decided this was the right thing and I had to go for it.

By this time however I had spent many days there and was due to fly back home the day after my tour around the site. Maureen spent the entire day chasing around, trying to offer the right price, waiting for phone calls. All of a sudden it all seemed to come together, both properties wanted to sign, we both signed on the same day. I signed the documents and flew back to England. The deal was done. As soon as I got home I said to Shelley, "I've just bought two places in Australia next door to each other, I don't know where we are going from here!"

Where the zoo would be based was betwixt two quite different areas. Kuranda is a well-known tourist area with many facilities though effectively it was in the middle of nowhere in many respects. Mareeba is a beautiful outback town with lovely people but effectively it is a service town for farmers and everybody else on the ranches in the outback so, in keeping with my love of country music and culture, here I was in a cowboy town with a rodeo ground. I loved it. Part of my decision regarding the area I built the zoo was influenced by the need for the animals to be comfortable. If I had chosen Cairns, as my original intention, it would have been very humid and muggy.

As you move further up the mountains the air is clearer and cooler which seemed to make far better sense for a gathering of animals and better for visitors too. The cost of the entire plot, both parts of the land, would work out at something like £250,000 which was a lot of money. Still, I was only using the profits from South Lakes to fund the zoo. While I was still in England Maureen was taking care of things in Mareeba, collecting rent from the tenants who were still living in what was now my property. I didn't know her at all yet she proved I could have faith in her, she was an absolute godsend. When I finally got back there in 2001 she helped me with a lot of things that I needed, things for the house, a vehicle, she helped with it all.

As I was visiting regularly Maureen, her husband Des and their extended family became like my family. I would go out to visit them every Friday night for a barbecue. We wouldn't watch television we would just all hang out together and talk. Theirs was a marvellous family - they all truly loved each other and were just happy to share their experiences rather than watch TV. Before actually moving there I visited a few times and whenever I saw Maureen and her family it was like I had never been away. She would even come to collect me from the airport and drop me off again.

It was strange because the whole idea behind buying the property in a country which I loved, doing a project which I loved, was to share the whole experience with Shelley. It was going to be a place for us to settle down together and make a life forevermore. Yet, Shelley never even saw the property I purchased. Apart from holidays she never came to Australia. It was not deliberate at the time, it seemed more that I had the business side of things to sort out, and Shelley would come over when everything was settled.

Coincidentally at the time I was trying to set up a zoo in Australia we had a kangaroo incident at South Lakes Wild Animal Park. A red kangaroo joey was thrown from its mother's pouch. Whenever we had tried to rear a joey in the past they would die because it is so difficult to recreate kangaroo milk. Often the joey will develop a digestive disorder which then leads to dehydration. This particular occasion however we were successful. Shelley performed most of the regular feeding around the clock and once we realised we had passed the danger point, we named the joey Poppy. The reason for her name was that she lived in a little backpack which included a hot water bottle – she would pop in and out of it with a joyous jump. Her story reached the local newspaper and was then seized upon by both BBC and ITV news. It was a cute, fun piece that made John Craven's *Newsround* and was then sent around the world. Within a few days Poppy became a worldwide star and everyone wanted to see her.

Poppy lived with us for many years. Sadly she would eventually develop cataracts and go blind as she had not had the exact nutrition she needed from birth. She had a male partner Nero, a wonderful kangaroo who took the responsibility of always being by Poppy's side. He would guide his blind 'wife' all over the Australian region of the park, making sure she stayed out of danger, especially with the pond so close to their environment. It was one of the most moving relationships between a pair of animals that I have ever witnessed. Poppy would never rear her own babies as she had the same issue her own mother had where she would throw out baby joeys. She was certainly a star in the park and loved by everyone.

I travelled to Sumatra once again at this time and it was a very political time for the Tiger conservation project trying to get permission to work in Indonesia via the Forestry Department of the Indonesian Government. So I spent much of my time in Jakarta, Java in Government building corridors waiting to meet ministers and managers of the huge Department. It was very difficult and extremely political and I constantly was left wondering exactly what you had to do to help the Indonesian Government to protect its forests and Tigers, but when you realise that at that time the Conservation Department was a part of the Forestry Department, this always seemed odd that the Department given the brief to protect wildlife and forests was controlled by the Department that was given the brief to cut and sell as much forest as possible for profit. The weather was atrocious and the huge city one of the largest in the world with an estimated 19 million people, at the time more people than lived in the whole of Australia. The sewer systems could not cope and were virtually nonexistent and the dirty water was on the surface everywhere, perfect conditions for disease to spread and indeed many people died of Typhus in the week I was in Jakarta. Neil Franklin that until this time was our Project Manager was feeling very ill and went to hospital for a blood test. This showed he had caught Typhus, the symptoms being very flu like but the after effects can be permanent and debilitating. If you are weak or infirm it kills very easily. I was due to return to the UK the next day and felt fine, I got on the plane for the 17 hour flights home looking forward to some English food that seemed so far away for so long. On the way I started to burn up, sweat poured from me and I must have looked like death warmed up. I was asked a number of times If I was ok, but I certainly wasn't, the shivers the heat the hallucinations all hit me whilst cruising at 30,000 feet. On arrival at Manchester a slight panic ensued and I was isolated and taken to Furness General Hospital directly. I was taken into an isolation area, actually a space between two sets of sliding doors whilst someone was found to examine me. I was left alone for ages and then finally I was taken to an isolation room on a ward. This consisted of a private room with two doors in between me and the rest of the patients. The nurses and Doctors had to change and wash before exit and entry as I had an unknown tropical illness. I had however been telling them the likelihood that it was Typhus since I arrived, apparently my logical diagnosis was not considered important to anyone.

I was struggling to breathe and it deeply affected my chest and lungs. Whilst I was staring at the ceiling and contemplating whatever the future held, a man's voice pierced the silence and said

" Do you want a newspaper mate? "

I said " How did you get in, this is high security and isolation?"

" I opened the door and walked in"

"Do you not realise the danger of what you are doing?"

"Selling newspapers isn't dangerous is it ?"

At this point I realised that intelligence was not a strong point of the man. I told him I didn't want a paper and he left, without washing his hands and taking any virus or contagious disease with him around the geriatric ward next door !

Isolation?

Well it was so ridiculous and yet serious in its failings.

I suffered with a desperately bad cough and difficulty breathing for about 6 months after this before I felt back to normal. Typhus is a very easy disease to contract in a poor country like Java but certainly puts fear into the minds of the Health Service here at the mention of it.

Chapter 18
A new love arrives in my life

My personal life was about to change immeasurably. In late 1999 I had received a CV from a lady named Caroline Jellicoe who wanted to come and work as a zoo keeper at South Lakes. She was worthy of an interview but I was quite annoyed by the implications on her CV. She had been working somewhere in the south of England and there she had been part of a team hand rearing lions and tigers. She had been playing with them and stroking them. Personally I don't like that, I think it is very wrong as it leads to a false sense of security with animals. In my mind it is the wrong way to educate people and it was the exact opposite of my ethos, which was to keep animals in their wildest, yet safest environment possible, and let them play out their natural personalities and instincts. I decided I would call Caroline in and give her a piece of my mind - explain to her she shouldn't be doing this and that it was bad for the animals. Realistically I couldn't see much of a chance for her to have a job here.

The day came for her interview along with a number of other applicants.

But then I actually saw her coming down the hill towards me. It is the most vivid memory I have of any person I have ever met. I can't tell you how I met most of the people in my life; I can't recall the exact circumstances or what they were wearing. But I can tell you all about Caroline Jellicoe. I was sat in the café, waiting for my interviewee and suddenly I saw her walking down the hill.

She had a pensive look on her face but she was radiating beauty. She had long brown wavy hair, and was wearing a white ironed blouse and pressed black trousers. I scanned her entire body from head to toe, I was completely transfixed. She was utterly beautiful! I didn't realise though that this was the lady who I fully intended to berate, to me it could just as easily have been a visitor. She walked towards me and I still had no idea who this was, though my heart fluttered as she came closer. When she introduced herself as Caroline I knew there was no way I could give this girl a lecture. I interviewed her as professionally as I could but my eyes could not avert their gaze. It was rather embarrassing as I was obviously looking quite longingly and my stare lingered a few seconds too long. She caught me looking and I am sure I blushed. One thing was for sure, I was happy to have her working at the park.

Caroline was eleven years younger than me, and I discovered she was living an hour away in Preston with a partner she had been with for some time. I was still with Shelley and had not strayed, or even looked at another female. Until now. I found myself besotted with the lady in white. I didn't know how or when it might actually happen but I knew on sight that I wanted Caroline.

By this point I had been with Shelley four years and we did have a positive relationship overall. I had remained faithful but I also started to act quite possessively with her which was the wrong behaviour towards such a young girl. She had not had the opportunities to go out and enjoy her late teenage years by meeting different people as she had already settled down with me. I can say looking back at our relationship that I could have behaved much better towards Shelley.

I was certainly jealous and possessive, it didn't help that she was young, good looking and surrounded by lads of her own age. By this time Caroline had been working for me for almost a year and I had become a good friend to her. All the while I had remained professional and our relationship was merely platonic. Most of the time she had worked at the park however, Caroline had been quite depressed, she often experienced problems with her partner. It eventually emerged that he did not want her working at the park - she had to drive two hours on top of her hours in work and he didn't like it. Worse still he was apt to get drunk and give her further grief whenever he was inebriated. A few times I had seen her in this state and tried to comfort her. One day I saw Caroline had been on the phone and she was crying her eyes out. I went up to her and put my arm around her, telling her I didn't like to see her always being upset.

"Something's not right, you've got to sort this out, if you need to talk, I'll be there for you. If you want to talk you can talk to me.

I was very aware of the latent ability of Caroline she was so interested and dedicated to her work and she had shown a deep interest in the Animal Record Keeping System (ARKS) and the Small Population Animal Record Keeping system (SPARKS), these are the worldwide computer record systems for breeding programmes and animal management for the world's top zoos. I was doing it all myself at the time and was desperate for assistance in this area of the parks responsibilities. I asked Caroline to come and see me about this and she took that offer up. Caroline came up to the zoo answering my request. It was a very cold night and I was in the house alone, Caroline had no idea that Shelley was away that night collecting a Tiger from another zoo. Around 7pm I heard a knock at the door. It was Caroline ready to discuss the role of Animal record keeper at the park, she had very quickly taken me up on my offer of discussing the ideas and it was a real confidence booster for her. We talked about many things positive and negative, telling me all about her home life and how things were going wrong and then looking at books and photos of the park and animals and talking of the career opportunities.

I was sympathetic and enthusiastic, but it suddenly crossed my mind, as we were sitting on my couch together, that Caroline was in my house and we were alone. I was captivated by her presence; there was nothing I could do to avoid the inevitable. I wanted Caroline and clearly she wanted me. We became closer and closer to each other, talking, looking into each other's eyes. Suddenly I couldn't resist any longer and we were close enough to kiss. I felt guilty by cheating on Shelley. It marked a turning point given I had never felt guilt like this in the past. I wondered what I was doing, and indeed what I could do from now on. I realised the only way I could even attempt to keep a clear conscience was to confess to Shelley as soon as possible.

When she returned home the next day I told her the truth. I didn't receive the forgiveness or understanding I naively expected however, the reaction was decidedly violent and unexpected. She was shocked but soon reacted by acting hysterically. Understandably I wanted her forgiveness, I wanted to be able to promise I would never do this to her again. But I made the choice of being honest. After that revelation she could never trust me again. She left the house that day and after this she was paranoid. Whenever she came into the house she would suspect I had been with Caroline, saying she could smell her or that she could see one of her hairs on our pillows. She was paranoid. I was distraught because I had destroyed my own happiness.

Shelley and I were married. It had only been a quick ceremony at a registry office in Barrow. The only people in attendance were Ben, Amy and my friend Stewart and his wife Christine. We went to an Italian restaurant afterwards, there was a special offer on at the time, and even with the champagne, the reception cost me all of £69. It was a mistake from Shelley's point of view that we conducted the ceremony somewhat in secret and didn't tell her parents. Her mother found out from the local paper - who photographed us coming out of the registry office - that we had become wed. The local paper had been aware I was going to be married as their office was right next door to the registry office and they obviously scanned the day's marriages. Our clandestine union caused a lot of problems within the family. We should certainly have been more upfront about the whole plan and perhaps had more of a big wedding, with all the family, but maybe due to the age issue I didn't want to court a great deal of publicity. Ironically that is exactly what I created by trying to marry in secret.

Publicity often seemed to come and bite me when I least expected it. For instance, when I returned from Australia in the early spring of 1998, a photographer came to the park and tried to start lining up all my girls for a photo together. He wanted a picture of all the keepers together. I tackled him and said, "Who are you, what's all this about?" "Oh nothing, I just want a picture of all your girls." "Why?" I responded. "Why would you want a picture of all my girls? It seems a bit odd, properly set up and everything."

It then emerged that he was a professional press photographer and he was interested in me and my work, as well as my love life. I should have grabbed his camera from him because he had already taken photos of me and my staff but I became irate with him and threw him out of the park. I then learned that he had been playing *Mission Impossible*, hiding up a lamppost outside my ex wife Alison's house. He had taken photos of her and the kids on their way to school. She realised someone was following her taking photos which was an upsetting event in itself.

This had annoyed me enough but it got worse when I then found out it was the *News Of The World*, that bastion of truth and humanity (it was no surprise and perhaps belated justification when the newspaper folded in 2011). I then wound up with the indignity of a double page spread in the newspaper. It was a cruel mock-up of my tragic incident with Zimba the rhino – they were even callous enough to produce their usual play on words with the apparent horny nature of my sex drive along with the rhino horn. True, masterful journalism at its best. I had already suffered through the incident and then its manifestation into the national press but now they wanted a different angle.

The papers all had the Zimba story wrong before even adding anything else. It was worse than Chinese whispers. They also completely neglected the very sad truth that the incident absolutely ruined my life, it was the worst day ever and emotionally shattered me. The story in the *News Of The World* could have compounded my already fragile emotional state, not to mention the sheer horror I still felt over the incident with Zimba. It could have ruined the reputation of the park – who wants to give money to a philandering animal killer who merely pretends to have the best interests of the animals at heart? Yet, it was encouraging that people saw through the intentions of the newspaper and actually complimented me in one way or another. Many people said to me, men it has to be said, that they wished they were me and not to let the paper get me down. People were telling me to live my life and to do what makes me happy. I received many letters and phone calls, it was quite astounding. I had no negative opinions or comments whatsoever. A couple of male letter writers asked if I would share a few of my women with them but that was the mentality garnered from *News Of The World* readers I suppose.

I think certain women were more vociferous in their disapproval.

It was something I had become used to by now. There had been a history of disapproving females ever since I transgressed from my initial happy marriage. When I had left Alison and Shelley moved in for instance, all of the young couples who I had been friendly with and who had helped us out at the park were the first to sever ties with me. They must have felt they had to show moral support to Alison. In that instance Alison had left the park and it had caused difficulty with others who used to frequent the place.

In hindsight I can view the *News Of The World* piece as something of a joke – you have to when something is so far off the mark with its portrayal. At the time however it was upsetting and frustrating. I felt it undermined me as a person as a zoo owner and a professional. I was suddenly a bad person because I had had an affair which I felt was unfair and unrealistic. It was also a very bad start to my portrayal in the press in general.

Up until the story on Zimba, everything that had come out in the press had been positive so it was a reality check and it was my first experience of how utterly negative and distinctly horrible the media can be when they get hold of a story and they want to exaggerate it. They can absolutely alter your personal life by the lies they print. It started a trend which has since continued in my life whereby I am seen as either hero or villain. I rarely encounter a middle ground view from someone; it is usually a case of love or hate.

Shelley tried her hardest to accept what I had done with Caroline, yet Shelley could not deal with my indiscretion, she just couldn't trust me again, and she could not forgive. She left me. I spiralled into a great depression. I couldn't deal with the fact my wife had left me, I had been so stupid and she wouldn't even talk to me. I went to see Stewart and Christine knowing they would listen to me. All I remember of this was being completely and utterly distraught that I had been the architect of my own problem and finding it impossible to work out why Shelley would not come back to me.

I was still feeling down. I had caused it all myself, a completely self-inflicted depression. I let myself down and I certainly let Shelley down. Yet, they say everything happens for a reason. I was just about to find out that Caroline and I was no one off. Caroline and I arranged to go to Knowsley Safari Park for a meeting with Nick Ellerton the Curator, who had moved from Chester Zoo to get information on drive through Lion enclosures to assist with my design of the new Australian development. We had a wonderful day and built closer ties and all the time after I still thought of her, the magical way in which we seemed to fit together. Fate was about to play an important card. Caroline was still having problems in her home life and felt it was so bad she thought it was about time she moved out. She had nowhere to go and I had a five-bedroom house which was lying virtually empty. It seemed only right that after all the turmoil going on in our respective lives, that Caroline and I should share our sob stories and draw comfort from each other. It was time she came to live with me.

Chapter 19
Building a zoo in Australia and a son is born

Caroline was not just a beautiful woman; she was immensely knowledgeable and impressive when working with animals. Regardless of my romantic liaison with her, Caroline stands out as one of the best to work for me over the years and I have some excellent and talented people working for me. She remains one of the most impressive employees I have had work at the park. She was young and passionate like so many of the other young girls I had working for me. But Caroline went the extra mile in so many areas. She had dedication, care, time, she had understanding. I do believe she also had a gift with animals. It was a major part of my attraction to Caroline, the fact that she was so immensely dedicated to her work with animals. She would drive 60 miles just to get to work, put in a full day's graft and then drive 60 miles home. Caroline had one unfortunate aspect to her behaviour and that was she smoked. It was something I could not abide and I told her so, that if we were to have a relationship she would have to give up. She stopped the day I mentioned it. That said something to me immediately. She had such a strong will that she knew what she wanted that she was prepared to give up despite the fact that she had been smoking for years and years but she just suddenly stopped that day.

Some people believe in destiny. In many respects it is not a factor I think rules my life, I prefer to live in the moment and change the course of life myself although as time moves on I am seeing that God has a real plan for everyone and yes we do make the choices when he places a crossroads, but there is a reason and plan. With Caroline I absolutely believe the planets were aligned and we were meant to meet, and destined to forge a dramatic, romantic union together.

At first I offered Caroline a spare room upstairs in my house. My charity ended there however. She had a couple of cats who she wanted to bring. But I said she couldn't bring those too. It was a bizarre twist but she decided to give her two cats to Amy and Ben. In fact they still have the cats to this day. Their mother Alison seemed to quite like the idea of Caroline which would seem bizarre given she is my ex-wife but it made sense. She viewed Shelley as her nemesis, as someone who had completely taken over her life in a fashion she did not expect or welcome, as someone who destroyed her marriage and her happiness. Anything that upset or removed Shelley was seemingly welcomed not just by Alison but by Amy and Ben, who were beginning to be influenced by Alison's hate. They began to hate Shelley too. Shelley was the one person in the world whom Alison hated with a passion because she took me away from her. Anything that caused Shelley the same distress Alison had experienced was very much approved.

On the surface Alison and I had dealt with the break up very well and almost like professional divorcees. We were as friendly as we could be given the situation and the kids seemed to handle it well, at least it seemed that way. I would later learn that there was a lot of resentment and bitterness and those things had affected Amy and Ben much more dramatically than I had believed.

I still cared a great deal for Shelley, whereas the animal magnetism which had welded Caroline and I together was in full effect. I was besotted by her and head over heels. I believe some people can convince themselves that they are in love with two women at the same time but the reality is always different. You can have a satisfaction or a *type* of fulfilment with a partner but it is not the same. The way I felt about Shelley by the time I knew Caroline better was not on the same level at all. As a person, Caroline was far more on my own level, which was no wonder given our ages were closer together. You cannot hide feelings for another woman. Your partner will always know too. There is a song called 'A Woman Knows' by Kenny Chesney which outlines this very predicament; that your partner will always know if you are in love with another person. As the lyrics go,

'Cause a woman knows, when there's another woman
She can feel her, all over her man
A woman knows, when there's another woman
You can't fool her, so don't try to think you can.'

It doesn't matter how you try and hide it, the love that you have for somebody - if it is deep and real love – will always be there. You can cover it up, you can hide it, you can shove it in a corner but it will keep bouncing out at you.

I did love Shelley and I still felt unbelievable guilt at what I had done to her. Yet, there was a good reason I did cheat on her. In my mind our relationship was not all it could be and I felt that Caroline was the one. There was no denying it. There had also been a discrepancy from Shelley's point of view. She had missed out on being a teenager, at least this is the impression she gave me. I couldn't provide the experience for her that another teenager could given I was twenty years older. There was no chance I would be going down to boogie at a club, it just wasn't me and I had outgrown that period of my life. Caroline was closer to my age and much more mature. Without her in the picture I might well have stayed with Shelley for a few more years but it would have broken down eventually because we were just a little far apart to make a lifelong commitment together. The spare room idea didn't last very long and we soon realised we were meant to be together and as close as possible, it took a while but the woman who had made my heart leap over a year earlier was now my partner and I loved it.

Our relationship got better and better, closer and closer and we were planning our future together. Caroline was as excited about Australia as I was and we arranged to travel there together. Caroline was deeply interested in the Tiger Conservation Programme in Sumatra so I arranged to take her there on the way to Australia. She was in her element, this was in her heart, in her soul and the first real experience of a truly wild place was an inspiration to her. We trekked through the tropical heat, through tiger country and slept out on a plastic sheet in the forest of Way Kambas National Park where tigers frequent regularly. One of the most exciting things I do in my life is to sleep in the wild with nothing but a ground sheet between myself and the animals, to experience the sounds and movement of the forests at night is an adrenaline rush that lasts for hours and Caroline just could not get enough of it.

After Sumatra I flew to Australia with Caroline to start the whole process of setting up the new zoo in 2001 and I recall speaking to Shelley on the phone. Caroline knew I had been speaking to her which wasn't the most popular thing to do but I needed closure. I needed to end it because Caroline and I were together. I found it very difficult talking to her but I remember us both deciding it was completely over, it had to be. The problem was, whereas Alison had been completely co-operative and agreed to a divorce quite quickly, Shelley did not want to. When I drew the divorce papers up for her to sign, she refused. With the time difference in Australia I would get up in the middle of the night to call Shelley and try and sort things out

When we returned to the UK it was apparent that the situation with Shelley was not "over" the guilt set in and a few attempts at resolving it were made, Caroline left the house for her mother's for a few weeks until it was finally resolved and truly "over". Caroline moved back to the zoo and we resumed our romance. It was in the time of our travels to Sumatra and Australia, the new beginnings and love that was deepening by the minute that Caroline conceived our child. I remember when Caroline told me she was pregnant it was a wonderful feeling to know that I was starting a family once again and this time with the woman I truly loved and was excited by, it just seemed to be the icing on the cake for us both.

Eventually, once Shelley found out about the pregnancy she came up to my house with a friend and finally signed the divorce papers. It was then I found total closure, in all respects. We have not spoken to each other since that day.

The closure enabled Caroline and I to fully enjoy our relationship together and from then on things just blossomed beautifully. We had some of the most wonderful times of my life in Australia. The photographs I have from that period in Australia are so revealing, they say everything about how happy we were in that period.

As part of our love nest I had gutted the whole house and rebuilt many parts – it was truly beautiful. The kitchen was all new and I decided to treat Caroline to a home cooked meal to celebrate the renovation. We had an electric hob with a propane gas oven. I wanted to light the oven but could not get the auto lighter to work; I persevered for a while until the smell of gas got very strong. I decided to wait a little while then try again. So this time I thought a match would do it. I couldn't see very well inside and asked Caroline to try and see exactly where the gas was coming from. I wasn't exactly following guidance from the handbook when I suggested she put her head in the oven.

Caroline bent down to look directly into the cooker. I struck the match, only to produce a complete *Tom and Jerry* moment. There was a giant boom as the gas exploded and Caroline's head came firing back out of the oven like a cannonball on a battlefield. As the smoke cleared I started to make out the outline of my beautiful partner, complete with a head of singed, burnt hair. She wore an expression of fear, surprise, anger and laughter all on the same face. I had to laugh, we both did.

We were enjoying completely natural fun in the most wonderful way and it was like a release mechanism within me, that I had finally released that burden, the burden of guilt which had taken so long to lose. Unfortunately that wasn't to last for long.

I took on too much though I didn't know this at the time. Hindsight is the best science ever. I was taking on Australia and taking on Britain trying to keep my businesses growing. South Lakes was already escalating at a ridiculous rate: 50,000 visitors in the first year, then 100,000, 150,000, 200,000, 220,000 - it was stellar growth. When I left for Australia I had to take on a manager to oversee things at the zoo. It had to be someone I could leave in charge for a number of months. I took on a chap called Roy Pirie. His daughter was already working for me as a volunteer at the park; she was a very passionate, dedicated worker. Her father had just been made redundant and had previously worked as a manager, somewhere within the public service industry. Roy's suggestion was very appealing and virtually impossible to turn down, the essence was that he would work for me in a management position for two months. If I wasn't happy with his work then I didn't have to pay him, but just to give him a chance. I thought that was a pretty fair deal, if he was worth paying then I would but if he didn't do a good job I was under no obligation. So I said, "Go on then, I'll give you a go because I desperately need to find somebody to take over the day to day management of the business when I'm not here because I can't run both."

At this time the Internet was becoming more and more a part of daily life and I was suddenly snowed under with emails as well as day-to-day activities and phone calls, meetings and letters. It's funny with hindsight because I remember that when we had just opened the park in 1995 I was making the food up at my garage whilst I was still doing almost everything single-handedly. A man came to see me and wanted to talk about tourism development and how I could spread the awareness of the zoo. He mentioned a thing that he was developing which was a web page for the Internet. He asked if I would like to get involved with this and I said, "What? What is that?" He then described it to me and I said, "By God, that'll never take off, there's no way I am putting money into that!"

It seemed so farfetched, it seemed like *Star Trek* to me at the time. Mobile phones were only just taking off. In my head because I was so bound in my world and what I was doing and animals and all the rest of it, I didn't take much notice of what the technological world was doing and in all honesty to this day I still don't, I couldn't really care less. I believed the Internet would be a limited market merely for the rich. I have been proven ever so slightly wrong with that view and it's become the biggest thing that ever hit the planet but I remember telling this bloke *that* will never take off.

It's so amusing to look back and see my business acumen has always been spot on!

This reminds me also that we didn't have computers then either, the first one I got would not hold a single photo from today in its memory and all we had a was a dot matrix printer in black. It really is amazing the speed of development of this technology in such a short time since the business began.

I went off to work on the Australian development and Roy Pirie stepped up to the mark and did a very impressive job. I got on well with him, he seemed a very friendly guy and he seemed to have a grip on what I wanted to achieve. He obviously took a more of a guidance role rather than ownership or leadership role so he didn't make decisions as much as he made sure my decisions were completed and fulfilled but that system worked quite well for quite a while.

For the first time ever in my life I realised I had overestimated my capabilities. I thought I was Superman, I thought I could do anything, I truly did. With my success I believed there was no such thing as the 'sky is the limit' – there was no limit. We had won the top attraction in the Lake District again for the second year running which was an absolute coup; no one had ever done that before. The Government Minister for Tourism actually came up from London to present me with a plaque and a certificate. My intention was to eventually sell up in England and use that money to keep Australia going, I did however have to keep South Lakes open because it was financing the development in Australia. An incident happened in 2001 at the park which did nothing to retain England's sense of charm. It was always a problem returning from Australia. The moment I walked through the gates to the park every member of staff seemed to have an issue that they wanted to mention, or something that needed to be resolved. There was one girl in particular, Lara Kitson who worked for the company as a keeper. She seemed to be suffering many ups and downs. From what I could gather the problem was in her relationship at the time. She worked on the cat section and every day Lara would climb a ladder in order to put the meat up four metres high for the tigers. When I returned from Australia, Lara told me she needed to talk with me. We moved into the hay barn and sat across from each other on two bales of hay. I had learned over the years that it was best in these situations to have another person as witness so I brought in another keeper who knew Lara quite well.

The conversation started and Lara was essentially complaining about people she worked with and issues she had at work. She told me she didn't know if she was happy or what to do about it. I told her that if she had any problems with others the best thing she could do was knuckle down and put the hard work in – it was the best way to answer criticism. I tried to be extremely positive to her. I tried to bring her into a frame of mind that told her not to let other people get her down. Lara began to cry but I told her things would get better, they always do, and not to worry, whatever was wrong we would sort it out. She got up and walked out of the barn. I looked blankly at the other keeper but in all honesty I just presumed she would get on with her work. Instead, she walked out of the park for good.

I said to the other keeper, "What was that all about? I don't understand." It didn't seem such a serious problem to overcome; in fact it was hard to ascertain exactly what the problem was. Many days passed and there was no word from Lara, until a letter came through the post revealing Lara was taking me to an industrial tribunal for sexual discrimination. In the document it said I was making it impossible for her to return to work because she was pregnant. This was something that had not been mentioned to me either in the meeting or around the park. I asked everyone whether they knew she was pregnant. Only one person knew and they had sworn secrecy, they confirmed that there was no way anyone could have told me.

I was accused of forcing Lara to climb up high poles while she was pregnant, which was strange because I would never knowingly do that and equally I rarely oversaw her personally. It ended up going to Tribunal and the young girl I was supposed to have as my witness said she could not go through with it as she was so scared of tribunals and courts. I said to her, "You've got to be joking, you're my only witness here. You were there. She never said it did she? Will you at least write a statement?"

She did so but it didn't do much good as she was not there herself to be cross examined. Suddenly I didn't have a witness. I also had a problem with another former employee, an older chap called John who was very lazy. He didn't want to work hard and eventually tried to con us by pretending to be sick, although someone I knew saw him in the town. The chap had supposedly broken his toe after dropping a flagstone on his foot, but he was seen walking perfectly. I knew he was really trying it on by then and sacked him. He ended up being Lara's witness, telling the tribunal that I had known she was pregnant and still forced her to climb up a four-metre pole. It didn't help that Lara took her baby into court with her. As I recall it two of them both cried throughout the trial, which didn't exactly help my cause, I was made out to be a harsh, uncaring brute. Unsurprisingly, the tribunal found in Lara's favour. I had to pay costs as well as lost wages and projected lost wages. The amount ended up at around £30,000. It was an obscene amount of money and I paid it for a mistake. My mistake had been to have such an informal chat, where I had tried to do the best by my member of staff. What I should have done, and what the Tribunal appearance taught me to do, was to have two witnesses and not do it in private. The meeting should be recorded both by audio and in written form and the person should be sent a letter detailing exactly what was said and whether they agree. I had always run my business with a certain informality, which was something I believed the staff liked, but Lara changed that. It also was the first experience I had of the serious injustice and failure of the English Justice system to be able to discern truth from lies and therefore make huge errors of judgement. Everyone in the park knew she was misleading the Tribunal but they were not allowed to be witnesses or place their views. I had total support from my staff over this and it was pleasing to know that confidence in me was so strong.

Though I was part based in England still my mind was rooted in Australia. I couldn't wait to have a zoo up and running there but it took an enormous amount of work, which was multiplied by the fact that it was ten times the size of my humble plot in Dalton. I had to virtually rebuild the house that Caroline and I would live in on site, look at procurement, find contractors, find suppliers and get the plans passed with the Council. We still found time to go to the beach and enjoy ourselves; it was an exciting time in my personal life, January 2002 onwards building a new future with Caroline. We had a baby on the way, there was a special future to come – it was an exciting time.

I still had my friendship with Maureen and Des from Mareeba and they both decided that they wanted to become involved in the project; it was like a family entity to involve them in my business. Maureen still remained in her work as a Real Estate Agent but she helped out with a few little things, such as checking the post and informing me of any developments. She would also talk to people on my behalf. Des became something of a similar figure to Glen Fitzwilliam, performing certain physical tasks which needed doing, such as organising boundary fences. Their commitment to me and the whole concept I had was unwavering and supremely enthusiastic. I also managed to enthuse the local Mareeba council who were bowled over that I had picked their little area to build such a huge animal attraction.

The mayor, Mick Borzi was a very enthusiastic participant in my ideas and plans and helped enormously. Mick understood promotion and tourism development. It was mostly down to him that Cairns acquired an airport, which in turn increased the tourism no end. Before then it had very little by way of tourist income, as it was so far to reach in a car. As soon as the airport arrived it became an international destination and Japanese tourists came in by the million. He became an iconic person in Mareeba but he was a very individualistic, inspirational person in his own right.

Mick really helped to integrate myself and my business idea into the area and enabled me to further my relationship with those in power in the town. I was invited to talk at various groups in the area. He wanted me to help and sit on some Council committees as an advisor. It was something I felt very positive about – it was very rewarding.

Things were cooking and Caroline and I returned to England to find Roy Pirie had made a reasonably good fist of things while I had been away. I was happy with everything and it was still ticking over, which during the winter period was about all you could ask for – it was a good time for me to go to Australia as in England there are very few visitors that time of year. My only real issue was to find someone who could look after animal records and so on. Caroline had been in charge of this side of things. Caroline was able to handle the animal records even from Australia but animal management was a different matter so I had to find someone to take over this task. It was a difficult position to fill – to even attempt to find someone who thought along the same lines as I did was a thankless task. I also needed someone who had experience of working with bigger animals such as rhinos, tigers and giraffes. I needed someone who had worked with animals, in zoos, for a long time so that they might understand my ideas and what I was trying to achieve.

We were absolutely renowned for the lemurs running everywhere, freedom for animals, space, mixed exhibits and I wanted somebody who wasn't going to come and change my strategy. Instead I needed someone who would just take my strategy and work with it because I could not stand people trying to change my way of thinking. This was no egotistical belief or anything, rather an inherent belief in what had worked for me and the park so far. The success had come big and fast so it was clear that I knew what I was doing. It worked. A bank manager once told me many years ago, never, ever to listen to anybody giving you business advice who has less money than you have. He was absolutely right. Never listen to anybody who is less successful than you are. Take advice off people who are more successful than you are because they have the right to give you advice. Anybody who is less successful than you cannot possibly assist you in your business.

It is a simple but logical point of view that seemed to fit with my own mission perfectly. Whenever anyone came and told me how to run my business I had very short shrift for them because I would say, "Hey, stop telling me how to do it. Look what I'm doing, look how successful I am. Don't try and tell me I am doing it wrong because I'm not, I'm doing it right." Some people saw that as arrogance. I had that thrown at me, that I was an arrogant person. I don't believe it was arrogance, it was a confidence. I knew my mission was the right mission. I felt I was changing people's lives, getting them enthusiastic about animals, getting schools involved, educating kids, charity work was raising money – by this time we had developed our projects in Indonesia and they were going well. In fact I made a yearly pilgrimage to Sumatra, Indonesia to check on the project and continuing to develop and improve it.

I wanted to be directly involved in my tiger projects and even though I was working with tiger conservation expert Ron Tilson, his license to work in Indonesia ran out in 2000. I worked solidly with the Government and everybody in Indonesia, to try and get the project going again but they didn't want Ron Tilson involved, it seemed they didn't like him. According to an opinion I was given, to them he was an arrogant, loud, dictating American with no respect for the Indonesian people. Unfortunately for Ron he could not get a deal done after that, whereas I took a different approach. Though our director Neil Franklin was an Englishman, I made sure the rest of my team were all Indonesian. It was a project based in their country and who better to know the land and the animals than the native people?

Neil was there to oversee the project but the team were all native, including an Indonesian manager. It cost a fortune to get the whole thing set up because I personally paid for the organisational costs. During the whole period where the government were deciding whether to allow Ron Tilson back in and there was no definitive agreement, I kept everybody in employment and made sure they had food on the table for their families. This went on for two years. You may wonder how on earth I had become financially solvent enough to the point of being able to take this project on as well as run South Lakes Wild Animal Park. Technically I was still borrowing money, though by and large the loans were paid off very quickly and I tended to use profit as development money in Australia, so essentially I borrowed far less than originally expected. Luckily my original strategy was not even followed through because the success of South Lakes was so far ahead of projections.

We were on a very strong footing and it meant I could run the park and tend to the projects in Sumatra. I strongly believed that I had a mission and that feeling became stronger as time went on. The success enabled me to fuel that mission even further – if it was working then I knew I must be on the right track and have the right kind of belief. As you have read when I started the park I felt I had a mission, to change the world a little and change people's perceptions of how humans can interact with animals.

I still desperately wanted to feel good about myself. I had been searching for it all my life, to have people acknowledge I was a worthwhile being on this earth, that I was a decent person. It didn't help that after the negative publicity from the *News Of The World* and the whole incident with Zimba that I had to fight again to establish credibility. It wasn't my primary motivation of course, the animals have always come first, but it was something I still sought, from my peers in the zoo world especially. The more effort and work I put into the conservation projects the more credibility I was afforded and the more I was seen as a decent human being.

It was highly important to me to receive recognition from my peers in the zoo world and I wasted no time in letting them know at every conference I attended, that I had been the one ploughing money into conservation work in Sumatra. I became known as the person investing money in conserving the Sumatran tigers. Every year I would make sure I spent two weeks in Sumatra and it was this work ethic in another project that I wanted to apply to the Mareeba project. It was clear to me that in order to establish respect and credibility I had to follow the same thought process which was working for the conservation. I applied the same logic as South Lakes and called my new project Mareeba Wild Animal Park. It is between Mareeba and Kuranda but I had to assert a specific place name and it is closer to Mareeba than Kuranda. I didn't want people turning up in Kuranda and being miles away. No one really knows much about Mareeba but at the time I thought I would establish positive relations with its people by including the place name in the zoo title. That strategy certainly worked. Today it is associated with Cairns because that is a far more popular tourist destination.

I had to apply for a four-year business visa to work in Australia – with the idea to later apply for citizenship once the zoo was established. The amount of work I was drowning under was immense. My mind was absolutely full; all thoughts were consumed by South Lakes, Sumatra and the logistics of setting up a zoo in Mareeba.

I had to develop new plans, drawings, ideas, concepts and get costings for everything. 24/7 my mind was in overload and it was overkill now I look back. I wasn't even sleeping the best or most consistent hours as I was often up in the middle of the night dealing with issues in Australia because for them it was the middle of the day.

I was suffering under the effects of stress but it was internal and I wasn't aware enough to acknowledge it to myself and I certainly wasn't about to slow down.

I was absolutely determined to do this, it was my future. Unfortunately in many respects I was *too* determined and too single minded. I started to experience problems in my relationship with Caroline. My mind was so full of my dreams, aspirations and activities that I found it very difficult to listen to Caroline, to listen to her needs and her wishes.

It took me a while to realise that I wasn't giving her everything I could, or everything she wanted from me. She loved me with all her heart which was restricting because it was this assurance that made me believe I could continue in the same fashion and it would be fine *because* she loved me.

I knew that when I had the time I would give her everything but in the meantime she would surely wait given she loved me so. I didn't listen to her and I didn't show her my love as I should. I wish I hadn't behaved like that but it was something that was out of control at the time. She was heavily pregnant which can cause all kinds of emotions and she needed me more than usual – yet it was at this time that I was so consumed with work.

During the build up to my future son Hari's birth, South Lakes was about to welcome four spectacled bears. The enclosure had been built in preparation. We were to have two arrive from Zurich and two from Paris. The two bears were flown in from Zurich whereas Caroline and I, with Caroline just a week away from giving birth, drove to Paris to collect the other two. We arrived at Paris Zoo and said hello to our two new arrivals, Mona and Alice. I have learned a lot of lessons about this kind of thing since, one of which was discovered on this particular day. Here we were driving back to Cumbria with two spectacled bears in the back of the truck. We arrived at the ferry terminal and the ferry ticket official asked me,

"What have you got in the back of there?"

"Two bears."

She called a higher official and they refused to let us on the ferry. They cited some rule from deep in their rulebook that said that exotic animals weren't allowed on the ferry so we were told we had to then catch a freight ferry which left the next day.

I said, "You can't do that, you can't keep these bears in these crates until the next day."

My protests were in vain, they maintained that they could and they would. I decided that instead of waiting and going with P&O I would drive over with the bears to Sea France. I didn't care what I was asked, I was saying nothing. I did have the correct papers but I thought it was imperative for the bears that we get them to their new home as quickly as possible. We bought the tickets and got onto the ferry, no questions and no problems. We made it back to Cumbria without a hitch and the bears started to settle into their new home.

A week later we were due to drive the van down to Heathrow to collect the bears flying in from Zurich. Once again Caroline was going to come with me – one week nearer to giving birth. As it turned out she was one second away. As she lifted her leg to climb into the van very early in the morning, her waters broke. This could have happened on the M6! Luckily it was just before. I still had to collect the bears however. So I called Roy Pirie and he and my ex wife Alison went to the Airport in London whilst I took Caroline to the hospital.

Alison had, by now, come back to work at the park. I thought I was doing the right thing to stay friends with her, she seemed to have accepted Caroline and I and it seemed like a good thing to do for the sake of the kids. As long as Caroline was okay with everything it seemed to be a positive scenario. It didn't seem to bother her but in reality it must have been a bit strange when Caroline was so heavily pregnant and we were planning on making a new life together and here I was with my ex wife working in the same place as me.

Now, when I look back at it, I would never have done it that way, never, because underlying, undermining and niggling her all the time is that somebody I was married to and sleeping with every night for twelve years virtually, was still there. It might have been good for the kids but it must have totally devastated Caroline to think that I actually wanted my ex wife around me. I felt it was an achievement to be able to keep my family together but in actual fact it was a mistake because it sent out the wrong message to the woman I loved.

By the time our son was due to be born in late April of 2002 it seemed a very tense time. I couldn't relax for the life of me and felt as if I couldn't just switch off from work and enjoy the process of seeing my son born. I feel somewhat ashamed to look at photographs of myself on that day. I should have been the proudest man in the world and I absolutely was proud, but I was extremely tense. I was worried about a lot of things and it manifested itself in tension, tension on my face, within my body and within the relationship. Perhaps it didn't help that I had been stressed trying to get the bears collected safely, also I knew what was coming whereas for Caroline, it was her first child. Far more difficult to actually give birth than merely to watch as well!

I kept getting sidetracked during the labour process, dealing with several work issues. It makes me upset to think I behaved that way. In my work drenched haze however I somehow believed that securing our future was more important than enjoying the moment and making the best of what was really important – our first child together. Hari was a wonderful and special addition to our lives but I should have switched off completely and enjoyed the time for what it was. I have since learned that the day is more important than the future because the day is what you are living now and if you don't get that right you won't even have a future, and certainly not the future you desire. It is one of the biggest regrets in my life that I did not listen or give Caroline what she wanted when it was within my grasp.

If I could do it all again the family would come first, my work would have to revolve around my time with family and not the other way around. I would take time out. Today I handle things much differently and always put my children first. Still, I ask myself if I would have been able to create a successful business during my thirties and forties if I had done this. The answer might well be no.

Chapter 20
Managers, cyclones and jealousy

I was coming up to 41-years-old. Caroline knew that I had missed out on my 40th birthday as it was around the time of the split with Shelley. Hari was just three weeks old and Caroline went to amazing lengths to organise a surprise party for me in the zoo. I have no idea how she kept it so secret but I was taken for a ride to Barrow for some obscure reason by Ben. I had no idea whatsoever of what happened next as I arrived back at the zoo the car park was full of cars and I was taken down to the restaurant. I walked into a surprise birthday party; suddenly there was a huge roar. There were all my staff, family and friends – it was a wonderful surprise (it is not easy to keep things like this from me) and a fabulous night. Caroline had spent all day making and hiding food and then told everyone to hide under the tables and erupt when I arrived, she wore a tshirt that said I love Michael (Jackson) and crossed out the Michael and wrote David. It was very special and Caroline and I were so happy with our new son Hari and the future looking so wonderful for us both, deeply in love and our new family.

Turning 41 might well have given me a reality check about my age but in truth I still felt as if I was still 21.

Caroline and I had many things in common. We had a little boy together whom we named Hari (pronounced Hah-Ree. The name comes from 'Harimau' and "Hari" which is Indonesian for tiger and day respectively), we both loved animals and crucially at this time in our relationship, we both shared the dream of running an animal park in Australia. Caroline saw Mareeba and Australia in general as idyllic: tropical beaches only half an hour's drive away, coral reefs, tropical rainforest, perpetual heat and sunshine, shopping centres that you could only dream of. Cairns is about the same size as Barrow-in-Furness yet has about twenty times the facilities of Barrow which is quite ludicrous considering its relative remoteness. It was quite a bump back down to earth coming back from there to Barrow.

I would work through the night and at a time when we should have been kissing and cuddling on the sofa I was dealing with things in Australia. I might get an email telling me, 'We have a problem with the fencing contractor, what should we do?' They were the kinds of questions that were impossible to ignore and too timely to leave until later. Despite leaving other people in charge there were always executive decisions that had to be made and they had to be dealt with immediately. If it wasn't problems or issues with the construction then it would be a financial issue – something would need to be purchased but they wouldn't be sure whether they could spend a certain amount of money without my say so.

Given this was a constant source of pressure and a time drain, I allowed Caroline to perform her role in the background of my life, presuming that she understood and knew why I was doing the things I was doing, and why they were being done this way. I assumed she knew it was all for her. From Caroline's point of view however, she felt neglected and she started to become depressed. I was aware of it but didn't take it seriously. I told her to pull herself together and see that she had everything going for her. I couldn't see that all she really needed was my time, effort and companionship. Though the doctors who saw her may have helped by giving her an outlet to vent her feelings, they couldn't give her what she truly needed – quality time with me.

It may seem quite simplistic now that I could not see what my own partner needed and it would seem as if I was all wrapped up in myself and quite selfish. Yet the truth is I was not living with complete awareness of myself, or seeking to please myself. On the contrary I wasn't feeling too pleased with myself, I knew there was still so much to do and I was existing in a strange netherworld where it was as if I was a separate entity. I wasn't thinking of myself, I was thinking of what I was achieving and what needed to be achieved. Sure, recognition, money and having something palpable to show for it was all part of the show but ultimately it was about the mission that I had and absolutely nothing could or would get in the way of it. It helped my belief when people questioned whether it could be done. To tell me it was impossible only drove me on to prove that it wasn't.

I managed to achieve this but the casualty of this achievement and mentality was that the fun and excitement I'd experienced at the beginning had started to wane and disappear. It might not be much of a consolation to Caroline but she was at least immune from me being drawn to any other woman. She was the girl for me and I didn't even think about being with another person. In fact there was a slight issue with Caroline and I which was that I felt she believed I was attracted to Maureen and Des's youngest daughter which absolutely was not the case. I liked the family but the daughter was not my type in that respect, not in the least.

In fact the family were dedicated to Caroline and I as a couple and as friends. Maureen would constantly talk to me, explaining that Caroline needed me and I was neglecting her, trying to get across the importance of keeping my partner happy. Strangely Caroline believed Maureen didn't like her but she was wrong. Additionally Maureen could see how I was behaving would affect my partner; she could see it from a woman's point of view. She tried to give me advice but I was on a one-way track with no brakes. I did listen to her but the trouble is, when you are so busy you can lose track very quickly. It is still an issue in my life where something can be said to me at 1 o'clock and it will become ancient history by 1:30 because my life moves at such a pace and can change so quickly it is easy to forget.

I bought Caroline a diamond ring to show my love – to make her my fiancée. In my mistaken haze I believed that would be enough to show her what she meant to me – enough to secure her love and her companionship forever. Although I proposed to her with as much romanticism as I could muster I see now that to her it must have seemed a little like, 'Here is my token gesture to you, I want to marry you, what more do you want? I can't give you the time, I can't afford to cuddle you because I am busy but here's this, surely this will solve your problems?'

Of course it couldn't do that because Caroline didn't want the house, the zoo, the car or even the ring, she wanted me. She wanted me to give my heart not to my zoo, not to my tiger project, she wanted me to give my heart to her and I didn't do that even if that is what an engagement ring is supposed to represent.

I am an old romantic at heart. One of my favourite films is *Pretty Woman* and I can relate to it in many ways. It is a very emotional film. It shows a business man who has had a hard life, he can't speak to his father or his family but he has a heart and he falls in love with a person so far outside of his realm of experience. It is a love story of immense proportions and in fact, Julia Roberts reminds me of Caroline (although not as the character in the film!)

I can't remember ever telling Caroline that my time was only going to be temporarily taken up while I tried to solidify my business, our future. I am sure I did at some point but it mustn't have come across in the manner intended. To her, the here and now was the important thing, and understandably so. Yet this was my strategy, and I knew that if I slowed down now from a work perspective the whole thing would fail. I was borrowing a lot of money because the nature of the project and the costs were really stretching the amount of capital that South Lakes could possibly provide, so there were multiple loans, somewhere in the region of £500,000. Although I knew that if push came to shove South Lakes would be able to finance Australia, I felt an enormous amount of stress on me, that money had to be paid back by me creating a successful animal park in Australia.

I was unaware of many parts of the Australian process which made my job immensely hard. I didn't realise until I was snowed under with the project that there were no rules and regulations in place for a zoo in Queensland, Australia, they made it up as they went along. Another aspect was the costs and standards of working in Australia. I used my previous strategy in the UK as a template because it had worked for me years earlier. Everything I did was based upon the UK cost of labour, materials, whatever I needed. I hadn't factored in the reality that we were based in far north tropical Queensland and therefore to transport fencing or the metal posts it would need to come from Brisbane, a distance of 2,500 miles.

Additionally the cost of labour in Australia at that time was double the costs in England. Given the excellent working conditions and the prevalence of unions it is no wonder people go out there to work because they look after those who have a trade and want to work hard. From my point of view the situation was dreadful, paying an electrician double what he would earn in England. Equally, I had saved a fortune doing the majority of jobs myself in constructing South Lakes. In Queensland this money saving option was not available to me. There, if you are not a qualified electrician you can't even fit a plug for your business. You can't fix your roof unless you are a qualified roofer.

Everything there was regulated and over the top. The state controlled everything. I felt it was the nearest thing to a Communist state that I had ever come across because it didn't matter what I wanted to do I had to get somebody else to do it or I would be doing it illegally. I tried to play ball but I would have crippled my chances of making this a successful operation so wherever possible I may have averted the technicalities somewhat. I didn't intend on shelling out for an overpaid electrician to fit a plug or do a little rewiring.

Des warned me constantly, "You can't do that, not over here, you can't do that." "Well it's too late," I would say, "I already have done, just look the other way."

"You can't do it, you can't do it."

"You look the other way if you think I can't do it."

There were issues with actually bringing the animals in. Once again, Australia kept its zoo world quite insular and everything had to go through the Australian Zoo Association (ARAZPA as it was then). They would control every part of the process of bringing animals in, which was something I didn't want. I didn't want to have to ask for their permission to bring in an animal I was looking after – if I did this I would have to ask permission for the simplest of animals, never mind a tiger. I wanted to be independent and the only way to do so was to build my own quarantine facility – which was a mammoth and expensive task.

In England quarantine involves isolating animals and protocols.

In Australia it involves air isolation. This meant that the air in the quarantine facility had to be pure and constantly filtered – there could be no pests or insects in the atmosphere or the facility. The building was already there, I just needed to modify it to the correct specifications which meant separate cages and proving that the room was pressurised so that nothing could come in or out. Therefore the facility was airtight and had to be separated from the world – water, liquid, everything. It had to be insulated for heat, everything had to be cool, it was quite a project! It was extraordinarily expensive but it was a real feat when completed, by far the best facility I had ever built at that stage.

All this time my children were coming out at different times, I wanted the kids to be a part of the whole experience in Australia. One of Hari's very first life experiences was flying to Australia when he was just a few months old. He would spend a few months in Australia and then come back to England for another few months or so. I was travelling a lot and so were the kids. I made sure I flew Amy and Ben out to Australia whenever they were on school holidays – they would come out unaccompanied on the very long flight and spend a few weeks at a time with me – they loved the whole experience and had a unique and special time with me in that land of wonder.

It was at this point that we had a fair amount of spare time before the main construction. One evening while both Amy and Ben were staying with us, Ben said, "Guess what we are doing at 7.30 in the morning?"

"What do you mean?"

"You know that you said you would love to sky dive? Well I have booked us all to 'Go Skydiving'." He had used my credit card to pay and because I never waste a penny, cent or any other currency we set off in the morning to the airfield at Cairns.

Despite thinking at every stage that the children would chicken out, they did not and I ended up jumping out of a plane at 10,000 feet and plummeting at staggering speed to the ground. The chute opened at about 3,000 feet to my utter relief and the glide to the ground gave me time to get my breath back. All I wanted to do once on the ground was get back up and do it again! It remains one of the most exciting things I have done, yet tame in most respects as it was prepared and planned perfectly unlike most of my adventures.

There were so many extraneous elements of my life and I felt I had to try and keep all those people happy who were important to me; it was like perpetual plate juggling. It was very important to try and keep Caroline happy. I believed it would help with her being in Australia with me; here she was alongside me helping to forge the business that was our life together and our future. I can see in hindsight that I should have held her hand a little more and given her a more specific guidance but at the time I felt she had enough to keep her occupied. The problem was she got a little bit lost. We were living quite a long way from anywhere. To get to the main town was twenty minutes in one direction or 30 in the other. Caroline felt a little stuck. It was an incredibly hot environment, so hot that she preferred to stay inside. She didn't make friends easily and became isolated in the house watching television, playing videos for Hari and generally concentrating solely on looking after our son.

When I think about it now, I did nothing with her. I was out there busy, so hard working. I came home every dinnertime, because we used to have a siesta after lunch. My day would begin at five or six in the morning and I would work until twelve. It was too unbearable to work in the blazing hours after noon so I would sleep generally until about 2:30. The temperature was around 35 degrees Celsius every day but on top of the heat was immense humidity in the wet season and dryness in the rest of the year. You couldn't escape in the wet season from December to March, the house was wet, everything was wet. Ironic really given that we did not see a drop of rain in the first two years we spent there – it was a complete and total drought. When it did come it was with a vengeance, 400 mm (about fourteen inches) of rain in one day for instance.

The design process of Mareeba was the principal cost. It was the biggest building project of my life. There was no water there which had to be addressed as it was crucial for the animals. This meant that I had to build two dams to block off two valleys on either side. Luckily I got permission to build them but one of the dams was enormous and incredibly expensive. There were masses of steel and concrete, a hundred truckloads of concrete altogether. Due to the heat intensity we were pouring concrete onto the dam spillway at 4am.

It was helpful that in Australia, building dams is de rigueur and it was easy to find a big company who were used to constructing dams in the middle of nowhere. Byrnes Earth Movers certainly knew what they were doing and they did indeed make the earth move. They devised an entire valley, which comprised the new lake – it was so vast that the lake itself was bigger than the entire South Lakes Wild Animal Park. The dam remains the largest engineering project I have ever taken on and it is still containing the huge volume of water today. It was completed in November 2002 just in time to capture the seasonal rains.

Unfortunately Caroline was struggling with postnatal depression. We spent right up to Christmas 2002 in Queensland. It was a very difficult time, I was working so hard. I was hot, frustrated, everything was spiralling out of control, money was slipping away like water and budgets were being overstretched and completely obliterated. I knew I had to employ a manager in order to keep track of the Australian zoo especially when I was so busy with other things and could often be in a different country. I employed an ex-zoo manager from Taronga Zoo in Sydney called Kevin Evans. We had a problem in that he was not remotely on my wavelength despite convincing me otherwise at his interview. He had worked for a traditional zoo and therefore was entrenched in that mindset. He had a different set of standards and expectations and in actual fact he cost a lot of money with his methods. He had only the experience of spending Government money, so profit and loss wasn't really important as the government always bailed out the big Australian zoos. For me every cent counted and if we didn't need it we had to do without. It soon occurred to me how people manage to get away with things when they are working in a team of twenty within a major zoo. When they are exposed on their own and have to do a job to a more exacting standard, they get found out quickly. Unfortunately this was made painfully obvious with my new manager Kevin.

He caused real problems because he could not follow my simple instructions. He knew one way to do things and could not adapt to a new approach. He was still in the traditional zoo framework. One example would be when he painted a line which was a metre away from a fence in front of a monkey cage, effectively ordering any staff to stay back behind the line. It was a very city zoo mentality and in truth it started to wear me down. He was unable to carry out my needs and often tried to cover up for his own failings. He did oversee the import of the large cats into the park during July of 2003 but only after huge delays with paperwork that he was responsible for. He could never admit when he was out of his depth, in this instance he didn't action the details when he should have. Eventually I found him out, we had a verbal confrontation and he left. He made quite an issue of the situation proclaiming I had sacked him when he was doing a good job but the bottom line was I cannot deal with people trying to change my agenda. It is the framework I have built and it works, most importantly it is best for the animals and for the visitors and involves working on budgets that are realistic. He had no idea whatsoever of how to manage a tight commercial budget and that could not be accepted.

The problem in Australia was just the same with a potential zoo manager as it was with a plumber. I was not allowed to bring someone in myself who was young, hungry and enthusiastic who I could train using my methods and template, just as I have done at South Lakes. The zoo authorities were adamant that I had to employ a person who was already trained and qualified as a zoo manager and so around August 2003 I had to bring someone in who had experience. Unfortunately that experience was tainted with pre-conceptions and misguided ideals that had been imparted from a major, traditional zoo. Around September 2003 I managed to find a replacement manager, Paul Whitehorn who brought his wife, Sam a veterinarian, with him.

During this period, the biggest scourge in my professional life was to come from zoo managers. No wonder really. I had built a zoo from scratch with all new methods and ideals, completely unique and rather alien in the zoo fraternity. I could not possibly oversee two zoos at opposite ends of the world on a daily managerial level and had to relinquish that control. But it was a difficult thing to do, especially when I couldn't find a soul that I could trust in that position. I was about to find a new level of frustration with a manager; only this time it was my staff who were going to feel the anger and aggravation.

I had to have an animal manager looking after things at South Lakes during the time I was in Australia and his name was Terry Bowes. He seemed a decent enough fellow and his assurance that he had a wide variety of experience in working with animals seemed to be enough for him to do a decent job. I employed him to oversee the animal collection while I was away and I told him quite categorically, "Terry, I'm in charge, you're looking after the staff and everything else but I want it doing the way I want it doing, I don't want anything bringing in from other zoos, experience or ideas. If you want to do that then we have to discuss it first because this place is so successful because of the way I do it, not because of the way anybody else does it." I wasn't harsh but I left it clear that he should follow the protocol I had laid out. He concurred that he knew how to follow those instructions.

While I was in Australia I started to receive emails from my staff at South Lakes. The content was alarming, telling me that Bowes was not doing things right, the way he works is causing distress to both animals and staff alike. He was putting animals in small cages, he had put them in the giraffe house, he was stacking animals two-four cages high. My staff were telling me that he wasn't the person I believed him to be. He was telling them how to do things and it was far removed from the way I would have wanted things done. The general consensus was that the staff couldn't stand him and that he was causing them all kinds of stress and disillusionment.

It had only been about two months from May 2003 but Bowes had already done untold damage to the zoo and relations among staff. He had tried to change regimes and diets and clearly he had absolutely no idea what he was doing. Effectively he was trying to play boss, make his mark and change things because I was out of the way. After eight weeks or so I received a letter signed by virtually every single one of the staff, bar Terry, and it demanded that either I get rid of him or they would all leave. I couldn't believe it. What the hell had he done? He totally, utterly, turned everyone against him and that's partly because my staff were loyal to me. They were loyal to the style; to the way we had done things. All of a sudden they had to deal with a chap coming in who wanted the traditional zoo methods and set up. I had no choice but to relieve him of his duties. It had not been a personal attack from myself, I simply responded to my staff telling me how they felt and that they could not carry on in this fashion.

Unfortunately Terry Bowes decided that he was going to get his own back. He wrote a standard letter which he sent to any important department he could. This included local councils, the Environment Agency, the police, HMRC, the VAT representatives, all the zoo federations, even the Australian Zoo Federation. Every organisation you could imagine that might get me in trouble, he contacted them. Everything he said was an outright lie. We were supposedly tax evading, using red diesel in my vehicles and breaking all known hygiene rules within the park. According to his letter we were breaching health and safety rules, animal rules, any form of documented rule that could be broken in fact. It was a steadfast and unpleasant campaign that assured that every possible department I was responsible to had a predication to investigate myself and the park.

We were then subjected to absolutely thorough investigations by virtually every one of these agencies but not one of them could find any evidence of anything that he ever accused us of. We were completely clean and he was just shown to be a very sore loser. In my opinion he was a pathetic character who could not take the responsibility of his own failings; he just wanted to blame me and all my staff, even though I wasn't there. The problems he created within the UK went away quite quickly but that wasn't the end of it.

I was already unpopular with the Australian Zoo Association because I was independent and they wanted everything to follow their own controlling regulations and requirements. As soon as I built my own quarantine area I was a threat because it was the only quarantine outside of a state zoo in the whole country. I could now effectively bring in any animal I wanted with government permits from wherever without their approval – something they weren't too happy about. The European Zoo Association (EAZA) were my allies predominantly because I had my own contacts that were focused on breeding programmes and working with them to find surplus animals. However I was not a supporter of all zoos because I had animals as my priority and sometimes my views were not appreciated by some. I was still forging an independent furrow.

One of the accusations that Terry Bowes made was that we had fabricated or forged some documents to export several lemurs and the fact is we did nothing of the sort. We had changed the I.D. numbers on them because we changed the animals we wanted to send but it had been done by following the proper procedure through the breeding programme. I even had a letter from the breeding programme to prove it had been done properly.

I'd had an employee working for me in Australia who saw himself as a future manager of mine. He often criticised and complained about the chap I had in as manager, which to an extent was acceptable, I wanted to know what was going on, especially if it could be damaging to the animals or the business. Yet it was a little snide and more like telling tales. Given the acrimony between the two of them it was only a matter of time before one of them had to go. I had to think of the business and ended up giving the younger chap his notice. He knew of the furore caused by Terry Bowes however, and decided he would do the same thing.

He then wrote to the Australian Zoo Association claiming that I had forged documents for an import, the same charge Bowes had levelled. The irony is he caught himself out because it was actually he who had signed the document in question! I hadn't even been there but it concerned a group of lemurs who were coming to Mareeba. There had been five coming, and we had all the correct documentation for that move. Somewhere along the line the five lemurs became seven. Instead of reapplying for a license for five lemurs he just altered the existing license, crossing out seven and putting five instead. I didn't know about this and to some extent, if someone is in a managerial position you assume they are doing this kind of thing properly and above board.

Due to the accusations ARAZPA kicked me out of the organisation without any proof whatsoever of any wrong doing, it seemed like any excuse to ostracize me. I said, "How can you do that without any proof it was me? If one of my staff did it, yes, punish that but you can't punish the zoo for the actions of one member of staff, who now doesn't work here, and has turned whistleblower. Ask yourself why he has done this. Can you not see that this is just a disgruntled person who is trying to cause trouble because he knew what he had done?"

I did eventually become reinstated but by now the government were going through everything with a fine tooth comb. Luckily the business was completely above board, though it taught me not to leave anything official to any member of staff unless I could trust them implicitly. These particular managers were certainly not trustworthy. The Australian troublemaker became a policeman in Queensland. Terry Bowes still lives and works in Cumbria but has never amounted to anything and in fact I still hear about him via complaints and concerns about his methods and actions even today.

I am not someone who holds a grudge and there are very few people in the world who I can actually say I hate but at the time I did hate Bowes for what he had done and the trouble he caused for all my staff both in the UK and Australia. I felt sorry for somebody who had to try and cover up his own failings instead of realising and actioning them, learning from them and being a better person for it. He just wanted to cause pain and difficulties for other people. The fact is he didn't just cause me trouble, he caused the whole park trouble, all the employees and everybody else and I suppose that gave him some sort of satisfaction. He did himself no favours with his behaviour however because everyone could see he was a troublemaker and in my experience a nightmarish character that they wouldn't want anywhere near their business. After the problems with managers I didn't want to employ another yet I was required to by the zoo authorities.

Chaper 21
Lions, Tigers and Baboons

I wonder how many people knew when they were relaxing on their flights from Australia to England that for almost a full day they were sitting above two tigers and five lions? Sitting in the hold underneath where people were stretching their legs worrying about deep vein thrombosis were Bastoni and Hari, two male tigers and their lion friends Mikumi and four others. This happened quite a lot, and no one would ever have known. In July 2003 the Mareeba Wild Animal Park erupted with new life, tigers and lions arrived from South Lakes Wild Animal Park to take up residence along with a few monkeys from Australian zoos. All of a sudden we had a zoo park and all my hard work seemed to be paying off. However my plans to create a park with rhinos, giraffes and other African Plains animals ran into many difficulties. The problem was the strict quarantine regulations for importing any animals to Australia, a situation I wish I had understood better at the outset. Hari, Bastoni, Mikumi and company settled extremely well into the airtight, insect proof quarantine unit, but could not see the light of day for over a month. When they did I don't think they knew what hit them, going from an Air-conditioned isolation unit to the full heat of the tropical far north Queensland sun.

I found a truly decent person to manage animal things at South Lakes Wild Animal Park in late 2003. Peter Dickinson was a gentleman with a huge amount of experience in the zoo environment. He had worked for the Welsh Mountain Zoo for two decades but he was unsettled and seeking a new challenge. He came to work for me and managed to build up a rapport with the staff – he was the exact opposite from Bowes, he even socialised with the staff. Despite this he was still an experienced zoo worker who had his own ideas about things and he seemed to find my style of management difficult. He had been working for a director who was long in the tooth and rather passive. Here I was with the zing of a teenager and a direct, hands on approach where I wanted to be involved with all aspects of the zoo, it didn't sit too easily with Peter.

I didn't help things because I had to be so strongly aware of what was going on in the UK when I was in Australia, I didn't want any further problems as with Terry Bowes. I was watching Peter like a hawk which really didn't give him a chance. I must have been over-powering and in return he came to the realisation that he couldn't be a manager with me breathing down his neck. In effect I was treating him like an ordinary keeper, though that had never been my intention. Still I had to admit that it was my fault Peter left and I also had to admit that for me to allow someone else to take control of my baby is a virtually impossible task. Peter then took grasp of his real needs and travelled the world and is a well known person around the globe. Today he is the creator of *Zoo News Digest* an Internet zoo news site that he runs from the Far East mostly.

I was having deep problems with the new manager in Australia. We had some monkeys offered to us from one of the zoos in Australia. They were their surplus but as I had experienced with South Lakes, I wasn't about to turn down a free offer of animals as I needed to stock the zoo. In zoo parlance the monkeys were sadly 'cast offs', there was something wrong with each of them. Some were too old, some were deformed, all were non-breeding animals. There was an assortment of cast offs, from Japanese macaques to a few male spider monkeys. These monkeys were brought in when I was in England during September/October 2003, so I had to leave very clear written instructions regarding how the animals should be released into the enclosures. These were of course surrounded by electric fences, and unfortunately none of the staff at Mareeba had any experience of working with animals and electric fences, regardless of how long they had worked in zoos.

I employed Paul Whitehorn and his veterinarian wife Sam, to attempt to make running the zoo easier but it was actually made more difficult. His wife worked for me for a short time but she was costing too much, we didn't have many animals and she was taking our funds that we needed so desperately everywhere else and I had to let her go. They seemed friendly enough but once again, when I was gone, they decided to do their own thing. By now I was becoming angry with this repeating cycle. One of the things they disrupted was my policy over electric fences. It was a very specific management technique, learned by practice and experience. I had learned an amazing amount about animals and electric fences, how to release and manage the animals into an enclosure with electric fences, a vital process because if you make a mistakes the animals go straight through the fences and disappear. It was difficult enough in England but in Australia, if the animals escaped they would be gone forever as there were thousands of acres of forest surrounding the park.

I spoke with Paul and Sam as well as leaving the written instructions. I pointed out that if they made a mistake it would be a grave one. They needed to follow exactly what I said because I had done it several times by now. Paul and his wife believed they could do better than me, they thought they could cut corners. They were supposed to allow one monkey at a time to go out into the electric fenced natural forest enclosure and then leave the others inside so it was attracted back inside to them. Instead they let them all out at once. The monkeys flew out at speed and they were confused and unaware of where they were supposed to go – the poor things were in a complete panic. Some ran up trees, some ran straight through the fence, some got electrocuted, one or two ended up in the lake. Some were heat stressed, some couldn't find their way back in, one had totally disappeared. It was a disaster.

I was sickened by it when I found out part of the detail by e-mail, because I knew instantly they hadn't followed the correct procedure, seemingly through an attack of ego. I was angry and upset, upset at the distress caused to the monkeys and angry because if monkeys were found on the loose, having escaped from my zoo, the authorities would have jumped on me like a ton of bricks and had the zoo shut down. The monkey on the loose was found in my next door neighbour's garden the next day and they managed to reign him back in. It was too late however as someone outside the zoo had already spotted it and a report made it to the authorities. I managed to cover up the whole thing from my end as I knew what it would mean for the zoo if it could be proven. It was then I realised just how impossible it was for me to do this in Australia with staff that just would not listen to the most basic instructions.

During this confusing, convoluted period I was trying to organise for two rhinos to come over to South Lakes direct from South Africa. I took Caroline and Hari – who was just one-year-old at the time - with me to Durban for the first time. We went to meet up with people who dealt with moving rhinos. They had some available on breeding farms especially for this purpose. We were taken all over the Kwazulu natal province looking at young rhinos for us to take back to England. We were looked after very well and it was a fantastic trip that we all loved. At the time Hari was just starting to come into his own, he was very active and vocal the whole trip.

We picked two white rhinos, who were sisters, from a ranch called Tala, just outside Durban. They had the same father but different mothers and they had been born just a few weeks apart. We decided this was perfect, two rhinos who knew each other well, they would be more comfortable travelling together and settling into a new life in Cumbria. It took a while for them to actually be introduced to the park in September 2003 as they had to go through quarantine in South Africa. The rhinos had quite a time of things. They had already travelled on a cargo jumbo jet together, at a cost of £100,000.

This money was merely for the flight and carriage alone, no money changes hands to purchase the animals themselves. In fact this is always the case, regardless of the animal we acquire. It is surprising to many people but animals are always exchanged without money changing hands and the zoo in receipt of the animals is always responsible for any transportation costs.

Most animals are part of regional or international breeding programmes and as such the genetics need to be freely available in a management programme. Therefore all animals in top zoos around the world have their details registered in a central database where the parentage, history, medical details and so on are all held, so that unrelated pairings can be organised by programme managers.

At South Lakes Wild Animal Park we manage seven studbooks

and in the past we have managed others. When we wish to obtain a new animal or species we first have to approach the species manager, utilising their advice on the 'best' pairing of available animals. We then agree the transfer and complete all paperwork which confirms the moves. This means the species is placed first and we also have viable groups for the future. EEP European Breeding Programme animals are not allowed to be traded at all by EAZA members and South Lakes has always been an advocate of free movement of species without trade. We have never sold an animal and work together with zoos worldwide to maintain viable populations of species.

Even though transporting rhinos via jumbo jets cost so much money it was worth every penny because we now had a true breeding programme in place – two males and two females.

My idea was to integrate the rhinos and giraffes with a troop of baboons. Sure we were mixing the exhibits and taking a risk and it took me two years of thought and risk assessment on my part to come to a decision, but I felt it was the right thing to do and it created an even more interactive living environment for the animals. Still the time delay that was involved in deciding in whether we should do this involved the practical logistics of how we could physically combine these animals together. How on earth could we have baboons, rhinos and giraffes and have all the gates work properly and co-operate with all the safety regulations? As soon as the gates opened for the rhinos there was the very real possibility that the baboons would run through them, therefore what size fence would be required to house the baboons and not interfere with the rhinos?

After two years I made an introductory little paddock for the baboons. The rhinos and giraffes were perplexed as to how they could make it up to the fence but not enter the same part of the field as the baboons. After about a month of this sectioned off paddock for the baboons I took the fence down, just before the females arrived from South Africa. The baboons didn't see me doing this so that when I did let them out they must have wondered where the fence had gone. It was funny because the baboons ran straight up to the boundary of that small enclosure marked by long grass and still stopped, even though there was no fence there. They had a moment of recognition and puzzlement – the fence was there yesterday, where did it go?

The rhinos also came right up and stopped where the fence had been before as if there was some invisible force keeping them there. Then all of a sudden they had a eureka moment: 'Hold on a minute there is a lot of nice grass in there that I haven't eaten yet.' They went into the new area, settling in perfectly and eating their new grass. Everything went smoothly. After two years of worrying about it and wondering how I could do it, everything that I put in place worked perfectly. It just goes to show that not everything can be made with a hasty decision; some things really do need to be planned for a long time. The whole situation with the rhinos, baboons and giraffes has worked perfectly ever since.

Chapter 22
Million dollar deal, over work and biggest visitor day ever

2003 was a year that nearly broke me totally in every way. The travelling in itself was unbelievable, the stress generated unwanted and immensely difficult to handle. We came back from Australia on 22nd December 2002, went to South Africa in April '03, to Australia again in the May, returned to the UK in August, the rhinos arrived in September from South Africa then we left again for Australia in October. What happened next was enough to take my stress levels out of the stratosphere.

In November of 2003 I couldn't believe the opportunity I was presented with. Just after baby rhinos had arrived at South Lakes I went back out to Australia. Almost as soon as I got there I received a phone call. A chap told me he was a friend of a guy from the Northern Territory, in a place called Tipperary Station.

He told me that his friend, a former successful businessman, had a fantastic collection of wild animals which he had to sell because he needed the money. It had to happen quickly because the land had already been sold to someone else and he had to have the animals taken off the land as soon as possible. He asked me if I would be interested.

"What have you got?" I asked.

"A pair of rhinos, pygmy hippos, tapirs, antelope, zebras."

Wow! These were animals you would seriously struggle to obtain in Australia ordinarily. Even better, the animals were already in the country and therefore would not need quarantine. I thought this was a decent opportunity already, and then he said that in all there were actually 2,500 animals.

He told me there were herds of different deer including Sika, Chital and Sambar deer, herds of water buffalo. There were herds of almost every herding animal in existence! I couldn't believe it. There were an herd of a very rare type of oryx, the Scimitar-horned oryx. I realised this was an opportunity I would never ever get again – it was a veritable ready-made zoo. Everything in place, all the animals you could possibly want or need and they were ready to go to my land.

I asked the million dollar question. Literally as it turned out. "How much do you want?"

"One million Australian dollars."

"Oh jeez! Well I don't have that kind of money."

"Well that is what it is going to go for."

"I'm sorry I haven't got that money."

"Well other than that we will have to split them up and see what we can get."

"Look I would love to have all the animals but really I don't need that many deer and buffalo."

He told me he would put me in touch with someone else who might be interested in those animals. It was a chap called Kevin Gleeson who had a game ranch called "Mary River Ranch" where people from all over the world, mainly America, paid a lot of money to go out and legally shoot buffalo and other herding animals.

My initial instinct was a huge question mark that hovered over my head. It wasn't something that sat well with me. Still I spoke with the owner of the ranch and he was convincing. He told me he just wanted the deer and buffalo. He wanted these because people paid a fortune for large buffalo horns and the big one: that if he didn't take them they would starve to death in the hot, dry and deadly dry season without grass and water. He told me that he would take the majority of the animals and leave me with just the exotics. I would then have the main draw type of animals for a zoo and he would be left with the main bulk of the collection. He told me he would sort everything out, all the logistics, I would just have to sort out the 40 or so animals I would be left with. He offered $500,000 for the herding animals.

Suddenly I was only paying half and I had the main draw animals. I'm not proud to have let animals go to a game lodge. It was a total compromise with my own life and lifestyle; it went against absolutely everything I believe in. Unfortunately the animals would have gone to the game ranch regardless as he had the money. I just managed to take those that I could. From my perspective it was the only option I had to obtain the 40 or so exotic animals.

I tried to rationalise the concept and treated it as if the animals were being farmed. It was akin to a farming business where cows and sheep are killed in order to be eaten; instead it would be buffalo meat and venison. These are people who kill with one shot, at least they don't go into an abattoir and have themselves electrocuted.

I once went to an abattoir to pick up meat for our lions and tigers. It made me feel physically sick. After being shot, within twenty seconds of being killed, of the last kick of their legs, the skin was being ripped off the cow's body. I wondered whether or not the cow actually had any feeling left in it at that particular time as they hung it up, put the hooks on and started ripping the skin off it. Some might counter that this would happen to any animal shot on a hunting lodge but the reality is quite different – an animal who is grazing and doesn't even know anything about being shot as opposed to the torturous, stressful experience of an abattoir.

All zoos have to cull their animals at some point. It is a serious issue which affects every institution that keeps animals. When another person who has suitable facilities to look after an animal cannot be found, action must be taken – it was in fact what I had spent years doing myself, taking animals from zoos who would otherwise have to cull their numbers. Euthanasia is, unfortunately, a recognised method of control within every zoo if every option is exhausted and the animal's life and welfare is threatened by its co-inhabitants in its environment.

We made the transaction in such a way that I didn't have to pay out the full million dollars at once, it was a simultaneous transaction so I didn't pay out money I didn't actually have. I now owned a bunch of exotic animals, though I needed all kinds of permits to more them from the Northern Territory to Queensland. It was a massive move and a logistical nightmare. The two States were barely in contact with each other and they had different rules and regulations.

On 26th November 2003, Caroline, Hari and I flew up to Darwin from Cairns and drove down to Tipperary Station deep in the Northern Territory (this was 'Crocodile Dundee' and "Australia" country). We inspected the animals and met up with the guy who was going to help with the round up on a huge area of many square miles of barren open bush land. This was a hot, dry desolate area at that time of year and yet floods could have drowned the roads. We therefore had to organise everything to co ordinate with the weather as once the dirt roads are wet out there nothing moves.

I owned Grevy zebras, a large, rare species, which pleased me no end. They were the only ones in Australia. Still, Queensland authorities only had permits which entitled me to move the Grants zebra, a smaller version.

I said, "Well, does it matter? Stripy horse, four-feet high, no real difference is there, can we not just import them on that?"

"No."

"Why?"

"Well it's just that we have to go through a process."

"What's the process?"

"Well it has to be approved then it has to go to government and it has to be approved by government in Parliament."

"Oh my God, I can't believe it. How long will that take?"

"It could take months. Months and months."

"Well surely it is exactly the same criteria as the Grants zebra. A zebra is a zebra is a zebra! They all eat the same, they all breed the same, just plagiarise that, just send it, it should get approved just like that."

"Oh no, not just like that. We have to go through all of the risk assessments and so on."

I couldn't believe it. They were worried about animals escaping and becoming feral. As if millions of zebras would suddenly breed and take over Australia. It seemed like a joke but they weren't laughing. They seemed to have a misguided fear of orang-utans escaping and taking over the world. I actually made a joke, quipping, "Have you been watching the *Planet of the Apes* recently?"

Again they didn't find it funny. I tried to explain that orang-utans take so long to breed, take so long to mature that if one or more were on the loose you would find them instantly but they just couldn't understand. I tried my hardest to speed up the required papers but in the end I couldn't get the animals moved quick enough and had to pay other people to look after and feed the animals. Once the new owners of the land at Tipperary realised that I was stuck they started to treat me like a sheep waiting to be fleeced.

They began to charge me hundreds of dollars a day just for feeding the animals and general maintenance. I tried to bring someone else into feed them who I would pay privately and they said they wouldn't allow it. They played innocent and acted as if they weren't doing anything wrong, which technically they weren't, but they knew they had me in a quandary. I realised then that they were mercenary and suddenly I was in urgent need to get the animals off the land because as long as they were there I had no choice but to pay them.

ABC News started to report falsehoods in local news programmes broadcast in the Northern Territory. The former owner had been charged with animal cruelty for not feeding his animals. Somehow I was sucked into the media coverage. They reported that the animals which were stuck there were not being fed or were struggling for food. My response was to be honest and let them know the animals were being fed alright, it was just that I was struggling to pay for it. In fact I attempted to use the publicity to my advantage and try to make an issue out of the fact that I was being extorted in order to keep the animals healthy. It ended up I was paying out about $20,000 a month just to have the animals looked after. It became a huge story in Australia and spread across different networks in the country – of course the news reached Queensland too. I did eventually manage to hire someone else to go in and look after the animals, it was difficult but it made things slightly easier. The owners of the land had by then extorted me enough.

I then had a problem with the game ranch because the guy who had bought all the herding animals started to steal some of the other, exotic animals. Whilst rounding up other animals he took the zebra and all my Scimitar-horned oryx. He took them back to his ranch for 'safe keeping' because according to him he was worried they would die if they were left out there so he just took them without asking me. I was trying to finish the deal and had legal teams working on everything but nothing could be resolved. I was stuck between a rock and a hard place. I couldn't move the animals, I couldn't re-sell them, and I was paying a fortune to feed them. From being the best deal that you could ever have done it turned into the worst nightmare. The hardest part was that I was dealing with two parts of an enormous country and they were literally at opposite ends. It would have been at least a three-day drive to get to the Northern Territory even if I had wanted to pick them up myself. There would have been a gigantic convoy of trucks and crates travelling across the entire north of Australia.

The whole situation was a financial mess. South Lakes was performing very well but Australia was costing rather than making money and ultimately I had to borrow the entire amount to fund the purchase of the animals. Thankfully I had a superb bank manager in England who understood the nature of the business and also realised what I was trying to do. He had been there for me in the past, supporting me through the financial ups and downs, we often used to have a good chat over a cup of tea. When I asked for half a million, he pulled out all the stops and it was done, just like that. I wasn't even there yet the papers were all signed and pushed through quickly. It seems bizarre to think that with such a profitable business which had really taken off that I was struggling with money but it was the sad reality and it was simply because I had gone so far over budget in Australia. None of the money was funded with my property in Australia; it was all paid for by South Lakes. I was under an immense amount of pressure; I'm not sure how I didn't explode. It was Caroline who felt the brunt of my unhappiness – I was near to tears a lot of the time because I had no idea how I was going to get out of the mess I had created and in turn it brought Caroline to tears being neglected in this way.

Things were becoming fractured with Caroline and I. I made things very difficult for her because I found it so difficult to deal with the stress and frustration I was experiencing. In fact she became the outlet for my frustration. All she heard was the incessant verbal bitching I would launch into the second I got into the door. I had been out of the house almost all day and yet when I did come in, when I should have been ready to spend quality time with Caroline I didn't see what she needed. I didn't see that she looked fantastic all of the time, I didn't appreciate that she was running around after me looking after me with drinks and sandwiches. She was my perfect girl yet I just lost her.

As I had done all my life, I ploughed myself into hard, physical work every hour I could get to it. This left me tired, exhausted in fact, and very irritable. When I got home all I did was let my frustration go. It would be immensely negative, slagging everybody off that was letting me down or pulling me down. It was so right but it was so wrong because I had the perfect place, all the animals ready to come, the lake was full from the wet season's rain but I couldn't keep financing it. By the end of 2003 Caroline and I had hit a real rocky patch and fell out – things were quite horrible. She was still feeling depressed and I wasn't looking after her, yet I felt as if I was the one who needed looking after. I didn't ask for sympathy and if anything I was trying to keep the stresses and strains away from Caroline. This was virtually impossible, so she felt all the tension but with little explanation. On a personal, romantic level I wanted nothing or no one but Caroline. Yet from a business perspective things were bringing me down and it took me away from my true love.

When I spent time with Hari it was often just him and I which was strange because Caroline had become possessive of him, understandably given she spent almost all her time with him alone. I spent a little time with Hari and Caroline at nights but whenever I did make separate time for him I wanted to be alone with him, which must have isolated Caroline even more.

All in all we were both losing our minds, losing each other, living together yet being so very far apart. Confused both within our own minds and within our relationship.

I thought that I knew what the problem was for me and I tried to focus on her a lot more. The problem was I wanted to do it but I couldn't because I couldn't get rid of the problem in the Northern Territory. I couldn't get rid of all the legal problems that I was having with the permits, I couldn't get rid of the issues, it was still a burden. Even though my head said I want to make this work, I want my family, I have got to find a way out of it, the world wouldn't let me. It was just an impossibility, I couldn't run away from it even though I wanted to, it was just there staring at me all the time. My money and time were both running out.

Even though I put a lot of effort into Caroline in that time, it wasn't anywhere near enough and I couldn't get rid of the stress. I know Caroline loved me but the zoo and my life totally got in the way. It was never just plain sailing dealing with animals either. In Mareeba we were about to receive an exciting new addition – two cheetahs from the United Arab Emirates. When they first arrived we placed them in a very large caged enclosure, big enough for a couple of tigers. I had an idea to try and implement my electric fence policy to surround the cheetahs. I'd managed to successfully keep very large bears in an electric fence enclosure so I didn't think cheetahs would prove a problem.

Cheetahs being quite docile I decided that instead of boxing them up and moving them into the new facility I would try and walk them through the zoo and in. I had dealt with cheetahs for years before and they were quite tame for such wild creatures – whilst feeding or cleaning them out they would never give you any trouble even when you were right next to them. You couldn't do that with tigers, they would kill you but I knew plenty of people who were able to walk in amongst cheetahs.

Early one morning, well before any one was around, we were ready to walk the cheetahs into their new home. We shut all the safety gates, and were surrounded by a large perimeter fence. We had mapped out the path for the cheetahs to follow, blocking off anywhere they shouldn't go or might be tempted to wander around. It wasn't a long journey and they walked all the way up to the new enclosure and went straight in just as I expected. This was just the first phase. The cheetahs were now in an enclosure surrounded by an electric fence, a novelty to them.

The male cheetah walked straight into the fence in a brazen display of curiosity. Yet, instead of jumping inwards he jumped the opposite way and found himself outside the enclosure. He then decided he wanted to get straight back to the female. As he was on

Toba, my first and favourite Sumatran tiger, in her prime

Egor the Amur tiger, attacking me at the fence just after he arrived

Toba was the inspiration for my mission to protect animals throughout the world

Shortly before the heavens opened and our near death in the river at Umbrawarra Gorge, Australia

Kakadu, Australia just seconds before an explosion in my stomach and disaster on the trail

Amy, Shelley and Ben, Eastern Australia 1998

2-day-old Sumatran tiger cubs born in Surabaya Zoo,
Java whilst working with the Sumatran Tiger Trust in 1999

Huubke and I in 1999

On an epic trek with my Sumatran tiger protection team where I would end up covered in leeches

African region of South Lakes Wild Animal Park in 2000

Hari the Sumatran Tiger, my son's namesake. 2001

Caroline and myself at Kali Biru, Way Kambas,
Sumatra on tiger protection patrol in 2001

Driving across a river in Tropical Queensland,
Australia in our Nissan Patrol

Caroline and I on the beach near
Mareeba, far North Queensland,
Australia in 2001

Poppy the red kangaroo.
Perhaps our most reported animal
in the park's history

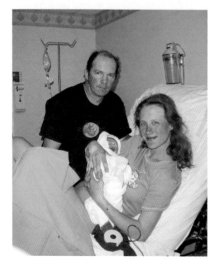

Caroline, Hari and I after he was born

Caroline, Hari and an eastern grey
kangaroo in Australia

Caroline watching the construction
of Mareeba Wild Animal Park,
one month after Hari's birth

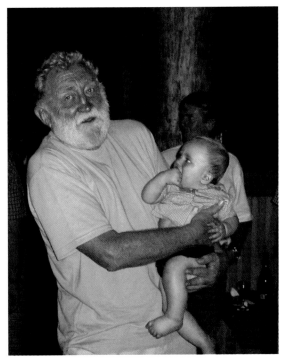

Dam construction in Mareeba,
an enormous venture, May 2002

Hari with Dr. David Bellamy OBE in Mareeba
Wetlands Centre, Australia 2002

Our house in Australia, June 2002

Taking a rare five minutes off on
the local beach close to Mareeba

My 42nd birthday at Maureen and Des Lane's house.
The couple were wonderful throughout my time in Mareeba

Caroline hand rearing a baby
Ring Tailed Lemur in 2004

Mareeba Wild Animal Park, Australia. 2003

Receiving a cheque for $491,000 from the Australian Federal Government in 2003

Syrian bears in a wonderful forest
habitat at Mareeba WAP

Skydiving in Cairns, Queensland

Very hot and tired siesta time in Mareeba.
Hari, Caroline and myself

Receiving an award for
Business and Commerce on
Australia Day 2004

February, 2004 when a cyclone dropped 15 inches of rain in 24 hours,
challenging the dam and lake in Mareeba

Mazungo, the father of our baby rhinos,
with me during filming for an
ITV series on South Lakes

Lemur feeding time at South Lakes.
The lemurs have learned to be fed at a
specific time and location

Pierre and Caroline looking on with trepidation during the great flood in Tambopata, Peru

The very special couple, my great friends Elisa
and Pierre, on the beach in southern Madagascar

Handing out millet food during the famine in Niger

May 2005 - the opening of the first walkway into the giraffes at South Lakes

Meeting the natives in Bukit Tigapuluh, Sumatra whilst on tiger patrols

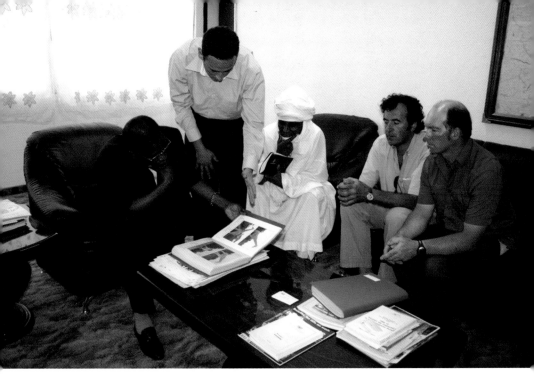

Meeting with the Minister for the Environment with Dr Kahlid Ikhiri and Pierre, Niger, 2005

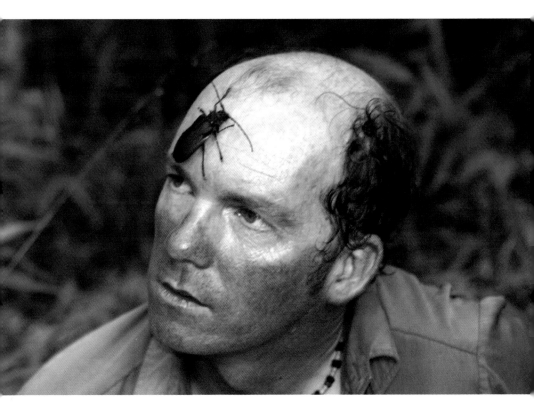

Wondering just what has landed on my head in the Madagascar rainforest

Opening a fresh water well in Niger, West Africa with many happy villagers. 2005

Pierre and I amongst the last few wild giraffes in West Africa

Tambopata Research Center, Amazonas, Peru shortly before a huge tree crashed down on the roof

"Dad whats that Tarantula doing on your shoulder?". Chaparri Peru

Iguazu Falls, Brazil with Carolina Sanin, Mauricio Fabry and his wife, Anna Croukamp and myself

October 2007 in Kanare, Niger working with the ASGN Giraffe conservation programme in my hotel

the wrong side, when he tried to get back in he got a real electric shock. He panicked and ran into the bush. I followed his trajectory and managed to ride a four-wheeler motorbike up around the other side and blocked him off. Surprisingly he wandered straight back into his enclosure. After this little incident, everything was quiet for a long time.

By now Paul had resigned due to the incident with the monkeys. He managed to do it before I returned to Australia, he must have panicked thinking I was going to take his head off given I was still angry at his behaviour. Someone reported me to the authorities for a cheetah escaping, as well as the monkey escape. That person even included a ringtail lemur 'escape' which lasted a total of about five minutes before the lemur missed his friends and came back in from outside the fence.

The authorities took it very seriously. Obviously they didn't understand it from my perspective. I was the director of the company and even though I wasn't there I was classed as being responsible. It went to court, even though I fought it, reasoning, "This is ridiculous, I have free ranging lemurs in my zoo in England, they run everywhere and nobody ever gets hurt." In Australia the rules were different however and I was fined for the brief lemur escape.

I was fined for the cheetah situation – they told me it was illegal for the cheetah to move out of its enclosure even briefly, even during a planned, organised move where no members of the public were in the vicinity. It was all political and technical relating to Wildlife Safety Legislation which was actually ancient legislation come the 21st century. Still, I was fined $10,000. For some reason they didn't even deal with the monkey situation.

We stayed in Australia for Christmas that year and shared it with our good friends Maureen, Des and their extended family who we had become really close friends. It was strange having Christmas dinner outside under the porch of a farmhouse, eating seafood and having a hose pipe fine spray us at the table because of the intense heat. Hari loved playing with the Lane children and I certainly felt like I had become an integral part of a new family.

By early 2004 I knew I had to open the zoo. We didn't have a huge range of animals but I had to get the place open to start recouping the costs of its construction. We had two cheetahs, two tigers, seven lions, three spider monkeys, five Japanese macaques, five ringtailed lemurs, three Sulawesi macaques, many birds, emus, kangaroos, wallabies and two huge brown bears. We had a fantastic entrance building built with cut trees so the branches were left on and formed a natural unique feel inside the gift shop; we even managed to secure a grant of $491,900 from the government in July 2003 before the opening as the project was recognised as a major new tourism development. Two Australian senators Bob Katter and Warren Entch gave me a tremendous amount of support. Katter in particular, became one of my greatest allies in Mareeba. He was desperate for the park to work and supported me no end. I even won the local Business and Commerce Award on Australia Day 2004 which was a real honour. The Shire of Mareeba is probably bigger than Wales!

Australia Day on 26th January every year was a huge event, similar to the 4th July celebrations in America. The magnitude of the event was not lost on me and I received my medal and certificate with pride. I felt real emotion as I sang the Australian anthem as loud as I could. It didn't seem to go down too well with a few locals however. I suppose I can see the irony, a chap from Cumbria, England winning the Business Award in Australia on Australia Day! There were a lot of complicated politics and procedures going on in Queensland at the time but I had enough problems to deal with. Still, the political reality was such that it would begin to interfere with my business. I had been recognised by the state to be doing a good job in their territory but the problems in the Northern Territory started to be felt further afield.

Although I could have done with paying customers on the gate I decided that the best way to introduce a new animal attraction to the people of far north tropical Queensland was to open the doors for free. It was the first time this idea had ever been used in one of my businesses and it proved to be very successful. I liaised with the local press and there were articles inviting all the people of the Cairns region to partake in the new zoo experience. Both Caroline and I were completely shocked by the response. There were 12,000 visitors in two days, 5,000 on the first followed by 7,000 the next. Modestly we had constructed a car park with spaces for around 300 vehicles.

The police weren't happy as the roads were blocked in all directions; there were cars atop of other cars as far as the eye could see. There were trails of cars for miles and miles queuing, waiting to get in. As prepared as we were in terms of food and beverages, it was no surprise that we sold out of everything, burgers, hot dogs, hot drinks, cold drinks. I had decided that one thing we would charge for was to ride the bus around the lion enclosure. When they had paid to get in this would have been free but given there was no fee to enter I charged $8 for this privilege. There was a queue a mile long to go on it. All day long that bus ride never stopped. Two buses going round and round and round. I made sure I had the buses as well as a road train (which we also charged for that day) that went through the park; similar to the South Lakes train we have today but with tyres not rails. The set up in Mareeba was fantastic; it was like a mini-safari experience.

We made a fortune that weekend with all the extras people paid for. It didn't go down well with my competitors or opposers however given it ended up being one of the biggest successes for any zoo in Australian history. Even Sydney Zoo or Steve Irwin's Australia Zoo had never had an experience like it. One of the reasons for this was that it was a completely new experience for the people of Northern Australia – there had never been a zoo in that area. There had never been a tiger or lion there, so the first time anyone got to see one, it wasn't from watching one on television, it was at the Mareeba Wild Animal Park. The fact that it was free instead of the usual $28 was a bonus too. I would later use this experience to further great effect in the years to come.

I was still waiting for the movement permits to get the animals from the Northern Territory, which it seemed the government were stalling over. It seemed deliberate to me, and despite our major opening weekend success I was still borrowing a ton of money and it was getting to crunch time. I needed to try and put some pressure on the politicians so I decided to go down the political route myself.

I did something maybe I shouldn't have done. I went to the newspapers and the television. By now they certainly knew who I was.

"Right, this is it now," I reported. "I've run out of time, I've run out of money, I've got all these animals up there, I need somebody to wake up quickly and get this pushed through please. I need to have this happen or else not only are the animals going to suffer, we are going to fail, everything is going to fail, it's going to go bang and everybody is going to be going. Why? Please, please, please government get this sorted out."

I then received an email from the Minister of the Environment (I think that was his title) telling me that I could bring the animals in as long as they were all sterilised or non-breeding single sex groups. There was then a brief game of email ping-pong.

I said, "That seems odd, they are endangered species in a breeding programme and you want the animals sterilised, why? Surely if they are in enclosures and they are in enclosures within a big enclosure with a perimeter fence they are safe."

"No we want to stipulate this."

"Well it's very hard, you can't just go and sterilise a tapir and a hippo, it's very difficult."

It was quite apparent that the minister wanted to make sure that animals were neutered so that we couldn't breed anything once they arrived. I informed the newspapers again. I mentioned that we were conservationists, with a breeding programme – how ridiculous to be up against the banning of my animals breeding when I had built the whole park as a conservation project.

I was informed that certain animals were allowed to breed but not all of them. For some reason it was perfectly acceptable for the lions and tigers to breed but not the smaller animals. I pointed out it was highly illogical and what basis did they have for drawing the line here? The papers and television seemed to understand and were interested in exposing the minister for his unfair treatment of myself and the park. Suddenly I was being interviewed for a news channel, though I believed it was just the local news. I was in debate with the minister concerned. I didn't realise at the time that in being clever and showing him up to be in the wrong I was actually making an extreme enemy who wielded a lot of power, something I really should not have done.

On the programme the minister claimed he had never instructed me to neuter some of the animals. I said in response that I would produce the email which came directly from him and show in black and white exactly what he had said to me. Later that night I saw myself on the national news! I wasn't trying to be controversial, I just wanted the process to go through and be over with, but this became a huge emotive subject, the fact that so many animals were stuck in the trap of a bureaucratic nightmare and they were the ones to potentially suffer. I went to bed that night hoping that I was going to have some sort of effect. To say it had an effect would be some understatement.

Chapter 23
Secret Police and escaping a nightmare

I've never taken drugs and I've never dealt drugs. I have no experience of being under suspicion from the police and I have never given cause to the authorities for suspicion. Yet on the morning of April 4th, 2004 at 7am I experienced what it must be like to be an enemy of the state. The front door of my house was knocked down with an almighty bang. I had no idea who or what it was. Then I saw a group of men who looked as if they were working for the Secret Service – suited and booted. To this day I have no idea who they really were.

I was pinned up against the wall in a rather painful, brutal manner. Caroline was also pinned into a corner. They then proceeded to turn the house upside down. I had no idea what they were looking for and they wouldn't give me an answer when I asked. It was as if they were looking for drugs or guns but I knew I had nothing like that, and why would they suspect I had? They took my laptop and every CD they could find, music CDs as well as computer discs, any disc they could find they confiscated. Every file, every piece of paper they could lay their hands on they took with them. Within a few hours they had desecrated our home and taken anything of any significance. All the office computers from the park itself were also taken. When Caroline needed the toilet they wouldn't even let her go alone, a woman went with her.

I was allowed to escape the clutches of the authorities but I couldn't open the park because I had no computers or any official documents or permits. Even my staff had been dragged into the melee, they were all trapped in one of the offices until every piece of equipment or paper had been boxed and removed. It was several hours long and was a tremendously frightening situation for all involved. It seemed like every one of the men in suits had guns with them, which was immensely unnecessary and over the top. The most upsetting thing was, it had all been for show.

I later found out that the national news channel had been told about the raid and had been there to film it all. The whole raid had been shown across the country. I was portrayed as a zoo owner who neglected animals and allowed animal cruelty to go on. Supposedly the animals were in a terrible state and the raid had been to trace as many animal records as possible to try and get to the truth about me, this awful man who couldn't care less about animals. It seemed especially naïve on the part of the press given just a week ago 12,000 local people had seen for themselves that my animals were in perfect condition.

I realised that what they were searching for was any records I had of the emails between the minister and myself. If I had carried through my revelations in the press and actually proved what had been said by him I could have ruined his career. I had some of my stuff returned to me, in dribs and drabs, a lot of things were never returned to me. When I did get my computer back, which had been sent to someone else, it had been completely wiped. I was still waiting for my laptop to be returned.

I also found out later that the search warrant they had for turning my house upside down had been illegal. It had been signed by a judge but the reason for the search was not filled in items on the agenda that they were allowed to take were different to those they actually did confiscate. My lawyers confirmed to me that the whole situation had been illegal, that they had broken every law in the book to perform their little show.

Soon afterwards, later in the afternoon I received a phone call from a person I did not know. All he said was that he was an ex-policeman who had worked for or had experience of the same 'team' I had been visited by. His voice was calm and calculated.

"I am going to tell you something David, and this is to help you. They've taken your laptop haven't they?"

I said, "Yes, how do you know?"

"I watched it on the news. I am going to tell you right now David, if you want to save your own life, you must get out of the country right now because I worked for that lot and when the computer comes back to you it could have a hell of a lot more on it than ever it went with."

"What do you mean?"

"Anything illegal, even terrorist stuff. You could have anything put on that computer and you would have to prove to a court that it wasn't there beforehand. I'm telling you David, before they come around and do it again, get out of the country because you will end up in jail, I'm going to guarantee you. Anything you do now, anything you say, any fight back you give, they will come and they will just hammer you into the ground because they won't give up on you."

His closing words of warning were, "Listen, I know how they work, when they want you they get you. That's how Queensland is."

I asked why he was telling me this and he explained that he felt ashamed because he had worked for them. He had done this to people himself and he wanted to give me the advance warning to save my life.

It was all the warning I needed. I was absolutely terrified. I quickly passed on a semblance of the conversation to Caroline and told her that we needed to go. We grabbed two suitcases and placed anything and everything we could of any worth that would fit in there. We took Hari and were about to set off in the car when one of the men who had been part of the raid walked up to me in the car. I stayed rooted to the spot, wondering what on earth was going to happen.

Slap!

He handed me a court summons.

One of the scariest elements of this was that they didn't inform you of the exact charges against you, which seemed to very much fit in with my informant in shining armour. I would have had no time to prepare a defence, as I didn't know what I was up against. In most other countries it would have been completely illegal yet Queensland really was a law unto itself, it seemed to me like they made it up as they went along.

I suddenly felt fearful that someone had seen us packing our bags. Here we were on our way to the airport to hopefully get out of the country as soon as possible, but if they knew what I intended to do they would no doubt stop me, I would be a fugitive, which would have put me in even deeper trouble. My head was spinning.

The night we left for the airport the surrounds were like something from a horror film. The winds were howling with biblical ferocity, there were landslides on the road. Warnings abounded on the news, as there was a cyclone with wind and landslide warnings for the whole of Far North Queensland. It was so bad I wondered whether we would even make it to the airport. We were driving up a mountain road that was smothered with landslide debris, and the same was true on the other side of the mountain. This time my preparedness had seen me buy a Nissan Patrol car which was built to deal with such problems. We managed to reach Cairns airport but all flights had been delayed due to the cyclone, there were no planes coming in or out of Cairns, the airport was saturated with people and we had to wait in order to hopefully find a vacancy on a flight, which seemed unlikely.

As luck would have it a flight came up quite quickly with a few spare seats. It was going to Tokyo but it could have been going to Iceland, it made no difference to me, I just wanted us to all get out of Australia. As soon as the winds died down we were on the flight to Japan. It was one thing to get on the flight but even then I didn't think we had made it. I knew I wouldn't be satisfied until we reached the house in Cumbria. I was looking over my shoulder every second, every minute through the night flight. I've never been back to Australia since that day. I had never been so frightened in all my life.

Chapter 24
Christening and personal failure

There was no way I could return to Australia. It was supposed to be a free country but in my experience there were enormous amounts of bureaucratic nonsense and red tape finished off with some exceedingly unpleasant behaviour from eminent politicians. I upset a very powerful person and paid the price. Luckily I managed to save myself and my family from anything worse. It wasn't just that I was an enemy of prominent politicians, the Australian Regional Zoo Association hated me and wanted me out of the way, not to the extent that they would set me up or have me killed no doubt, but I was still a problem. They didn't want an independent voice or business, they wanted a state run, autocratic system which they could manipulate. I wouldn't sing along to their tune. I wanted other things to happen. I really felt that the Australian Government didn't have a mandate. They would act as if everything had to go through them but when you read the law it didn't. According to the law, things had to pass by the government department not through ARAZPA. I requested that it didn't go to ARAZPA because they had no right to have any say in it – my lawyers made sure that this happened which probably upset them even more.

They knew I could bypass them altogether. They didn't like me. It was ironic given I had won the business award and brought in much needed interest to a barren area. The park and myself seemed to be popular in general, I was even friends with the highest politician in the area. I have no doubt that Bob Katter had no knowledge of the coup, which was unleashed upon me, we were friends and I trusted him. When I spoke to him about the situation he couldn't understand it. Still, there was little he could do to remedy a now impossible situation. It was obvious that I needed to sell the park and upon advice it seemed that the best manner was to voluntarily put the company into liquidation.

The whole period upon my return was a depressing time. I had failed, the business had failed, Caroline and I had seemingly failed in our dream to live a life out in Australia. Perhaps on some level I took to blaming Caroline for the way things went, using her as an outlet for my feelings of frustration. There was nothing she had done wrong, but she was the only person I felt close to. I had a feeling of wanting to get rid of everything around me and start again.

Throughout all my success in England, well before things went wrong in Australia, my dad had never acknowledged me in any way or told me he was proud of me. He visited the zoo for its opening ceremony, though he was merely a peripheral character. After that he didn't come again. For many years after my divorce with Alison, dad fell out with me and wouldn't talk to me. One Christmas when I was in Australia I rang and spoke with my mother, but he would never tell us why he hated me so. From then on if ever he answered the phone I would put the phone down. Eventually Mam answered and I said, "Mam, I just wanted to say 'Happy Christmas', I just wanted to say I am thinking about you."

It made me cry and I struggled to deal with the emotional let down of having this happen with my own family. Why did my dad feel the need to treat me this way? I told my mam, "Tell Dad I have rung up because I just can't understand why he won't speak to me. It's just ridiculous and I want to stop it."

"I will tell him," my mam replied, "but I can't help it." This went on from 1997 all the way through until 2002.

Dad wouldn't have anything to do with me, he wouldn't acknowledge me, wouldn't say anything to me. I was banned from going to my parent's house at Christmas. My mother always had a family gathering on Boxing Day and all her children came and all their children came – it was something of a tradition with our family but I was banned. One year, when I had not been invited my dad had suggested that everyone get together for a family photo but all my brothers and sisters refused. They said to my dad that if I wasn't there then it wasn't the whole family and they didn't want a picture taken without me. Even they could not understand what his problem was. If he had spoken with me and explained we might have been able to get somewhere but he never would.

On 6th October 2002 we decided to have the Christening ceremony for Hari and I sent an invite to all my family.

Come the day of the christening, all the family were standing at the back of the church, waiting for the ceremony to begin. All of a sudden there was a clunk and the door squealed open. In walked my mother and father. I couldn't believe it. He didn't say anything, in fact he looked downwards, but I smiled at my mother and she came across. It was an irony given this church was the one that both Mam and Dad attended every week, they knew the vicar well. I struggle with the reality that some people can go to church every Sunday and then have different rules once they get out. At least the christening went ahead and it was a delightful ceremony. More delightful still was the presence of Caroline. She looked amazing, with the most beautiful dress – she looked adorable. I have photographs from the time which I never tire of viewing.

After the service I invited everyone back to our house where we had organised a buffet. I made sure to invite Mam and Dad. My mother said, "I think we have done enough for one day." It seemed that might have been the end of it but within a couple of weeks my mam called me to see if we would take Hari round to see her and my dad, which we did. The situation was still strained however, Dad would make himself invisible while we were there and when he was there he would barely talk.

I did eventually get to a stage where we could have a chat, though it was a very forced six or seven words. I knew I had to pick a subject that he is good at. My parents were cruise fanatics, for many years they often went on two or three a year. So instead of talking about my life, or the zoo, I managed to talk to him about cruises. One time I went round to my parent's house and my mam wasn't in. Dad and I talked and things seemed okay, in fact, it was the best conversation I had ever had with him. The conversation was still enforced, and I didn't receive any respect or interest from him regarding my life but at least it was civil. It seemed that my appearances in the local papers was enough for him to know all about me and what was going on – I know he read them. Yet he could never directly talk to me about my life and I was desperate for his attention like a small child.

When I think where I came from, a poor family with very little in terms of job prospects, it staggers me to think that my father would not be interested in something so special as creating an animal park from the ground up. So many people stop me and say, "Oh, how's your dad doing? I used to work with him," I always have to say, "I don't know," to which the person responds, "what do you mean you don't know?"

"Well he has not spoken to me for years so I don't know."

"Oh, right, well, sorry to hear that."

"No, don't be, don't worry about it." They obviously feel quite embarrassed but extremely surprised too, no wonder considering.

Something which perturbed me at the time was when my dad was awarded an MBE. It was a very proud day for him and us all to have to travel to Buckingham Palace and receive his award from the Queen. He was allowed to take my mother as well as two of us five kids. There was no discussion as to who might go and there was no chance of names being drawn out of a hat. He chose Alison and Karen without telling anyone why and it was a bugbear for me that I got over quickly. It was impressive to receive an MBE, no doubt about it, and it was garnered by his work with youngsters – but my take on it was that he received an MBE for his community work and looking after the safety of other people's kids instead of fishing with me and I wish he had spent more time with me. Dad and I were talking but it was always stunted and never seemed to progress beyond anything other than vacuous small talk. Still, I did manage one or two family gatherings, especially at Christmas. The fact remains I am not upset about it anymore, I have not been for a few years but all I ever wanted from my Dad was recognition, support and love.

The difficulties within my birth family meant that at a time when I most needed support there was nothing for me from my parents. My brothers and sisters were there but had no real concept of what I had taken on. When I returned from Australia I felt very isolated. I felt stunned by the whole Australian experience and had no idea what to do next. It was one thing to disappear from the country but I still owned a business out there and couldn't just leave it to rot.

Perhaps it was a feeling of guilt that somehow I had caused the downfall of our perfect life together in Australia, but I started to push Caroline away.

She was surely the one person who could have given me the support and backing I needed yet I felt as if I couldn't live with her anymore. She could have helped me, she was my future, yet I found myself at odds with the woman I loved. There was no major fallout or argument, no specific incident; I just felt I couldn't continue living with her. I can only speculate as to the reason as I didn't even understand my own feelings at the time but for no apparent reason I asked Caroline to move out.

Something kicked in and in knee-jerk fashion I removed her from my every day life. I owned a house a mile or so away in Dalton and I asked her to live there with Hari. I feel guilty to even describe the fact that I made my soul mate go through this isolation and neglect of her own but it was what I needed at the time. She still worked at the park so we came to the agreement that we would work slowly at rebuilding our relationship. There was no specific problem other than we had been dealing with a continually fractured relationship that, if not halted in some way, might tear us apart for good. With all the best will in the world however, this is exactly what threatened to sink me next.

Chapter 25
Kangaroos, Bears, Coatis and receivership

2003 and the beginning of 2004 had been a very traumatic period. I would hesitate to say I had a breakdown but there were certain emotional issues that had to be healed and I didn't know how to heal them. I certainly felt guilt in some way as to how the Australian experience had turned out – I felt like a complete and utter failure. It was a hard feeling to come to terms with because at that point in my life, everything I had ever attempted from a career point of view had succeeded. I didn't know how to deal with sudden failure. I can rationalise now and say that I felt that sense of abject failure in front of Caroline – she knew better than anyone how things had gone and that effectively, it was my fault for getting us into the mess. I couldn't look her in the eye as my soul mate, as the person I so deeply loved, and deal with that perceived rejection. I wanted Caroline to see me as a hero rather than a failure and instead of dealing with it head on; I tried to run away from dealing with it.

From a work perspective I was saved in the form of a fly on the wall documentary that ITV wanted to produce on myself and South Lakes Wild Animal Park. I had only been back from Australia for a week and was straight into filming with ITV – it gave me the perfect opportunity to focus on something completely different. There were cameras following me and watching events at the park for a few months, which seemed such a long time for a six-part series.

28th May 2004 was our ten-year anniversary at the park. We had a party to celebrate and it gave cause for me to reflect on all that had happened in that decade. Most events had either gone well or I had managed to turn a negative event into something positive long term. The one thing still lingering in my mind was the unmitigated disaster of Australia. Despite the ongoing filming by ITV and the opportunity to get my teeth into a little showmanship, displaying the wonderful surrounds of South Lakes Wild Animal Park, the protracted negativity of Australia still loomed. Even when filming, after a while the cameras become invisible and nothing is planned or pre-considered, life just goes on.

I wanted the problem from Mareeba to disappear but I felt the harassment of lawyers and business people, all wanting a decision or, more often, money. It was thousands of miles away from me, my family and my life, it no longer felt as if it were a part of my existence yet I knew, logically that I simply had to deal with it. I couldn't just wash my hands of the situation and I could never return to the country – I felt that if I did so I would end up in prison for sure. Every time I received a legal missive asking me to come back and sort things out, my response was always the same – 'no chance'. I was still frightened to death by my mysterious caller who had outlined so graphically what would happen to me if I stayed in the country, and that was not the kind of message that changed or improved with time.

I took stock and asked my ally Bob Katter who sat in the Australian Senate, to look into police records to try and find out if there was a warrant out for my arrest or any other official call for my capture. He assured me with all sincerity that he had looked into it thoroughly and there was nothing. Despite that assurance I was still terrified for many years that if I went back I was history. It did briefly occur to me to question what the mystery man had told me but I was already in an extreme state of fear and disharmony even before his call – having your door knocked down and being pinned against the wall by a team of government suits will do that to a man.

It is ironic to witness the films of myself in the ITV documentary. I appear to be relaxed and even happy. Inside I was torn apart, fearful and confused but I managed to convince everyone of the opposite. People who know me would be able to tell whenever anything is wrong but thankfully for those I dealt with in a professional sense, they would have had no idea about my difficulties, and I certainly didn't mention them on the documentary.

I even managed to deal with animal issues within the park. We started to have a problem with our Andean bears. We had four female bears – two sets of twins, as well as one large male called Snoopy. The females started to gang up on poor Snoopy for some reason – mainly two of the twins, Mona and Alice – and after a while it started to get out of hand to the point where it became quite violent and I became very worried for his safety. This particular evening they were fighting and it started to go dark. I knew it couldn't continue and that we would have to try and separate them before leaving them to it for the night. I had my head keeper Jo Dennis with me as well as keeper Gavin Clunie.

I turned the electric fence off and said to them, "I'm going in."

I tried everything I could to get the females away from Snoopy – I shouted at them, ran at them, even threw sticks in their direction – nothing was working and, for me at least, this seemed to go on forever. Suddenly, Mona and Alice turned and looked at me. I could see the hint of recognition in their eyes that this was no fun for them and they were going to stop this stupid man distracting them from their bear-bating duties. It was the first time in my life that a bear did not run away from me, and instead, ran right towards me.

I panicked and started to run like crazy, diving over a ditch through the electric fence. I'm not sure how I sneaked through the gap of the fence but it was a good job I did, I could have been sliced like an egg in an egg slicer. The bears followed hard behind me before reaching the fence and stopping out of habit. Although I think they were worried before I got on the other side of the fence, as soon as I was safe Gavin and Jo found it extremely funny, in fact, years later they are still laughing about it. It was a sobering lesson to never put trust in a bear, especially bears with hormonal imbalance. Though it is a natural state for certain females of certain species, they don't quite know or understand what is happening to them, and react accordingly, with confusion and violence. They are not themselves, the hormone rush can drive them insane. Poor Snoopy suffered the consequences of this female onslaught but luckily for me I managed to escape it, one of the few occasions where the only thing damaged was my pride.

In Australia I started to deal with the liquidators, both of whom were mercifully decent people, one in particular, Gerry Mier from KPMG in Cairns, felt for me. He said that we would have to sell the whole business as soon as possible.

"We have got to get the animals from Tipperary, that's the first thing, and then we have got to try and sell it as an ongoing thing or," he said disturbingly, "hang on...hang on long enough until you can come back."

He offered me a solution to feeding and looking after the animals in Tipperary – I paid him a fee to sort everything out for me. It might not seem such a helpful gesture when I say that the total accumulated to over a million Australian dollars, but I was grateful for someone to take over for me at the time. Considering the project was not sold for over two years, it is no wonder the maintenance of the animals cost so much.

There was interest from many businessmen but as soon as they learn of the reality of owning a zoo and the expertise they will need, they are naturally reluctant to go ahead. It is a specialised field and there are simply not that many people around the world who can do it just like that. Anyone walking in to that environment without experience would undoubtedly fail miserably, something any successful business person would pick up on. Of course a smart businessman can buy and retain ownership of a zoo but in order for it to run smoothly they need a team in place to perform the necessary work, and how many people would have a readymade team of animal specialists? Selling the zoo was made doubly difficult because the park was in such an out of the way place.

Sadly I was about to deal with yet another egocentric 'expert'. The liquidators had to employ someone quick smart and they found a so-called expert zoo consultant, named Tim Husband. I learned about him from a conversation with an old boss of his at Canberra National Zoo. He wasn't enamoured with his former employee, telling me he didn't work for him anymore and that there was a good reason for it. He apparently was an arrogant chap who decided he knew better than his superiors and had no respect for his boss so they parted company. Still, this was the person charged with looking after my zoo and he moved from down near Canberra, into my house in Mareeba in order to do it. The liquidators felt there was no other option and I had to agree; besides they would be monitoring him. The government were watching and the liquidators had to show that they were following the correct procedures. Tim Husband seemed to actually do a reasonable job.

I wish I had Gerry Mier in my corner before because he then performed a miracle in procuring the correct permits from the government. He used a little Australian diplomacy, warning the government that if they didn't comply it would be them who looked bad as they had quite clearly forced me out of the country.

They concurred and so Gerry organised for a convoy of trucks to travel to the Northern Territory. With a huge array of crates the drivers picked up the rhinos, hippos, pygmy hippos, tapirs and a number of deer. There was, sadly, one pygmy hippo which they couldn't find – he was nowhere to be seen. It was presumed that maybe he was hiding in the water somewhere and they had to leave without it as the other animals would have overheated in the crates. Only recently it was found, someone believed it was a large pig and shot it. It had been living somewhere outside of the zoo for years. It came on the news and I knew it was my hippo. It was part of a clip on *Weird Stories*, about this idiot who shot an animal he believed to be a pig, and it turned out to be a hippo, in Australia of all places. It was terrible.

Finally, I no longer had to pay for the animals in Tipperary to be taken care of, though Mareeba was an ongoing concern which still had to be financed. The government initially tried to have me change the facilities to comply with their specifics, which I would have done had I been there. Seeing as I was thousands of miles away and that the park was no longer open to the public, they allowed the animals to stay with the facilities as they were.

In Mareeba I still had an ace up my sleeve – I still had my friends, Maureen and Des Lane there to keep an eye on what was happening. Tim Husband started to think they were spies and indeed they were, I needed some form of observation from people I trusted, to see that my money was being spent as wisely as possible. The property might have been going through liquidation but I still legally owned it and therefore it was my money at stake. Husband confronted Des and started to cause a little trouble. He became an immensely negative influence and he pushed everyone who might have been able to help him, away. If he was doing a good job there was no need for him to react so aggressively. Unfortunately Des had enough of his attitude and left him to it.

During this period one of the worst things that could possibly happen to a zoo happened in Mareeba – a lion escaped. Once again it was down to staff negligence, where they could not follow simple rules and procedures. The fences should have been checked every single time before a lion was allowed out. One day when the lion had been let out he found a glitch in the fencing, a weak spot which had not been found, never mind fixed, and he pulled the fence up, before escaping. They managed to control the lion and return it to the zoo but someone somewhere spilled the beans and it made the national news. No one likes to hear that a lion was on the loose as it conjures up so many images of terror in the streets and the possibility that the general public might come face to face with a killing machine.

Around six months later it happened again, this time there were four lions that found a hole in the fence and were on the loose. Tim Husband decided he wanted to blame me for his own bad management, calling the welfare of the animals into question in the pages of the local newspapers, and asking what on earth I was doing in abandoning them and not taking adequate responsibility. He was merely trying to cover his own tracks and justify his own mistakes. He made it seem as if there was a problem with the fence but the fence wasn't the problem – it was designed to last twenty years. The problem was in the management, or lack of. The manager was responsible for checking fences to make sure no wires were loose as, in the immense heat, the wires can easily corrode. It was something I knew was a potential issue and it featured in our zoo protocol.

Tim Husband made himself out to be quite special on his website and through his mannerisms, but really it became clear to me that he was just an inadequate human being with a big mouth who always blamed others for his mistakes. He slagged me off to high heaven but did not handle the escapes and dangerous situations caused under his 'watchful' eye. These were nothing to do with me, they happened on his watch. He thought he could get away with it and blame me. He even set up a little organisation in Mareeba that he had in place just in case I was to return, it was a threat I made a few times, mainly to see if he might start to do his job a little better. Not that it made any difference. In fact he started to contact the papers about my terrible management and wrote a libellous article in *Thylacinus* magazine which is a zoo periodical. Eventually he would disappear from Australia himself after I understand being very closely aligned to the disgraced 'Lion Man' in New Zealand.

After two years of struggling to find a buyer there was finally someone who came forward who showed genuine interest. Udo Jattke was a property developer and he wanted to buy it for his wife. I thought, "Oh my God this is no good." I obviously wanted animal lovers, experts or those with previous experience – it was not supposed to be a rich boy's plaything, or a present for a spoiled wife.

Gerry interviewed the couple and admitted to me that it was not the best situation, or best pair of buyers I could find but he stated the obvious – I didn't have a lot of choice. The couple were quite willing to take on a recognised manager to oversee the zoo; in fact they were going to keep Tim Husband in a job.

"I need to get out of this," I said to Gerry. "If they come up with the money then I will happily do it because it's not my business anymore. In fact it's none of my business, I have got to escape." I was losing money hand over fist paying out for absolutely everything that needed to be spent in order to keep a full time zoo, only there was nothing coming in. Almost every penny made in South Lakes was going into a venture that was totally dead in the water. South Lakes Wild Animal Park continued more or less out of habit – there were no advances made in terms of expansion or new animals because there was no financing which could be used. Literally all that changed at South Lakes in 2004 was the first breeding of bats, agile wallabies and babirusa, which was nice but not in keeping with my usual lofty plans.

Eventually it became a moot point when the couple who were itching to buy came through with the funds and the new owner became Jenny Jattke. The first move Jenny made was to change the name of the park to Cairns Wildlife Safari Reserve. I received the money which enabled me to recoup a lot of my costs in acquiring and maintaining the property over the last two years. After the repayments of all the loans to the bank in England I actually managed to have a little cash left, though this was notwithstanding the ridiculous costs that had been paid for Tipperary.

One of the main reasons I did well on the return deal was due to the exchange rates being so much better by the time I sold the park. Today I would have been in debt still! Jenny paid a few million overall for the park, something I could never have expected would happen after all I had been through but I luckily found someone with too much money who wanted a posh play set with animals – it was something for her to play with, 'I've just bought a selection of tigers and lions…' She was a nice enough lady but as it would later turn out, her business sense left a lot to be desired.

The legacy of the park in Mareeba hadn't quite been extinguished however. The press situation got out of hand because the press there, as happens in most small places, love a good story to get their teeth into – they won't let it go if it helps them sell papers, even if it is not actually based on truth. The quality of the park had been outstanding and everyone who visited realised it.

There is no way that we would have been allowed to have a quarantine facility if our conditions were not 100% as good as they could be, it just wouldn't have happened. All animals who come into Australia are deemed to spend the rest of their lives in quarantine, so the facility would have to be top notch. Even Gerry, the liquidator, said to me almost as soon as he looked into the details of the case, that he did not understand how it could be said that we kept our animals in bad condition.

It upset me and irked me that people try to blame others for their own failings and shortcomings. There are very few people in the world who seem to be able to take responsibility for their own actions and don't seek to blame others when something goes wrong or they make a mistake. No one is perfect and I would be the first to admit I have made a great deal of mistakes in life, I will admit where I went wrong. I struggle with the lack of responsibility most other people can live with, how their conscience can remain clear I do not know. Equally, many people seem to be able to live with themselves when they steal from others.

People made allegations to me about Tim Husband, indicating that he was siphoning money from the business. A lot of tools and other equipment from the zoo mysteriously disappeared. Perhaps this was the reason he did not want me spying on him or returning to Mareeba! It could also have been other members of staff and it is something I will never know with 100% clarity. All that is certain is that when Des took an inventory there was a lot of stuff missing.

Maureen and Des were so loyal to me; I felt I had to repay them in some way. I gave them my Nissan Patrol 4WD and let them have all the furniture I had in my house. I wanted them to have it rather than anyone else. I remained friends with them and have always kept in touch with them since; they were one of the only positive parts of the whole experience.

I was out of Mareeba, out of debt and out of all of my obligations to the zoo I had created in Australia. However, this was not quite the end to the saga. Jenny Jattke wasn't quite out of my life just yet.

In 2010 Jenny Jattke made contact with me after four years of running her own Wild Animal Park, the same park I myself built from nothing. The Cairns Wildlife Safari Reserve had been an ongoing concern for Jattke and it seemed that the people of Mareeba still had an animal attraction that seemed to do reasonably well, despite the immense negativity in the press from my time there. Jenny told me the park had not taken off in the way she had envisaged – tourism in Queensland had supposedly tapered off and there had not been much additional investment in the park.

She asked me if I would possibly be interested in either coming back to Australia or at least buying back into it in some capacity, even if it were just with a view to an investment or partnership. With the benefit of time I seemed to somehow dislodge the fear and pessimism which had once been associated with my time in Mareeba. In fact, Jenny's proposition really peaked my interest. I told her I wanted to see the details regarding the idea but that in essence I was very interested. I wanted to see the park I built, that was my own idea, continue to grow and do well.

Two things put me off the idea. Firstly, by 2010 I actually had a good grip on most things in my immediate life and didn't need to go back to a situation of such glaring uncertainty. The second thing was that Jattke's business nous seemed to be a little awry, which was no surprise given her lack of experience, particularly in the business of keeping animals. The park was in debt having made a financial loss every year.

Eventually I told Jenny, "I'm sorry, I can't. I can't do it because it would ruin my life again and I have just found myself. I am doing ever so well here, I don't want to jeopardise that because things are fantastic at South Lakes." I even made the point of telling her that the people who had criticised me during my time in Australia should take a look at the things I had gone onto achieve at South Lakes.

"I have doubled the turnover in my park," I explained, "I am making great profits, I am re-investing, it's growing and I am about to expand to three times the size here so why would I really want to be involved with Australia again? Still, good luck to you."

The Wildlife Reserve had been placed on sale because Jenny wanted to spend more time with her new husband and her children, which I certainly related to, but somewhere along the line the finances were askew and Jenny was asking way too much of anyone to part with $3 million to buy the place which is the price at which it went onto the market place. I calculated that it was not worth any more than $1.2 million with the very best of intentions.

My initial idea for the park was never made a reality, which was hugely disappointing. I had great dreams of what it was going to be and to my mind Jenny did not have the same marketing vision. They say 'never go back' and there is a great sensibility to this notion, it is a true-ism. For one thing, Australia still holds a great element of the unknown for me but for the park itself, things just weren't meant to be. The lesson I learned from the whole experience concerns another old adage, 'look before you leap'.

I should have researched the entire process much more deeply before jumping in and just doing it. It is one thing to just grab the bull by the horns and go for it, it is in fact something I have made a habit of quite often through my life. But sometimes it is far more important to take your time and consider the consequences, not to mention to look thoroughly at what something will cost!

I have a beautiful house and home in Cody, Wyoming in the USA. People often ask me if the reason for this is so that I can build a zoo in America but the reality is that was never in my thoughts. Cody is somewhere for me to go and get away from it all, a wild and natural place that is very dear to me. To taint it with building a new zoo and attempt to do the same thing all over again would be something I'd never risk. I have recently invested in a Horse Ranch called the UXU Ranch on the Yellowstone Highway only 15 minutes from my home. This business is a dude ranch and established with a great team working for me and a wonderful place for my family to relax and have fun in the summer months. I have always been a Cowboy at heart, from riding ponies and horses in my younger years a little to loving western films I had a yearning to shout "Yee Haa" ,wear chaps, Stetson and spurs with my belt buckle and boots whilst cracking a whip on the trail. I love the whole lifestyle of the west in the USA , it is still a community that cares, a lifestyle of laid back living but hard work and wilderness all around. There are only 500,000 people in Wyoming and it isn't so far off the size of England and that has about 65 million squeezed in. I have made some of the most caring friends in Cody found love and new family and it is so hard to leave and come back to the UK from such a piece of heaven. However I would love the opportunity of assisting with the development of a Community Educational Wildlife Centre if the chance arose as I know that I still have an urge to achieve things in life. It is a great place for me to visit in the warmer months, however it is somewhere I am unlikely to settle year round. For one thing the persistent snow and cold is hard to deal with through the winter – minus 30 degrees Celsius with a six-foot coating of snow does make you wonder about the day-to-day reality of such a harsh life. Secondly, I would miss my animals too much. I will say that whilst it may seem that it was all bad in Australia the fact is in between times Caroline and I had some fantastic times together and wonderful memories in the zoo, out in the bush and in the town of Mareeba. We had some favourite places to go for barbecues and picnics and found love and fun there and I know that Cody would be a perfect place for the family to live it ticks all the boxes.

South Lakes Wild Animal Park was always a source of tremendous activity and, at times, immense pain, but for some reason I was always a glutton for punishment and nothing would deter me from working with my animals.

One time, one of our grey kangaroos had a septic foot; somehow the poor thing had stepped on something unpleasant and developed a deep infection. We had to find a way of draining the kangaroo's foot and cleaning and treating it. I always wanted to avoid drugging animals if at all possible which was beneficial for them, but not always the humans in charge of their care.

It became a raid like something out of a western movie. Myself and five keepers tallied together with a noose, ready to down the kangaroo. Our plan was for me to plant the noose around the top of the kangaroo's body, stultifying its arms in the process so he could not do very much, at which point we would jump on him and grab his legs. We thought that with six of us we could manage to curtail a kangaroo and treat him without having to use an anaesthetic. It seemed a foolproof plan. I went to the front of the team, a team I trusted and had complete faith in. I noosed the kangaroo and shouted to my faithful team behind me,

"Right now everybody on him."

I started to pull him down and as I looked behind me, wondering why no one else seemed to be with me, I saw that everyone had run out of the building. I had no idea what happened but learned afterwards they had been terrified by the size of the kangaroo and by the noise he was making. He was growling like a bear and his claws were as big as a bear, hanging on the end of his huge hands. Kangaroos look fine and dandy hopping along playfully with their two front feet draped in front of them but their claws are enormously powerful and incisive. Most people worry about the back legs but it is the front which are equally as dangerous.

"I've got him, I've got him!" I shouted in anguish, "Come and stop him!"

I was no match for the 'roo however. He gripped me around my arm and tore it open with his penetrative claws, with two swipes the insides of my arm were exposed – he may as well have used a knife.

I was still determined. "You're not going to beat me, mister. We've got to treat you. You are going to die if we don't." Here I was, doing it for the poor creature's own good but he didn't care. Nor it seemed, did anyone else, although eventually a keeper came back in once I screamed out for assistance yet again. Now they came back in with confidence and one after another, we had enough manpower to sink the feisty 'roo. We treated his foot and he ran off the victor.

I, on the other hand, was dripping blood all over the floor. I strapped it up myself and did not go to the hospital. Luckily there was no permanent damage other than a few large scars which I still bear today, though the incident taught me a huge lesson which is now imparted to all of my staff. You must never let your colleague down because the after effects can be deadly. Thankfully I was never abandoned again when trying to treat an animal. In fact, in the park today, I utilise my courageous Deputy Animal Manager Niall. He now has the chutzpah of the old David Gill. I let him jump on animals and get bitten first, which has happened quite often. I've learned there is a fine line between bravery and stupidity and precautions and forethought must always be carried out. The power of even the cutest animals must never be underestimated.

We must also endeavour not to underestimate the powers of escape of certain creatures. One such mammal is a coati, which is a South American omnivore with a long striped tail and a long nose. I've had them for many years and love them. I know all about their potential and abilities but there was one coati in particular who surprised me completely. We received a regular report one time from a home owner about a mile away cross country, who described a strange animal which kept visiting them at night. It was only ever at night and I struggled, at first, to believe the sincerity of this report as we never had any animals missing the following morning.

One night I got a call saying there was a strange brown animal with a long nose and a stripy tail, walking down the road. The next morning I asked for a coati count, as it was pretty clear this was the mammal witnessed, and each one was present. Every night and every morning all the coatis were there but one night I received a call that revealed the coati was there, in this person's garden, right then. I drove to witness this escapee coati and I saw one of my coatis digging holes, searching for worms. For whatever reason the ground was softer and he was quite happy searching for worms here. He was obviously making a pilgrimage for a new class of worms, having his fill, and then returning to the park, with us none the wiser. A true *Escape From Alcatraz* coati. He was so good at avoiding capture that he wouldn't even come to us when we were there – we had to set a trap.

This was known as a live trap, where chicks and eggs are used as bait. It took a few days but in the end we did catch the wiley coati. To this day I cannot fathom exactly how he escaped from his enclosure every day. For a time we kept him inside to break his little custom. Once we allowed him out once again we kept an eye on him and he never did escape again. It is continually amazing to me the abilities that animals have – abilities that we don't really appreciate and understand about their sense of direction and how they can find a new area which they want to explore, yet being able to find their way back to their real home.

South Lakes also featured a mysterious escaping porcupine which was finding his way out every night. There were signs of it everywhere. We saw spikes, porcupine spikes and spines in places. We saw chewing marks, but our porcupines were always in the enclosure when we saw them. This went on for a long time with none of us any the wiser. One night I went down into the zoo in the dark, I walked round the corner with a torch and nearly walked straight into a porcupine. He was trundling around the park every night for a wander before going back in his enclosure during the days to sleep. Perhaps it was an inadvertent measure to avoid meeting the general public!

Chapter 26
Amazon floods, conservation partners and a babirusa attack

Throughout my horror time with Australia, one thing had remained true to my heart – animal conservation. I had maintained my work within tiger conservation. I had been investing between £80,000 and £100,000 a year into the tiger conservation project through income generated by South Lakes Wild Animal Park. It was something dear to my heart and a special sideline which maintained even through my difficulties elsewhere, it justified the whole idea of my parks.

The background to this was the ongoing success at South Lakes. One of the major discoveries I had made, which thankfully fit in with my initial hopes in running an animal park, was that people truly loved the interaction with the animals. Walking in with animals, having various creatures running around them, being able to feed them. This became more and more apparent that it was the secret to the success of South Lakes. Every time you asked visitors for feedback they would say, "Oh, this is so different, we love it, we come all this way because it is different. You are not stood far away, you are close, everything is close, everything is right in front of you." This response made me feel like I had a magic formula that was working but it was *my* formula and it seemed a constant struggle against everybody, even the staff, to stop them from changing it. Everybody wants to make everything a bit easier. What we do at my zoo is hard, it's difficult and the paradox is that it is hard because it is simple.

If you want an easy life in a zoo you put an animal in a cage, then you know where it is. At South Lakes, at the end of every day, the staff have to find everything. They have to check that the tamarins aren't running round and they are inside. They have to check the lemurs are there, that they are not up trees and they are in their housing. Everything needs to be checked because the animals are in an expansive environment, not an easily assessed trap that can be ticked like an inventory box. These animals can take a long time to put back in their enclosures for the night – it is not a case of bang, bang, close the gate and go home. Sometimes the staff can be up to two hours late in going home because they can't find the animals after closing time; this can particularly be an issue in the summer.

The larger zoos could not possibly do this, or would not attempt to at least. It would be a logistical nightmare so they would rather not even try it. Therefore, they possibly do not create an environment that is best for the animals; they probably create the environment best for the humans who take care of the animals. I want our animals to have as much freedom and ability to express themselves. I want my animals to do what they do best. I want gibbons swinging through trees, monkeys diving down on branches that move and feeding off berries and picking insects off the trees. Even if it is made harder for the staff, I want the animals doing what they want to do, to the point that they have no idea they are in captivity. We have a completely unique set-up – even when other zoos introduced walk through enclosures they never truly let the animals free.

The animals are all monitored so that there is no possibility of overfeeding. The feeds for the likes of the giraffes and penguins are managed so that the public can join in at the animal's designated dinner time. The animals which are fed throughout the day by visitors to the park, such as ducks, peacocks or wallabies, won't overfeed by default.

In 2005 I had the idea of building a walkway which went all the way out into the giraffe enclosure. Instead of just walking around the giraffes and rhinos, my idea was to immerse people into their world by coming as close to the animals as they could. With the giraffes leaning right in towards and even over visitors it would enable a true 'wow' experience rather than the anti-climax of seeing an animal at distance. I wanted people to go home with a true buzz after a fantastic, special day and be moved to contribute to our projects around the world.

I had to think long and hard about how to integrate the animals alongside people who were coming into the park. Obviously they could not literally walk up to tigers or rhinos but there had to be a way to retain my unique idea for being up close and personal with the animals. An idea finally came to mind of a pier which stretches out into the sea. Just like that, a person can suddenly be in the sea with the safety of a wooden or steel structure beneath them. This feeling is always incredible, to be within the sea itself, albeit safely. It occurred to me I could do this with the more dangerous animals in the park.

I tried my first experiment with this in 2005. The first pier was built in amongst the rhinos and giraffes. The pier was low enough that the giraffes could lean up towards the people and stretch their heads almost over the barrier. It worked perfectly and there were no mishaps at all. I decided there was no reason it could not work over a big cat. At the time I thought the safest animals to attempt this with would be the cheetahs as they are not that aggressive and can't jump too high. All of a sudden people could climb in amongst the cheetahs. The piers cost a lot of money, even though we built them in house, and I found a fantastic contractor named Adrian, from AK Fencing, who works a lot with building metal and wood works. He started to work on the lion enclosure for me, building the new piers, which were already a hit with the public. Adrian and I got on very well as I always respond well to those who work hard. As Adrian was working he would come up with new, intriguing ideas and I would roll with them. It was gratifying to see his confidence build and the new piers work even better than the ones before. Every time we built one they seemed to work perfectly so it was time to go one step further and build one over the tigers. It would be where you could see tigers naturally moving around in a natural environment, unencumbered by mesh or glass. This was clear, clean and still so very close to such a wild, dangerous animal. This was one of the best innovations in the park's history because the public fell in love with the concept and couldn't get enough of such unbridled access to wild animals.

The new perspective also gave the public a chance to see how fit and agile our animals were. I decided almost at the inception of the park to keep our animals as fit as possible. I knew in order to do this they had to be kept active, so they would not just vegetate; rather they would expend energy in trying to find their food, just as they would in the wild. I knew of a man called Graham Law who placed raw meat high up a pole at the former Glasgow zoo, with the intention of making the tiger chase up the pole to retrieve the meat. The benefit for the tiger is that in climbing the pole it strengthens every part of its body and has the same effect as if it had chased down a large deer. South Lakes started to perform this task regularly and it worked wonders. Since then we have done this every day, even Christmas Day. We put the same theory into place for all the big cats so the lions and jaguars also get the same workout. In the wild tigers don't have an ounce of fat on them, nor in fact, do any animals which need to chase down prey. If they carried fat they would not be fast enough to catch the prey and my logic was to keep our animals in the very same condition. Therefore, not one of our animals carries excess weight.

The true benefit for the public comes in watching the awesome power of our tigers chasing up a pole for their food. In the early days however it was always a problem because there would be a couple of thousand people all congregating at the same time and many people could not see the tigers as there would be row after row of people. This can happen at most zoos whenever there is a particular spectacle that everyone wants to see. The beauty of building the walkways in and around the tigers was that it created an enormous amount of space for people to leisurely watch the tigers. It was in fact just like having a grandstand view over a football pitch. There were terraces and then higher levels which could accommodate so many more people than in the past. I also believe this attention to detail has encouraged more donations to tiger conservation because people feel a stronger awareness of the tiger, and possibly even a stronger bond.

Very soon we took the very same concept and used it so that people could enter into the bear section. Here, visitors would enter into the bear's own world, in amongst their trees and natural habitat. This was also continued throughout the monkeys and lemurs, enabling people to get an entirely unique view of such creatures swinging through the tops of the trees.

The cost of innovation has always been a source of concern to me. I always wanted the very best in my business but always felt it could be approached from the point of view of saving as much money as possible. As outlined earlier in the story, the essence of this was to do the work myself as far as possible. Whenever I have had to watch others do the work, I have learned and taken the approach of learning for the future, I always intended to do the work myself the next time around. A case in point was when I bought the first building for the park. It was a standard agricultural building with a steel frame. There were block walls and an asbestos concrete roof. I had no idea how to erect the building myself and had to hire a specialist company. Unfortunately the mud was very wet at the time and their digger got stuck, they had to wait for the weather to dry before removing it and this wasted a lot of time, several weeks in fact.

When they were digging the foundations I watched every single move they made with the belief that next time around I would do the job myself. I watch, learn and save a fortune. It has truly been the essence of our success. An example of just how much money can be saved by doing the job on your own terms would be comparing the cost of an outsourced quote for building a new giraffe house, versus the figure it actually cost me and my trusty team to construct.

Most zoos hire contractors to perform all the jobs they require, most of the time at an extortionate cost. One zoo was building a giraffe house which was very similar in style and size to the one at South Lakes. It cost them £500,000. I hired contractors to put in the frame of the building but everything else we did in house. It's a very large building with excellent insulation and an upper section and a great amount of metal work. I designed and built the building myself – there were no architects or other specialists to pay and the cost to the park was just £30,000.

There was no danger of me making a mistake in whether the giraffes were adequately housed because I had made mental notes of every single giraffe house I had ever seen at other zoos. Giraffes evidently need height, and they also require reasonable heat. They need to be kept warm and out of drafts during cold spells of weather. My secondary wish with the giraffes was to have a platform whereby people could see their extraordinary height from the best perspective. Although we have various walkways out over the top of the giraffes, the giraffe house itself has a public area that is on the ground floor, this way the magnificent stature of these splendid animals can be seen in all its glory. It was very important that we provide access to giraffes even in winter, when they are much more likely to be inside.

My focus has always been South Lakes first and foremost, but conservation was really an obsessive sideline for me. I enjoyed what I had been doing in this respect but I felt the need to develop it in some way. I had been put in touch with the Chaparri Andean Bear Project once we received our spectacled bears in 2002. I was very interested in what they were doing and we sponsored a rescued bear for a few years. It was a small project that was taking confiscated bears and releasing them back to the wild, or trying to. At a European Zoo Conference in Leipzig, Germany, I met up with Pierre Gay – a tall dark Frenchman – who I knew was also very interested in this project through the Bear Taxon Advisory Group meeting. Pierre and his wife Elisa, run the Doue La Fontaine Zoo in France, now called Bioparc Doue La Fontaine. Pierre asked to meet with me as he believed that the two of us had similar thoughts and interests.

I had known of Pierre for years but it was not on a business level. When Pierre was at conferences he was always one of the noisy ones who had a few drinks and the French always sing the same songs, they only know three, 'Frere Jacques' and one or two others if they are lucky! They certainly really get into the party spirit. I would watch Pierre and his French compatriots and admire their attitudes and approach. Whenever I went to conferences abroad I wouldn't sit with English people.

In my eyes I was there to branch out and broaden my horizons so there was little point talking to Brits who I already knew. I always sought out people from other countries and I would sit next to them for meals or sit next to them in a meeting and start talking to them, find out who they were. This is how I started to build my contacts. In fact it was a double down side with the Brits because they formed their own little cliques and I didn't see much point in doing this when you were supposed to socialise and learn about other countries and their methods, not to mention their personalities. There were many cliques but I stuck out on my own. It was fine with me however and I often became embroiled alongside the Dutch or the French crowd at the gatherings.

Although Pierre knew me as a peripheral figure to some extent we didn't truly learn about each other until the designated meeting. Here we were in Leipzig, a French and British pairing who had so much in common and had never truly realised it before. He owned a private zoo and so did I. He desperately wanted to do more for conservation, he was doing a lot and wanted to do more yet found himself limited by the amount of money he had. I felt the same – we were involved in a fantastic project but we needed to do a lot more, we couldn't just focus on tigers – we had to do something further.

Peggy, Pierre's assistant who organised our meeting, is brilliant at her job, in fact if Pierre was not my friend I would snag her myself to work at South Lakes. Peggy sat down in between us and told me, "This is what we want to achieve." I said, "Wow, you could have written that for me. What a fantastic opportunity – we should work together." I know they are French and inferior to us English but...I jest! I love the French people, though they certainly do seem to be particularly aware of every single historical event, every single sporting occasion that their fellow countrymen have ever won. That is true patriotism!

Pierre was ten years older than me but he didn't act it. Together we were a great team – we both had immense energy and intense passion. I also helped in terms of structuring the project in Chaparri. Pierre was a whirlwind of energy but he needed help in organising the project and achieving more. I like to think I also helped Pierre to better control his finances. If it were up to him he would be bankrupt himself in a week by giving everything away. He had enormous enthusiasm for the projects, but I was often the voice of reason, counting the cost for our partnership.

Many people involved in zoo conservation were on ego trips which was the opposite of Pierre who is a person who likes to involve everybody. I found it quite difficult inviting other people into our project whereas Pierre would often welcome others into the fray, hoping they would help. I often had to hold him back from doing so because it was our uniqueness that made the partnership special – there are no two zoo directors in Europe who think the way we do.

Pierre opened my eyes to so many things, one of which was that people were the ones who caused all the problems so we needed to work with people to resolve the problems while working in conservation. When you travel the world it becomes very apparent that tigers don't wipe out tigers, elephants don't wipe out elephants and monkeys don't wipe out monkeys. People wipe out everything because of the numbers and the needs and the demands that are our lifestyle has given us. It is an absolute truth but the way Pierre reacted was to say, 'Well they're here, we can't get rid of them, we have to work with them.' Thanks to Pierre I felt a completely new approach to conservation.

With tiger conservation you can't have people living with tigers. They eat people. If you have too many people the tigers will attack them. So tiger conservation is far more about keeping people out of the tiger's domain. Although the people have to live in the same country or territory as the tiger, as with Sumatra, it is all about educating them to being able to live alongside the animal harmoniously. Pierre taught me a very different way of conserving species than I was used to.

Pierre is a very resilient person who I admire in many ways – he will give his time and effort for anybody. The first time we went to Madagascar together, we visited Maroantsetra. Here we met a family who had a young girl called Natachat whose feet were badly deformed. She was struggling to walk as her feet were actually upside down, the soles of the feet were pointing upwards. Pierre and Elisa fell in love with the family and felt immense compassion for the little girl. The parents were wary of the Gay's offer to help out; I think they couldn't quite believe it. Pierre and his wife Elisa eventually convinced them to allow themselves to be helped and they managed to take the girl to France to begin a series of operations to correct the position of her feet. They allowed the girl to live with them while she attended the hospital and then recuperated. Together they have also set the girl up in business in Maroantsetra to help her in the long term. It must give Pierre such satisfaction to see the girl now being able to ride a bike and do all the usual things so many youngsters take for granted.

It was October and given our joint enthusiasm we immediately agreed that we would take a trip together the following January. It wasn't just a cosy liaison between Pierre and I; there were quite a few others who tagged along. It became a family event; I brought Caroline, Hari and my daughter Amy. Pierre had his wife Elisa with him who is a wonderful lady. There was also a French National TV newsreader named Manu, a friend of Pierre's who had always wanted to see Machu Picchu. It was classed as a work related trip but considering the people we had with us, and the fun we had, it could have been a holiday. This was my first major trip to South America.

As we were ready to drive down to Manchester airport from Cumbria, we were driving on the M6. The winds were atrocious, blowing at 100mph speeds. Although we were in a large, sturdy Range Rover, the winds were so powerful that we were being blown all over the road. Just before we reached Wigan an articulated truck was blown over completely. It became sandwiched in between the side and middle crash barrier. There was no way any traffic could pass. The traffic began to build and meantime, we were completely trapped in the vehicle. Our flight was due to leave in two hours. Eventually when I got out of the car and moved to take a look at any damage the wind blew the car door straight into my head and face, I was bleeding all over the place. I was wearing a Ferrari cap at the time which I loved and in the ridiculous winds it blew away and I never got it back. This probably annoyed me more than my crashing or having my head cut open. Another annoying outcome was that we missed the flight.

As anyone knows who has missed a flight – especially one that can be such a logistical nightmare such as a Peruvian trip, with family in tow – knows that airlines can be less than sympathetic to the fact that you missed your flight. Somehow, regardless of what happened, it is your fault. I was sitting in the airport lounge with my head bleeding, looking quite the dishevelled mess, and British Airways stepped up to the mark admirably. They managed to reorganise our flights so that we were able to join the next available flight to Heathrow, before adding the next leg – a flight from Heathrow to Miami and then, Miami to Lima. In the end we were only eight hours behind Pierre and his party and we managed to meet up before the last leg within Peru.

When we landed in Lima it was so stormy our Cusco flight was cancelled anyway. So, the first time I met Pierre and Elisa on a trip was at the airport but we had the most fantastic trip, it was one of my best trips ever. We visited Manchu Picchu first of all, staying in an amazing hotel. This was a wonderful beginning to our trip and produced some fantastic memories. It was a magnificent experience but I was about to have an experience that I would never forget.

The Amazon basin is the most enormous landscape; it really has to be seen to be believed. It is so vast. We travelled to a place called Puerto Maldonado at the fork of a tributary river of the Amazon called Tambopata. When we arrived it was a beautiful, hot, sunny day. After a brief time to settle in we were then taken by truck to the jetty into the Tambopata River. The river was calm and the weather continued to be the tropical dream I had expected. We reached Posada Amazonas, a beautiful lodge in the middle of the Amazonas forest, for an overnight stay. It started to rain heavily, the sound of the lashing drops echoed around our dinner table conservation, but I didn't think much of it – tropical rains come thick and fast and they are a part of life out there. We had to be up early the next morning, earlier than an early morning newsreader in fact – 3am. The reason for this was because we had to go out to an oxbow lake in the river – it was a long walk to the river through the dense forest, then a boat ride up river and a further hour long walk through the dense forest.

Along the oxbow lake we spotted giant otters – parents as well as their young – one of the rarest animals in the world. We were on a raft and fishing for piranhas. It was fun feeding the piranhas with bacon bits. Luckily Hari was not fearful of the fish with such vicious potential and razor sharp teeth – it was just a bit of fun. We watched the otters for a very long time; it was such a privilege to see the impressive creatures in their natural habitat.

We then walked all the way back to the river climbing back onboard the riverboat for a six hour journey up to the Tambopata Research Centre (TRC). It is one of the most amazing sights on the planet – here is the biggest collection of parrots in the world, which land there every morning to eat clay from a natural clay face. David Attenborough had in fact filmed a documentary there a few years before which I had watched on TV. It then became quite well known, with the presenter describing it – quite correctly as I can confirm – as the most colourful, noisy place he had ever seen in the world.

The weather had calmed after rain from the night before and had remained settled throughout our day. However as we were moving further up river, there were large planks of wood and pieces of trees floating past our boat. The river then started to turn colour. It changed from fairly clear to dark brown, muddy, becoming worse and worse. The boat was struggling against the current as the river started to rise, rising further and further. Eventually there were full sized trees careering down the river towards us as we desperately tried to steer around them. It started to become scary but we had come too far to turn back. The journey to the research centre took much longer than it normally would but eventually we made it, walking 35 metres up from the boat along the banking to the TRC main building, constructed from logs and bamboos.

It was by now quite late in the evening so we settled ourselves in our new surroundings, unpacking before having a bite to eat. We could see from our lofty position in the social area of the building that the river was continuing to rise. Given my experience with water in Australia I knew full well what could happen and that night was one of the most frightening of my life. I cannot adequately describe the sheer immensity of the river – something like half a mile in width and the level rose by some twenty feet. In just a matter of hours the river rose to a staggering height with immense speed and power that is impossible to describe.

The river climbing so high was one thing but when it started to eat away at the banking it was time to really worry. It explained before my very eyes why such large trees had been floating down the river – they were falling into the river from the eroding banking further upstream. By now it was falling at our very feet. The force of the water was enough to break the jetty up and crumble it into the water. The banking was falling further and further down. By now the water was a raging torrent.

We sat having our meal with everyone saying,

"What's going to happen, what's going to happen?"

"Oh don't worry if it gets any closer we will just move, we'll move further up into the forest. Don't worry about it, it's bad but it's not that bad. Let's sit here and wait and see, it can all change very quickly."

Dr. Don Brightsmith, who runs the project, seemed the pinnacle of logical calm. Although Don and his colleagues had not seen anything of this magnitude for many years, they were quietly confident that we would be safe.

Although it was January of 2005, the simple reality was that we were seven hours up river bang in the middle of the rainforest; we had no contact with the outside world. There were no satellite connections and the radios were intermittent, only working at a short distance. After our meal Don made a presentation about the research project with the macaw parrots, using a generator to power his laptop.

We were in the middle of Don's presentation when all of a sudden an almighty creak started; it was quite literally the sound of a giant tree falling down. If a lumberjack had caused it he would doubtless have shouted 'TIMBER!!!'

Although we were mercifully protected by a thatched roof made with banana leaves, this led to us having no idea exactly where the tree fell from, or quite where it had fallen to. Regardless, it was certainly very close to us. It amused me, even at the time, that Pierre fled straight under a table as it occurred to me that if a tree hit the table he would have been dead anyway!

We all ran out to see where the tree had dropped. It was an enormous tree that was leaning over the roof of where we were staying. Amazingly none of the big branches or boughs hit the building that we were in. It hit either side and left us completely unscathed with a huge tree leering over the top of us. We could all have died.

Suddenly, panic really set in. It was dark and we couldn't really see what was going on. What we could hear was thunder. It was getting closer and closer and we could still hear the banking falling in. All night we sat on the veranda watching with our torches. The banking was falling further and the water was rising higher. By the next morning we had around ten metres left of the eroded banking between us and the river. "Oh, it's got to go down," someone said helpfully, "it can't come any further, it's done more than it's ever done in twenty years so…"

We went for breakfast, what we could actually digest. It was a sobering thought that when we arrived we had had to climb twenty-feet or so to reach our building. By now the water was level with our dwellings. Planks of wood had been placed on the floor so we wouldn't all get covered with mud but by this stage they were floating away. We were trying to eat breakfast, with the river water bubbling under our table. We were sat with our wellies on having our breakfast with the water underneath the table, part of the river now. I couldn't work out where the current was though it was still penetrative.

Eventually reality dawned and it was decided that we had to move. We could only really grab our basic belongings, moving forward in single file. As we moved forward we unfortunately found a section of the land which was clearly lower and so all of a sudden we were trapped by the water, which was now cutting us off from returning. We tried to plough forward but out of the blue Manu disappeared completely, falling straight down. We found out afterwards that he had been attempting to step onto a footbridge but couldn't see because of the depth of the water. He missed the bridge and fell straight into the river. It was hard enough for a man on his own, but I was carrying Hari and trying to keep an eye on Amy and Caroline too.

We all started to panic, there was no way we could go back. Even if we wanted to we wouldn't be able to get back. The thought crossed everyone's minds – how on earth do we get out of this? We had no boats, no radio, nothing. For the first time I actually saw fear on the faces of the people who were with us. For so long it had been a shrug of the shoulders, 'this happens, don't worry about it' mentality. But now, even they were scared. Even the animals were panicking – they were appearing around us out of nowhere, sodden and full of fear. They had been pushed out of their territory by the flood. They were swimming for dear life.

As if things could not get any worse, we had been struggling forward for so long that it started to turn towards night time. It was bad enough when you could see what the problem was but in the dark everything was magnified and the water seemed to take on an even darker power and the noise increased considerably. The river was still coming towards us and the ground on which we were standing was constantly being eroded. Every single person in our camp was convinced we were going to die that night. The water seeped right under the veranda and we all knew that as soon as it took the foundations under there away the entire building was just going to collapse like a house of cards, into the water where we would doubtless drown.

We were praying for dear life. This could be the last thing we were ever going to do because we knew damn well the moment we dropped in that river we would never be seen again. There were billions of gallons of water flushing down the river at torrential speeds and with biblical ferocity. It was the most horrendous thing I have seen in all of my life. We have all seen floods on the television in news reports, or portrayals of tsunamis and their aftermath. But no matter what I have seen through the safety of TV, I have never seen anything as bad as we experienced that night. The cosmopolitan group was unified in our abject fear and we all held a vigil through the night. Sleep was an impossibility, we were all thinking of our loved ones and whether we had just minutes more to live.

As the light dawned it became clear that the storm which had seeped down from the mountains must have eased as the water levels were dropping. It seemed to fall as quickly as it had risen. In just four hours the level must have dropped by ten or fifteen feet. The locals told me that the 30 metres or so of the banking which had been eaten away by the water was a complete one off event – this had never happened before, even in this tropical rainforest. I had lived through a once in a lifetime storm.

By now you might think I felt like I was jinxed in some way. Or perhaps the opposite, that I was immortal. I didn't feel either of these things. I have a fairly philosophical viewpoint on the happenings that have occurred in my life. I may have put myself in some bizarre positions and had some frightening experiences but the reality is that I am involved in working with and around nature. Nature can be cruel; it is unpredictable and ferocious occasionally. Other times it is tranquil and beautiful. You have to take the rough with the smooth – live for the moment, and sometimes abandon all logic and just pray!

Nature is uncontrollable. For many people it is sunshine or desert and for other people it might be incredible floods. For some it is ice and snow but wherever you are in the world there is something that is going to be an extreme. It perhaps makes it seem more dramatic because the United Kingdom's climate is the least dramatic climate there is. When compared to Australia for instance where it can remain dry – completely desolate – for two years. When it gets above 28 degrees in the UK there is often a hosepipe ban enforced!

The next morning we managed to hop aboard the boats – we wanted to go and observe the parrots again. But they had all flown away, they weren't as inhibited as us mere mortals and they obviously didn't like what they saw. All we saw was an unbelievable deluge of mud and felled trees. Whenever I see the people who accompanied us that day we always reminisce about the famous flood. For Caroline, Hari and Amy it was one of the most dramatic experiences of their lives, something never to be repeated. For me it was just another in a long line of outrageous happenings and I revisited the same place over one year later in October 2006. I found out there had not been a single flood since, not even a mild gush. The banking had remained in exactly the same place as where it was when I left. They learned the lesson from the flood however and rebuilt the research centre further back into the forest and much higher above the ground to avoid a repeat should there ever be another flood of those proportions, but, so far so good. I visited once again in February 2011 with my son Indiana and the river rose dramatically once again, though it was nothing like 2005 and there was never any feeling of danger at all. That is indeed why it is called the rainforest!

From there we moved down river once again, quite quickly as it happened, which was a mighty relief. We visited Chaparri at the other end of the country in the north and chilled out for a while. There I met Heinz and Ana Plenge, a wonderful couple who have since become good friends. Heinz is a world-renowned wildlife and culture photographer, he produces his own books which are amazing, colourful hardback designs. They have dual languages, English and Spanish on each page. Heinz is Peruvian and has German heritage but speaks very broken English and obviously Spanish, and he married Ana, a Peruvian lady. They live in the most amazing landscape which they are thoroughly dedicated to preserving. It is a completely different part of Peru, very dry forest "Bosque Secco". It is an unbelievable environment with huge cactuses and the most arid desert, but when the rain comes it can bloom into even greater beauty. This might only last a few weeks and suddenly it turns dry again. It is a peaceful landscape but despite its remoteness and extreme heat the most amazing wildlife exists – I have seen some of the most wonderful birds there, scenes I have never witnessed anywhere else in the world.

For the first couple of visits there it was a true refuge, as you could not even pick up a mobile phone signal. This suited me just fine. Unfortunately now, with the increase of satellites and masts all over the place even a region such as Chaparri can produce a phone signal. I have had some beautiful, peaceful times here because of its isolation – it is possibly one of the things I most need for love to blossom fully. Whereas with my first wife Alison shied away from the adventurous nature of my calling in life (she still has not flown in an aeroplane on holiday to this day that I am aware), Caroline loved adventure and loves wildlife. She reveled in the kind of life I lead. She wanted to continually travel the world and work with animals; she wanted, quite literally, the wild life.

I returned in 2006 to the same regions in Peru, where I stayed for almost a month. That time however Caroline was not with me. By then we had started to grow further apart from each other. There were many distractions still in my life – the most distracting was the continuing saga of Australia that was draining all my resources and slowly killing my business, there was the every day running of South Lakes which takes up the majority of my time. There was also my conservation work, and then there was the attention I seemed to receive from other women. If a girl so much as smiled at me Caroline became suspicious.

I still loved and wanted Caroline and she was always on my mind. In retrospect I shouldn't have become upset with Caroline any more than she should have become angry with my female staff. I should have talked to Caroline more and tried to reassure her that I wanted no other – if I had given her the confidence and belief that I was after no one else then perhaps her actions might have been different. In reality I didn't quite know myself where we were in our relationship.

I saw it as a negative and interfering action from Caroline but in reality it just showed how much she loved and cared about me and didn't want another woman to have me. Given her behaviour however I felt more distanced from her than ever, we seemed to have a communication block which kept us apart. At the time however I was busy making a complete mess of my life, not knowing which way to turn and how to address the reality and the function-ality of a loving relationship.

Caroline harboured anger from her childhood and I look back and I think of the errors of judgement I made, what I didn't see and how stupid I was. Though I had no idea how to remedy our disparate existence I loved Caroline enough to try and make it work somehow and I couldn't have a relationship with another woman.

Still, I was lost and confused and I felt that Caroline and I could not make it work. I sought companionship, I wanted someone to accept me, like me and give me the unbridled, non-judgemental attention, nothing I did seemed good enough for her.

I was searching. South Lakes was doing ever so well, the best year ever, I had finally sold Mareeba Wild Animal Park and everything was going amazingly well. I did have one physical problem caused by a brutal pair of Babirusa however.

Their names might not have spelled fear and terror but Brussel and Sprout were capable of causing more than wind.

South Lakes Wild Animal Park featured two breeding male Babirusa: affectionately named Brussel and Sprout. They got on just fine usually but the female in their little group Kota, was in season and it caused a violent reaction, Brussel and Sprout started to fight each other. The problem with Babirusa is they have astoundingly sharp tusks, four altogether. There are two long sharp tusks which pop up from their mouth and then two curled tusks which pop up from the bridge of their nose, they are quite amazingly different to most animals in this respect.

The two males were thrusting the top tusks into each other, slicing parts of each other all over the place – they were making a lot of noise and causing a very unpleasant, gory mess. People were asking me what I was going to do about it. Clearly, I had to do something. I entered their territory armed with a yard brush which was my first weapon of choice to try and tear them apart. It didn't work, so I tried a hosepipe. This too had no effect whatsoever. I dropped the hose and went up to them myself trying to push them away from each other in desperation as I knew one or both of them might die if I didn't do something quick.

It was a long time after I interfered in the gentlemanly duel of the Babirusa that one of them stopped, turned and looked at me. Now I had got their attention and they didn't like it one bit. There wasn't a lot of room between me and an escape route but I backed up at the speed of light, tripping over a log and falling onto the steep banking behind me. I landed disconsolately with my legs apart facing a charging Babirusa.

He ran straight at me, tusks down and ran straight in between my legs. Although I didn't see this as he approached his mouth was wide open and he bit me hard between the legs, before scampering off.

It was at this point in my life that I could prove anyone who says you can't hold your breath for more than three minutes is fibbing. It must have been ten minutes before I caught my breath.

Brussel had bitten right through my scrotum. He had carefully missed both testicles but put a hole clean through from the front to back. I was bleeding profusely and in considerable pain. As any gentleman would know, any slight alteration to that part of the body leaves you in a state of pain and shock that no woman could ever understand.

I dragged myself up, slowly yet purposefully, I had to make it over the fence just in case Brussel, or even Sprout decided to come and finish me off. Somehow I climbed over the fence and lay on the floor, still trying to breathe, whilst the throbbing pain soared through my groin.

Here I became aware of the bible tale, The Good Samaritan, as person after person – witnessing a man lying prostate on the floor, bleeding from his groin, winded and punctured – walked right by me, leaving me to die in the open air. It took a very long time for someone to come and assist me.

I could hardly walk but I reached my house a few hundred metres away and hobbled into the bathroom where I cleaned the wound as best as I could. I decided to keep it clean with the anti-septic cream Savlon and keep an eye on it. People might think I was mad not to go to hospital but I knew from my days on the farm that you can slit a pig's scrotum with a scalpel, remove the testicles and feed them to the dog. All that is required is a few antibiotics and the pigs walk away. My theory was a pig's a pig and a man's a man, what's the difference? There was some bruising and pain for a while and I had an ever decreasing circle in the skin of my scrotum, but it did eventually heal.

The moral of the story is when animals such as Babirusa are going crazy trying to kill each other, don't disturb them, unless you have a groin protector.

It just shows the speed, aggression and reactions that animals have when they decide to do something. If the situation happened again I would take a plywood board with me to make sure I had that between myself and the animals.

Chapter 27
Colombian experience and Sumatran trek disaster

In a business sense 2005 was an absolutely epic year. We returned home from Peru in February and then it wasn't long into May when Pierre and I went to Colombia for the conference of the Association of Latin American Zoos (ALPZA). Pierre had been invited to speak and I too had a slot to speak at the conference. My subject was all about how a small zoo can still contribute a massive amount to conservation. The theme of my talk was all about how a small zoo might think they can't make too much of a difference when in reality, of course they can. South Lakes Wild Animal Park was living proof of this.

Pierre and I visited Cali Zoo in Colombia and we were made so welcome by the director of the zoo, Maria Clara Dominguez, and all her staff. She put on such a fantastic conference there and I met many extraordinary people. Up until that point I had made no great strides into learning another language, not since my foray into Italian 25 years earlier. However, I had been enthralled by the Spanish dialect, from spending time in Peru and then Colombia it grew to the point where I knew I wanted to learn as much as I could and start to try and communicate in the native language when I was in these wonderful countries. South American Spanish is quite different to European Spanish, it doesn't have the same inflections and it is actually a lot simpler, in my view at least.

I really enjoyed Colombia. I met a lot of new people, I went out for meals, we went dancing, it was an experience that was extremely influential to my being. I was immensely surprised by Colombia. I had this vision of the country as being laden with danger – the way it has been portrayed by the media is as a haven for guerrillas, drugs cartels with danger and murder in abundance. You hear so much about it. Bogota was called the murder capital of the world, Medellin wasn't far behind and it crossed my mind that Cali might well be fraught with danger too. I felt incredibly safe though I did later learn that Cali Zoo had gone out of their way to make us feel welcome and protected. They had provided terrific services for Pierre and I, a beautiful hotel and unbeknownst to us at the time, we had armed bodyguards behind us, following our every move.

Whenever we went for a walk, for a meal or to a bar or club, these guards were there just a matter of feet behind us. We could have been kidnapped, threatened, or succumbed to any form of violence. The fact that we weren't actually told this meant that we could enjoy the trip. If we had known we would have been seriously terrified. We felt quite relaxed, it wasn't something that occurred to me at all – Colombia seemed beautiful and peaceful by my reckoning. While we were in the conference there was quite a big event taking place only a few miles away where the guerrilla used an infant school to launch an attack on the army. The army patrol went one way, an infant school and guerrilla on the other side and the guerrilla fired rockets at the army. There were many deaths and they had used the kids as a barrier so the army couldn't fire back. It was just a few miles from where we were and around ten people lost their lives. It made the news but the whole event seemed to be reduced to a very brief topic of conversation, which in hindsight was to probably help us feel safer. It wasn't just Pierre and I who were outsiders, there were a few other Europeans as well as a couple of American conservationists at the conference and they didn't want any of us panicking.

From the conference we flew up to Medellin and met a guy called Carlos McClean. Carlos had set up a foundation, he was very passionate about Howler monkeys and the saddest thing about a lot of places in the world is that animals are used as pets even when they require a degree of expertise and people don't realise what they have got themselves into. They buy a tiny, little baby monkey from the marketplace and it grows up into a big, very dangerous and wild animal that they cannot possibly keep in their house. They don't stay tame. They have a tremendously difficult diet because Howler monkeys eat tree leaves, quite far removed from a human's requirements. So, very often these babies come, they go into houses, they die very quickly, because people feed them what they would feed a child or a dog or something different, they don't have a clue how to feed a baby Howler monkey. It is a very sad trade. The baby monkeys only cost five dollars and yet the mother is shot and killed before the baby is taken away to be sold.

Carlos saw all this going on, decided he wanted to do something about it and worked with the Environmental Authorities in Colombia, in that region, and set up a project called Ecolombia. The idea was to rescue and to rehabilitate the Howler monkeys and also to involve the local people via education, by helping them with employment and so on so that when he released them the community didn't just automatically take the monkeys again. Carlos was a very pleasant fellow and totally passionate about his Howler monkeys. I saw a number of amazing people making a real difference in these kinds of projects, the likes of Medellin Zoo who were helping Carlos with the project, from the veterinarian side of things.

Carlos was quite a wealthy businessman. He had a shrimp growing business and had a lot of influence in the business world with connections in the USA. We were invited to stay with him at his house in the Colombian mountains – it was a delightful property that influenced me to the extent of changing my own house, it was that good. It was the first time I had ever stayed in anyone's house that had an en-suite bathroom in each bedroom which meant you didn't have to go traipsing over the house in the middle of the night. I took to this idea.

I also loved the colours in the house. The design of the house was incredibly dramatic. The colours were bold: reds, yellows and greens and it spoke to me on some level. It was very different to what I was used to, the usual off whites in every room. The house was also very much open plan, and I thought to myself, 'I am going to go home, I'm going to knock my house to pieces and start it again' and I did. I came home, I had the plans drawn, I knocked my house into open plan, I put bold colours on the walls and I put en-suites into all of the bedrooms, all of which came from Carlos' house where I had such an enjoyable time.

While I was in Colombia I realised that it was the dance capital of the world. It was the first time I had really been exposed to true, all out, full on dancing and I loved it, not that I had a choice. I found the culture quite astounding and markedly different to Britain. In Britain everybody sits around the edges of the dance floor until they have had too much to drink and then they forget themselves and only then do they go and dance. Very few people get up to dance because they like to dance as a partner and also in England, people tend to dance on their own a lot and the whole notion of dancing with a partner has all but died out, unless it is for a programme like *Strictly Come Dancing*.

In South America it is wonderful because everybody is immediately on the dance floor. It has nothing to do with bravado, or being drunk, it is merely that this is their culture. They are dancers, they are not frightened of dancing and they are so happy to do it, not only do you dance with your girlfriend or your boyfriend but you actually swap for the next dance. You meet lots of different people, talking and dancing in a moving, changing atmosphere, the whole experience is tremendous.

I got up to dance and I spent ages and ages entertaining people with my wobbly bum and my legs that never coordinated properly. They were constantly trying to manoeuvre me to do it but I must admit I should have started a lot earlier in life because to dance like they do is near impossible. I think it is something they pick up naturally and I really struggled to do it. I was attempting to do it as best I could and may have managed it to some extent, creating a few laughs along the way, but I am never going to dance like a native Colombian.

One of the people who worked for Ecolombia, Margarita Vallejo, struck me as being a fantastic worker. In actual fact they were struggling to pay her so I paid her wages for a couple of years to make sure she stayed involved. Eventually she ended up coming over to England for a placement in the zoo for quite a few months and enjoyed it and learned a lot about England. She returned to Colombia and now lives a happy life as a married mother of one.

Another time where I saw a lot of dancing was at the festival in La Pintada village where we hold a Howler Monkey Festival every year. It is funded by our conservation project and brings the whole community together. There are many different groups and school children involved.

The event features art, dance and music and it is all linked to how important nature is, how crucial it is to live with nature rather than destroy it. They learn that their lives will be better in the long term, as the forests remain, they are not destroyed by pollution or erosion. The event brings fun, games and dance to raise awareness of a serious issue. I loved this attitude from the Colombian people.

I witnessed one humanitarian issue which really concerned me in Colombia. They have no such thing as a welfare state; therefore any woman who has children and becomes widowed or has a husband who leaves her can end up unbelievably vulnerable. She cannot work as she has to look after her children and suddenly without a male to go out and work, she will have no income at all. Colombia might well be a modern society but the catholic, family lifestyle is all pervasive and the attitude towards relationships and marriage is very orthodox which is a positive attribute.

One of the things that was being done by Ecolombia with our support to help these unfortunate women was that a small factory was set up to send a batch of different materials to these women at their homes that they could then stitch up to make soft toys. It provided work for many single women with children who otherwise would have really struggled. They suddenly had a future and regular work. The idea from our point of view as conservationists was that we would buy the soft toys directly from the Colombia projects in order to sell in England and France. It isn't much of a financial benefit to us as we make next to nothing but I knew it was more important to keep those women in a perilous predicament in regular employment. The main idea was to keep the community together and to let them realise and appreciate that if you look after the animals the animals will look after you.

When I returned from Colombia I had such fond memories and was pleased to have my pre-conceptions utterly obliterated. I hadn't presumed it would be such a beautiful, diverse country. I can also say with all sincerity that the Colombian people are some of the most wonderful people I have ever met in the world. They are very loving and caring. When you meet a Colombian they don't want to talk about themselves, they want to know about you. They are always looking for a way they can help you or your family. They also enjoy life to the absolute maximum and it influenced me in a very positive fashion.

Before Colombia I had been feeling down about life in general, I was busy and my whole life felt like very hard work where I found it near impossible to relax and enjoy myself. To visit Colombia and find I could release myself from myself, to forget home, forget stresses and actually let go was a wonderful experience. I hadn't done it for such a long time; in fact I couldn't remember the last time I had let myself go. To give over to such pure and simple fun, there was nothing else to it but having a really great time so it was no wonder I came away from the trip refreshed and reinvigorated.

From a business perspective I was bolstered by relationships with the zoos in the country, to the point that we now exchange animals with my contacts in Colombian zoos. When I returned to the country I started to help them re-design their facilities and exchange ideas in order to build better zoos for their animals – instead of the usual cage system for keeping animals I showed them the animals could roam free with just a boundary of electric fences to house them.

A month after Colombia I travelled to Sumatra for the tiger project which was a full two weeks at a completely flat out pace. Of all the countries I find myself visiting I find Sumatra is the hardest from a physical perspective. There are three different centres of operation there, one in the north, one right on the Equator and one in the south of Sumatra. Sumatra is a surprisingly large island and the roads are terrible, so bad in fact that you can barely use them. It is far more effective to fly; yet you have to fly back to Java each time as there are no flights between Sumatran cities. I don't see much point in going all that way to sit in an office or hotel and discuss things. I want to get out there and see things for myself. I wanted to meet people, ask them about how things were going, get into their heads and view their every day lives. I want to go to the problem areas and if they are suffering, I want to know how and why. I want to put myself in the same position they are in; if they are uncomfortable I want to feel their discomfort. It is almost never that I will stay in a hotel when visiting one of my conservation projects. I want to lay alongside those who have it hard, sleeping out in the forest under a piece of plastic with large ants crawling all around you. I still don't think I truly feel it the way they do as I am there for a few days before jetting off to the next destination whereas these people can sometimes do it for two weeks straight, living off rice and soy sauce.

I don't just want to sit at home in England and agree to send money, I want to be stung, sunburned, to sweat, to feel so tired you want to just drop to sleep at any time. I don't think if I did that myself that I could truly appreciate how hard the people out there work.

As part of my commitment I travelled to Sumatra in 2004, aiming along with a ten-person crew to travel to Datai village for the first time. Here we intended to build schools and employ people to look after the tigers there. This was something we eventually managed. Our first foray into the area however was fraught with difficulty – at least for me. Included in our party was an ITV film crew which consisted of one woman who did absolutely every job – camera person, sound editor and so on – all by herself.

At the time there was no access by boat and the only road to the village was a complete mess - and ended 20km from the village - there were huge ditches and divots, gravel, stones and mud spread everywhere. After a while of attempting to drive across the infernal path we all decided it was so bumpy and awkward that we would be better walking.

It was a mere 27 kilometres. We were laden with backpacks; the temperature was soaring, with sweltering humidity. Unlike Niger which has a burning intensity, even when it is a mere 35 degrees – 31 degrees in Sumatra can seem like a devil's cauldron. A few steps and you are already dowsed in sweat. The only comparison between the two climates is an overwhelming need to rest at all times as the climate just zaps your energy.

We followed an old logging trail through the jungle for what seemed like an eternity, before eventually reaching our destination.

We just had time to have a quick wash in the river before having something to eat and crashing out for the night. The next morning we were offered the chance by the locals to go and visit a waterfall, which they seemed very proud to show us. It was a precious thing to their tribe and they had developed a close bond with the beautiful natural wonder. We were flanked by our tiger protection men in uniform, carrying guns, which made us look like we were in a military operation.

We were treading through completely virgin forest with no trail to follow. At certain points we were walking alongside a small river, and before long we were walking through the river, knee deep in water. It is indelibly hard to persevere, walking through a flowing current. There is natural resistance from the water, the stones move beneath your feet and it is all you can do to try and remain upright.

We walked something like 10km before reaching the furthest point in the jungle, finally reaching the fabled waterfall. It was one of the remotest parts in the world and the realisation suddenly hit me. I felt like an explorer – a true discoverer of new lands. The area was obviously populated by a few indigenous locals but they had rarely had any interaction with the white man. It is rare – even throughout all of my travels – that one can truly feel as if they are the first person in a location but that day I felt as if I had truly traversed the earth and found something new. The waterfall itself was blindingly beautiful and was worth the awkward trek. Unfortunately I had injured my knee in the process, feeling a snap at one point on the walk and quickly realising that I had damaged the cartilage in my knee. It may have been the wear and tear from the walk the day before but whatever the cause, I could feel two or three parts of my knee floating around inside the skin.

The pain was agonising. My leg locked and I couldn't bend my knee. I swiftly realised I was as far deep into a jungle as you could go and the beauty and pride at having come so far suddenly gave way to fear. I felt very aware of my unexpected vulnerability. I couldn't be carried or helped in any way, and we had no painkillers. For the position I was now in I may as well have broken my leg.

We were due to walk back in another hour or so but I felt that if

I was going to make it back to the vehicle I best start walking right away.

They wouldn't let me set off alone without the protection of a gun as there was such great potential of an animal or even having an accident where I could fall down a hill and disappear forever. With hurried fervour the team set off on the return journey.

It wasn't too far to Datai but we then had the 27km further before getting back to the vehicle. During the first leg back to Datai I was in agony, with tears streaming down my face. When we reached Datai I managed to find a bed to lie on.

My leg was swollen and I could barely get off the bed, when I needed the toilet I had to virtually lean over the edge of the bed. Once again I was struck with fear. How on earth was I going to get back to the vehicle? The path back was not even flat; it was a mountainous road up and down steep hills, with logs across the path and river crossings.

I thought to myself, without trace of humour, 'I am going to die.'

We set off back towards base camp with my brain on just one thing – making it back to the vehicle. I knew that as long as we could back to base camp I would be able to take some painkillers and rest. Though no one else was suffering with any injury, there were several rest breaks taken on the journey back. I felt however, that I could not stop. I desperately wanted to – I felt numb with pain from my head to my feet – but I knew if I stopped I might not get going again. I kept pushing myself, trying to get through the pain barrier.

We finally made it back and amazingly I wasn't the last one to arrive at the vehicles. One chap who was younger than me took so long he was an hour behind me, we had to wait for *him* even though I was desperate to return to base camp. When we finally made it I swallowed some much needed painkillers and put a cold compress on my knee before resting for a few days. It wasn't too bad, or at least I told myself so because it was a long trip and I needed to keep going. I never did have treatment for my knee and today, if I push it too far I get the same pain again, though nothing could ever be as bad as that long walk.

On the same trip we travelled to Way Kambas and camped out in the Kali Biru area of the forest, which has become particularly well known for its concentration of tigers over the years. During the night whilst lying on the plastic sheet and covered with little but a shirt I woke in the pitch dark to feel something sniffing at my toes. It was a terrifying moment as I suddenly wondered whether a Sumatran tiger could be deciding on whether to risk eating my foot.

I had my camera by my head and slowly took hold of it, clicking to take a photo facing down towards my feet. The flash forced the animal to run for cover. Back then camera film took so long to develop that I had to wait for weeks to find out what animal had been at my feet. When the film was developed I saw it had been a civet, a largely nocturnal mammal – it was beautiful. The night was made even more memorable as once we were packing up camp in the morning we discovered tiger urine on a tree no more than ten metres from our camp. A tiger had been close but had not sniffed my toes, thank God.

Chapter 28
Sumatran Tiger Programme,
building schools and flooding ordeal

My job in Sumatra had expanded somewhat from just a few years before when Ron Tilson had initially been in charge of the projects. As I was the main one who was interested in taking over from his role, it fell to me to take on a mountain of work. Ron Tilson was actually a good example to me of what *not* to do when visiting the conservation projects. Whenever he visited Indonesia, he preferred to stay in the capital Jakarta. He would make the field workers come to him so they had to travel from Sumatra – a very awkward journey. They would then meet in hotels for meetings and talk about budgets and policy strategies. He also genuinely believed the Indonesian people needed them and could not perform any conservation work without them, which I didn't agree with. Yes, they needed a little assistance but they were more than able to carry out the work of their own accord. To me, I had always wanted a strong team of Indonesian people to carry out the work, to the point where the original team assembled in 1996 is still working for me today.

My approach was something rather different to the established norm. I embraced not only the locals but also those in power. I met the Minister of Environment and Conservation, a guy who we had made quite good friends with on the tiger conservation side as he was something of a novelty – there aren't many people within the Indonesian government who are interested in tigers or their conservation. Most people in that government were no different to many other third world governments, they were interested in anything that made them money and nothing that would cost them time, effort or that they had to fund. There was corruption as in many other countries but at least I found an ally with this particular minister. He was a nice fellow and very supportive of us and what we were doing.

I also had meetings with others who were high up in government, the Director of Conservation, the Director of Forestry – I met them all a number of times. My attitude to them was to treat them with the utmost of respect, to talk to them and when I talked to them to say, 'This is *your* country, this is your tiger not ours, I'm only here to do what you want me to do and to help you to do what you want to do'."

Those previous to me handled the situation differently, they went in and said, 'This is what we are going to do, this is how we are going to do it and you will do what we say.' It wasn't the most helpful attitude - the Indonesians saw them as controlling – and it was therefore much easier to see me as someone more sensitive to their own preferences and ways of doing things.

The whole idea of my project was for it to be ultimately run by the Indonesian people. Our senior person on the team, Muhammad Yunus, is an Indonesian university graduate. He has made great strides himself to court favour with the likes of the Director of Conservation as well as local universities. With our project being seen as a local concern, it is far easier to be granted permits and the like, the UK is merely the country funding the project. Other than when I go out there myself it is completely local and self-sufficient.

It is far easier to ingratiate yourself when you are willing and wanting to work out in the field with the people who are running the project. I spend days at various camps learning about the people and even their families. I always seek to leave the hotel as quickly as possible, the hotel is just a base and really it is going to cost money to sit around indulging myself. The other thing I insisted upon which is generally much different to how previous people were dealing with the projects, was to not use the project fund to pay for my expenses, I did that myself. I saw all too often that zoo money from various places around the world, was being used for hotels, drinks and meals which was just such a waste and not remotely what that money should have been for.

I once had an argument with a representative from a zoo in

Europe, because I saw him claiming travel and hotel expenses from a project's conservation budget. I wrote to the project to say, "You shouldn't be doing that. If you are that keen to run a project you should be doing that for the love of it or your zoo or your employer should be paying for it as their contribution to your project, not out of people's hard earned gift to you." I refused to join in with the project because I thought that was wrong. When people give money to help an animal they want to help that animal, they don't want to pay for a flight or a nice hotel or meal for the zoo representative. People contribute hoping their money will be used for protection, or cameras, something in the field that will benefit the animal concerned.

The kinds of activities that donations can provide might be something such as remote cameras which can be used in the field. Our tiger team was the first in the world to use remote cameras. The team perfected the process to the point where they then began to teach everyone else how to use them. In 1996 we became the first group to capture a tiger by camera trap. We were the first people to photograph wild Sumatran rhinos. We were the first people ever to film a live video of a wild Sumatran tiger. We were the first people to video moving film of a wild Sumatran rhino. We have become notorious for achieving a lot of 'firsts' within the animal and conservation world. All of this is helped by sponsorship. The Trust I created ended up pledging over a million pounds. Without that money the tiger could no doubt have become extinct or at least very close to it.

During 2006 I visited Sumatra twice – this second time with my own team of people. We had to go up river from Bukit Tigapuluh which means 'thirty mountains'. Here they have a National Park where we run one of our tiger projects. Tribes of natives live, virtually untouched from the Western lifestyle. The project has also enabled us to build schools in Datai. It was while travelling on the Datai River to reach this small group of villages which is some six hours upstream that I encountered one of my now familiar problems with water. With me was Roy Pirie, a member of South Lakes staff as well as a good friend and trustee of the STT, Ian Collings. There were eight of us altogether.

We set off up the narrow river in canoes which had just one seat in them. They were distinctly uncomfortable, but by now I was used to such low level courtesy travel in such remote parts of the world. The water flowed down the slim river way but as we were quite a way into the journey the weather started to change and the river became rougher, stronger and higher.

We were making stupidly slow progress, moving inches up the river. The heavens were truly opening with thunderous power – lightning forked over head and the noise was frightening. Each of us held tarpaulins over us to try and keep dry – not just for ourselves but for all the equipment and food we had in the tiny canoes. The once bright day was now turning to a ghost story – dark, punishing skies throwing endless water down upon us. Everyone was starting to become scared. In this weather we should not have been on the river but there was nowhere to stop and shelter, it was keep pushing on or stop dead in the water and drown.

Eventually after several endless hours in pitch darkness we came towards a stopping point called the Sadan Orchard, which had a very small contingent of local people. We could see the tiny village shining like a beacon through the thick forest but before we could get there the outboard motor had had enough and flew off the back of the boat into the water below. Our driver, who was already doing a sterling job in keeping us alive, obviously thought the motor was more than his life was worth. We all heard the noise and the boat ground to a lumbering halt. We all lifted the tarpaulins up to see what had happened. Without blinking the driver jumped into the river and, somehow in the pitch darkness, retrieved the motor. He popped back up into the boat and fixed it back on. Amazingly the boat started again. He managed to steer the boat back on course, still in total darkness.

Everything was soaking wet, even our food. We could barely see in front of us as we pulled the boat up towards a banking. The rain and noise was relentless with thunder and lightning crashing all around us in the middle of a forest which could have snapped a few trees upon us at any second. Though we knew the name of the area we had no idea where we were going and it was still utter darkness, we were simply following noises ahead of us to try and reach a sign of humanity. We came up to a muddy hut which sat on stilts. A poor unsuspecting tribal member opened his door to a gang of eight degenerates, wet through with a raft of luggage, looking and feeling fearful and worried. We were invited in to stay the night, a remarkably hospitable reprieve.

The reason for this was simple. The tribes here believe that houses belong to all men, not the individuals who live in them. Thus travellers have a right to stay – it is a rule of the forest, whoever asks to come is welcome. The next day we thanked the tribesman profusely and headed to Datai on a now much calmer river. We should have had two days in Datai but by the time we reached there after our dramatic excursion, we had just two hours. Our proposed six-hour river trip had taken almost 22 hours.

We had to navigate the same river on the way home, which was now moving much faster as we were moving with the current. Thankfully conditions were calmer meaning there was little danger of falling out of control, even on such a fast flowing section of water. However we ran into a problem with an enormous tree which had fallen in the river. There was only a two-and-a-half foot gap between the tree and the passable river.

We couldn't see the tree until we came around the corner at some speed however. We all heard cries of "Lie down!" in Indonesian and we obeyed, sliding down as horizontally as we could manage at speed. As we did so the bottom of the gargantuan tree trunk skimmed my nose as we sailed underneath. No question, if any one of us had hit the tree full in the face we would have died.

Luckily the tree missed everyone. The driver had saved our lives yet again and in order to save his own he made a remarkable escape, perhaps the most impressive I had ever seen.

He was the last to have to navigate the tree and as the tree came toward him he jumped with one foot on the tree and the other foot propelling him over the tree before he landed on the boat on the other side, it was as if he had a magnet on his feet. It was a miraculous escape.

Roy Pirie was still working with me at the time but he struggled on the trip and it was his first and last with me. But he didn't tell us until afterward the epic journey upstream that he couldn't swim.

Why he didn't tell us I don't know, he could have had a life jacket but looking at the photographs of the journey it is visible on his face that he couldn't swim!

Early in 2005 we had finished the new penguin enclosure that had been built on the site of the old Coati facility. The time had come to go for the penguins that had been allocated to us from the Black Footed Penguin Breeding Programme or EEP as the programmes are known in Europe. We had been allocated a group from Stuttgart in Germany and we also had to collect some Swamp Wallabies from Zurich in Switzerland. We had for a long time had our own animal transportation facilities and a vehicle passed by the authorities to do international animal transports and rabies quarantine. The van was a long wheel base high sided Transit, looking back, a very difficult vehicle to drive at the best of times with no 5th gear and no real power in the engine against the wind. This journey was to prove one of the most difficult ever taken on as it soon became apparent at our first fuel stop we had a major problem with the ability to start the vehicle. The starting mechanism and battery stopped working, so we had to do the whole journey without stopping the engine at any time if we could avoid it, as the only way to get it going was to push it and bump start it. When we got to Dover and the ferry it was a dilemma and embarrassing as clearly when on the ferry we had to stop the engine, once at Calais we held up the exit of most of the vehicles whilst we tried to push the van uphill and start it, this was impossible. Eventually people came over and helped and we with embarrassed smiles and waves embarked on our drive down through Europe to Switzerland. I had taken Ben with me , he was by then 17 and had passed his test and wanted to help me with the long drive as we had a tight timetable and wanted to try to do the round trip without stopping anywhere to get the animals back as quickly as possible.

On arrival at Zurich there was a foot of snow and with 300mm of snow driving the Transit was very difficult and I was conscious that if we stalled it would be impossible to bump start on ice and snow. I was so tired on arrival all I wanted to do was sleep after driving all the way from Dalton with Ben taking a few spells for me. I slept in a room at the Zoo Zurich and we parked the van on a hill that had been cleared of snow. The animals were loaded and we set off before dark after a flying run around the zoo. We had targeted being in Stuttgart at about 5pm but it took a lot longer in the atrocious weather and we landed at about 9pm and the keepers there helped us load up the 20 or so penguins. With our fishy smelling and extremely noisy load, they are not nicknamed "Jackass" penguins for nothing as they sound just like a braying donkey; we set off into the dark, wet and windy night in a van that we could not stop. I remember driving in snow and ice, feeling desperately tired and not allowing Ben to drive until the road was clear. We made it back to the zoo the next day and completed the quickest run to Zurich and back that I had ever undertaken straight there and straight back and our new exhibit was populated. The van was fixed on our return and we decided to change it soon after because this was the fourth European drive the van had done when something major went wrong with it and that was enough.

Chapter 29
A Ferrari and a Bentley

From a personal point of view in recent years I have to admit that I have been known to spend a fair amount of money on myself, though at least it's my own money. I'm not a flash person but I do have a decent car. The story behind those purchases is in keeping with my lack of convention however. After my experience in Australia, I chose a different way to spend my money, instead of investing it in my zoo I ended up taking a rather large chunk of money and buying a car.

At the time my son Ben was seventeen. Naturally, he had been living with his mother for quite a few years by this time and it was a disturbing change to his character that I saw from afar – Ben became quite arrogant. I don't feel too proud of this aspect of his character, he was extremely opinionated and did not see another person's point of view easily. He would not listen to others and once he had an opinion he would not change it for anyone. In this respect he is very similar to my father. My father is unfortunately a person who, once he has made up his mind, would seemingly die before he would change it. Even if he realised he had made an error he wouldn't admit it and Ben, I feel, is very much the same. He is a person who feels very much that he is more knowledgeable, more experienced than anybody else and even at that age he was forming this air of superiority, something which I vainly hoped and believed I might be able to change.

One day in late 2004 after our return from Australia in a hurry, I took Ben and Hari to Old Trafford to watch Manchester United, his favourite football team. Personally I only went so that I might see them getting beat. Every time I saw United play they won and I was desperate to see the opposite outcome. Worse still, they were playing Birmingham City that day and they have become a team I feel an affinity with. My brother-in-law John is a staunch Birmingham supporter and every time I spend time with him and my sister Karen we seem to end up at St. Andrew's to watch a match. It's given me a liking for the Blues. So here I found myself at Old Trafford desperately hoping for an away, and most unlikely, win.

At the time I had a BMW. In the past I had always driven second hand Range Rovers, which I found were practical enough for my needs. Yet I suddenly realised I wasn't catering for the needs of family so I actually ended up buying my first saloon car, a BMW 750i which was the biggest and most luxurious car BMW made at that time. It was a flash car but I found it from a second hand dealer and it was relatively cheap.

As we were parking near Old Trafford we happened to see the Ferrari garage. Ben saw a Ferrari and started to pester me, "Dad, dad go on you've got the money. Come on get something for yourself, do it for yourself, you need something to let yourself go, you can get out in this and it would be amazing wouldn't it, a Ferrari!" He made sure to repeat the last phrase again, "Think Dad, a Ferrari – every man's dream car."

I knew deep down I didn't really want one. I had always been an impulsive person yet given I had to think about this one, it was a sure fire indication that I shouldn't really do it; it wasn't really me and was, to my way of thinking, a good way to waste a large chunk of cash. Yet Ben's persistent nagging progressed to the point where I wandered into the garage and asked them what deal they would do on a car.

At the time the finance deals they were offering were better than inflation so in effect it was cheaper than using your own money. I thought I could do it without too much inconvenience. I didn't have to worry about spoiling my cash flow as I could pay for the car over a longer period of time. I signed up there and then and the car was delivered a week later. I could not believe myself that I had a bright Rosso red Ferrari 360 Spider, an iconic car which many men would love to have. Somehow it didn't feel right however. Though it had a few running in faults and I had to take it back, I felt quite special when driving it. It was the most powerful, noisy and absolutely amazing car. When I accelerated my head threw back with a whiplash – and I didn't mind the rabid attention where folks could not believe this car and often took photographs.

The thrill was short lived however and for some reason, I began to feel guilty driving around in such an expensive motor. It seemed somehow a conflict of interest. There I was, a conservationist, putting money into tiger conservation, trying to save the forest, trying to save the earth and driving a Ferrari, it seemed hypocritical on some level. Yet I soon realised that everything in my house was second hand – settees and tables and chairs that had been given to me or cost me next to nothing. What had I ever done for myself? On some level, Ben had a point. It was then that I started to reward myself a little and spent a little money on myself, buying better quality furniture and upgrading my house. The guilt over the Ferrari dissipated somewhat.

It was some time later in February 2005 that Ben and I went to another match at Old Trafford. This time Ben was pushing me to change the family car and suggested we go and look at the Maserati. I didn't question his motives at the time; after all he didn't actually ride in the Spider with me, so I presumed he genuinely wanted me to have a good car for myself.

This time when we got to Old Trafford there was now a Bentley garage which had sprung up, obviously with the lure to highly paid footballers. Given we were going to watch a football match we weren't exactly dressed in dickie bows, I was wearing jeans and a leather jacket, plus a baseball cap. Ben had very long hair at the time and he had what I would call a ribbon in his hair, otherwise known as a bandana. He was wearing a baggy top with even baggier jeans. I also had Hari with me who at nearly three-years-old seemed to have a perpetually dripping nose. We did not seem as if we were that well to do. The chap in the pinstriped suit who was the chief salesman was obviously muttering under his breath at our apparent poverty. He must have thought, 'Please leave quickly and do not touch anything on your way out.'

Still he was a polite gentleman and we began to chat. I mentioned that I was hoping to change my car and upgrade a little but I wasn't quite sure whether it should be a Bentley. Suddenly the salesman started to look a little nervous. It was no wonder given Hari was jumping up and down on the back seat of a Bentley, his nose running everywhere with the glass covered in snot. Ben was carefully trying to reach over and pull Hari out though he was persistent. He enjoyed wiping his nose all over the £185,000 car. I apologised profusely as we pulled Hari out as soon as I had spotted the price tag. Now we truly weren't welcome, but I persisted.

"I don't know what you can offer me or what we can do," I said, "do you have any second hand ones?"

"Well, sir, they are very, very expensive."

"Well, yeah I know they are but…"

"What do you drive right now?"

I think he intended to make a comparison with my presumed Fiat T reg – 'Yes sir, let's compare that with a Bentley.'

"Actually that's my car there," I said, "the BMW 750i." Yes, the one with private plates I thought. "Oh, is it?" he said, suddenly sounding slightly more interested.

"Your name?"

"Mr Gill."

"Yes, I see the plate GIL, yes. What do you do? What's your…"

"I own a zoo."

We continued to chat and I had to throw in the fact that I also owned a Ferrari.

"A Ferrari?" he said fawningly. "What sort of a Ferrari?"

"A 360 Spider."

"What year?"

"Oh it will be one year old now."

"Well, Mr Gill, please come over here. I can show you a car that has just come in and I'll take you into the garage where there are some more further round."

All of a sudden he was interested and saw me as a genuine potential client. Once he realised we weren't about to trash his garage his whole demeanour changed. I learned his name was Jan Casey and he was extremely polite and helpful. I've known him for a few years now and bought a couple of Bentleys from his garage.

I fell in love with an electric blue Continental GT. It was only about a year old. Jan told me the price and I had to clear my throat a few times. The car was astounding however; it had specialist wheels, 6 litre W12 550 horsepower. It was the fastest most powerful 4 seat car that money could buy. The name Bentley is iconic and many people will concur that they are the best cars you can buy. Jan offered me a very good deal on the trade with my BMW. I decided you only live once and that I had been through enough hassle and hell with Australia. For twelve years I had worked with my family's future in mind and never done a thing for myself. The Bentley was clearly not a family car – it was a four-person vehicle but predominantly it was for the driver and a single passenger. I loved it.

About a-year-and-a-half later Ben came to me again ranting and raving about Bentley, they had a brand new car called the Flying Spur. "It's much bigger than this one," he said referring to the GT Bentley, "it's got the same engine but it's more of a family car, a big saloon, limousine type car. It's the fastest four-door car in the world, Dad you've got to have it, you've got to have it." I told him I wasn't interested, as I loved the Bentley I already had. Still, he managed to persuade me to visit the garage and take a look at the car. I made a mistake that day and swapped my beautiful electric blue Bentley for the Flying Spur. The very second I handed over the key I regretted it and I never did really enjoy that Flying Spur. It might have been the fastest four-door car in the world but I was never happy with it.

I stuck with it for one year however but by 2007 I decided I didn't want to drive it anymore and I was really going to do something for myself. I was invited to a Bentley convention at a private golf club in Cheshire where I rubbed shoulders with top footballers such as Manchester United's Ryan Giggs and the former Blackburn, now Tottenham Hotspur goalkeeper Brad Friedel. In fact Brad Friedel believed he knew me, which he didn't as I had never met him before. He walked over to me, shook my hand and said, "How are you doing, I haven't seen you for a while." He soon realised he didn't actually have a clue who I was, but it was an amusing situation which Brad himself found funny. He asked all about what I did and seemed interested. I then ended up speaking with Ryan Giggs and I found him a genuine, down to earth, nice guy. If I didn't know who he was I would have just presumed he was a regular guy – he didn't act any differently to the man in the street, there was no superstar aura around him at all.

We were at the convention because it was the launch of the GTC, the convertible.

It was the first time it had been launched in Britain and I said, "Are you going to get one then Ryan?"

"Actually yes," he replied, "I'm going to get one for my wife, I've put my name down for one."

"That's lovely that," I said. "I wish I could just buy one for my wife."

I must admit I found the night a little strange as it was so elitist. It seems a touch inappropriate to be in the same privileged bracket as Premier league footballers when I came from a little terraced house with five kids and three of those tucked up in a tiny room in bunk beds. Here I was in a truly superstar environment where everything was fancy and expensive, it was a tad unusual, though very enjoyable. Having said that, I had been used to working alongside well known TV presenters such as Michaela Strachan and Philippa Forrester and many more, even having dinner with them – for behind the scene purposes, nothing romantic!

In my eyes I didn't feel star struck, just highly aware of my roots. But it occurred to me that the reality is if you work hard enough you can get anywhere. The footballers put as much physical effort in as I had to get to where they are so perhaps in a way we were on a par with each other. Either way I eschewed my humble roots regardless and thought to myself, if Ryan Giggs can buy a GTC then so can I, so I put my name down for one.

I should have had to wait for the car for around eighteen months for them to completely customise the vehicle though my new friend Jan managed to have a car ready for me within a year. The process for having your car custom made is very special. I had to go into the Bentley garage and sit in to design the car in every possible aspect. The basic design remains but the extra design features are customised: the colour of the steering wheel, colour of the trim, the leather, the wood interiors, the gear sticks, the pedals. You could choose whether you had TV screens in the car, or an automatic opening boot. Everything is on screen and when you decide they press a button and start to manufacture the car to your specs. The car was a brand; spanking new Bentley GCT straight off the production line and it became my baby.

In August 2007 I received the car personally delivered and ever since then I have been in love with it, I cannot see myself ever selling it. I know the effort that went into producing the car. It does still seem at odds with David Gill the zoo owner and conservationist but everybody has to have a little bit of something that's different in their lives and you have got to enjoy your life. Whereas in the Ferrari I felt ill at ease, I have never had the same feeling in the Bentley.

There is perhaps even more of an allure to the public when you drive around in a Bentley. It catches a different kind of eye than the Ferrari; it is of a higher class than a Ferrari in many ways – more for a discerning motorist. It is a dream to own one and was certainly not something I could have imagined when I was first starting out. My first car was a Ford escort, which blew up. Now I have a Bentley with a 6-litre W12 engine, 550 hp, it is luxury at its absolute highest level. I do feel like I have come somewhere after a long journey. It may be more powerful than a Ferrari and even more elitist but I don't feel that way when I am driving. It is comfortable despite its immense power and somehow I feel I've earned the right to own one through sheer hard work and dedication.

348

Chapter 30
Giraffes, African deserts and a Madagascan Adventure

In July and August of 2005 I remained in England working at South Lakes Wild Animal Park. I had had some unforgettable experiences travelling the world but felt I should stay at home for the busiest time of the year, the summer months.

In September each year there is a conference for the members of the European Zoo Association EAZA, in 2005 it was held in Kolmarden in Sweden, in previous years in Holland, Germany, France, Belgium and Denmark. Kolmarden is a beautiful place on the coast line of south Eastern Sweden, it is miles from anywhere and has a wonderful zoo. The conferences are hard work with sessions and meetings all day long for 5 or 6 days they discuss breeding programmes, conservation issues and strategies as well as training, new science and technologies. It was attending the conference in Alphen aan den Rijn in 1997 that really set me off on my conservation road for ex situ programmes, that being animals in captivity. I took on the European Studbook for Lar Gibbons, the European Breeding Programme for Geoffroy's Cat and the European studbooks for 7 kangaroo species. I really enjoyed the social aspects of meeting all the other zoo directors and owners from all over Europe from the far east of Russia to Portugal and everywhere in between. The highlight of the conference social calendar was the grand dinner and entertainment and it was at Kolmarden in 2005 where the social side suddenly was taken into another realm. We were taken by bus to Stockholm where we entered a huge building that was in the past an industrial factory site on a grand scale, a cavernous but warm place for a formal dinner for nearly 400 people. The dinner was nothing special but the entertainment after was exceptional. On the huge stage there appeared ghosts from the past in young versions of ABBA the group that was so huge throughout my childhood. From the moment they struck up they had the audience captivated and dancing, it was just like the real ABBA in every way possible the sound, the looks and the atmosphere. The night was very special and will always be etched on my memory, but not just for this musical extravaganza but what followed also. We left the venue very late by bus to travel down the coast to our accommodations. My "room" was actually over five miles from the Zoo and conference venue and along with a few others we had been put in log cabins in a forest and small local hotel. Mine was a cabin set in forest by the coast a really beautiful setting. I had taken two other staff for the conference as was usual and they had made friends with other attendees and decided they were going to make a night of it and go back to the conference hotel and finish the early hours dancing and living it up. I decided to have a drink with a few friends from Holland and then walk from their small hotel to my cabin in the forest about a mile away. The night was very cold, frost was in the air and I had a light silk shirt and trousers on and nothing else, so getting home to the cabin was brisk and direct. On arrival I suddenly remembered that I had asked the others to hold my key in their bag at the dinner. Now , then I had a problem, on my own, in a forest, minus temperatures and with only a silk shirt on , no phone and nowhere to be found to shelter from the very cold wind at 2 am in the morning. This is where the only person you can get angry with is yourself, although it did seem easy to get annoyed at the others who had made that decision to go to the other hotel. I did manage to find an emergency phone down in the central part of the site, but as it was off season it wasn't manned and only in Swedish anyway. The cold set in and I decided to have a good check round all the cabins and building for any shelter at all, eventually I found a truck cab that was open, I climbed in and moved the clutter from the seats and sat, freezing, but thankfully now out of the wind and damp night air. By this time the cold had got right through me and I was in pain from it. I fell to sleep with the pure tiredness and cold. I was woken in the morning by the sound of talking and saw it was the other two returning, they had not even realised that they had my key and been oblivious to my plight whilst they danced and chatted all night. I let fly at them both for leaving me like this, they looked at me in shock and disbelief but within minutes we were all laughing at the whole thing, I can assure you it wasn't funny at the time, but in hindsight I had to admit it was all my own fault. The rest of the conference was really enjoyable but I made sure my key was with me at all times !

By the time October 2005 rolled around I was ready for a new challenge. Pierre and I travelled to Niger (pronounced Ni-jher) in West Africa. It is an exceedingly poor country, one of the poorest in the world. There is a lack of infrastructure, with a poor state of education and health care. The climate in Niger is intense with temperatures often reaching over 40 degrees Celsius. On average the country only sees just over five inches of rain a year and this often comes in just a one or two month period.

Despite the hostile landscape and ongoing military occupation the people of Niger are warm, friendly and, surprisingly, happy. Niger was my first experience in a sub-Saharan country. It was an experience that has changed my life.

Pierre had been involved for a while with the ASGN (Association to Safeguard the Giraffes of Niger). Pierre wanted to do more and the whole idea intrigued me too. We discovered that the number of giraffes in the whole of West Africa had declined phenomenally in the modern age and there were actually only 41 giraffes known to exist in the region. There is a part of Africa which sticks out from the main body of Africa and in the entire of that Western section there were just 41 of the magnificent creatures, it was quite unbelievable. At their peak there were thousands of giraffes all over the west.

Those that were left were all confined to a small part south east of the city of Niamey, the capital of Niger. We decided we would go out there to see how the organisation was performing. Pierre and I had our partnership in Peru, as well as Colombia and he wanted me onboard for Niger, together we seemed to be making real strides.

Niger is both the hottest and the poorest country I have ever been to. Try and picture the likes of Heathrow airport with its multitude of different corridors, rooms and levels. Everything is high quality with flashing lights and signs. In contrast Niger airport features signs which are all hand written in shortened pencils: 'Customs' or 'Passports Here'. It is so primitive, there were no computers – everything is just on scraps of paper which they stamp. Niger is like this even today; the whole country is in turmoil – they are an unbelievably poor people. We moved from the airport to the Catholic Mission in Niamey, a very basic refuge station. We then went out into the field, which is quite a long drive out to a place called Kanary where we first caught a glimpse of the giraffes. Niger was then the poorest country in the world. Today it still ranks in the top ten though in reality the difference in the poorest African nations is fairly interchangeable.

The people in Niger were living the most basic, poverty gripped lives that I have ever seen in my life. These houses were nothing but little mud huts. Their residents had to walk miles for water, through virtual desert. They were attempting to grow millet as a crop but on sand dunes it was near impossible; it was quite staggering and sad to see. There was one tarmac road that went between the two cities of Niamey and the next city which was much further along and it was here that the giraffes lived. It was a wonderful sight to see. I had seen them in their natural habitat in South Africa but I was truly moved to see the rare group of specialist desert giraffes that existed in Niger.

I then discovered the reasons why the giraffe had become so rare in the region. The villagers reacted because they believed the giraffes ate their crops. They pushed them away or they killed them, and even ate them. The villagers were also cutting down trees for fire wood and in order to cook. For the giraffes this was bad news as there was less for them to eat. At the time in Niger, there was also a very dangerous famine.

Pierre and I had taken some food with us to give to the locals. We presented the famine ravaged families with the food which consisted of bags of millet. They did not react like I expected. When viewed on television, as and when aid or food is handed out to poor peoples they are always shown to be scrambling and fighting over the bags – screaming and reaching for the food. The people of Niger had a great dignity. They queued patiently, no one argued and everyone was smiling, despite the fact that they were starving.

We moved onto a number of different small villages and I was struck by how well dressed the people were. In particular the Puerl tribe dressed immaculately. They lived in mud huts in the desert, but brushed the sand level and clean every day. They wore beautiful bright colours. They were so proud and happy with their homes and their ability to always look their best. I wondered how they could be so happy. They had nothing. It was millet for breakfast, dinner and tea. If they were lucky they managed to catch a grasshopper and eat that but somehow this couldn't bring them down.

I started to really think about everything I could do for the people who live in these scenarios. At a full gathering of the village one evening I asked everyone I came into contact with, from the whole tribe up to and including the chief: "What are your dreams? What are your thoughts? What do you want from life?"

Every single person gave the same answer: fresh water. It struck me like a ten-ton hammer. In the UK people moan about everything they possibly can, from the weather to the health service. We have the NHS, which is one of the best health services in the world, yet people whinge about everything that goes wrong.

These people have absolutely nothing, they have never seen a doctor ever, there are no nurses, no hospitals, nothing. If you get something wrong with you, you die. Their only want or need was something that we take utterly for granted. We flush it down the toilet like its going out of fashion and yet these people have to walk two kilometres each day, every morning and every night, just to get water that isn't fresh but filthy because it came from the river bottom. Yet they were happy.

I was staggered by it all and so impressed that I promised them I would provide them with fresh water and build them a well. Suddenly I was lifted up and carried around the village above their heads while they were doing a dance and singing. It did briefly occur to me that I might get placed on top of a pole and eaten or something but they were treating me like a king because they were so happy. Just £3000 and these people could have fresh water. Suddenly a village of 200 people had fresh water for the first time in their history.

We moved into other villages and did the same thing. We also brought them grinders to enable them to grind the millet properly. It needed to be ground as fine as possible because they were eating grain that was too thick and couldn't be digested properly which was bad enough for adults, but a big problem for young children.

The people were immensely grateful and were also taught quite simple procedures that they knew nothing about. We taught them that any water spilled from the well could be used for the garden where they could grow tomatoes. We taught them how they could vary their diet by using waste so washing up water could be disposed of in the garden to be put to use instead of just being thrown away. Niger is a place Pierre visits far more often than I do given they speak French there so he became chief communicator for the two of us.

Since we first made our presence known in Niger the numbers of giraffes have risen to 250 in the area. Since we prevented the local people from killing giraffes, every single one that has been born has survived. Those that have been born are then able to reproduce themselves after three years. The numbers are therefore slowly but constantly rising. It is wonderful to see. On a personal level the experience in Niger changed me exponentially. I returned from the trip a completely different person. On a general, day to day level I felt that I had much more empathy for other people, the reason being that I had just spent time in a country where the residents had absolutely nothing. On top of this it made me feel as if perhaps I had too much – I didn't need all the things I had surely? How could these people live without anything that we all hold so dear. It was refreshing to experience time in an area where modern conveniences did not exist and life came down to its very basics – humanity and compassion. I suppose when you grow up with nothing , expect nothing and have no advertising telling you that your life is incomplete without their products you do have a chance to see the most important and basic issues of life , that being love and community. Something I fear we have lost completely in the west due to the focus on consumerism and Governments encouraging everyone to expect far more from life in the way of possessions and materialistic things than is necessary.

On arrival back from Niger, I felt decidedly ill, I went to bed feeling very tired and drained, it wasn't long before I had to make a fast visit to the toilet with the runs, however this was more than that, I lost so much fluid in a few hours I collapsed in total weakness just managing to get to the telephone and call the hospital as it was late at night. I had clearly picked up a very serious bug that just ripped my body apart in its need to reproduce in my intestine. I wasn't sick but the effect was to confine me to bed for a while. The antibiotics and rehydration treatments all got to grip within a day or so, but I had a real scare and had it highlighted to me that the bugs hanging around such countries were far more virulent to us westerners than I had ever thought. Personal hygiene of washing hands before any food , never touching your face and the unknown of trying to source food that was prepared correctly became a feature of my trips after this , however, the damage done to my stomach and intestines was obvious and created a weakness that affects me to this day. It is very rare now that when travelling to the third world that I do not suffer badly with stomach or intestinal problems, a recent trip to Madagascar was the first time in years that I wasn't sick or had stomach issues. I travel now with a full treatment and recovery pack for dehydration and loss of bodily fluids, it is an essential !

After Niger, Pierre and I went on to Madagascar, clocking up a few extra air miles. 2005 had already been an incredible year. Pierre had been working to set up a Non Governmental Organisation (NGO) in Maroantsetra which is situated in the far North East of Madagascar. A tropical place with lush forests and a wet humid environment for much of the year. The idea was to visit the project and make progress with its organisation and objectives and then have a fact finding tour round most of the huge dramatic and unique island. For the "holiday" part of the trip we were lucky enough to be looked after by a fellow called Monsieur Jean de Heaulme, who was from the colonial times when the French colonised and took over the country he owned vast swathes of land that were cleared for Sisal plantations, a cactus looking plant that is used for its fibres to create the backings for carpets among many other uses. Over the years the family had become extremely wealthy. He took us to his own private island at the foot of Madagascar. He had his own private chef who he took everywhere with him – the food he made was utterly divine.

We visited a very famous destination for lemurs, Berenty, in the south of the country. This was owned by Jean de Heaulme. We stayed at his sister's house; it was an absolutely idyllic place. We visited Antananarivo, the capital on the east side of Madagascar, and we met up with Henry de Heaulme, Jean's son. We were asked if we could help Henry to develop a conservation project on some land in a very dry part in the west of the island. We travelled in two vehicles; a Toyota Land Cruiser and Mazda pick up truck from Henry's home in Antananarivo down to Morondav. We were travelling on one of the very few passable roads which reached cross country. All in all it was a three-day drive. We went through enormous swathes of nothingness, mountains and just barren desert. When we stopped for our overnight stay it suddenly struck me how cold the central high country was, something I did not expect. We were so high up in the mountains it was a distinctly chilly night.

The next day we set off and Henry, who was driving, became sick. He started sweating, he had to stop and get out to throw up. He suffered from malaria and was having a particularly nasty malaria attack. It was so bad in fact that I was scared he was going to die. We stopped the car for a while to see if he would recover but in fact it was worsening, he was almost unconscious.

Given how far across country we were already we had to keep going. Henry was stretched out on the floor in the back of the Land Cruiser with his wife by his side. There was a problem with the vehicle and it got decidedly worse, I was the one driving but suddenly the vehicle would not go into drive, the engine was spinning and the car wouldn't go anywhere. It was the first time I had ever driven a left-hand drive vehicle and it was when I was in the middle of nowhere in Madagascar with a man in the back who I thought was about to die, in desperate need of medical attention. It was starting to go dark and the car just would not move.

Luckily our party featured another vehicle, the one with Pierre and his wife as well as another chap from France, Jean Marc Lernoud. We found a very thin piece of rope in the car which was hardly the stuff of towrope fantasies but we managed to tie the pick up to the Land Cruiser. When we set off there was quite a long distance of rope and driving like that was something I had never done before, especially in these circumstances.

Suddenly the road ended and we were on sand, just endless desert. It was getting darker and I was driving over mini dunes. Given the rough terrain I was almost hitting the pick up in front of me which meant I had to keep slamming the brakes. Each time I did this the rope got a little shorter so I was edging ever closer to the vehicle in front.

Henry was still very ill in the back and we were all panicking, we drove all night till about 2am in order to get to the town and safety. Every time I misjudged the ground beneath I almost hit the pick up, though I somehow managed to stave off what would have been an even bigger nightmare. Somehow the rope whittled down to just about a metre long. It was all I could do to keep my eyes stringently focused on the pick up, desperate not to hit it but coming ever closer to doing so.

I had the most horrendous night. I was so tired and greatly stressed. Eventually we reached a village on the coast and found somewhere to sleep. I was so tired I couldn't even talk to people and they were patting me on the back saying, "Well done, well done!" By the next day Henry had thankfully recovered, though he still wasn't in the greatest shape. The village we were in was exceedingly primitive. I think the local garage might have been lucky to have a hammer and a spanner in their workshop. The chap in the garage seemed undeterred by this equipment deficiency however and causally took the differential apart, fiddled with the insides, added something and put it back together again. It worked! At least, it worked enough to get us to our next destination where we would need to get it properly repaired. This man had a garage with almost nothing in it and somehow he fixed our car, I could not believe it, but I was immensely grateful. The next day after sleeping in a mosquito infested room that drove me mad all night we had to travel to Analabe north of Morondava to the plantation of sisal and broken forest that was being looked at for a eco tourism project to protect amongst many other species lemurs, sifakas and the Fossa, the only large predator on the island. We had limited space because the Land Cruiser had been left in Morondava so I volunteered to stay on top of the truck back that was full of equipment, fuel and food for our trip. Whilst at the time it seemed like a wonderfully wild idea to be out in the fresh air taking in the sounds and smells of Western Madagascar, I had not bargained on the vicious strength of the mid day sun and the dryness and heat of the sandy roads and surrounding fields. The heat was intense, the sun was draining and the vehicle relentlessly drove on and on deeper into the dry landscape. I just hung on as the truck threw itself all over to stay on the rutted dust road. In these conditions sun block just has no effect, the sun burnt me to a cinder, the power must have seeped deep into my body and as we arrived at Analabe I virtually fell off the truck, not knowing where I was and suffering from heat stroke. This condition is awful , I have had it twice in my life and both times it put me through hell , it took a full day to get my feet again and feel up to eating and drinking a day of severe uncertainty so far from home. The day after this our group of Pierre, Elisa, Henry and his wife along with myself went out for a drive to survey the region, it was another scorching hot day and this time I made sure I was totally covered and protected from the sun. However whilst driving through a patch of dry forest we hit a fallen tree that had dropped right across our only route. Henry and Pierre decided to go back and get a chain saw to clear the road and dropped Elisa myself and Henry's wife so we could explore the forest and surrounding area on foot whilst they made the journey back which we expected to be about an hour.

The hour came and went, then another, then another. Real concern stepped in as we had little water, it was searingly hot we had no food and the day was getting late. We had a short little conference and made a decision to start walking back to Analabe through the forest. It was so difficult to walk in the hot loose sand following the road we had come along, hoping that when they returned, and we had no idea why they had not, that they would find us. The talk started to get difficult, both women started to think the worst about their husbands and why they had not returned hours before to collect us. I had to step in and stop the talk between them as they were not helping each other and we needed to keep confident and focused on walking out of the wilderness we were in. We passed snakes, chameleons, butterflies and a myriad of unique wildlife on the walk before suddenly around a group of trees the truck appeared in a cloud of dust and sand.

The relief was immense, the day was becoming dark and it was revealed that on the way back with the chain saw they had a major puncture that caused them to get stuck and they had to wait for a passing vehicle to take them to get it repaired before finally retuning to find us along the same long dry road. Another day, another adventure, another night to reflect on what might have been and what thankfully we had avoided. The sifakas and lemurs in that region were still doing well but in small islands of forest left after cultivation. This is the problem for most animals in this world today they are now surrounded by people and have nowhere to go and are trapped awaiting the fate of localised extinction.

The main reason for visiting Madagascar however was not to indulge, but to organise and manage our Lemur Conservation project near Maroantsetra in the north east of Madagascar. There we worked with a group of locals who were educating the villagers about conserving their forests and wildlife. This was another project where water played a real driving role in the conservation of wildlife. We helped villages to construct small dams on streams to irrigate fields close to their villages in order to grow rice effectively and efficiently. The traditional methods were to slash and burn forest and grow one low yielding crop of rice before doing the same again, destroying forest and habitat for the lemurs. They also hunted and killed lemurs for food and it was our intention to get them farming ducks and chickens in order to stop killing wild animals.

The first Lemur Festival of what has become an annual event took place whilst we were there and many thousands of villagers attended from far and wide, many walking for days to get there.

The aim to provide free loud music, dancing and fun and in between giving messages of conservation to all that attend. The highlight being a great feast where we provide great barrels of rice and a soup made from a number of cows provided by us for the occasion. This concept of a free meal and entertainment based on taking in lemur and forest protection messages has been a great success and local villages now vie with each other for the honour of hosting the annual Lemur festival. It was at this first festival I met up with Miranda Richardson the actress who has appeared in such films as Harry Potter, she was doing a documentary on Aye Ayes and lemurs and the festival and our involvement was a part of the documentary in the series "Last chance to save". The feeling of humility and sense of a need to help overwhelmed me in 2005, the poverty I saw and lived amongst was simply the most influential impact I have ever felt and it changed my whole view of my own life.

The Madagascar project was in its infancy and over the years has become a huge influence in the region.

2005 saw me visit a huge variety of countries and destinations: Peru, Colombia, Indonesia, Africa, Madagascar, I felt like I had discovered the world.

In my personal life I didn't know what the hell I was doing. In early 2006, though the issues with Caroline were still prevalent and I was still in love with her I started Internet dating. It was in this haze of cluttered thinking that I made one of the biggest mistakes of my life.

PART THREE

Chapter 31
Big mistakes, internet friends
and more mistakes

In April of 2006 I made a serious error of judgement, a mistake of such gigantic proportions that it was the most expensive error both emotionally and financially I have ever made. Caroline was impossible to deal with, her emotions were up and down in minutes. I never knew where I stood and Hari became the ball in the middle. I felt I needed help to protect Hari's time with me so I went to the courts. I had spoken with my solicitor and, naturally, his advice was to go to court – it seemed logical enough.

I now have to tell you the reader that many issues I would have liked to have made comment on cannot be mentioned here, because the rules surrounding Court Cases in the Family Court in England and Wales prevent the publication of details of contents or proceedings in the public arena, it is said to protect children from harm. I have written the section to conform to that ideal and confined myself to the opinions, effects and emotions surrounding my experiences but sadly in effect it also protects the people involved in the Family Law system and prevents the reporting of the failures of the people who decide the futures and fates of children in broken families in this country. These are my opinions of the hell I have experienced at the hands of the Family Court system, the legal system and the inadequacy of the Social Services that I have been forced to deal with. It is not meant to be in a vindictive or revengeful way, but in an objective and helpful way to anyone reading, because quite simply, I would not wish what has happened to me, to happen to anyone else and if I can help to prevent any family from entering the Courts system and find a solution for themselves then I feel I will have saved a family and children in particular from potential disaster and given them hope of a better future.

I see now in retrospect however that from the start the solicitor's advice was geared towards me spending my money in becoming embroiled in a legal situation which should not have even existed.

I should never have listened, I should never have done it, it was a huge and costly error in every aspect of the word and as I already stated by far the most devastating mistake I have made in my life.

It started a court battle which has raged for five years. A court case that during that time has only ever produced one outcome – complete unhappiness – though there is a bonus for the lawyers – money. They don't want to settle anything. This is the point in my life where I allowed my stupidity to take this route and have regretted it ever since because from that moment on the Legal system took hold of our lives our children and took away any chance of happiness or family life.

I blame myself for that decision, without question it is my fault. I should never have taken it to a Court. I should have treated Caroline better in the first place. I should have recognised the love that she had, I should have opened my mind, I should have stopped, I should have ceased being the stupid idiot who thought there might be something better. I do think I should have gone back there, should have seen the unbelievable depth of love that she had for me. I was blind, I was stupid, I was an idiot. I couldn't reciprocate the love she had for me. Yet, her anger, vindictive approach and inability to talk made it happen.

It was all a little accidental how I clicked onto a dating website, a pop up ad at the side of my messenger application, I thought it might be a bit of a laugh and it seemed appealing at the time. In the end it became a little addictive. There seemed, on the surface, to be so many people with similar thought processes to mine, similar interests and pretty women too. In the end I went on around fifteen dates with various ladies. A couple moved onto a second date but all I seemed to talk about was Caroline, which would probably go down as a dating 'don't'.

One thing in my mind was that I felt guilty for even being on the date so it ended up being all I could talk about. Several of the ladies said to me at the end of the night, "Do you know something, you should be with her because that's all you talk about!" It was true; I should have been with her. That's why it all went wrong. I met some good people through the dating site, though I also realised straight away, that I would never want to see certain people again as well. The whole dating game was a failure and it was always destined to be so seeing as I loved Caroline. Yet the relationship was dysfunctional and her anger got worse.

In 2006 I didn't stop travelling or yearning to discover more. I actually stopped for breath to have a holiday in July 2006 though it still involved travelling and animals. I took Ben and Hari with me to Durban in South Africa, from where we drove north to the Bonamanzi Game Reserve. From here we drove every day into the Hluhluwe-Umfolozi Game Reserve where we saw rhinos and elephants in their natural splendour. It was a wonderfully relaxing trip and one which Hari enjoyed to the full. He became a keen animal spotter throughout his time in the bush, his favourite was the zebra.

Perhaps the relaxing holiday spurred me on to revisit Peru. I didn't want to be beaten by my previous experience there so I returned to Tambopata in October 2006. This time Amy took her turn to travel with Hari and I. I didn't want to be frightened by something that I knew logically was a complete one off event – nature wasn't going to get another one over on me. I revisited the TRC and also made sure to revisit the parrots. We went early in the morning in order to see the birds at their very best because at that time there was beautiful weather in Tambopata. I just so happened to be visiting on the best day of the year for parrot numbers – they informed me in fact that they had never seen so many. There were thousands of brightly coloured and very loud macaws, Amazon parrots and more, a sight I will probably never see again. We then visited Chaparri. This trip was to become, along with Sumatra, the backbone of my travel, and an annual event.

What I did not realise at the time was that all my dedication to conservation and my constant need for travel was jeopardising my family life.

2006 saw Caroline becoming ever more worried about our future together. I was doubtless not helping matters by flying all over the world and showing that I would always want time with Hari, even if Caroline and I never made it together. At South Lakes Wild Animal Park the new restaurant was being built, and the grounds were being expanded as visitor numbers were still on the increase.

It is clear in hindsight that I had replaced one chaotic, time draining activity, i.e. Australia, with another. This was to devote all my waking energy to working on the development of South Lakes as well as travelling here there and everywhere, working in conservation and taking in the occasional holiday. In truth however I never really switched off. My mind was so full but I wanted it that way. I wanted the horror of Australia to disappear and the only way I could see myself dispersing this incredible disappointment was to remain busy. I should have devoted more time to Caroline and Hari. It was one thing taking him away with me but what he could have done with was time with his dad in the UK. One of the rules I have learned about life is to put your woman first because if you do that your children and your life will come with it. If however you put your woman second or third then you are always going to be in trouble. In a legal sense Caroline and I were still in an ongoing dispute over our family situation because once the Family Law system gets hold they just don't seem to ever let go even when you want them too.

I see the reality now but I didn't see it then. The work that I was doing, especially within conservation, was actually getting in the way of my family. It is easy looking back but at the time it is so hard to understand why other people cannot understand you. At the time I presumed I would receive more respect, I hoped for a little tolerance. I felt that I was trying to save lives in Niger, trying to save Howler monkeys in Colombia, trying to protect giraffes in

West Africa, trying to save lemurs in Madagascar, trying to build dams for rice fields. As I saw it I was making a difference to thousands of lives and making their world a better, safer place to live. In the village in Niger I helped provide water wells that gave fresh water to 20,000 people. I also provided the same wells for everyone in the wider local area. I expected the people who were close to me to see what I was doing and appreciate it, if not acknowledge it. But the truth of the matter is all those people could see is that time which could have been spent with them was being donated to others. In a strange parallel it was a similar situation to the one I had suffered with my own father, the difference being I had the love and shared it with my children but my time was being stretched.

Thankfully, even at the time I was aware of this potential hazard and when I was in England I spent as much time with Hari as I physically could, he lived with me for half the week at the zoo when I was in the country. I tried to involve him as often as possible and make sure that we did lots of little things together as father and son, perhaps this was even a reason that I often wanted to be alone with him instead of including Caroline as well. From a business perspective it wasn't the smartest move to keep Caroline away from the park. She had phenomenal talent and could and should have been allowed to continue putting it to good use in my business. It is something I deeply regret in not allowing her back or creating the ability for her return.

I struggled with uncertainty at the time, to my mind, if we were having problems then perhaps there was someone better suited to me out in the big wide world. I was often attracted to other women, or at least I could acknowledge their attractiveness, but I did not feel a magnetic pull to spend the rest of my life with them and yet Caroline was an 'angry' person and that ruined the peace.

When I was in the process of discovering Internet dating I did meet a wonderful lady of another kind, which perhaps was destiny's reason for me going through such a thankless task. I came across a lady named Linda Hill. Linda was interested in animals and conservation. She lived in Madison, Connecticut, USA a sea town in New England in quite an affluent area. Her passion was wildlife and nature. She had worked for *Rolling Stone* magazine as a writer interviewing all kinds of famous musicians, from Aerosmith to Elton John. She then moved on to work at a well known book store in her local town where she often was charged with bringing in various famous authors for book signings and so on.

Though everything between Linda and I was completely 'electronic' I didn't help myself by what I did next, especially baring in mind Caroline's continuing jealousy. Given I wear my heart on my sleeve Caroline knew I was becoming close to Linda. Linda and I had been enjoying regular Internet and telephone contact and after several weeks of enjoying each other's company, she invited me to meet her. It was suddenly quite a big issue that we lived so many miles away from each other. It wasn't as if I could pop round the corner and have a cup of tea.

"Why don't you come to New York?" Linda suggested. "I used to work in New York, it's two hours from my home. Come over, meet the family, see the place I live and we'll see if we like each other."

Though it was quite a distance, after all the travelling I had done in recent months, it didn't seem like a big stretch to catch a plane to the east coast of America. I had a free weekend coming up as I had spent the weekend before with Hari, so I packed a bag and headed from Manchester to New York on March 2, 2006.

Linda was a year younger than me and looked good for her age. In fact it crossed my mind that she looked quite a lot better in person than on her photos, they didn't do her justice. Normally with Internet dating, as I was by now more than aware, the photos tend to make people look a damn sight better than in person. With Linda it was the opposite. She had long blonde hair and was wearing a long black overcoat given it was snowing in New Jersey and minus twelve degrees. Though it was quite a thrill to go such a long way for what was something akin to a blind date, I felt somewhat embarrassed and a little out of my depth.

Yet I felt quickly relaxed and content in Linda's company, she was a wonderful, entertaining lady. We spent the day as tourists in New York before travelling up to her home in Madison. I met

Linda's daughter Kendal who was softly spoken and beautifully behaved, as well as her dog and a couple of cockatiels. The house was beautiful, the setting was exquisite, the town was stunning – I felt very at home. We went out for breakfast in the morning to the local coffee shop and it was traditional old time America, like something from *Happy Days*. I met with Linda's parents and had a meal with them. The whole trip was idyllic. Yet, as lovely as Linda was, as much as she was a successful, attractive woman, I could not forget Caroline.

I have remained friends with Linda until very recently when she told me she was getting married and we felt it better to end the friendship on a happy note. She is now quite happy to impart that she knew from the first few minutes of talking to me that I was in love with another woman. Caroline was all I talked about. I still returned to New York many times in the next months. We went straight to Madison and spent time together again, walking on the beach, sharing our lives and meeting up with her extended family once again. The whole time all I talked about was Caroline.

Unfortunately I wasn't aware that I was doing it. It was like a knee-jerk reaction and an addiction, I could not help myself. She was on my mind so often that she entered into the conversation regularly. It was the same old realisation. I would meet a woman, find myself getting on with them very well, but they knew, as well as I did, that I had not let go of Caroline. The simple reality was that even when I came close to finding another woman they were so aware of my love for another that they would say, "You don't seem ready for this, you haven't let go of Caroline."

Linda herself did indeed marry and I truly hope she finds happiness. She is a good friend who I respect a great deal. Who knows, if things had been different perhaps we could have had a relationship, we had quite a lot in common. One of Linda's favourite places was Jackson Hole in Wyoming, not too far from my own little piece of heaven in Cody. We were good for each other but it could never progress beyond a friendship; Caroline's grip on me was ever pervasive. I have been back a few times to see Linda. If I was going through New York I always rang her and we met for lunch or coffee.

From the moment I was with Linda and her family in their town my whole idea of America improved from any negative pre-conceptions I might have had. New York wasn't really my kind of place but Madison, Connecticut struck a chord with me. Some of the time I was there I would go playing golf with her dad while she was working, and the true beauty of the real America hit me, the patriotism, the caring and the community and great fun people.

In October 2006 back at home I began work on a personal dream project – designing and constructing my own indoor swimming pool. It was like a positive beacon shining through all my personal difficulties. In just a year I finished the pool and the following October I swam in it for the first time. I worked on the pool constantly at the weekend and most evenings. I felt that it was the best building project I had ever completed and was extremely pleased with the results. It has become a special place for myself and my children. I had hoped when I built the pool that it would mean my children would come up the house more often; it was a true family project rather than just spoiling myself with a car. I also decided it would be something of an 'open' pool for other family and friends to come and swim in whenever they desired.

All through this time Caroline and I were still close and getting closer. I felt as if I was falling in love with her all over again, she looked so beautiful and it seemed as if all the difficulties had dissipated. We spent great time together and I felt as if maybe things had come back on track.

We were passionate together once again and were getting on as well as we ever had. I noticed she was still driving around in a battered, white Renault Clio car and I suggested we get her the car she had always wanted, a Toyota Rav 4. I told Caroline I wanted her to be safe and happy, so we travelled to Wigan to buy a model we had found on the Internet. It seemed like a big step forward in us reconnecting. On the January 20, 2007 however things were once again moving too quickly. Caroline told me she was pregnant again.

This caused a lot of strain in our relationship simply because we had not found an answer to all our issues and problems even though we loved each other. We ended up over the next months separating again and we certainly had an on / off relationship because of the pressures that we faced with the awful intervention of the court and family lawyers who just would not let go of us and stirred the pot constantly, turning us against each other at every chance.

When in England I often took Hari to school, on set days I would take him and pick him up. People had got to know me at the school and often asked me how things were going at the zoo. There was one woman who was always in line at the school at the same time, Alison Creary. At first I didn't notice her and didn't talk to her too much Alison's daughter Amy was in the same class as Hari so we often crossed paths. It began with a simple hello but I said hello to everyone. Hari had coincidentally been invited to Amy's birthday party in February of 2007 as were all her classmates and I took him there. I spotted Alison's husband and assumed they were happily married, and kept myself to myself eating small sausages and pineapple chunks. I often heard her in the school yard talking to people and then most of the mothers came with their children to the park for Hari's fifth birthday party, which was held there. I'd shared a cup of tea with Alison and her friends. There had been nothing untoward in our friendship, in fact that was all it was.

Much later into June Alison said she wanted some company but didn't want to come up to the zoo for some reason. So off we went for a drive in her car to a quaint little coffee shop in the southern part of the Lake District National Park. It was a nice afternoon but on the way back Alison was at pains to make sure no one in the Dalton area saw me in her car. At the time I did not know the reason for this, it seemed a little strange to me as we were just having a coffee as friends.

I continued to talk to Alison whenever I saw her at the school and eventually invited her to bring Amy and her other daughter Alicia up to South Lakes with her. Caroline and I were certainly in a true on and off relationship at the time.

I started to distance myself from Caroline despite her pregnancy. I was terrified of the consequences of having another child and not being in a loving, caring, marriage. We were as far from that as we could have been which was mainly due to the complete grip of the courts constantly producing tension and negativity via solicitors.

We told the lawyers and social workers involved: "We want to stop this now" but because of the aggressive, negative approach of profit making solicitors who rely on a case to be extracted as long as possible to make their income they wouldn't listen and neither did anyone else. Most of them in my experience are just so removed from everyday reality to understand that finding fault in a court is without doubt the worst possible way to find a long-term positive solution for children.

The court process for families is very sadly and damagingly based on causing people to find faults with each other and keep them at loggerheads full-time. It is their modus operandi. The Family court system was not designed to help people or children find solutions, all I have experienced is a need to win from lawyers who have a vested interest and this has to be the worst aspect of the system as the children are simply lost in the mêlée. When Caroline and I should have been co-operating and finding the best way of raising our family, the court system was driving us apart. The English Family Court system is adversarial in its roots, it is adept at ruining family life, totally destroying relationships and completely destroying the future of any children involved as the cost emotionally and financially of just trying to resolve issues is paralysing to ordinary people. An ordinary man in the street realistically has to just walk away from his children if the mother decides to take them as he has no chance whatsoever of finding the extortionate costs of legal representation and in my experience of representing myself that is not an option as I was treated as if I didn't exist!

Many times over the years we had opportunities to pull together and find a happy life and the whole thing was ruined by the fact we were forced, by the law, to go through court and turn against each other again, it all happens far too slowly and drags the emotional nightmare out over a very long time. If one side decides to fight rather than resolve it forces hell on the family.

To begin with I employed lawyers who were helpful and positive. This didn't seem to get me anywhere because Caroline had a lawyer who was negative and aggressive towards me and tried to rip me to pieces. So then I employed a lawyer who was aggressive but she was *so* aggressive she wanted to destroy Caroline. I *loved* Caroline, why would I want to destroy her? So, I had to sack her, I had to get another lawyer. I was going through lawyers all the time because I couldn't find one that was right and because the last thing on earth I wanted to do was destroy Caroline as a person. Yet it seemed any half decent lawyer would be looking to do exactly that. What I actually wanted was to find a positive way to love her and get stability in our lives. Nobody helped us to do that. From my experience of the court system, CAFCASS (The Children and Family Court Advisory and Support Service), lawyers, nobody wanted to help us find a way out. It was obvious to me that the people assigned to help children in cases have nowhere near enough time to find out the real situation so relied on the adversarial notes from biased lawyers on each side and possibly psychologists (who have shown to me that they are amongst the most arrogant and self important people I have come across as they feel they can assess a person's life, character and whole behaviour from a 2 hour interview in an alien office somewhere.). It is actually sickening to see how much weight is given to these frighteningly inaccurate reflections on a whole life by a person who claims to be able to write every word you say at the same time as you say it and still, concentrate and understand? No wonder the factual content is so often in question, I am not saying they get it all wrong, but what they miss is huge and sometimes miss the whole point even the major issues and men always be aware the male / female bias is staggeringly obvious in many of these people simply because it seems to be an accepted principle that men are aggressors and women victims, yet as many men will know that certainly is not true. Sadly accusations that are not reality are treated as fact and decisions are taken on unproven hearsay. I felt like there was no justice for anyone, particularly the children.

There is no help in the way of mediation or counselling. There is no help for people in that situation, only destruction of the family, finances and children's lives.

My advice don't go there and sit down and talk and find solutions for your families sake. Find compromise and balance, winning is resolving it amicably.

I was not only reliant on the legal system however. I tried myself to instigate some form of reconciliation between Caroline and I directly. I approached Caroline all the time. I wanted to talk to her, I wanted to resolve the problems so I would visit her and we would discuss the problems, sometimes we even came to an agreement. But then we would face a hearing at the court which was already in place – we would both have to make statements which were then influenced and procured by the lawyers and we were back on the same merry-go-round and the anger flowed from Caroline again.

I tried to point out that one really damaging issue was the court process was so long and drawn out itself was a contributing factor and was *making* us argue. I would say, "We make progress and then you keep bringing problems to us, reminding us of problems, then asking us questions about things we had resolved weeks ago. You bring it back again and you make it worse."

The problem stretches far beyond two adults unfortunately when there are children involved. But the system in my view is not designed to help children either in the long term as the real consequences are so far from the agenda. It seems to me the system is so pre occupied with the past events it has no way to observe and accept change, or a will to find solutions and accept a need for an objective positive view it is so wrapped up in "protection" it can actually inflict problems of a family that never existed before.

As time rolled on Caroline and I both wanted to walk away from the whole sorry situation but 'contempt of court' could have seen one or both of us go to prison.

It had been said by some that I was a controlling personality and therefore this was a bad thing for the family. I have to admit I was, I could never have developed the business and the charities without having a "controlling" aspect to my life. To be successful it needs control or the visions would be lost. I do not accept this makes a person a bad father? This would suggest that everyone with a controlling nature and there are millions of us are inherently bad parents a conclusion I would have to defend strongly as not being the case. However I would be the first to admit I had my issues, as outlined earlier in the book that had to change, my whole focus of my life needed adjustment but sadly I could not see that then, I now can take the responsibility for the things I have done wrong and the mistakes I have made, but I cannot change Caroline.

By the time I found the answers to our myriad of problems in my mind in 2008 it was too late. The "system" had taken control and was dictating absolutely everything to us.

I was sometimes made to feel like a criminal rather than a father desperate for help to find a solution.

The people working for CAFCASS have a multitude of families to see and attempt to 'repair'. Therefore they cannot by the simple laws of physics give the "required" attention or time to any one family. The system is not set up to achieve this. It is like having a problem child in a classroom full of 30 kids. They are unlikely to get the individual attention that they need in order to improve and blossom. Instead they will be left to go off the rails because no one has time to give them or show them they are important.

The CAFCASS people did not have time to really find out what the issues were, they merely scratched the surface and made quick, ultimately rushed decisions because the process dictates it.

I was made completely aware of just how busy they are and felt immediately how you are merely a number on their list. I did not feel that I was treated like a real person or made to feel as if you or your situation is important. I felt like we had been lumbered with a particularly bad CAFCASS employee. This person seemed to me to have the opinion that the mother was the only figure of importance in a child's life, that the father was insignificant. In the end I had to make a complaint about the person and I wasn't the only one. We seemed to be in agreement that this "social worker" was a big reason why things were getting worse and worse. Unfortunately by then it was too late. I wonder myself how many other families' lives might have been ruined by that person's ineptitude and attitude. What struck me was the fact we both were crying for help to resolve our problems and in my opinion all that ever was handed out was punishment, no assistance was ever offered to us.

My relationship with Alison Creary was developing during

August 2007. We spent simple, quality time together which made me feel as if I still had a somewhat normal family life. We would meet up at the weekend, with her two children and Hari, and we would walk around West Yorkshire and the Lake District. It was a refreshing experience after everything I was going through with the courts. Alison seemed to relax with me and as I learned more about her own troubled life it seemed that this was a positive development for her.

All we were doing was meeting up for walks in the country, which I thoroughly enjoyed.

Every time a court hearing was coming up I would feel immensely stressed and tense, it was always an appalling feeling and Alison brought relief from Caroline and negativity.

Chapter 32
Brazil and white water rafting

In June 2007 I attended the ALPZA (Latin American Zoo) conference, which was being held in Sao Paolo, Brazil. Sao Paolo is one of the biggest cities in the world and a quite amazing sight. It was immediately apparent flying in over the city to land that it was gigantic. Being the intrepid, experienced traveller that I was by now, I decided that Brazil was going to be very warm indeed. All I packed was shorts, t-shirts and thin shirts. It was freezing! Brazil gave me an instant surprise by being so cold and windy, I just hadn't expected it. Every night when I went out for social drinks in the bars – which were all open plan – with other delegates, I was shivering cold.

While I was catatonic with cold I had to find the Sao Paolo zoo in amongst the sprawling metropolis. I had landed on the opening day of the conference and after managing to find the zoo I was welcomed with open arms. Being so far away from home it was a great feeling to be recognised – which was a compliment after all my work with foreign associations – and acknowledged by everyone. I had been working on my Spanish and was able to follow it quite well during the conference. There were parts which were in the native Brazilian dialect of Portuguese, but mostly the speech was Spanish as it was a general South American conference.

About halfway through the afternoon a girl came in and I recognised her immediately as Carolina Sanin who was the educator at Zoologico de Santa Fe in Medellin. She also recognised me at once from our work with the Howler monkeys. Carolina didn't know anyone else at the conference so she sat with me. I soon realised just how beautiful Carolina was, both physically and mentally. We got on very well. We talked throughout the afternoon. I asked Carolina if she was staying in the same hotel as me.

She told me she was staying with her brother. The journey took her almost two hours to reach the conference but she was obviously doing this to save money. She had only received expenses for her flights from the zoo, not her accommodation.

I remarked that she would miss out a lot on the social activities that were so important during these kinds of conferences. Colombia's hospitality and events were by now legendary and I expected the same kind of South American hospitality whilst staying in Sao Paolo. I told her she would be crazy to miss out and that I would pay for her to stay in my hotel. I explained the work she was doing for us in Medellin was first-class and she could accept it as a reward for all her efforts. She managed to enjoy the conference properly, without having to worry about a four hour round trip to travel there every day.

After the conference I had planned on meeting a friend of mine, the director of the Santiago Zoo, Chile who was planning on holidaying at the Iguazu Waterfalls, which border Argentina and Brazil. The waterfall is one of the most amazing sights in the world – it is almost two miles wide and just under 300 feet high.

Myself, Carolina, Mauricio Fabry and his wife were invited to stay by the lady who owned Parque des Aves, a bird park situated at Iguazu Waterfalls. Ana Croukamp was of German origin and her husband came from the Isle of Man where they owned property. They had made their money from mining in Africa and they had bought a beautiful bird garden in Brazil for their retirement. From such tranquillity we were suddenly cloaked by a completely dark underbelly. The family were somewhat paranoid. There had been many kidnappings in the area in the past in order to demand ransom money, so security ringed their house, with a permanent armed guard. It seemed a very dangerous place to live but we enjoyed ourselves regardless.

The Iguazu waterfalls are often used in feature films, though always from the Brazilian side of the border. They are thoroughly spectacular but quite different when viewed from the Argentinean side. I would personally recommend it as one of the 'must see' places in the world.

We spent a few days in the Iguazu area and at one point; we went white water rafting down the river. It was one of the most raging torrents I had ever seen; in fact we were travelling down the river on one of the most difficult stretches that feature on the rafting scale. I had thought Sao Paolo was cold but the forest at Iguazu, whilst tropical; was very cold in the morning. The water of the river was much warmer than the air. I dove in with just a wet suit and padding for company. It was an amazing and privileged experience to sail down one of the largest, most violent rivers in the world. I was invited by the raft captain to jump in a float down the rapids for a while, I swallowed some water doing this and thought nothing of it. That night I flew back to Sao Paulo and then back to Paris and onto Manchester. I spent virtually all the flight of 10 hours in the toilet violently sick, I then worked out that the river that flows over Iguazu falls goes through a number of countries on its journey from the Rainforests of the Amazon to Argentina, with many millions of extremely poor people using it for a toilet, bath, washing machine etc etc, to swallow a drop of this concoction of chemicals , bacteria and viruses was "lethal" and attacked my defences with impunity and aggression. It was then that I wished they had TV in the toilet !

While I was in Brazil I met a young lady, Ana Faria, who was working for the nature department of the Brazilian Government. She was a very interesting, pleasant young woman. Over a period of five days I got to know Ana quite well. We were sharing a bottle of wine one night with Pierre and she told me that she had been saving for several years to go to Africa. It was her dream to see African wild animals in their natural environment.

But six months before she met me her mother, who lived in Rio de Janeiro, had been burgled and her entire house had been ransacked. She had been held at gunpoint and was left with nothing. It had been a nightmare for Ana who had given up all her savings in order to help her mother get back on her feet again. The poor girl had been devastated that she had lost her dream to travel to Africa.

I thought about this for quite a while and it really moved me how she had sacrificed so much for her mother, she had given up everything that she had wanted for her mother and I was truly moved by it. I felt immense compassion and said, "Me and my family are going to South Africa in July, would you like to come with us? I'll pay for you to come because that is a wonderful compassionate story. I don't want to see you lose your dream that you were looking forward to because some thug ruined everything. I want to do this for you." She was absolutely taken aback; she said she didn't know if she could accept my offer.

A few weeks later she contacted me by email and asked, "Is that offer still on? I've been thinking about it non-stop, is it true?"

I said, "Of course its true."

I made all the arrangements and met her at Heathrow airport where we flew onto Durban. Ana roomed with my daughter Amy, while I shared a room with Hari. It was a wonderful trip and Ana was so full of thanks and gratitude the whole time. We spent time driving around South Africa, looking at various game reserves and all the beaches. She and Amy got on very well; it was such a positive, enjoyable trip. It cost a lot of money but it was worth every penny to see her so happy – she was smiling the entire time. She was married the following year. We kept in touch for a while afterwards; though we sadly have lost touch since.

I had had an interesting summer in 2007. Travelling to Sumatra, South Africa and Brazil was wonderful but it might seem somewhat irresponsible as Caroline was heavily pregnant

I didn't know what to do with regards to Caroline and our unborn baby. I am sure Caroline resented me going all over the world enjoying myself. When I look back now I can see that I was selfish to do those things and I feel truly terrible about it. I wanted to go to the scans Caroline was going for during the pregnancy but I couldn't, and by the time she was due to give birth, I wanted to be present.

There were a lot of complications with the women in my life at this point. I still had a residual friendship with my first wife Alison. After my divorce from Shelley, Alison had been a friend of mine once more, even working at South Lakes for me as the shop and restaurant manager. Eventually I did make it known that it just wasn't right for her to still be working for me and that it gave the wrong impression but when it was Alison's 40th birthday, myself and the kids decided we would throw a surprise party for her. She was totally shocked by the gesture, so many of her friends and family travelled from miles around and Alison had a thoroughly great party in the zoo.

I took Alison Creary with me to the party which was probably not the best move as far as my relationship with Caroline was concerned. In fact it would turn out to be one of the deadliest moves I could have made.

Chapter 34
A deadly attempted murder

The night of my ex wife Alison's birthday party 17th August 2007; I had Alison Creary with me. It may have seemed to everyone at the bash that this was my new girlfriend and I was having an affair, cheating on Caroline. No doubt this was how Caroline interpreted the invite. To me however the motives seemed far more innocent. I was friends with Alison by now, I didn't think anything of inviting Alison to spend the night at my house. Given it was a party and many people were helping themselves to a little booze, Alison did the same – she had a liking for a drink. She had sent her kids to a sitter as was her usual habit when she wanted to go out and have a drink and was supposed to be driving home but I didn't want that after she had more than a drop of wine so I suggested she stay at my house. I wasn't quite aware at the time just how much Alison had been drinking but as it turned out, she had been turning to booze as solace for troubles in her marriage as many people were very aware.

She had split up with her husband in January of 2007 and she had been drinking to numb the pain. It was only afterwards that I was told by people how often and how much Alison would drink. She would, in fact, drink until completely unconscious. There were times where I had to literally carry her home because she was so drunk in front of others. I tried to get her to stop but the sad fact was Alison seemed to me to be dependent on alcohol and there seemed to be no way she would stop drinking. It was new phenomenon for me to deal with; I had never been around anyone who drank to excess since I was a 12 year old on the farm and had no real comprehension of what its implications were.

On the night of my ex-wife's party I knew little of Alison Creary's dependence on alcohol, I just presumed she had had a little too much to drink and I knew the right thing was for her to stay right where she was.

Hari had been worn out by the night's events; he was so excited with all the running around at the party. I thought it best if I settle him so I climbed up the stairs and into bed with him to help him get off to sleep. Hari's room was upstairs, he had a huge double bed and I thought he might have been a little disturbed on his own. As Hari fell asleep, so did I. Alison, slept in a downstairs bedroom of the house.

I awoke with a start, it was after 2am hearing a noise in the house as if someone was up in the kitchen. It occurred to me that perhaps Alison was getting herself a glass of water or something. I thought the noise might be because she had no idea where anything was; so I decided I would go down to see if she was okay.

I walked about three steps from the bed; just reaching the doorway of the bedroom. It was then I heard somebody coming up the stairs. I assumed it was Alison. As I turned the corner, thinking I was about to meet her, a very big, strong hand grabbed me by the neck. The person with the grip pinned me to the wall, obviously trying to strangle me. It was happening so fast I didn't have more than a second or two to think and the only explanation I could come up with was that I was being burgled.

I couldn't breathe, I couldn't say anything and then the man said, in absolutely no uncertain terms, "You're shagging my wife and you're going to die." He then plunged a knife straight into my neck. I felt it puncture my neck and felt the blood spurt out, it splattered onto the wooden laminate floor, I could almost see it. I could feel the knife enter my flesh and there was a dramatic heat which came from the feeling of my blood rising to the surface and then leaving my body.

I was in a complete state of panic but somehow I managed to push his hand away from my neck. I then held onto the left side of my neck with my hand. I knew I had to keep the blood from leaking to the point where I could bleed to death. I held that puncture tight, for dear life. Had I not done so I wouldn't be writing this now.

The man, who I had by now realised was Alison's husband, stabbed me again in the neck. This time I reacted more quickly and pushed him away instantly. He stumbled at the top of the stairs as I pushed past him, sliding in the pool of my own blood which covered the floor. I ran down the stairs, screaming in hope Alison would hear the commotion.

"It's your husband, it's your husband, he is trying to kill me!"

She had been asleep, in an alcohol coated fug. She came out of the downstairs bedroom completely bewildered by what was running towards her. She was stunned but started to shout at her ex-husband. In my mind, I thought I should go into the bedroom to protect her. He followed me into the bedroom, still white hot with rage. He had been carrying both a carving knife and a Stanley knife. For whatever reason he didn't actually use the carving knife on me.

He came towards me and punched me like a sledgehammer, straight in the face. Once again, he said, "You're shagging my wife and you're going to die." He lunged forward with the Stanley knife, aiming to stab me again. This time I ducked out of the way, and the knife just caught the side of my face. I lashed out at him and knocked the Stanley knife from his hand. It flew across the bedroom into a pile of clothes and he bent down trying to find it again.

By now Alison had called 999 and the police were on the other end of the line – though I didn't know it at the time. Her husband, who I now know as Richard Creary, started to scream at me, "You're going to die, you're going to die!" all of which was recorded by the police. I quickly determined that he wouldn't kill his own wife and the best thing for me to do was to get out of the house. I was dying. I knew I was dying. The blood was flowing from my neck like a waterfall; I had to hold it with a cobra-like grip.

As I was leaving the house, he started to hit Alison. I couldn't defend her. I had no choice but to keep hold of my neck. I also knew I had to go and get help quickly. I hadn't known at the time that Alison was on the phone to the police and the main thought I had was that Hari was still asleep upstairs. Richard Creary seemingly didn't know this or he could just as easily have stabbed Hari in bed.

I was terrified for Hari, it was the only thing on my mind. It had been bad timing as we were building the extension onto the house and there was no lock on the door leading to the extension.

I ran out of the house. I ran and ran. With a burst of adrenalin I jumped straight over the seven-and-a-half-foot gate at the entrance of the park, all the way across the car park and down the hill. I was still barefoot and bare-tousled as I ran all the way down the hill. I sped across the bridge in pitch darkness to the nearest place I could think of, which was Jack Dent's farm.

By now it was 2:30 in the morning. I'd been running across tarmac with bare feet and I was caked in blood from head to foot. I knew the lady of the house, Anne Johnson but this particular night her husband wasn't home. She must have been terrified to hear my fist, pounding like a jackhammer on the door. She could not have expected the sight of a half naked man covered in blood as she opened the door. As she opened it I collapsed on the floor. I had lost that much blood I couldn't hold on any more.

I was still semi-conscious so I spoke to Anne. I said, "He tried to kill me, tried to kill me, get the police please, Hari is up at the house." It was all I could do to try and save my son, not to mention Alison. Anne soon found out that the police were already on their way which was a great relief. She told me, "Hold tight, the ambulance will be here very soon. Keep the wound pressurised."

When the ambulance finally arrived I can clearly recall the paramedic saying to me, "Don't take your hand off there, do not take your hand off, don't lift it."

He calmly explained that he didn't want to even attempt to look at it, that it was best if we waited until I got to hospital before they examined the damage. Clearly, the paramedic didn't want my death on his conscience, surely mindful of the fact that if I let go half of my neck might implode.

The Police Inspector came into the back of the ambulance and calmed my fears, saying, "Don't worry Mr Gill, we've got him. Your little boy is alright and the lady is alright. Don't worry, we have got him, he is in our custody. He is no danger to you or to your family anymore." I then learned that Richard Creary had left Alison and my son at the house so that he could run after me to try and finish me off. The police had apprehended him half way down the hill.

Once in the hospital it became apparent that I had been quite lucky, though I had saved myself in part by keeping the pressure on the wound. When they finally released my hand from my neck I didn't even bleed, the immense pressure I had applied had made the wound bind itself. It appeared I was indeed very fortunate that my assailant had used the Stanley knife rather than the carving knife, as the position of the knife wound was just a quarter of an inch from my jugular vein. He had all intent to kill me; of that there is no doubt. His words said as much. Yet, somehow someone was looking out for me. Had he plunged the carving knife into my neck I would have been dead instantly.

Hari slept peacefully through the whole thing which was a great relief. During the whole clean up operation, which was taking place during the very early hours of the morning, a policeman kept guard outside Hari's bedroom. That way, if he had have woken up he would not have seen anything that was going on. It took many hours for them to clean up all the blood.

The worst part about the incident was the simple truth that I wasn't sleeping with Richard Creary's wife. She stayed over because we were at the party, which was the only reason, it was not even planned. She had had a bit to drink and stayed over with me, we weren't even in the same bedroom, never mind the same bed. He had followed her that night and found out where she was – putting two and two together and coming up with fifteen. Richard Creary had apparently been out drinking himself and his mates had been egging him on to come up and sort me out. There had been local rumours that his wife was having an affair with me and in an ill-conceived act he had come looking to restore his male pride.

I later learned from the evidence collected that during their fairly acrimonious separation, Alison had been placating her husband. She didn't tell him there was no chance of them getting back together, she had been somewhat pliant towards their potential future, mainly because she was scared of him as he was such a violent man. I didn't know this. He had numerous previous convictions for violence. He had beaten her up on several occasions, so she later said, but at the time I had known nothing of their violent companionship. In his mind he fully expected the two of them would get back together and somehow he had completely lost it when he believed she was sleeping with me. The incident made the national press, with the *Daily Mail* reporting that Creary had whinged, "He has a Bentley and a zoo, how can I compete with that?"

I soon learned that Richard Creary had not just stabbed me with intent to kill; he had also covered every single piece of my electrical equipment – sound system, video and television system, everything – with washing up liquid. It had seeped into every section of each electrical item and ruined the lot.

He had also stabbed two tyres of my brand new red Bentley, presumably to stop me driving away. In fact this was all he seemed to use the carving knife for, which was quite idiotic considering he could have scratched the vehicle to pieces and caused much more damage. Nevertheless, overall he caused over £3000 worth of damage to things I owned.

The main physical damage apart from the scars on my face that I suffered afterwards was severe injuries to my feet, I could barely walk. I had glass and stone buried deep in both feet, they were shredded and I wore a lot of plasters on them for many months to try and help them heal. I had run like there was no tomorrow so it was no wonder.

Richard Creary was taken into custody right away. He was sent to remand in Preston before the case came up a few months later. Once again the courts did me no favours. Creary was given the option of pleading to a lesser charge in order to guarantee a conviction. Instead of attempted murder, which is what he was arrested for and absolutely what he should have been charged with, he was found guilty of aggravated burglary. This could have still meant a life sentence. He would not admit attempted murder, this was despite the fact that the police had the very clear evidence on tape that he purposefully told me he was going to kill me. Coupled with the blood loss from so close to my jugular vein, I am not so sure what more evidence they would need for attempted murder.

I learned that in order to secure a conviction of such a grave offence, the evidence has to be pre-emptive. Therefore, if he had been overheard in the pub beforehand claiming he was going to kill me, then a jury would have found him guilty without question. I personally do not believe a jury would have needed such irrefutable evidence to have convicted him of attempted murder. How much more apparent does it need to be? He also admitted to battering his wife, and all in all he received a five-year sentence. Today as I write he is a free man, though there is a restriction order that prevents him entering the Dalton-in-Furness area. I was appalled by the decision. I wondered what on earth a life is worth. Five years? He could have killed me, killed my son and killed his wife.

The incident will live with me forever. Every night before I go to bed I check every single door and window. Sometimes in the middle of the night I check them too. I can never sleep unless I know those doors are locked and if I have a doubt in my mind I have to get up. For a long time I did it three or four times a night. It was the most traumatic feeling being unable to relax in your own home. If I heard the slightest noise during the night I would wonder what was coming, it was a persistent terror.

In fact, many local people felt the impact of the incident. Suddenly, a generally safe area with next to no crime was just as dangerous as anywhere, if someone could try and murder another human being then no one was safe.

Chapter 35
Birth of my daughter, Galapagos
and septicaemia

I had a trip planned to Niger but I had made sure to book it ten days after Caroline's due date, I thought that would be plenty of time for her to have our baby and for me to hopefully spend a few days with them before flying to Africa. Shortly before I was due to go Caroline was rushed into hospital with labour pains. I sped to the hospital myself – with Hari in tow – but it was a false alarm.

As it happened the situation was taken out of my hands. I hadn't told Caroline I was due to go to Niger and as time wore on it was clear she wasn't going to give birth before my proposed travel date. I decided I should go, even though I knew I would not be able to see her. I travelled to West Africa, a small village called Kanare to a simple campsite in the middle of the desert. My 'hotel' sleeping quarters came in the shape of a sleeping bag with a mosquito net draped over the top.

Quite remarkably given its isolation in the sub Saharan desert, you could just about pick up a mobile phone signal at a certain point on top of the roof of the project building. As I was standing on top of this remote spot I received a text from Caroline.

"Can you come down to the hospital right now please? I have had our baby," it read.

'Oh damn' I thought to myself, 'how can I possibly get there.'

I texted her back. "I can't, I'm in West Africa, I've come to the giraffe project and I can't. I'm so sorry I want to be there and I am desperate to be there but I can't."

I was in tears because I could think of nothing I wanted more than to be there.

She asked me to think of a name for our baby girl.

That day we were distributing micro credits to all the villagers in the local area and I was seeing the various names of each person coming up. One lady was called Kadi, pronounced Kah-dee. Kadi was a middle-aged lady who had a wonderful disposition and, as is the custom there as no one can write, she 'signed' for her micro credits with a stamp of her thumbprint. I fell in love with the name Kadi.

I sent Caroline a few different names via text later that day. One of the names, for which I expressed a preference, was Kadee, which was how I spelled it phonetically to Caroline. She liked the name but asked if we could pronounce it Kaydee. She also told me that Hari wanted to call our little girl Rose because his favourite film was *Titanic* and that is the name of Kate Winslet's character. In fact, if Caroline had given birth to a boy he would have been called Jack after Leonardo DiCaprio's character.

I felt a rush of pride and happiness because I had named our daughter. I couldn't wait to get back home. Every time I went to Niger it was always a relatively short visit, usually a week. Niger has the harshest living conditions I have ever experienced. The poor diet, the lack of hygiene and the persistently high temperatures – of up to 45 degrees in the shade – it is a difficult place to say the least. I completed the very important humanitarian work we went to organise and the continuance of the programme to protection of the last Giraffes in West Africa because it is a deep personal commitment that I have made to these desperately poor people and the Giraffes of course. Some of the poorest most isolated people on the planet live in that region and yet some of the happiest people and that has always impressed me about the natives of Niger, the fact that they have nothing, but they ask for nothing except for food and shelter. They have no pressure on them to have material objects and therefore no disappointment when the world does not give them more than they have in their families and homes. No television adverts telling they are a failure without the latest gadgets or Governments that promise standards of living they can't deliver and leave expectation and ultimately in our society disappointment and disillusionment. A basic existence with no medical cover, no shops and a reliance on nature to allow them to live their simple but content lives is what I witness and in many respects there are so many positive things about the traditional ways.

I came back home and went to see Caroline and Kadi as soon as I could. I loved Kadi right away. I apologised for everything, expressing to Caroline that it had just been a series of ongoing complications, which was the story of my life.

Directly after the stabbing back in the August of 2007 and resulting stress and worry I suggested to Alison we escape from the media attention and trauma and go on a long trip away together, Caroline was pushing me away I thought and it seemed the right thing to do at that time in the confused and lost place my mind was. In early September, well before Kadi's birth, I had booked a trip to South America, visiting Peru and Ecuador during the October half term holidays for a couple of weeks.

I booked a trip to our bear project in Northern Peru. I also organised a trip to the Galapagos Islands, something I'd always wanted to do. It was a luxurious trip which lasted more than two weeks. I wasn't exactly sure what I was getting until we arrived as I had left a friend of mine in Peru, who owns a travel company, with the responsibility of booking the trip. So despite Kadi's birth and Caroline asking me to visit, I already had this pre-booked, quite stupidly and blindly I continued with it.

It turns out my friend had performed wonders. We were treated to an almost exclusive private yacht, there were only two other people on the boat, a German couple. The seven of us had the whole ship to ourselves, with two private chefs, sixteen crew members and all the necessary equipment for diving. It was incredible luxury. We could eat anything we wanted, if they didn't have it on the menu they would find it and cook it regardless. Hari seemed oblivious to this range of choice and settled on scrambled eggs most of the time.

We sailed around the Galapagos where I could dive and swim at our leisure. I swam and snorkelled with sea lions, and also swam with manta rays, stingrays, tiger rays and turtles. We were up close to every single type of bird, lizard and virtually every other wild creature which lives there. The activity which impressed me the most was swimming with sea lions – it was quite staggering to have these very wild creatures swim around you, beside you and sometimes through your legs. I did feel a slight panic; it could have been the quickest vasectomy on the planet, far worse than a Babirusa!

Swimming with stingrays was interesting and you need your wits about you at all times. All rays are exceptionally dangerous because they all have a spike on their tail which can inject poison into you. If it hits you in the wrong place it is lethal, as Steve Irwin found out to his cost. Whenever I am swimming with any rays, I always like to swim like above or below and to keep a good distance and stay behind them. This way you don't antagonise the rays by any quick movements – you have to shadow them. You can then just glide along.

It was no surprise to me that Steve Irwin ended up dying from his own bravado. This macho culture is a true part of Australian living.

Steve was certainly a showman. He was a showman that later on in his life did enter into the business of conservation and though I think he used this to justify his position a little, he did buy a lot of land with his money and did some good in Australia. I did think his motives sometimes were very dubious. One time he came to Indonesia to canvas the people in the areas that we were already working on conservation. I am told by my staff there that his intention was a little strange; he wanted to remove some elephants from Way Kambas elephant camp to take to Australia. He was desperate to buy them and therefore offered a sweetener that he would help with conservation work there.

I didn't know Steve personally but I have heard one or two stories which, along with some of my own experiences, make me wonder about the kind of person he was. In Australia I employed a couple of people who told me some stories, as one of them was a personal friend of Steve's . In the early days when Steve was starting out this man went on film shoots with him as his assistant.

They were on a shoot somewhere in the Northern Territory, and there was a lizard of which they desperately wanted a close up shot but it was too high up a tree. They were there to promote conservation but Steve Irwin just cut the tree down! I was told he could not believe it and there were a number of thoughtless incidents such as this which led him to tell him that it was not nature working with Steve Irwin, it was showmanship and he couldn't continue working like that.

A lot of the time the filming was geared towards the showman aspect rather than actual reality. Many times for instance Steve would be 'filmed' putting his hand down a hole and retrieving a snake but the information given to me was he never was that crazy – there were merely clips integrated to make him look more like a daredevil.

What I particularly did not like and heard many stories about was Steve Irwin's roughness with the animals. It was apparent to me that he had no respect for them whatsoever. Animals being roughly treated or roughly held was part of the norm and I had to agree once I saw Irwin's act on film once. He was in the Australian desert attempting to capture a camel. What I saw sickened me. They wouldn't dart the animal as it would not have provided enough excitement on film.

Instead, they got a big pickup and took a big noose on the end of a long pole. The idea was to go and catch a camel by its neck – they chased and chased it for quite a while before eventually noosing it, all for the excitement of the film.

The poor camel was nearly dead when they finally did get it because it had run and run under unimaginable stress. Finally they necked the camel and pulled it down. It couldn't move, its tongue was hanging out, it was frothing – it was absolutely horrible. Yet, Steve Irwin sat on top of the camel, proclaiming, 'Finally got the beast.' I thought it was sick. There are so many other ways he could have captured the camel which were safe and efficient, but he just ran it into the ground. I could never think of him with any respect again.

When I was in Australia I almost worked with Steve Irwin, it briefly occurred to me that it would be a good publicity drive for the zoo but then I realised I would be as bad as he was if I had done that – working for the money and showmanship. It wasn't me.

Even in Irwin's zoo the set up was too gladiatorial for my liking.

Animals were dominated and the idea was that man was superior. It certainly was a showman's domain, not a conservation place. At South Lakes Wild Animal Park we feature events and get people involved but the idea is to make sure the animal is seen as the tremendously powerful sensitive thing that it is and that man should not try and dominate these creatures. Animals have skills and abilities that we do not have. Just because we have guns and vehicles and the ability to overpower most things, when it comes to skills, most animals can outwit us every day. When you think of the ability of other animals to do things that we can only dream of, for instance, to guide yourself across from one end of the world to another and land up in exactly the right place. That's a skill we do not have, unless we are given a GPS.

The whole time in the Galapagos I wanted to be close to a shark. I knew there were many there, we had seen many from a distance. There were tiger sharks and we were told they were relatively safe. I was diving off the boat in a bay with a cliff edge that hung over the water – I was told that there would most likely be a shark hiding under this particular cliff, which continued deep underwater into a cave.

I felt quite safe. All of the crew on the yacht were professional divers and strong swimmers. I left Hari skirting on the top of the water wearing his armbands supervised by the crew. I wanted to see a shark and I got my wish. I could see him up ahead of me and suddenly I was dead set on the shark which appeared much larger than I had expected. He was roughly three times longer than me. I saw its mouth, its eyes and I could just see its teeth and I thought to myself, 'Did I really want to see a shark?'

I decided that perhaps it was time to go back. I started to back pedal and began to lose my breath. Somehow I managed to propel myself with enough force to make it back to the boat. I had seen many sharks in my time, especially when swimming and snorkelling in Australia. But this particular shark gave me the willies, it was so massive, it terrified me. It was a close call.

It was a strange time in terms of my family life especially when I had Alison with me, a person so domesticated. She was the exact opposite of Caroline in that respect – she didn't like the wild life, she didn't care about conservation, she found the wild life quite a chore in many respects. She was of the mindset where life was not as good when you didn't have hair straighteners and make up.

There was no mobile phone signal in Ecuador but once in Peru I recall receiving a phone signal in the isolation of Lambayeque, Northern Peru and all I wanted to do was talk to Caroline, to find out how she and Kadi were I managed to exchange a few text messages and was so happy to have contact with Caroline. Alison started to turn on me towards the end of the trip because she sensed that I had been talking to Caroline. I assured her I hadn't. I felt bad to lie but the trip had at least shown me as always that I wanted to be with Caroline. No matter how much time I spent with Alison, no matter how many glorious destinations we visited together, when I returned home the first thing I did was to go and see Caroline.

Once Kadi arrived – I wanted to spend as much time with her as I could, feeding her, changing her nappy and generally being dad.

Kadi had been born 2nd October 2007 and though the in-between times had been a little disjointed; by Christmas time all I wanted was to spend time with Caroline and the kids. They came to my house for Christmas and we spent a wonderful time opening presents. Ben and Amy were also there. I have some tremendous photographs of that day. It means a lot to me because it was to be the last time I ever had all of my children with me.

In late January 2008 I became extremely ill, I found myself in searing pain in my shoulder, it was beyond words for me to describe, the pain turned to infection and the poisoning of my whole body. Septicaemia from an infection in my shoulder bone marrow was diagnosed. I was drugged up by the Specialist to get rid of the pain and infections. I was left to recover at home and Caroline was doing a great job looking after me. I really cannot remember much at all about one whole week of my life as I slipped in and out of consciousness. One aspect which was a precursor to future events does stick in my mind and was the first real clash between Alison and Caroline. How it came about I do not know but Alison tried to displace Caroline as my "nurse" and her aggressiveness leap out at

Caroline in front of my eyes in my own home. This was awful for me as I could not even intervene I was so paralysed by the pain I could not move from my permanent position. I seem to remember the Police being involved in some way and Alison was extracted from the situation and peace was restored. It was the first time I had seen Alison lose control and be so aggressive and angry but it would not be the last.

During early and mid 2008 the Court system sadly had its usual negative influence on our lives once again, the process being sickeningly slow and laboured and so far behind real time events. The lawyers get involved again and it is like explosives being let off in a peaceful town square, turning calm and happiness into carnage on a battle field with the two sides aiming to do as much collateral damage as possible without ever considering the effects on the children. Despite wishing it would all go away the pre arranged hearings just seemed to be timed at the worst possible time for Caroline and I as a couple and the lawyers had the ability to ruin all our lives in seconds. Help was all I ever cried out to everyone, but my pleas were lost in profit making business accounts of Legal Firms who's needs for profits were far more important to them than finding amicable solutions. Caroline and I were forced further apart once again by the "system".

Chapter 36
Counselling and Colombian dancing

Before the attempt to kill me I had been feeling in desperate need of help and assistance to find a way out of my seemingly never-ending trauma. I started a self-realisation process in the July of 2007, just as I was becoming friends with Alison Creary. The whole situation that was taking place made me decide that I needed to talk through my feelings and try and get to the bottom of my seeming irresolvable family situation. I approached my GP who had known me since I was fifteen-years-old. I told her I needed to explain my feelings to a trusted stranger. I needed an independent view of my situation to try and find answers to how I felt about Caroline and what I could do about it. The Doctor said she could refer me to a Counsellor on the NHS. I agreed and I started to talk to a counsellor called Jim Smith, who was brilliant. I needed someone impartial to see my life objectively from the outside looking in – most people I knew had an opinion and would side one way or another. It didn't help me in the least, I needed some objectivity. Altogether I had six sessions through an NHS programme.

The first thing Jim said to me was, "What are you coming for? What's your objective?"

"I need to get out of this circle that I am in. I am going in a never-ending circle," I said. "I just seem to find happiness then it turns wrong, then I move away, then I want it back, and so on. I should jump off, I can't, I end up where I began, I end up there the same."

"The sad situation is," I continued, "that this court system brings us back to the same circle all the time. I need to find a way out and break this repetitive situation and break away from this vicious circle in my life."

I talked and talked and began to truly let go. I really wanted to find that solution and Jim was very good but couldn't carry on beyond the six sessions so I had to start paying him privately. Every Thursday evening I would go to Jim's house and talk. I found it very useful because he really started to open me up and find out who I loved and who I didn't love. What did I think? What did I not think? On and off I went and visited Jim for a year until July 2008. I had honestly believed that the stabbing incident had been causing me grief since the August of 2007 but in the end, despite the many hours of discussion, it didn't once come up. Perhaps it was some buried trauma but I didn't feel it pertinent to try and lessen the burden of such a major occurrence, I was convinced, as he was, that the answer lay in my problems with the way I was with the women in my life.

Somehow I wanted to erase the past, all the damage done, a lot of the upset I had caused. On some level I hoped that perhaps Jim could do something for me in that regard. But no one can wave a magic wand, the problems were mine and I had caused them. Talking was the first step towards realising that and changing my life. Jim was there to help me release the information that I needed in order for me to realise and make changes, and to move on.

Unfortunately no amount of talking could offset some of the stupid decisions I had made. After the stabbing, Alison felt isolated and alone in her living circumstances. She was residing above a pub her mother ran and desperately wanted to get out. She was waiting on a divorce settlement but had no money until that came through. I felt sorry for her but in all honesty we were not in a relationship of consequence. So I came up with a deal after having a discussion about it and her wishing she had a way out of her housing situation. I offered to buy a house but make the arrangements through a bonafide legal contract, whereby she could make rent/loan payments to me and then buy the house outright once her settlement came through. Everything was signed, in front of witnesses. I went with Alison to look at a few houses and she settled on one which was a fairly new build quite close to the zoo. Not the smartest move I could have made, but I helped a friend and she was happy and relieved to escape the life at the pub. That was enough for me at the time.

In early May 2008 I stayed over with Alison in her new house one night, the consequences of which were far reaching and the result was my son Indiana (Indi). I had a sudden realisation that this development was going to be one of the most significant moments of my life and relationship with Caroline and it sent ripples of fear through my body knowing it would be devastating for Caroline to find out this news. When I told my mam and dad that Alison was pregnant with my child Dad went berserk. He was still of the opinion that the biggest mistake of my life was made when I left my first wife Alison. I told him it was my life and that I didn't agree that was a mistake. We were different people. He told me in return that he didn't want anything to do with Alison number two, or the baby. It struck me like a sledgehammer. It hurt me like crazy that an innocent child was going to be affected by my own father's ignorance and selfishness. He could have said what he liked to me, but when he told me that he wanted nothing to do with my unborn child I felt like there would be no going back, he could not find the compassion for an unborn child.

It must also be said that, though my counselling was helping me to get my head straight and come to certain decisions about my life in general, the idea of the counselling was not look at one issue but my life as a whole, the way it was balanced and the need I had to keep everyone happy all of the time and to be successful at work, an impossible task as most will know. I have no idea what was really controlling my mind at this point I certainly had not found any answers from counselling. Many people wondered how I could be friends with a woman whose husband had almost killed me – it didn't seem like the most sensible move, especially when at that time I had no intentions of settling down with her happy ever after. Was it to fill the gap when Caroline wasn't there ? It was certainly looking that way to others.

I was learning all through the counselling but it was not as if there was a huge bright light switched on in one go. Through the sessions I was picking up little things here and there which only came together at the end of the time I spent talking to Jim. I had had enough twists in my life but it was another strange twist and development to find out I had another child on the way, to another woman.

In late May 2008 I returned to Ecuador for a Latin American Zoo Conference. It was held in Quito, the capital of Ecuador. I loved the Latin American conferences and they were always full of such outstanding characters. These people did not blend in; they were just so individual, colourful and full of life.

I flew to Ecuador completely shocked. I already had Hari, who was six-years-old and Kadi who was not even a year-old and here I was with another baby on the way to a different woman.

I didn't have an enjoyable experience at the conference, my head wasn't in the right place and I didn't pay much attention to what was going on. I spent a lot of time walking around the city, I spent a lot of time doing virtually nothing constructive and looking for things to do outside of the conference because I just couldn't focus.

I went out dancing which was enjoyable but somehow or other I was in a void because I knew that Alison being pregnant would do so much damage to any plans or any thoughts I had with Caroline. After Quito I flew directly to Colombia to visit the Howler Monkey Project again. There I saw Carolina Sanin and other friends and locals who were doing so much good work. Colombia gave me the personal refreshment I needed, as it always did. I had always given unique incentives to my staff at South Lakes. If they did a good job through the year then I would take the best performing staff members with me to a conservation project, whether it be Indonesia, Peru or Colombia. This particular time I took a member of my keeping staff, Vicky, who stayed with a friend of hers in a different town, while I stayed in Medellin. My time in Medellin was absolutely fantastic, with people who seemingly picked up on the fact that I felt lost within myself. Everybody seemed to put a lot of effort into looking after me.

It became one of the few times in my life that I have drunk alcohol past a couple of glasses of wine. I am not a drinker, I can have the odd beer and then I won't have another, I'll have a glass of wine but I tend to have not much more than one, rarely I will have two. I went out with my friends there and in Colombia there is a traditional way of drinking. You buy a bottle of rum and place the bottle in the centre of the table and just keep drinking it until it is finished at which point another bottle of rum comes to the centre of the table. Your rum is constantly topped up with Canada Dry and ice by ever attentive waitresses. Given so many people are sharing the bottle you don't really have awareness of what you are drinking and you soon end up drinking quite a bit – way more than I would ever normally drink.

I drank a lot for me but still, strangely, did not feel as if I was out of control. The reason for this was probably the constant dancing, every two seconds someone would pull me over to the dance floor, so I was diffusing the large amounts of alcohol almost as soon as it hit my system. There is nowhere else in the world I believe I could actually drink that amount and still be able to function normally. Only in an environment where you are sweating to death with the perpetual dancing can that amount of alcohol be evaporated! I have only done this once and never again !

I also visited another project called Projecto Titi which I had been interested in for a number of years. It was created for Cotton Topped Tamarins, one of the rarest and smallest monkeys in the world. There I met the director of Barranquilla Zoo. Rosamira Guillen, who I had known for a number of years, had done a lot of good work for this project. We travelled around the forest together watching the monkeys in their wild, natural habitat. The project was also sponsored by the Disney Foundation who were performing the research and looking for a partner or buyer for the forest.

I really liked and trusted the people working there and I made a commitment there and then that we would start funding the project. I hadn't forgotten my personal difficulties completely but I certainly felt reinvigorated by the Colombian experience yet again.

When I came home my eldest daughter Amy, then 22, came to see me and told me she was pregnant. At the time she had been working for me as an animal registrar. She had worked her way up through being shop manager and restaurant manager. When she was just 21, Amy raised the restaurant profit by £100,000 in one year. She had learned a lot from me about budgeting and management and utilised an obvious natural talent to put it all into practice. I was so pleased and proud of her.

She then took on the gift shop and re-designed the layout, increasing the turnover there. She was very talented and I honestly thought she would become General Manager of South Lakes Wild Animal Park at some point. She then started working on animal records and helped South Lakes become one of the top five zoos in the world. Caroline had achieved this accolade in previous years and Amy got us back there.

This meant, thanks to Amy, we had some of the most accurate animal records (which record an animal's parentage, their birth dates and other details) on the planet.

Amy loved her work and she loved working with me. Every morning at ten o'clock she would come out of her office, we would meet in the café, she would come and give me a cuddle – even though she was now a fully-grown woman she was always my little girl.

When she told me she was pregnant I was a little taken aback. The person she was with, the aptly named Barclay Bland, was not a communicator, or at least he could not seem to communicate with me. That set alarm bells ringing as it made me question his intentions for a long-term commitment. I think if your daughter's boyfriend can come and talk to you and they are reasonably open it shows they are genuine. It didn't say much that he could not come to me, with Amy, and show he was going to do the right thing now he had made my daughter pregnant. When my first wife Alison became pregnant we went, hand in hand, and told both our parents together.

I told Amy I only wanted the best for her. No doubt she might have expected I might show my disappointment but I had no right to react in that manner, I had been there and made similar mistakes myself so I had to accept Amy could make bad decisions too. Ben my eldest son had been at University and was taking a business degree and had just qualified and got his degree around this time.

I booked a holiday for July 2008 thinking that this would be the last time we could all go as a family. Now Amy was pregnant she would be busy with her baby and she might get married and move away. The trip was going to be unlike any other holiday I had ever experienced. I was constantly being bullied by some family and acquaintances and more especially by people involved in the "Family Law System" to get Caroline out of my life and move on, it was a pressure excerpted on me that I fought hard against but it had its effects so I decided I would take Ben, Amy, Alison, her two girls and Hari with me in a road trip across America. I had seen the Robin Williams film, *RV* (*Runaway Vacation*) a comedy where the luckless Williams has to endure many mishaps while driving an RV to the Colorado Rockies. I decided, despite the comedy of errors in the film, that this was the best way to see America. We had done this in Australia years before of course.

I liked the idea of having a huge camping truck where we would have the freedom to just go where we wanted when we wanted doing everything ourselves but having the true adventure spirit. I am an adventurer, I don't want to have something that is predictable, I never have. I have never been on a trip that was really predictable in my life or where you know where you are definitely going to be. You might start there but are you going to finish up there? Most people go on a holiday and they start there, they stay there and that's where they are when they end but I don't do that, nor would I want to. I travel in between; I am never in a hotel or anything for more than a night or two nights. I certainly don't fancy a two-week all-inclusive in Benidorm and it wouldn't matter who I was with – I wouldn't be able to do it, I would go berserk by the second day.

I booked our trip on the Internet partly and was really looking forward to taking the kids for the summer holidays. I was still attending counselling and I still had the courts to deal with. I was due in court on 18th August and it was not something that they would let you just change your mind about, once the date was set you had to go. It was made even more ironic by my counselling sessions because I felt as if I had settled on who I was and what I needed but the court system was ever running and never changing. Though I had found some answers, the system just kept on making it difficult to move on.

When Jim and I were putting all the pieces together of our sessions in early July 2008, one thing became abundantly clear and it was as if now, finally, a huge light came on.

The conclusion was that the problem was me.

It was like putting the pieces of a jigsaw together and suddenly seeing the picture clearly. I remonstrated with myself:

'It is me that has caused all of this. I didn't take care of Caroline when she needed it, I didn't look after her when she needed it, I didn't listen to her when she needed it, I didn't support her, I didn't love her when she needed the love, I didn't put my arm round her, I didn't do any of this and when it came to this particular point I was the one that should have put more into it and done this. I should not have argued, I should have gone to look for the better alternative, I did it wrong.' I never understood her anger at her past or had tolerance for it.

I finally looked inside my heart and realised where I had gone wrong. Where I had once blamed Caroline I realised with all sincerity that a lot of things had been caused by my own stupidity or selfishness. Then I realised with absolute mind blowing clarity that I loved Caroline so much. I didn't ever want to lose her. It dawned on me that she might have been waiting, hoping I would come to my senses and make the right decision when all along I was making continually misinformed judgments, and acting like an idiot. From that moment it was like a ten-ton weight came off my shoulders. I could not escape the problems with the courts because they were ever running but within myself I finally accepted what I had caused.

It was a ridiculous and strange time to be setting off on a holiday with another woman but that was the reality. Despite the fact I was going on a pre booked family holiday with Alison I felt, as we were travelling to America, that I knew the right thing to do and that things would work out. I knew I wanted to marry Caroline.

Chapter 37
The RV road trip from hell

Manchester to New York. New York to Las Vegas. I had never been to Vegas before, it wasn't even somewhere I wanted to go but I had seen it on TV and thought that at least I could say I've done it. I'm not a gambler, I've never put a penny on anything in all my life, in fact I have always been against gambling so, if anything Vegas held only a freak value for me. It was a distinctly hot environment, we spent a full day and night there, wallowing in the casinos and breathing in the acrid, white-hot atmosphere.

The next day we were to collect our RV, camper van in English parlance. The beast was 31 feet long. It had four double beds which would sleep eight people comfortably and had all the same facilities you would find in most hotel rooms. As I was starting to pull out of the bay at the yard of the rental site I saw the warning that there was a huge dip in the ground. It was ridiculous really because with such a big vehicle it was impossible not to scrape the ground and that was exactly what I did. Within the first minute of driving an RV I had scraped the bottom of the vehicle on the tarmac which made one hell of a racket. It was a precursor of the bad luck to come.

We drove down the main highway out of Las Vegas towards the border with Arizona, from Nevada towards the Hoover Dam where the border lies. Unusually for America, especially in desert country, the road started to get narrow and quite windy – there were crash barriers on either side as we were approaching Hoover Dam. I had never driven a vehicle that long before and I slightly misjudged a corner, which meant I caught the side of the crash barrier. My heart jumped. Nothing was particularly damaged and we were all okay but it meant I had my wits about me to the highest degree afterwards as it had scared me a little. It was precursor number two.

After some time at Hoover Dam where we took photos and revelled in the heat we stopped at a camp site where the kids went swimming. It gave me one of my funniest memories and I couldn't help but take a photograph of a sign I saw. Normally you would see signs that forbade diving or jumping into the water but only in America could you see one that read, 'If you are incontinent please wear rubber diapers or watertight pants.' It astounded me to think some people might think it perfectly acceptable to soil themselves in a public pool merely because they were wearing adult nappies. One thing the sign made sure of – I was not about to get in that pool.

After all the years of watching Country Music Television and furthering my knowledge of country music by constantly buying and playing country music both in my home and at the zoo, I was now something of an expert. Whenever we were driving through the States and the radio was on I would know every song.

We travelled through Arizona where I wanted to make sure we saw Monument Valley and the Grand Canyon before moving off the tourist trail a little and utilising our own transport to explore some of the lesser driven roads. We found a very basic camp site near to the Grand Canyon which had one distinctive feature: a dry toilet. There was no water or anything else of any consequence. The kids went and found a few pieces of wood and pine cones so we could set a fire – it was a very basic and wild night, but enjoyable nonetheless. We managed to see wild deer the next day, watching the sunrise from the edge of the canyon – it occurred to me that this was exactly what I wanted from the holiday.

The next day we travelled to Monument Valley, a very special place made famous in John Ford films with its astounding geological landscapes in a Navaho Indian Reservation. We were hot and tired from all the day's driving and walking. As well as my own children we also had Alison's two daughters with us. That night, Alison, Ben and I sat outside at a table while Hari and the girls started to quibble a little. Alison had a different viewpoint than I had regarding computers. She allowed her daughter to have a Nintendo DS, whereas I had always thought it was not the best thing for a child to be absorbed with morning and night. There were three kids but only two Nintendo's, which was not the best mix. They were starting to get a little rowdy so I told them to calm it down as I didn't want them making too much of a noise on a public camp site, especially at night time. The children started to fight over the games and a small battle ensued leading to Hari grabbing the game and Alicia chasing him and forcibly getting it back. It was just kids scrapping as they do. I left it to Alison to make a decision and she made the right one, she confiscated them so no one could play with them.

Suddenly Ben turned to me and said, "You let him get away with everything don't you?"

I said, "What do you mean?"

"Well, you should have hit him for that, he pushed Alicia over."

"Yes but it was Hari's turn and she wouldn't give it up and then when he took it she nicked the thing off him. Basically it was swings and roundabouts, six of one and half a dozen of the other. I mean you can't punish one without punishing the other - and they were all punished."

Ben by now was 21, but he had been opinionated from his teenage years. Our debate continued with me wondering why on earth Ben felt the need to push the issue. "Ben," I said, "you can't physically punish a child for just fighting over a toy. They are punished enough, they have had the toy taken off them and that shut them up and they have gone to bed now."

"But you should have hit him for that, for what he did."

"No, Ben, corporal punishment like that is restricted to the most severe things. Even then you have to think very hard before you reprimand a child because it has to relate whatever punishment it gets to what it did. If the child can't relate it to what it did they will never understand why they were hit then the child grows up thinking that hitting is just something that happens out of nowhere."

I made it clear I didn't think that was any good for a child, it taught them nothing – potentially it would only make them violent. I said that a tap on the hand might be warranted occasionally but that usually, a raised voice is enough. "If it isn't enough when they get to this age," I said, "you have to be very, very careful about corporal punishment because it can be misinterpreted and it can be too much. There is a time and a place for severe punishment and that certainly wasn't it."

Ben continued his arrogant stand, insisting I should have hit Hari. I was getting fed up with it. "Ben, I'm his dad, you're not. I make the decisions about his punishments, you don't. You are his brother, you have no right to take part in any punishment." I said that was enough and said he should go to bed. As the saying goes, you should never go to bed on an argument but I honestly thought that would be the end of it.

That said, I found it hard to forget about the altercation and I questioned why on earth he was so obtrusive. It kept turning over and over in my head how alike he was to my own father – that he could never change his opinion or see your side of things. If you said white was white or water was wet he would find a way to disagree.

We woke up in the morning and it was very tense. Ben was slamming things around, banging the doors. I said, "Come on, this is no good. I don't want any of this. Sort yourself out." He wouldn't concede that he should change his behaviour and the belligerence continued. We had to find a supermarket to stock up on a few basic provisions. Normally when we pulled in to a store, everyone would get out of the vehicle together and all go into the shop but Alison, Amy and Ben didn't move. I decided I would just take Hari in on my own. I came back to the vehicle, fed up of the searing tension.

"What's the matter with everybody?" I asked. Everyone seemed stunned and no one would answer me so I decided to just get on with it.

As I drove away I came to a section of the road that started to tilt steeply downhill. It was the first time I had experienced this after the generally straight and easily navigated roads in that part of America. This hill was especially steep and I misjudged the entrance to a gas station where I intended to pull in to refuel. The vehicle was moving downhill with me trying to keep hold of it in order to turn in. I slammed the brakes quite hard and caused a scene which would have been perfect for the *RV* movie. The cupboards opened and plates and cups fell out – glass and porcelain banging on the floor. No one was hit with anything but it was a close call where the vehicle tilted to the side a little.

Poor Alicia, who had long been highly strung since her parents splitting up, burst into tears. She was quite hysterical which was no wonder given the noise. I stopped the RV at the garage and asked if everyone was alright. I said I was sorry and that I couldn't believe how that had happened – the floor of the vehicle looked a mess but actually only one glass broke. Everything else had fallen on the floor but not actually broken, so it wasn't as bad as it sounded. Alison said we would have to get out of the vehicle, Alicia was inconsolable.

Amy was sitting at one of the dining tables, somewhere she shouldn't have been sitting while we were travelling. She was sitting on a seat without a seatbelt and she said she had bumped her pregnant tummy on the table when I braked. I was concerned about her and asked her several times if she was okay, she kept telling me she was fine. I said everyone should go into the garage and have an ice cream or a drink and compose themselves while I cleaned everything up.

Everyone got out of the vehicle but as I was starting to put things back in their rightful place the door of the RV flew open. It was Ben. He squared right up to me, within inches of my face. "If you ever hurt my sister I will kill you," he said. Something about his manner and his glaring, burning eyes told me he meant every word. It unnerved me.

"Ben, do you think I did that on purpose?" I asked incredulously. "My God, how stupid that I would want to do that on purpose. Think about it logically. It was a stupid little accident, I misjudged the bloody corner – that's all there is." Ben walked away. When the others came back in I checked if they were okay. Amy told me she was still fine, she was touching her belly but promised that she was not in any pain. I told Alison about Ben's actions and I thought long and hard about what to do, I felt that the best thing to do was drive back to Las Vegas and send him home – he was still fuming and I had no desire to spend the rest of the holiday with him, after all we were only three days in. Then I thought about the situation logically. To get back to Las Vegas would take at least two days and then it would be another day or so before he got a flight, and it would affect all the plans we had of where to go. I decided that we would just have to work it out.

That day we drove all the way across Arizona before reaching the border with New Mexico. There was an Indian Reservation with Indians selling their wares. Hari and I had a walk round in one direction while the others went the opposite direction – it seemed a very 'us and them' situation. In many ways I believed this was Ben's problem – that he was jealous of the time and perceived favouritism I showed towards Hari. He was only a young lad and to me it was a natural thing to keep my attention focussed on him, but Ben didn't see it that way, he saw it as a rejection.

After this for almost two weeks Ben and I didn't hardly speak.

Everyone else seemed to mellow, in fact I spent a lot of time with Amy, going on long walks around various geological sites. All she would say about the situation is, "You know what Ben is like." Ben spent the majority of his time on an I-Phone, which would have been one of the very first. He was clearly uninterested in the holiday or learning anything, he spent all his time online. He wouldn't go for walks or take part in anything, he just isolated himself.

One of the best aspects of the whole trip was the remarkable geology we were witness to. Western Australia was truly amazing but going through the west of America was something else altogether. Seeing the sand dunes and gigantic mountains of Colorado, through the stunning canyons of Utah and the Arches National Park was a tremendous experience. Hari was so interested in geology and natural life. He was only six-years-old yet he was taking in everything I was telling him. I was talking to him about wind erosion, soft sandstone, hard rocks. He was watching everything I was doing.

"Dad, what's that type of rock?"

"That's igneous rock."

"Dad, what's that type of rock?"

"That's sedimentary rock."

Every time we went to a different valley the colours of the rocks would be different, it was unbelievable for Hari to see red, yellow and white rocks all in the space of a few hours.

As we were nearing the end of the trip my mind started to drift towards what would happen when we got home, where I would tell Caroline that she was all I wanted. I would have to tell Alison that our future could only be as parents to our unborn child. As we reached Las Vegas again, with a little time to kill we ironically passed a number of wedding chapels. All I could think about was taking Caroline's hand in marriage. For the first time in the entire trip I switched my mobile phone on.

I texted Caroline saying, "This is going to sound crazy to you under the circumstances, but I want you to know that I love you more than anything else in the world, I want to marry you. Would you please be my wife?"

Much as it seemed like a good idea at the time I can see in hindsight how naïve that way of thinking really was. To expect Caroline could ignore the fact I had spent two weeks on holiday with another woman, a woman who was pregnant to me. This is how Caroline saw the situation and she reacted to my text quite sarcastically.

We were due to catch our flight in a few hours and decided to stop for a meal before travelling to the airport. All through the trip despite Ben's antics and rudeness I had been paying for every meal that we would all eat. His attitude to money had been eating away at me through the entire trip. He would always choose the most expensive food and drink on the menu, every single meal time. It was absolutely deliberate, his attitude being that I could afford it, so what did it matter?

He wasn't thinking about the cost of the holiday itself. I paid for us all to go driving around America for two weeks and it certainly was not cheap. By the end of the trip his desire for spending my money was becoming particularly irksome.

As he plumped for the most expensive option on the menu yet again I said, "Ben you have really got to start valuing money and stop just thinking it grows on trees because, if you just treat money like that one day you will spend your last pound and you will realise you've got nothing else to spend the next day or invest in anything." It was something of a lecture but it was long overdue. I started telling him the important of investing and saving, no matter how much money you have. I told him to think about his life and the consequences of spending money.

"Well, I need more money anyway," Ben responded. "I want to do my Masters degree in business." He had already completed his business degree, and I was very proud of him for the achievement. Ben's mother Alison and I attended the ceremony for him and we all went out for a meal to celebrate. He was pleased with himself and I felt the pride along with him. After all I had put him through university and I had even bought him a Mini Cooper to replace his basic mini for his 21st Birthday because I felt he had done well.

I thought I was doing the right thing to ask Ben to work a little for his regular amount of money from me. I wanted him to do some kind of work for me, whether it be on computer or even driving the train at South Lakes Wild Animal Park. He rarely worked to earn the money I was paying into his bank account every month however. He would come into the park in order to work but then I would walk down to where he should have been and find out he had just disappeared. It was a terrible example to set in front of other staff, his work ethic was non-existent, the complete opposite to myself.

Although Ben has lived much of his life with Alison and without me as a direct role model for his influential teenage years I still do take a great deal of the responsibility as to why he is this way. I was too soft with him, I should have been much harder, I should have imposed greater discipline and not just given him the gifts that I did. I never received a gift from my own dad and had to work for everything I owned which was ultimately a great lesson. I wanted to spoil my kids because I never had that for myself but it was a big mistake to give them things which they did not have to work for. Ultimately the same thing would happen with Amy.

According to Ben, even after our hellish experience in America together, he needed £16,000 for his Masters degree. I couldn't believe it but figured that after accommodation and all the requisite fees that it would not be all that surprising.

Nevertheless I decided enough was enough. "That's a hell of a lot of money Ben and I'm going to tell you something now, I think today is the day where we have to make a stand. From the age of ten-years-old I have earned my own money. I had a paper round, I worked on the farm and I did everything for myself. I never got any money off my parents, I never had any assistance from my parents, I did it myself so everything I bought, my motorbike, my car, everything was mine. You are already having your car and insurance paid for, and everything else."

Ben was nonplussed, staring at me. It was time he truly realised the reality of life. "You don't realise what it really costs to live in this world," I continued unabated, "and you won't really value how much this holiday has cost me either and how hard I have had to work to get this for you. So, today is the day it changes and I think you should go and get yourself a job to fund your Masters. I think you should take on a student loan to do it, and then pay it off when you can. That way you will value it because you'll say, 'I did that for myself, nobody helped me, I achieved it'."

I told Ben that this realisation in my own life created a great sense of pride, the fact that everything you have achieved has been done by your own hard work. I felt I was being a caring father in trying to help him see the world as it truly was instead of continuing with the handouts. I also wanted to see some respect from him instead of the feeling that I was being treated like a pariah by my own son.

Ben did not like what I said which was no surprise. He made it very clear that he didn't like it and was so angry after this that he never spoke to me that night. This incident was the culmination of the negativity surrounding the whole trip. From the moment Ben squared up to me and showed me such little respect our kinship was in real danger. I tried to forgive him for his behaviour but realised it was not about forgiveness. I merely accepted that this was how he chose to behave. It didn't mean I had to be around it for the rest of my life. It was up to him to change.

After the flight from Las Vegas to New York I was in the baggage hall looking to leave our bags for the day as we had twelve hours to wait for the flight back to England. Out of nowhere Alison came storming through the baggage hall, past the scores of people between us, right towards me. She was screaming at the top of her voice.

Everyone was looking and I was feeling utterly embarrassed, not to mention confused. Alison ran right up to me and pushed me clean over. I pulled myself up off the floor.

"What is going on?" I spluttered.

"You! What are you doing telling Caroline that you want to marry her and that you love her?"

I thought to myself, 'How has she found that out? Did I press send to the wrong person?'

"Ben's just told me."

I tried to play innocent. "What's Ben saying that for? Why? He is just trying to cause trouble, you know what he's like he is always trying to cause trouble."

"No, I've seen it with my own eyes. Caroline's Facebook page". Ben, who was friends with Caroline on Facebook, had read her wall post stating, "I've just had a text from David in America who is on his holidays with his pregnant girlfriend, asking me to marry him."

Though Ben was friends with Caroline online he didn't like her and neither did Amy, they had a long history of conflict between them from the point many years earlier when they realised I loved Caroline and wanted to be with her. They much preferred Alison and thought she was less of a threat to them for some reason. So doubtless Ben was enjoying causing the friction, thinking he would get rid of Caroline for good when in fact he was only going to push Alison away.

The whole situation became rather farcical. I went over to Ben to ask him why on earth he had told Alison that, why couldn't he speak to me first, or at least wait until we got home? Ben then started to get pushy with me and quite loud. Then Alison joined in, becoming violent with me again, shouting and pushing me around. I said I wouldn't fly back with them having them do this all the way home, and I didn't want Hari to see any more of the conflict. So I took Hari and we went around New York on our own. I was stunned and could not believe how the situation had developed. There were no other flights out of New York available that night and I just could not sit next to them for seven hours, so I decided to call Linda Hill in Connecticut. She told me she would come and collect me and we could stay with her until the next available flight.

Before Caroline realised I had gone to stay with Linda for a day or so, she texted me.

"David, I would love to marry you." My heart just went through the roof; I thought things were finally going to be alright. She told me she wanted me home as soon as possible, but naturally, I told Caroline about the shenanigans in New York and I told her where I was and a contact number. I texted her back saying we would be home in a couple of days.

Hari was enjoying swimming in the pool at Linda's house and we spent a wonderful time walking on the beach, I was in love and I was about to finally marry the woman of my dreams.

What I didn't know was that Caroline had found a permanent house in Manchester while I had been away and as soon as I handed Hari over to her she took him all the way down to Manchester. They moved away and they left me. It gave me a wake up call. I had had the clear and total realisation of the things I had done wrong but when I was finally ready and aware, Caroline turned and left me, quite simply the relationship with Alison, the hell Alison gave her behind my back and the need to escape the town of Dalton forced her away.

All of a sudden I had lost two women and all my children in the space of a couple of days. The whole situation with the court system suddenly seemed ever deeper and more severe and suddenly no one would speak to me. Even Amy would have nothing to do with me. When I tried calling Amy her boyfriend Barclay was abusive to me and would tell me she wouldn't speak to me. Ben wouldn't speak to me.

I tried to ring Alison my first wife, she sent me a text back saying, "If you phone us or come here we will ring the police."

"What have I done?" I asked. "What have I done that you have to ring the police? I want to come and talk to you; I want to sort this out." I was told not to bother. All I had said to Ben was I wouldn't give him any more handouts. Beyond that the issue I had was between Caroline, Alison Creary and me. It didn't need to involve the children or my first wife. I was baffled, hurt and upset. When I got home Ben's car was waiting in the car park of my zoo, with the keys handed in at the office. A few days later Amy's car turned up too.

She went into the office at the park with her work computer, to hand it over to a member of staff. It was covered in several work related notes, fully up to date and spotless. Once again whenever I tried to get in touch they either would not speak to me or I was threatened with police involvement.

I felt completely isolated; I couldn't even talk to Caroline. No matter what had happened in the past, Caroline would always speak to me, even if it were just through a text message. Now, even she would have nothing to do with me. I had always been of the mindset that if there was a problem you should talk it through in order to come to a solution. There was never a need for communication to dry up. But suddenly I was the bad guy and no one would give me the time of day. It was ironic that after all the realisations I had experienced, all the heartache I had endured and the conclusions I had reached by now, no one wanted to continue my journey with me. The only way forward was to go it alone.

Hari with Nyala who was born 1st June 2008 - our first rhino birth at South Lakes Wild Animal Park

Viewing hippos with Hari, Amy and Ben near Hluhluwe-Umfolozi Game Reserve in South Africa

Hari and myself taking in the natural power of the sea in South Africa

Pierre and I handing out Micro credits to women villagers in Niger, West Africa

The only place I could get a mobile phone signal in Niger. I had just learned Caroline had given birth to our daughter

Happy families - Kadi, Hari and Daddy

25th September 2008 Zimba joins Nyala with both mothers on the African region for the first time

Hari with Nyala, 2008. The next day Hari was taken from me by the family court

The long walk deep into the jungle where my knee gave up whilst on Tiger Protection Patrol

2008 An October night in the swamp forest, Senepis Bulahala, Sumatra with the tiger protection team

Sumatran war zone, the war against deforestation and tiger poaching

Monument Valley, Arizona. Within a few hours my world changed.
Ben, Hari, myself and Amy

Indi, Alison and I in the USA
in 2009

Indi and I in Chaparri working for the
Condor conservation programme

Hari (with Indi in his arms) and me
at South Lakes

Alison on a camping trip
in the USA

Andean bear programme, Chaparri. Hari or Indi and I have visited here every year since 2005

Indi and I having a chat with Zimba at South Lakes

In Chaparri reserve, Northern
Peru wearing a traditional
hat given to me by
Heinz and Ana Plenge

Indi making research notes at the macaw project in Peru 2011

One of the dams and irrigation schemes we
built in Madagascar

One of our Tiger Patrol
boats in Sumatra

Checking a Camera Trap to monitor and research Tiger populations in Sumatra

Over night camp in the Sumatran Jungle, a Tiger rubbed
up the side of the plastic in the night

Peralta Giraffes in the desert of Niger where the temperature was over 40 Celcius

The second school I built in the remote jungle of Sumatra

Educating children from the native tribe to equip them for the world they face in Sumatra

Children walk for over 2 hours each way to get to our school in Bukit Tigapuluh Forest

Our Tiger capture and relocation team setting a trap to
catch a man eating tiger and move it from people

This beautiful Sumatran Tiger cub caught on remote camera in
the jungle is what we work so hard to protect

Protecting Tamarins in the Colombian Jungle

Cotton Topped Tamarin in the wilds of the Colombian forest

Community employment project in Santa Catalina, Colombia

Rescued baby howler monkeys in Medellin, Colombia, waiting for rehabilitation

At our reintroduction project in Colombia for Red Howler monkeys

Silvestre the first successful wild birth of a Red Howler from released animals in our project

Illescas protected area, Northern Peru. Our work made this a National Reserve in two years

Indi meeting a Condor awaiting release in our project in Chappari, Lambayeque, Peru

Our rhinos enjoying winter sunshine in 2010

2 month old Kadi at South Lakes Wild Animal Park

September 18th 2011 my very first day out with my 3 young children in over 2 years, the children and I loved every second

On the UXU Ranch, Wyoming in November 2011 at over 7000 ft up with Clyde my steady riding partner

Chapter 38
Family turns on me and
a dramatic reaction

My hearing, which was to decide the future contact arrangements for my son Hari and baby daughter Kadi, was due on 18th August 2008.

I had made mistakes, getting another woman pregnant when I loved Caroline was quite high on the mistake scale. Caroline had her reasons for taking the children away to Manchester and this was all because she could not stand to see me with Alison and the constant verbal and emotional harassment she was getting from her in the school yard and town. From her perspective I had made another woman pregnant and taken her on holiday. All Caroline wanted to do was escape from me, Alison and the situation I had caused.

Today I can understand Caroline's viewpoint but at the time I could not. All I saw was Caroline still fighting me when I was so willing to resolve it. I found my children against me when I was desperate to find out why. All I had done up to the America holiday was love them. I would always help them and give them the support that they needed. For twenty plus years I did so without any problems. I gave up everything for them before I built the zoo and gave them opportunity after.

The days preceding the hearing were my lowest ever. I felt completely desolate and depressed. The woman that I desperately loved and wanted to marry me rejected me; my son and my daughter rejected me and were actively conspiring against me.

Time wise, it would be next to impossible for me to see my children very often – however often I could make it, it would be nothing compared to seeing them as much as I was used to.

The hardest part for me to deal with was the fact that no one would open a dialogue with me. Being ignored was one of the most difficult things to deal with – everything was now going through the court system. It seemed patently clear to me that all the "system" had done so far was to make everything awkward and difficult – the exact opposite of helping our situation. To involve them further seemed asinine, to ignore me during the process seemed antagonistic and childish. Whenever I tried to make contact with Amy and Ben I would be threatened with a police visit.

I looked around me. I had a gorgeous home, a zoo, a Ferrari and a Bentley in the garage. Yet I had nothing. How had this happened?

I wanted Ben and Amy to talk to me. I wanted it so badly at the time that I did something particularly stupid. I decided I would make them wake up, I'd see whether they love me or not. I wasn't suicidal, but I decided to make out that I was fully intending to kill myself.

I sent Ben and Amy text messages, saying the same thing. The message said that they would never see me again and the implication was that I was about to take my own life. It must sound crazy but my hope was that they would rush up to my house and attempt to 'stop' me – it was the only way I could think to get them to talk to me. I was going out of my mind simply because I loved my kids with all my heart, all I had ever done for them was love them, give them a great unique life and now they were isolating me without so much as an explanation why? I wrote a note, which was a huge stream of emotions towards them and how they had affected my life. It occurred to me on some level that the kids were thinking of themselves in terms of; whoever I married was entitled to 50% of my zoo and my legacy. They wanted me back with their mother because it would benefit them. Me marrying Caroline would mean they would probably see far less money – at least in their eyes. Ben has often made it clear he feels I "ripped his mother off" in our divorce, but it was amicable and fair at that specific time in our lives.

I told my kids that I would sit in my car and listen to music until I fell asleep forever. Unfortunately my threat did not work. I got into my car and put an Eagles CD on. There were two important distinctions from a man who wanted to kill himself however. The first was that I left all the doors open to the car. I also left the garage wide open. Well, I didn't want to asphyxiate!

Secondly, I made sure I left both of my electronic security gates slightly open so it would be easy for someone to walk right through and come to 'save' me. The reality is, anyone who wants to kill themselves would do so without telling anyone first or enabling someone to come and stop them doing it.

My children did not come to the zoo as I had hoped but, they told their mother (my first wife Alison) who called the police instead. I recognised one of the policemen immediately. He was a police sergeant whom I had known for many years as a local bobby. I instantly felt incredible embarrassment. Once again it had gone completely wrong – I had wanted my kids to come running and instead I receive a visit from the cops. Nevertheless I continued in my stupidity. I shut my eyes and pretended to be asleep.

Given the threat passed on via my children the policemen did not see a man having forty winks, they saw a man who was attempting to kill himself. They presumed they had to act quickly to try and bring me back to life. They pulled me out of the car with such speed and force that I thought they would pull my arms off. They banged my head accidentally. I was still so embarrassed I just kept my eyes shut.

They tried talking to me. "David are you alright, David are you alright?" I was wondering what on earth to do. I started to make a few groaning sounds. I knew I was acting like a complete idiot but I had gone to far to hold my hands up as having made a stupid mistake. The ambulance was by now pulling into the zoo car park. My two sisters were following close behind, in tears because they believed I had tried to kill myself. I felt awful.

They put me in the back of the ambulance. As soon as we set off I jumped straight up out of the stretcher and said, "I don't need to go to hospital, I'm alright, I'm absolutely alright, there's nothing wrong with me."

They told me we would have to go to the hospital, I couldn't get out now, they needed to check me out.

We soon reached the hospital with my sisters following behind. As soon as we arrived I jumped out and said to them both, "Alison,

Karen, I am so so sorry, I'm an idiot, I've done this, I'm stupid, I've not tried to kill myself, I just tried to get my kids to come and talk to me."

As it happened it would become just another reason for my sisters to be annoyed at the way Amy and Ben had treated me. They were already angry at them for their behaviour. My sister Alison, a nurse, was very worried about me – at the time I am not sure she believed that I had not actually tried to kill myself. Regardless, I was clearly in a confused state of mind to even pretend to do such a thing. The one thing I could not believe was how on earth my kids didn't seem to care, even when I was apparently going to die.

The police sergeant came to see me next. He asked if I was alright. I told him the full story and apologised profusely for wasting police time. He told me he wanted to sign me off straight away but that it needed a clarification from a psychiatric team at the hospital. He told me he didn't want me to have to go through that but it was either that or I go to the police station.

Before I knew it I was in a hospital ward that had locks on the doors. I waited on my own with the walls closing in, wondering how on earth I had ended up here. Eventually I had a captive audience with various professional types, including a consultant, nurses and a social worker. I told them the honest, uncomfortable truth. I apologised to them and said that regardless of what I had done, I was certainly safe to go home. They left me again to discuss the situation before returning in a matter of minutes. The doctor told me I had been through a kind of post traumatic shock after the treatment from my kids. He told me that the confusion and shock was a fairly common reaction, even if my method of dealing with it was unusual. I was told I could go home.

During the interview my phone had rung. It was Caroline. She was panicky, making sure everything was okay. Of all the people I thought maybe would care Caroline was the only one who actually called showing she truly cared and loved me.

The police sergeant was kind enough to drive me home and a couple of days later I called the other officer to apologise profusely for putting him through the whole situation.

It didn't help my position with the court system however. As I can not reveal any of the Court proceedings you have to use your common sense to imagine what the Social worker assigned saw and took from this silly event, I think you will understand that it didn't help me at all and would be something that could be used to suggest I was an unstable person who didn't deserve to see his kids. This – in my opinion – heartless, uncaring and cold person made comments in essence about our whole lives and futures and after all of this I was so distraught I couldn't bring myself to attend the hearing. It was the biggest mistake I could have made.

Looking at all the evidence, which was completely stacked against me, and seeing that I could not even turn up and apparently must not have cared about my children the Court made its order. I cannot discuss the judgement here once again due to secrecy/privacy laws in the court system, but I can tell you the result that Caroline received full custody. I was banned from seeing my children for a minimum of five years a situation that was described to me as draconian in measure. I also ended up not being allowed to contact in any way, shape or form Caroline, we couldn't even email each other. If I broke the order I would be sent to prison. The outcome I do not see as a secret as everyone in my life , my wider family and in the workplace was aware of the situation from that moment on. How can one keep such an outcome secret from family or work colleagues who then wondered where Caroline, Hari and Kadi were when they didn't turn up at the zoo?

Obviously everyone around me in my life was devastated by this result because in effect it meant that my children were taken from my whole family, the life they lived and the father they loved and yet all this was my own fault , I didn't do anything to my children but love them, I made huge mistakes in my decisions in my life and finally my children were chosen as the ones to suffer the consequences. I was in a fragile state of mind and in my opinion it was the worst decision possible for the children and myself. It made everything so much worse. I may not have actually intended to kill myself but clearly I was in a mire of depression. How could the "system" believe that his judgement would help me or my children in any way? The last thing on earth I wanted to do was hurt my kids in any way emotionally or physically. In fact everything I was doing was trying to avoid hurting them but the "system" couldn't see it or find a way to assist me towards peace, because that is not even a consideration in the system I was a captive of, or the person assigned to "look after our children's interests". I was lucky to find the support of family and close friends. My sisters, my friends, Ian and Gay Collings, Stewart and Christine Lambert, all rallied round me. They gave me the strength to carry on believing.

I put my heart and mind into work again, it was all I had left. I designed and built the Tropical House and set off with my excavater digging out the area immediately. We had it completed in five months and it helped me enormously to have that focus as well as filming TV programmes and my animals around me.

Chapter 39
Baby Rhino's, unwanted gift and South American adventures

"When you feel that you have reached the end and you cannot go one step further, when life seems to be drained of all purpose:
What a wonderful opportunity to start all over again, to turn a new page."

Twenty days after the court hearing I had to go to visit my solicitor in Knutsford, Cheshire so I arranged for my car to be serviced at the same time. I dropped the Bentley off at the garage for a service as it was also in Knutsford, and picked up a courtesy car for the day. I broke the Court Order virtually right away by contacting Caroline , how can love of that depth be simply switched off ? It is impossible so I made sure Caroline knew I was going to be close to Manchester and she sent me a message saying she would like to meet. We knew we had to be careful as we weren't actually allowed to see each other. The date was a historically significant one – September 11, 9/11 as it is known, which was a date that would become significant in my personal life too.

It had been almost three months since Caroline and I had seen each other and she let me know she had missed me. She virtually pulled me into the house, threw me into the living room, onto the settee and smothered me with affection. I seemed to have timed my visit quite well as Kadi was asleep upstairs and Hari was at school so they did not get drawn into the situation. Caroline and I shared a wonderful time together, it felt so good to know just how much she had missed me. It also put everything into perspective at just how we loved each other – it was everything and everybody else that was conspiring to keep us apart.

I was bubbling with excitement, my heart was bouncing, I had butterflies and I believed my future was starting all over again. Just a month earlier my world had crumbled around me and now it seemed I was going to be back with the woman I loved. I thought this might now be the time where we could finally get married.

As I drove back to the Bentley garage to pick up my car I was smiling to myself, thinking that every cloud has a silver lining. When I got to the garage there was a phone call for me. One of the rhinos at South Lakes Wild Animal Park had been due to give birth and just as I arrived I received news that Tala's waters had broken and she was about to give birth. I desperately wanted to be there and quickly asked if anyone at the garage had a computer with Internet access. We picked up the feed on the South Lakes web cam, on a TV screen. Myself and the staff at the garage watched our rhino give birth in my zoo from the Bentley garage in Knutsford.

It was also being screened live on the BBC website. Over the years I have done many television programmes for mainstream TV , usually one every year at least. We had been working with Channel 5 TV to produce a couple of children's animal programmes that summer, both of which were presented by Michaela Strachan. It was a real coup to have the BBC and Channel 5 at the zoo for the birth and it made a wonderful programme.

It was such a beautiful feeling, and a feeling of redemption in many ways, after the tragedy with Zimba. I had carried a feeling of guilt with me for a long time. The only thing that could have possibly made me feel any better about the death of Zimba was breeding another rhino. I named the baby boy Zimba in his memory.

We were lucky enough to have had two rhino births in the space of four months. Rhinos endure a sixteen-month pregnancy which is one heck of a long time to wait to see a result of the breeding. The rhinos were getting bigger and bigger throughout the end of 2007 and beginning of 2008.

On the 1st June 2008 I went to my friend Stewart's house for a meal, we actually eat in the high quality restaurant which he has on his farm in Kitridding, near Kirkby Lonsdale. I was about five miles away from my own house when my phone rang. It was one of my keepers. "David you'd better get back, we think Ntombi is about to give birth. We think her waters have broken because her back end is very wet all of a sudden. She's out in the field and she's standing funny."

I turned my car round as if I were driving in a movie chase scene. I sped back to the park. As soon as I saw her I knew she was about to give birth. The first thing we needed to do was to separate her from the other rhinos that were standing with her.

It was now that my gift with animals could really pay off. I decided to do something no one else would, or perhaps could, have done – I walked into the field myself to separate Ntombi from her fellow rhinos. I brought Ntombi inside and made sure she was all alone except for a selection of human company. We had been preparing for the impending birth for quite a while and were ready to provide everything necessary for a smooth birth. There was a large straw covered area with a deep litter. There was a web cam once again which everyone was watching intently on a TV screen. Personally I felt that Ntombi would benefit from being calm and I made sure I was there right by her side throughout the birth. It surprised even me that she was so accepting of my being there. Everything just seemed to go perfectly.

I held my camera with anticipation and as the new rhino came into the world I took some treasured photos with an unprecedented viewpoint. Being there when the rhino was born was one of the most moving experiences of my life – it was just the same as going through the birth of my own children. As happened with the birth of my children, I was in tears as the baby rhino appeared. It was a rush of vindication in many ways. The tiny rhino appeared without a horn (this would take time to grow) but huge feet. It was as cute as could be. I knew then was time to make myself scarce to give mother and baby time and space to bond. I continued to watch from the office but felt a surge of fear as I saw Ntombi unsure of how to be a mother – she was nudging the baby quite strongly, I had a sudden fear that she might squash her. I was panicking, hoping to God that she wouldn't kill the baby. Thankfully things settled down and the baby got up for its first walk before settling down to feed. It was a perfect success, despite the fact that many of the surrounding aspects of how we deal with the rhinos at South Lakes Wild Animal Park are somewhat unusual.

There are no other zoos for instance which feature two large adult males running together with two females, but it is something we have long done. Most zoos have one male; if they do have two they will keep the two apart. Ours are always together and it has never been a problem. Once the baby, whom we named Nyala, was born I thought about how long I should leave it before introducing Nyala to the other rhinos. When she was ten-days-old I decided to let her out into the field. It went like a dream, with Ntombi following and the males grouping around in complete acceptance of the new addition to their extended family. We thought Tala would give birth much closer to Ntombi than would turn out to be the case, but it was still a wonderful moment to have had two white rhino births within a few months of each other. It was a coup to have white rhinos breeding concurrently, especially when all could live in harmony. There is also harmony with myself and the rhinos as from the very beginning both of the mothers have allowed me to go in with them and their babies. I played with Nyala and little Zimba from day one and today, often enjoy getting them to roll on their backs while I tickle their tummies.

Every time I go back to the garage for a service they always remind me of that special moment that we all shared. It was magical. Jan, the salesman who I had met when buying my first Bentley, was there too and always likes to talk about that wonderful event. September 11, 2008 was a great day.

My daughter Amy had made it quite clear she didn't intend to come back to work at South Lakes Wild Animal Park. Nevertheless, perhaps in some misguided hope she might return, I kept her on the books for several months. I knew we should follow the correct protocol and issue her with a P45 but before I could make the decision there was a Tribunal summons that came through the post. Amy was suing South Lakes Wild Animal Park for unfair dismissal. I could not believe it. I had even offered her a review meeting via letter which gave her the opportunity to come in and discuss her issues with another senior member of staff. I didn't hear anything back from her whenever I tried to come to a positive solution.

When ACAS (who deal with employment disputes) became

involved, initially as mediators, it was clear Amy had no basis for her claims and the case was dropped. By now Amy had apparently spent well over two thousand pounds on legal fees. It was coming up to Christmas and I decided I would try and make peace with her. I gave my sister Alison a letter to take to my mam and dad's Boxing Day do. In with the letter was a cheque, payable to Amy, to cover all her debts.

In my letter I told Amy that she was welcome to come back to work, that I loved her and wished to see my new granddaughter. I said I hoped we could go back to how things used to be. I wanted my little girl back. I didn't hear back from her and the cheque was never cashed. I waited four weeks thinking she may change her mind. Eventually my accountant asked me what she was to do with this lingering cheque which hadn't been cashed. It was obvious Amy did not want the money so we called the bank to cancel the cheque – the main reason being it could fall into the wrong hands.

Before I knew it I received a letter from her solicitor saying that I was going to be sued privately for cancelling a cheque that belonged to Amy Gill.

I was astounded. I even showed the letter to my sisters and my friends – no one could make sense of it. It didn't make sense that she would be so aggressive instead of just talking to me when I had given her every opportunity. I decided to fight it myself instead of employing my lawyer; I really didn't think I would need one over a cancelled cheque. We ended up in a small claims court. I had tried one last time, this time through a mediator, to speak to Amy but the mediator returned telling me Amy wasn't interested.

The court appearance was a strange occasion. Amy, who is usually very quiet, came bounding in the court laughing with a group of people by her side, including her mum. I was sat on the opposite side on my own.

I said to the judge, "The first thing I want to say to you is I really wish I wasn't here. This is my daughter, I shouldn't be in court fighting my daughter about money, we should be talking. I have given her everything all of her life, what am I doing here? She is saying I owe her £3,000 which was my money in the first place. I gave it to her as a gift to help her."

The judge asked me whether it was a gift, or a commercial deal. I told him it was a gift which he said would make things difficult. Because I had offered a gift, and of this there was no doubt, then I did not have the right to take it away.

It became a pernicious technicality. "I didn't try and take it away," I said to the judge, "she never claimed it. I didn't take it from her, she never had it."

"Well I am sorry but there is a technicality of law here and I have to side with the law." The judge openly said he felt empathy for me and understood where I was coming from but this was the law and I had to pay Amy the original £3,000 as well as her court costs.

Prior to the fallout with Ben and Amy in America I had also helped Amy out financially so that she could buy a house. At the time the mortgage market was going to make it extremely difficult for her to buy one on her own merits, so I told her she would be able to take out a mortgage via South Lakes Wild Animal Park. I bought my friend's old house in Cleator Street, Dalton and I told Amy she could have the house and pay the mortgage to the company directly. There would be no need for a deposit and we would do everything legally and above board, albeit with far better start up terms than she would have had with a bank or building society.

After the fallout in America, when we returned Amy just gave up the house. She sent the house keys back to me and moved everything out, leaving it empty. After this I sent Amy an emotional letter and text messages expressing my surprise and deep upset but saying I still wanted to sort everything out – to forget, move on and start again. I was extremely frustrated.

Despite the ongoing problems in my life I could not slow down at the zoo or in my travelling escapades.

I visited the Howler Monkey Project in Colombia for one of my most bizarre trips yet. With me was my Animal Manager Jo Dennis. Something I have long offered my South Lakes staff is an incentive if they do well during their work they can accompany me on trips around the world – I have taken staff all over the world. It gives me great joy to give them something special that is so much more memorable than a monetary gift.

On this occasion Jo was with me to finally see Howler monkeys in the wild. This was something we did eventually manage to see but the antics along the way were quite amazing. It was searingly hot in Colombia, and humid, perhaps more than usual. As with some of the more exotic trips I have been on, I didn't know what I was letting myself in for.

We were taken to the new site of our project in Jericho, travelling in a cable car to the mountain top, through dense tropical jungle. It struck me how unusual it was to have a cable car in such an area; it would normally be reserved for a ski trip in the Alps. It was a beautiful site and it was no surprise to learn that they were attempting to develop local tourism. Gorgeous as it was, there was no point in trying to attract foreign travellers as hardly anyone goes to Colombia for a holiday.

We reached the top and the locals proudly revealed they would like to show us the site for our reintroduction project. We began to cut a trail through the mountain forest. We may have climbed several hundred feet courtesy of the cable car but we were now going back downhill at some pace given the steepness of the path. The angle was not the only problem – the rocks were covered in moss and algae so it was all we could do to stop from sliding to our deaths. This was incredibly difficult as there was nothing to hold on to. The only thing flanking us were sharp tree branches which were more dangerous to grab hold of than leave well alone.

We seemed to have been walking for quite a while and we began to wonder how much further of this watery death trap was left to traverse.

"It's only another 100 metres down!" our guide helpfully said, too many times for our liking. In fact, it started to become a comment of derision and one we couldn't take seriously.

I was wearing an altimeter which I kept glancing down at.

"Just another 100 metres!"

I could not believe we descended 3000 feet down the mountain without a break. Any one of us could have broken our ankles but somehow we managed to remain intact. It was by now something of a joke between Jo and I that she only ever seemed to accompany me on crippling walking trips, though it can't have been much fun for her either.

As I was trying not to fall down the hill I started to feel my knee start to go yet again. As we slowly and carefully travelled metre upon metre my knee became more and more painful.

"Only another 100 metres!"

Jo and I finally reached the bottom, along with the others in our camp. We took a much needed rest before having to wait for an eternity while everyone else followed behind us at a snail's pace. Some were two hours behind us. The speed with which we had traversed the incline took its toll afterwards however.

I'm not sure what the locals were thinking by having us travel down such a steep mountain. To add insult to injury, all the official delegates met us at the very bottom of the mountain safely tucked up in their cars. Luckily there were cars to pick us up for the two-hour drive to Medellin. It wasn't my thing to stay in fancy hotels but this time one had been organised for us and for once, I was grateful to have somewhere to relax properly. But first, I had to get out of the car.

The ridiculous walk and two hours in a car had done nothing for my groaning body which had by now seized up. I could not move my leg to get out of the car. The comical sight then emerged where several people were trying to extricate a man in his late forties out of a car. Passers by were treated to the even more humorous sight of the same man not being able to walk up a few steps to the hotel. We had to laugh. Well, everyone else did at least. I could hardly even move my mouth to giggle.

I must have looked some sight, like a diseased explorer with parts of the Colombian jungle all over me. A helpful woman ran over to me and in a breathless Colombian Spanish tone said, "Can I get you an ambulance? Do you need the hospital?"

"No thank you," I replied, "a hot bath and a good meal and I'll be fine."

A short while after this visit to South America I travelled there again with my close friend Pierre, this time visiting Peru for the Bear and Condor Projects in Chaparri, Lambayeque, North Western

Peru. This as usual was a very positive and productive visit as the release and rehabilitation of Andean Bears is going very well and the management is very committed. At Chaparri we met a young lady called Raphaella, she was the daughter of an Ecuadorian businessman who has a passion for wildlife conservation. They had set up a private reserve on their huge estate over the border in Ecuador. We were being invited to visit the site and give advice on its future. Raphaella had driven down to collect Pierre and I, the drive north on the Pan American Highway was over 12 hours and we were in the back of a twin cab truck with our legs cramped in the small space. A couple of stops for Ceviche (A Peruvian delicacy of raw fish, seafood and lime juice) Pierre's favourite dish, I love it but I have to say after Ceviche for a number of days, a change is welcome. I cringe at the thought of Pierre getting to the bottom of the plate or dish and then drinking the left over juices of the raw fish and limes, mmmm to him and ughh to me! that drive was certainly memorable not for the desert scenery that is constant up that west coast of South America but for the lack of comfort and excessive heat. Ecuador is so named as it lies on the equator, as we crossed the border the scenery started to change and the region miraculously became a more tropical environment. We drove close to Guayaquil and stayed at the Hacienda of Raphaella, they bred wonderful prancing horses on the Ranch, but the main activity was a huge Banana and Cocoa Plantation along with shrimp farms. They were doing an excellent job of providing a safe haven for the protection of Brown headed Spider monkeys and the Guayaquil Macaw. From there we were met by a man called Ernesto Arbelaez, Ernesto impressed me the first time I met him at a Latin American Zoo conference in Cali, Colombia with his enthusiasm and determination to protect and conserve his local fauna , especially amphibians and reptiles. Ernesto had set up a small Herpetological centre in the bottom floor of his family home in Cuenca, Ecuador and he wanted to expand his ideas to building a small zoo in the very historic city thus enlisting both Pierre and I to give him some guidance and assistance. Ernesto arrived at the hacienda in his car, a two door small compact that seemed to be held together with black tape and cable ties. He intended to make us feel very comfortable by telling us of how proud he was that it was on its second engine after completing over 200,000 km on the first. On the map the road from Guayaquil to Cuenca looked relatively easy and not too long so when we forcibly squeezed both our bodies into the back of the vehicle hitting our chins on our knees and extracting wheel jacks and spare wheels used as cushions on the seat, we were resigned to putting up with the pain for the journey. Ernesto had his girlfriend, Amanda with him and we all engaged in good conversation about the local conservation issues and his ideas. We started to climb up steep roads getting higher and higher, sharper bends and very steep drops, the weather closed in dramatically and the rain that had been light and misty turned heavy and damaging. Ernesto seemed to take all this in his stride not slowing down, yet I couldn't see out of the windscreen as the wipers struggled to push away the volumes of water. I looked at Pierre and he looked at me and we both expressed faces of concern. Ernesto ploughed on swinging left then right, the wheels slipping on the wet corners and the deep mountain valleys appearing too close for comfort. The dark arrived so very quickly as it does on the equator and this just frightened us even more as it really didn't seem to have any effect on Ernesto, he knew the road and clearly felt comfortable, well that was until we came round another bend and suddenly came face to face with a mud slide, but he just calmly drove round the edge placing the car precariously on a wet edge with a thousand feet to the next stopping point down the mountain. The road was deteriorating, the weather washing away the surface and making deep ruts in the carriageway. We had numerous heart stopping slides across the road towards the staggering drops. The small basic bone shaker of a car had made it this far, but every bump in the road made us bang our heads on the roof, every swerve right and left created bruising on our sides and arms and the sheer claustrophobic feeling of being trapped in the back of this car with no door to escape and on the side of an extremely high Andean mountain in the dark and tropical rain was overwhelming. I have never ever felt that kind of vulnerability before except of course when trapped in Australia in the camper. This car was still moving and up a seemingly never ending mountain road, I tried to close my eyes and thought that the best way to deal with it was to not look and try to sleep through it. Amazingly and due to the excessive heat of Guayaquil and the very long day and possible lack of oxygen at the altitude and small car I drifted off into oblivion and woke to the city lights of Cuenca one of the most ancient Cities in South America with a history of about 5000 years and where the Incas once ruled and dominated in the 15th Century. The centre of the city is a UNESCO world heritage site for its historical buildings.

We stayed at Ernesto's family home with the small Reptile and amphibian zoo below us. The experience was enjoyable, the ideas very ambitious and we gave him as much guidance as we could regarding developing his site for the conservation zoo he envisaged. The return was so ordinary compared with the journey to Cuenca I cannot even remember where we went from there or the journey back as the dramatic drive across the Andes to Cuenca was so powerfully etched on my mind !

Chapter 40
Another son, anger and politics

After our dramatic reconciliation in September 2008 Caroline and I started our relationship over again, dating each other like two love struck teenagers. Every weekend I would drive the 100 miles to see Caroline and we would go out on day trips with the kids, visiting the likes of Martin Mere Bird Reserve and Tatton Park, a stately home in Cheshire. Caroline was worried about bumping into someone who might know that we weren't supposed to be seeing each other but I would try and calm her fears, saying that we should just forget about everyone else and enjoy ourselves.

We had to take care but not forget to enjoy our time together. It had been so long since we had our relationship in such a positive state. It was an immense pleasure to spend time with my children too, doing the simple things which I had missed for so long such as playing football with Hari and Kadi while Caroline had some time to herself. We had an idyllic time together, driving for sunny days out with the top down on the Bentley. The sun seemed to shine for weeks on end, and though we were breaking the court order everything seemed right.

Despite our wonderful times together we both knew that the birth of my child with Alison Creary (who long before then had reverted to using her maiden name, Rushton) was imminent. There was no getting away from it. We could put it off all we liked but the reality was, my child was going to be born to another woman. My conscience was too strong to decide to have nothing to do with him just because I wanted to be with Caroline. I wanted to be at the birth, I found this hard to explain to Caroline although I am certain she knew that the child was an innocent party. It was a difficult situation to keep both women happy but I was trying hard, I was trying to do the right thing by my child.

Eventually I had to be honest with Caroline and tell her that I wanted to be at the birth. It upset her but there was no way I could abandon an innocent child. I couldn't really blame Caroline for not wanting me to be involved, she obviously saw the new child and Alison as a continuing threat to her own happiness and we already had our family unit which she did not want disrupting. I could understand that but I had to be there for my new baby when he was born. Alison was due to give birth in early December 2008.

Caroline brought the kids up to my house for Halloween weekend in late October. It was another perfect family gathering with Hari and Kadi dressing for the events in the park where there was always entertainment during Halloween week. While Caroline and I were both getting on so well Caroline fell pregnant again.

It was just four weeks before my child was due to be born to another woman that Caroline revealed this information. I love my children but this was another dramatic turn in what was already a virtually impossible situation to live with I was happy that Caroline was having our child but left sat wondering just how I could extract myself from such a complicated web of issues. I could not believe that I was in such a tangle of emotions and babies. My Christmas present to myself in 2010 was a vasectomy, and about time I hear you say!

Suddenly the union I had with Caroline was a potent threat to Alison. There was increased tensions in the long-standing war that Alison had waged against Caroline, which was hellish for all concerned. A few weeks before Alison was due to give birth, somehow she saw Caroline drive past her house on the way up to see me.

Alison jumped in her car, with her kids, and followed Caroline up the hill to my house. She was right behind Caroline as she came through the security gates. Before I knew it the two of them were having a verbal and physical altercation in my garden. It was all Alison she just lost control and was giving both Caroline and me abuse. The kids were watching as Alison was screaming at Caroline and pushing and shoving, at first I just wanted to hide, I knew it was all my own making and had no idea at all what to say or how to escape it all. Nonetheless after a short while I tried to mediate, keeping them apart. Alison stole my house keys and so then I took the car keys away from Alison as I truly believed she could harm herself if she drove whilst so full of rage, she didn't seem to be of sound mind, she completely lost her cool and was liable to hurt herself driving in a rage.

Alison started to leave, and as she did she ran down the hill in the dark and tripped and fell down (she was eight months pregnant at that time). I told Caroline I would have to take her to the hospital, I felt terrible that the bad blood could possibly harm our child. I knew Caroline wouldn't like it but I didn't feel I had a choice; I wanted to make sure Alison and our baby was healthy. She had tests done at the hospital and they took precautions with an overnight stay but thankfully she was okay.

I went down to the hospital the next morning, after spending the night with Caroline at my house with our two children, and picked Alison up. As I was sitting next to Alison's bed talking to her before she could be discharged, I noticed Neil, one of my zoo keepers walk past us. He had just been dropped off at casualty; in agony after the door to the rhino enclosure had fallen off and almost flattened him. In the end thankfully Neil was fine too.

In amongst my personal travails I was still running into the occasional problem at South Lakes.

It was the 8th December 2008 and was the first really cold night of the winter and the keepers were making strides to bring in all of the lemurs making sure they didn't get too cold. Around 8pm I was in my house and I could see a strange light outside, something was flashing. I looked out to see a huge orange light along with plumes of smoke. I suddenly realised the lemur house was on fire. I had to call the fire brigade right away.

I knew I had to do something so I grabbed a coat and ran down to the lemur house. I couldn't believe the raging inferno that greeted me. It was so bad in fact that I could not get anywhere near it. All the glass had melted and the roof had collapsed, it was even hard to tell exactly which lemur houses were on fire, I could only really see three of the six units. I took a deep breath and ran in to the first lemur house, I suddenly saw that three were completely dark and had yet to be breached by fire. I was met by a wall of smoke. I tried to open the slides of each house to see if the lemurs would come flying out but nothing came. I was fumbling around in the pitch black then attempting to grab any lemurs I could. I found something and I grabbed it. It bit me, but I threw it out of the door and then I grabbed something else and threw it out the door. I had to come out for another breath. I was barely breathing but I knew I had to go back in and grab as many lemurs as I could. Out of the lemurs I could see they were just sitting there observing the smoke enveloping them.

The smoke was ever present, ensnaring me like a plastic bag tied over my mouth. I had to get back out into the air to breathe in again. I repeated this several times before I finally found the lemurs huddling together in the top corner of one of the houses. I didn't care where they went in the zoo, I just grabbed as many as I could and threw them out of the door. I thought I had got them all. The fire was still whipping through the wooden houses. I saw a blue light approaching and felt relieved the fire engine had finally come to help. It soon became a worry that they might not actually be able to do anything; it was such a distance from the accessible part of the park to the lemur houses. By the time they actually extended and attached all the pipes and hoses there was barely anything left of the houses.

My lungs were full, I could hardly breathe, with a constant feeling that I was going to be sick. I was given oxygen. I was still in a daze over the events, worrying whether the lemurs had all escaped. I hoped perhaps a hole had burned into one of the houses where they might have escaped. For me, I was just trying to breathe properly again. I was told to go to hospital but decided to go back home and recover there.

First thing the next morning I went out with tools to clean up the rubbish and rubble. One by one I found all of the 31 lemurs that had perished. They had been completely roasted and were virtually unrecognisable. I could only tell what type of lemur it was from the building I was in. The fire had been so strong that the aluminium ladders in the house had completely gone save for two steel clips.

The worst thing of all was that one of the lemurs had given birth to triplets which she had raised separately. She and each of the babies had died.

The fire removed the entire breeding group of Red Ruff lemurs, the main breeding group of black lemurs as well as a whole group of ringtails. Some of the lemurs had been with me for thirteen years since they were babies. I knew them all and they had all been home bred. I was devastated.

The fire had been caused by sawdust in a thermostat because it was a wooden building. The irony was we had been constructing a metal building for the lemurs and in just a couple of months all those who died would have been in a new building which would have never caught fire. The one good thing to come out of the tragedy was that we learned to always clean the thermostat. The chances of a tiny bit of sawdust causing the spark in the thermostat were miniscule but anything can happen. It is something we are now always aware of.

Those lemurs which did survive changed in their behaviour. They were so used to seeing their fellow lemurs who just disappeared one day – it was very perplexing for them. Ultimately we would introduce another group of lemurs from Holland to create a new group. We are now almost back to the 100 lemurs we had before the terrible fire. We have only recently managed to have a breeding group of Red Ruff lemurs again however which is a real shame as it is this species that I work with in the wilds of Madagascar. Thankfully by 2012 the lemurs will be breeding again. The trauma of that night was devastating and the shock must have reverberated through us all as the very next morning Alison came to the park to inform me she was feeling labour pains. I calmly drove her to hospital thinking that it would be many hours of waiting as had happened with all of my children previously.

I had only been waiting for around twenty minutes at the hospital when my son's head appeared and just like that, Indiana Darwin came into the world. After the convoluted build up we had been blessed with a smooth birth process. We chose the name Indiana, which was based on the fact I wanted my lad to be adventurous like his brother Hari, and who more adventurous than the perennial fictional daredevil Indiana Jones? The Darwin part came from our time in the Galapagos where the Darwin theory was developed. Alison initially disliked the name Indiana but after a while she came to terms with it. She did offer two alternatives – Harley or Harrison – but they were a little too close to Hari for my liking and I questioned the intention of wanting a name so close to my older son, but she never provided any other alternative so Indiana it was.

I felt an immediate special connection with Indi – I loved him from the moment I saw him. Alison didn't want to feed him herself and so I was given his very first bottle to feed him and loved every second of it. I was so glad to have been there for the birth. Alison and Indi were in hospital for just one day after the birth with me going to visit. When she was discharged I asked her what she was going to do next.

"Do you want him for the night?" or words to that effect she asked. It was a strange question in hindsight, and a suggestion which most mothers would find immensely difficult to understand.

At the time however I did not question the sanity behind such a suggestion, I merely reacted as I saw fit. I was happy to take Indi home with me. Alison came up to the house with him, I already had a cot and baby room set up at my house because I knew he was on the way and I expected to be involved, although I did not know how much. It was a stroke of good fortune to me to be given the opportunity to take responsibility full time. Alison left with her girls to return the next day to see him again, but once again left Indi with me for the night and this carried on.

I had certainly held my fair share of babies but for some reason, perhaps the overwhelming nature of having to look after him all by myself, there was a certain fragility about Indi. I was particularly conscious of how tiny he was. I felt vulnerable and alone but loved every second regardless. I was immensely lucky. I placed his cot at the foot of my bed but Indi only woke up once every night, usually at about 2am, and after this he would sleep until 7 or 8am. He was a perfect baby, he never cried, he was a pleasure to have. Alison would come and see him and also take him out for walks on her own. I often expected she would ask to have him back whenever she returned to my house with him, but she never did. To my mind I felt that Alison was desperate to displace Caroline and the way that she felt she could do so was by making sure I had as much contact with my son as I could, to have as tight a bond as possible so that when my other child came along I would be less involved.

Caroline didn't say much after Indi's birth but we kept our relationship going through it, however it was a delicate balancing act that was simply too difficult to expect to run smoothly.

Christmas was difficult as you can imagine but Caroline and the children came up and we all opened our presents, four days after Christmas Day. Caroline had no problem with Indi and she told me and showed me as much by the way she was with him, she just didn't want Alison to be around which was totally understandable. It was of course still impossible for me to get rid of Alison from my life when she was Indi's mother. Caroline was quite happy to push Indi around the zoo in his pram, all of my staff and friends saw that she was making the effort with another woman's child and at this point I was extremely happy, it all seemed to be coming together. Alison still saw Indi, but only during the day and when it suited her. Indi became my full time job and changed my life because all of a sudden I had the singular responsibility of bringing up my son virtually alone. I had wonderful friends around me who gave me support and assistance.

It might seem that I have a very awkward relationship with the authorities but, in 2009, I made a step to try and change my local community. In my local area many people seem to have an opinion – just as they have an opinion on me it seems – on what kind of relationship I have with Barrow Borough Council. In 1993 when I first put in my plans to build South Lakes Wild Animal Park, Barrow Council gave me their complete support. It truly seemed as if they wanted me to help improve our local town and surrounding areas. As time went on and circumstances changed however, with society being run with greater red tape and bureaucracy, it seemed petty little jealousies started to arise. A story which became a big deal locally involved my applying for permission to tarmac the South

Lakes car park as it was a mass of grass and gravel. I wanted the car park to be smooth as it was a nightmare for families with strollers, not to mention disabled people. It cost £120,000 to tarmac the car park but safety came first. Council officers approved the scheme but there was one councillor, Councillor Gordon Murray who seemed to have a jealousy problem. His old house stood next door to my zoo and, though he sold it to another buyer, apparently the two were in cahoots to oppose my plan – for some reason they didn't like the zoo being there. Murray took it to an extreme, pursuing against me with venom, and somehow he managed to turn everyone against the idea and eventually my plan was rejected. It had all been approved by planning officers and was completely logical yet Murray had scuppered the final approval.

Suddenly we were refused permission to tarmac the car park. I took it to an appeal which cost a lot of money but it was worth every penny as the case was overturned, in fact, the Appeal Inspector claimed it was one of the most clear cut cases he had ever witnessed. It was obvious we needed the car park and it was clearer still that it did not impinge on the landscape, as Councillor Murray claimed. I took things further and asked for an investigation as to why he had been so staunchly against our plan.

Ultimately he defected from the Conservative party after pressure from them to oust him. He moved to the Liberal Democrats, and lost his position as Chairman of the Planning Committee. There was clearly a personal problem which no one could understand. I knew he might cause a lot of trouble for myself and the park in the future. A person who I shall not name came to me and asked,

"David, do you want to stop this man from causing you trouble again on the Council?"

"Well, yes it would be nice because he's just being obstructive. He's not doing what's right for the community and Councillors are supposed to do what's right for the people who voted for them and everybody knows that wasn't right."

"Right, why don't you run for Councillor then, in the same Ward, in the same election and see if you can beat him and then he can't do it again?"

I thought this was a very good idea, although I rarely considered political affairs unless they directly affected me or the business. Life gets in the way of politics unless you are involved on a direct level. It was perhaps the time for me to become involved. In the build up to the 2009 local elections I attended the local Conservative Party meeting and I soon realised I could offer a lot to the community. I found a good team in place and there were six seats available. I assisted them in organising everything including leaflets and publicity. I had always erred on the Conservative side because they seemed to be supportive of local businessmen trying to further themselves. They had certainly supported me when I was first starting. Despite this loyalty I had no true interest in politics. I helped in the campaign and come election night my fellow five Conservatives all won their seats. When it came to the decision on my proposed seat I was up against Murray and another chap who had set up as an Independent. The Independent and I both received the exact same number of votes. I asked for a recount and when they did so it emerged I had won by three votes. Then my opponent asked for a recount. He won by a single vote.

I asked for another recount, which was by now well into the next day. He again won by a single vote. It was a personal view into how a political system such as a vote count is not infallible. It was only by votes three and four that they found consistency. If he had not asked for a recount I would have been elected. Instead, he won fair and square and I shook his hand knowing he would do a good job. I felt relieved as I knew he had the time to create an impact with many of the same ideas I had, whereas I was always struggling for time as it was. Thankfully, the best aspect of my running was that Mr. Murray rolled in far down the rankings and couldn't find a seat on the council. It is quite astonishing to note that he defected to Labour and had therefore ran for all three colours in the space of two years or so.

Sadly he was re-elected in 2011 which only served to show me that people vote for the party, not for the individual representative. Murray is now back on the planning committee, still causing disruption as he in my opinion misuses his position, throwing personal grievances into a professional situation and with his history should not be allowed to be on Planning decisions about the zoo.

Nonetheless, overall, working with or alongside Barrow Council has been one of the easier elements of my business life. Apart from the situation with the Rhino in 97, I had never really had a problem with them contrary to popular belief, until very recently that is. Situations that were once easy are a lot more difficult nowadays and there is an awful lot of red tape but that is the scourge of modern society. The Planning Department however have been very helpful and positive about our future. The council have some individuals who are very confrontational and sadly, at the time the relationship had hit an all time low. Common sense is not being applied and a "jobsworth" mentality sometimes erupts. I am so glad I am not dealing with these issues directly anymore and take a back seat, it certainly is a challenge trying to operate a business or employ people with the red tape and regulations we are burdened with these days. To be very open I would never live in this Borough and I would have left many years ago if it was not for the zoo. The whole attitude in Barrow since the demise of the Shipbuilding industry has been negative, backward and must be the worst place in Britain for encouraging innovation and private enterprise. The mentality of the present councillors seemingly is to stop all business development, job creation and wealth creation, but we are stuck here and we have to hope that a change of administration and now a total clean out of the older Managers in the Council may herald a new brighter, positive vision for the Borough.

I just keep smiling and trying hard and it always wins through in the end. We need new young, enthusiastic innovators on the council in this borough to turn this long held negativity around and we are happy to help achieve that aim, local community is very important to me and we are keen to find ways of involving the community in our work and assisting the community to use our facilities in as many ways as possible, from free school visits to local schools and Church services on site to hosting youth events and charity fund raising days, it is all a very important part of our place in this local community and we all have great fun doing all these things.

One such annual event is "Dream Night" a special evening

in June where we invite children with special needs and families of disabled or seriously ill children. The whole staff give their time and make it a magical night for all involved. Usually 600 people attend and it has become one of the very special days in our years.

Chapter 41
A violent feud, losing
my children and Yellowstone

Unfortunately the issues with Alison and Caroline were still ongoing. Out of nowhere on the 30th May 2009 when Caroline was up at my house with me – seven months pregnant – Alison left her three children, including Indi (as she was having a rare few hours with him), home alone and came storming up to my house in her car in blind uncontrollable rage. She had previously stolen a remote for my security gates that I was unaware of and used this to enter my home. She totally lost control of herself. As Alison was running threateningly towards Caroline, Caroline was in the house quickly shutting the door behind her. Alison ran up to the now locked full glass door and started screaming, banging at the door with hands and kicking so hard with her feet.

"What are you going to achieve by doing this?" I shouted at Alison through the glass. I honestly thought she was going to hurt herself, she was going berserk. "Go home and calm down, we can talk things through later," I said.

"I need to sort it out with her," Alison replied, almost feral.

"You are not fighting, she is seven months pregnant, you are not fit, get home now." "I'm not going home until I have sorted it with her once and for all."

I told Caroline and the children to go upstairs out of the way.

Alison and I continued to remonstrate with each other and after the children were safely upstairs Caroline came back down. Alison picked up a large rock and with the rock in her hand swung it at kitchen window towards Caroline, smashing the double glazing. Unbeknownst to Alison I had called the police when I saw how ferocious she was and after she had refused to leave after breaking in to my property. The police turned up just in time to see her launching the rock at my front window. She turned on the police, swearing at them, resisting and, all the while becoming quite agitated with the officers. She could quite easily have been charged with attacking the police. She was instantly arrested and taken to the police station in Barrow. I was informed by the Police that she spent the night in the jail cells. I should have pressed charges against her but she was still Indi's mother and I had no desire to make the situation any worse.

As I understand it Alison was allowed out on police bail with certain conditions attached but was told in no uncertain terms that she could not come up to the park – she wasn't allowed near me, Caroline or the kids and she would have been hauled into court at the speed of light if she decided to trespass. Because the children had been there during the incident however, the police report was immediately passed on to Social Services. Caroline received a call two days later that she was required to attend an interview with Social Services in Trafford , she was supposed to be staying with me for the week with Hari and Kadi and we had been having a wonderful time and I desperately didn't want her to leave. Caroline was terrified that if she didn't go to the meeting they might do something to her, whether it be take the kids away or something else as we had been breaking the order for nine months and despite us doing fine without the interference of the court system, all of a sudden Alison's anger and violence had brought it all back to us with a vengeance and Alison in effect got what she wanted.

Caroline was very fearful. I was distraught. I reacted badly at Caroline's decision to leave and I tried to stop her. I didn't want to lose my family. It had all happened because Alison had brought the police into the picture by her own behaviour. This now was the pattern that Alison managed to cause so much trouble for Caroline that it ruined our relationship, Alison had been doing this consistently for nearly two years , giving Caroline hell in the school yard or in any way she could to get her out of my life. Caroline always maintained the only reason she moved back to Manchester was to escape Alison Creary and the gossip that she procured around the school yard and in the town. Her aim had been achieved. Alison's ease of having angry outbursts and taking out on others was a major part of the whole situation Caroline and I were in from a courts perspective, the anger from Alison just erupted and ended up getting the attention of the court, amazingly not for her but for Caroline and I.

What a mess I had made for everyone by my own actions getting two women pregnant at the same time , I look back and try to understand what emotions I stirred . I had to face the music and because children were involved I was stuck with it or abandon my children which was something that was not even considered as I was their Daddy and I loved them .

I still felt guilty about seeing Caroline regularly while the court order was hanging over us. I decided to tell the truth and ask for assistance for our family as we had done so well for the previous nine months without the Court system involved. So I approached CAFCASS (The Children and Family Court Advisory and Support Service) and said I wanted to talk to someone high up who might understand. I told the person the full extent of what had been happening, even that in both our views the previous CAFCASS representative had not exactly had our best intentions at heart. He came to see me and we spoke for six hours. I truly thought he understood where I was coming from and that he could see I had changed. I did this to ask for help but unfortunately he told me he was now obliged to tell the courts I had broken the law.

I asked that he at least give the Court the breakdown of what we had spoken about and that I was in a better place now – I told him all I wanted was a positive resolution. He promised me he would do his best. The Court however was presented with a piece of paper which told them I had broken the order and I now know that one of the worst things you can do is to break a court order and anyone reading this take note, breaking court Orders is a sin you will always regret, so do not do it .

Once the law had been broken the whole situation obviously went downhill just as before.

All of a sudden I wasn't allowed to see my children again.

I could give them so much love with me at the zoo and yet the "system" and the people in it could never see how important I was to my children. Surely, it did more harm than good to separate the kids from their father? They were the victims of a feud waged by one woman on another that I caused by my irresponsible actions and yet importantly the children were the ones punished. No attempt by the "system" to find a solution to the real cause of the problems , no attempts to look for alternatives to the "draconian" separations, just a straight forced separation against both Caroline's and my wishes and without any doubt against the wishes of the children and to their detriment as shown later.

We live in a society where the "experts" always claim to know best and who checks out these "experts" ? no one, their opinions are Gospel, their views accepted as always factual and lives ruined, destroyed and children's whole futures and minds messed up because of these frighteningly powerful "experts" who just go home at 5pm and get their meals and watch TV unaffected, but with a huge fee in their pockets whilst our family is devastated, separated and the children left distraught and lost by the whole events.

A court hearing was set up for October 2009 and I didn't see Caroline before it took place. I then never saw my children again since that very moment. I never had sight of them, nor spoke to them. In fact I had no contact with them at all since June 1st 2009.

I desperately tried to be involved with Caroline when she was due to give birth – once again I wanted to be there. I asked for permission from the social workers but was told that I was not allowed to be present because of the Courts decision, I was in an impossible position. Toba James was born on 25th July 2009 but I never held him or was able to hug or kiss him.

After this Caroline would not talk to me and break any orders, understandable as the Court system is a very frightening place for anyone and especially for people who have witnessed the power and control it has over your life. By September 2009 I decided it was about time I faced up to the bare facts. If it was the decision of the "system" to permanently separate Caroline and I and my children then I can't go back down the same road and I must find a way to escape the nightmare the "system" created for us all, then I would be doing the best thing for me, not to mention Indi, by moving on. I would think that most reading this would not know the power of the court to break up relationships between adults by force.

I wanted to return to America. It had been a terrible personal time with Ben and the family during my RV trip but it hadn't spoiled the love I had for America itself. The scenery was never less than superb and I felt at home there.

I asked Alison if she would mind if I took Indi to America. It was clear she would agree if they all came with us. I thought it would make life a lot easier so I agreed. We decided we should get another RV and this time, go north from Denver, Colorado into Yellowstone, it's something I had always wanted to do. In September 2009 we spent two weeks in the west of America. We travelled through Jackson Hole in Wyoming. I loved it. We spent five days in Yellowstone witnessing mind-blowing scenery. There are more geysers there than everywhere else in the world added together; there are more geothermal features than anywhere else on the planet. The colours, the smells and the scenery are second to none.

We left Wyoming taking the Bear Tooth Pass into Montana before coming back down into Wyoming. We came through a town called Cody, a small cowboy town – it is the Eastern gateway to Yellowstone. There was something about the place that I loved. Though we only spent just over 24 hours there I felt a strong affinity with Cody. We camped in the town and watched a cowboy show, 'Cody Cattle Company'. After Cody we drove back into Denver, Colorado, our starting point. We travelled through the Rocky Mountain National Park where it was snowing heavily.

The scene around Cody reminded me of *Lonesome Dove* which is a TV mini-series based on the Pulitzer Prize–winning western novel written by Larry McMurtry. Robert Duvall and Tommy Lee Jones are the main characters who portray old Texas Rangers, who are retired and finished. They learn of a gathering of a few thousand cattle in Southern Texas and Northern Mexico which are available for whoever can take them.

They drive the cattle two-and-a-half thousand miles up through the middle of Indian country up to, through Wyoming, through Yellowstone and up to Montana. The story is epic and involves a lot of pitfalls; it's a real cowboy adventure. But it is the love story which runs simultaneously through the film that particularly appeals to me. My all time favourite film.

The whole trip was a marvellous experience and Alison and I got on very well. Indi was only nine-months-old and had to contend with a lot of time in a car seat but he was remarkable, perfectly behaved the whole time. He was such a good kid; he sat in the RV, perfectly happy while I drove 3,000 miles in two weeks. I was wondering when we returned, if maybe there was still something for Alison and I and whether I truly could move on from Caroline.

Caroline and I had such a difficult time. The way I saw it everybody was against us, especially my older children and especially the heartless, unemotional so-called professionals who dictated and controlled our children's destiny. Everybody wanted to spoil it so I started to wonder whether I should stay with Alison. The sticking point was that there was no way I could ever forget my three kids with Caroline. The one compromise I was never willing to make was giving up my children.

Chapter 42
Soldiers, deportation
and a Madagascan cyclone

Caroline turned up to the court building in October holding Toba as she was breast feeding she could not leave him at home. It was the very first time I had seen my son and he was three-months-old. I couldn't touch him or go near him; the closest I got was about twenty-feet, it was so emotional. I was told after this that another hearing was due in December after up to date investigations were made into the family and whether I should now be allowed to see my children in the future after all. This gave me hope and seeing Toba lifted my spirits.

Directly after my court hearing in October 2009 I flew to Niger with Pierre. There seemed to be a military clamp down going on and when we arrived there were soldiers everywhere. It was news to me. I also did not know how difficult it would now be to obtain a visa. Usually I walked straight into the minister's office and picked up my visa before entering the harsh, hot terrain of Niger. I was friends with the former Minister for Education of Niger and he usually personally saw to it that my visa was granted, but he was out of the country.

Just as I was about to take my bag off the luggage carousel I was accosted by a tall, armed soldier. I was told I had to go with them immediately. "What about my bag?"

"Leave your bag. This way," he ordered in French.

I turned and looked forlornly at Pierre. Pierre had his visa and was allowed through.

I was taken into a room. All around me were men holding machine guns talking very loudly in fast flowing French. I was being moved from room to room without a shred of explanation.

Eventually I was moved through another set of doors and out onto the runway.

I saw that we were heading directly towards a plane, though I had no idea of its destination. In the blink of an eye the plane started up. We were in the air and the next thing I knew I was in Burkina Faso. I didn't know where Burkina Faso was, but I saw that this is where we were once we landed. Their explanation, when I finally received it, was that I did not have a visa on arrival and they had to deport me.

I had to wait in the most uncomfortably humid, sweaty office for a couple of hours before I saw the right person who could help me get back to Niger. I explained that my bag was full of spectacles.

"What?"

"Second hand spectacles," I explained, "I am here to help the people of Niger. I came here with a bag full of spectacles and bandages and things like that to give to needy people in Niger." The man looked at me, intrigued. "Here I am being treated like I am a criminal, it is absolutely appalling."

"Well I wish you had come to Burkina Faso with those things because we need them just as much here," the man replied. Luckily he was a helpful chap who understood I was a humanitarian, looking to help all peoples. There was no favouritism towards Niger. He told me not to worry, that I would be able to go back to Niger. The arrangement was quite simple. Pay them 1000 euros and I would be able to catch a flight back to Niger.

Back onto the plane I went. It was a relatively short flight and I would later realise, Burkina Faso was directly next door to Niger, a landlocked West African country. After a brief flight, I felt happy to finally be allowed to walk legally into Niger. I reached the door of the plane, where I was met by more soldiers with guns. "Mr.Gill!" one of the soldiers shouted aggressively. Through the open door of the plane all of my documentation, and my returning luggage, was thrown at me.

"You are not getting off this plane!" the soldier barked. He wasn't lying. I was marched back to my seat and the plane turned and flew back to Paris. Within 24 hours I had experienced a very frightening amount of uncertainty and terror, only to end up back where I started. I still had a bag full of spectacles.

The regime was clearly very military and it encapsulated one of my most fearful experiences through all the years I have travelled. To be held at gunpoint when you don't even know why is about as scary as it gets and unfortunately my good friend Dr. Khalid Ikhiri (who is the President of the Association to Safeguard the Giraffes of Niger and the Niger Association for the Defence of Human Rights) was not in the country to assist me with an explanation of my position and consistent humanitarian help to the peoples of Niger. In a country such as this under such draconian measures, you really do wonder whether you might get kidnapped, or killed and left. Your body would certainly decompose quickly in the scorching heat. During the celebrations for the 50th year anniversary of Pierre's zoo I spoke with Khalid. He said this experience I had in his country was so unfortunate and he apologised telling me that, contrary to my belief at the time, he could have resolved this with those who were causing me problems. I should have utilised his influence, all it would have taken was one phone call and it would have been sorted amicably. What a difference one phone call can make !

Even when travelling into the country had been safer there was always the language barrier. I thought I could pick up a fair bit of French until I was in a room with the Niger Environment Minister speaking his native dialect. Once, when Pierre and I were in a meeting with the Minister he was talking so fast it was impossible to follow what he was saying. I politely smiled as I looked around the office at the pictures on the walls, wondering what on earth he was going on about. I didn't think it would matter as I could ask Pierre at the end.

After the meeting Pierre and I were walking down the corridor and I turned to him and said, "Pierre, I never got a word of that, not a word. What did he say?" "I don't know," Pierre replied, "I couldn't understand him either!" It was such a strong, unusual dialect of French that even a native Frenchman could not follow a word, though we had both shaken the minister's hand thanking him profusely as we left the office. We both laughed and asked our native staff to help.

As soon as Pierre arrived back from Niger the two of us flew from Paris to Madagascar. I hadn't been for a couple of years and I had a wonderfully rejuvenating experience where I forgot about all the things which had been going wrong. We set up our new forest projects and designed the eco-tourism chalets. We spent a little time going to the Masoala Peninsula where lemurs ran wild. We went on long night walks and saw all kinds of unusual animals that are endemic to Madagascar, including Aye-Aye and mouse lemurs to name a few. It was a magnificent trip but just as it seemed to be helping me come to terms with all that was going on there was another twist.

We set off to go to the Masoala Peninsula where we knew a storm was forecast. There was very little communication to speak of so unbeknownst to us as we were climbing into the small boat; the storm had been upgraded to a cyclone. The water was so up and down that our guide, who had been through the stormy conditions hundreds of times before, threw up in the boat. Several hours in a tiny boat was enough to test even the most able seafarer. Pierre and I had prepared for the storm by not wearing any coats, so the rain quickly soaked us through. The weather was in fact atrocious once we reached the Peninsula but we saw some amazing animals such as Red Ruffed lemurs and giant scarlet red millipedes and actually had a great time.

For those who wonder why I would not pack a coat with me I must say that the chances of rain at that time of year were actually very minor before we set off. The chances are if you pack a coat the weather will be stifling and hot and all you will be doing is carrying it with you everywhere. And in terms of looking ahead at weather forecasts, we were in a place where people lived in little mud huts with no television. Even if we looked on the Internet at the forecast it could not possibly show a storm on the way, these things can develop in the space of a few hours. Therefore, when I visit tropical locales, I tend not to pack a coat.

Though we had a wonderful time on the Peninsula we still had to traverse the water for another seven hours to get back. As we set off the sky became darker and darker, the wind blew stronger and stronger, the waves crashed higher and higher and our little boat, every now and again, peaked at the top of it. It was like something from *The Perfect Storm* though we were only in a tiny boat. Occasionally we would see a slight glimpse of the land in the distance but then the rain would come in again and eradicate that sanctuary.

It started to become a little frightening. It was as if we had no idea which direction we were travelling – bouncing thirty feet up and down in the boat – I had no idea how our guide could realistically know where we were going or how to get back. The storm continued for hours and eventually ruined everything we had with us, including my camera. I managed to salvage the memory card with all the photos we had taken, but the camera itself was useless. The guide was throwing up all the way back as the boat bounced up in the most ridiculous sailing conditions I have ever seen. The boat almost tipped over completely countless times.

Eventually we made it back safe and sound. I still loved Madagascar and its people. Separate to our conservation projects there is a humanitarian project run by a lady, Violette, who buys disused 100-gallon oil drums. She has gathered all the disabled people she could find from the streets of Antananarivo, the capital of Madagascar. This includes the blind, deaf and those with limbs which are damaged or missing. She has given them work cutting the oil drums up into pieces, welding it into shapes which can be made into furniture, light shades or statues etc. They make the pieces in Madagascar and Violette then comes to France and sells them. Pierre and I visited her and each year bought many pieces from her to sell in our zoos. With the profits she has made, the disabled people and their children now have buildings to live, a school and work in reasonable comfort. She has become very revered in Antananarivo, she is something of a Mother Theresa: Mother Violette.

Pierre, Elisa and I also travelled to mountain villages. We knew that we wanted raffia toys making, but that if we went to a dealer the people would get next to nothing. So we travelled to the villages to deal with the villagers directly so they would receive the best price. We gave the same size order to each family in the village. Soon they made enough toys to put into a container that would be shipped back to France and England. This ensures the whole community directly benefits from the work.

Elisa is a truly beautiful lady, in every which way. She has a heart of gold and is, like her husband, very caring. Each year Elisa helps by organising all the logistics of transporting all of the products we buy in Madagascar.

The beauty of travelling with Pierre and Elisa are the amazing highs and sometimes, one or two scary moments. Pierre and I are like two peas in a pod. I generally fit my schedule around his and follow his lead as to when we travel. He will say we have to go to Madagascar, Niger and Peru and I pretty much allow myself to be told when and where to go to these projects by Pierre and his assistant Peggy.

Chapter 43
Inept social workers, children who turned on me and formal complaints.

After my exotic travels I had managed to somewhat postpone thoughts of my upcoming court hearing, though it was never far from my mind. In most cases it is common process for the "system" to request for a special report on the family. Usually the local authority is asked to do this work and investigate in detail the family and then produce a report that will be the basis for any decisions. I was aware that any report, as it would be with any family, would be to find out whether we were both caring parents and capable of sharing care of the children . I was very confident that we were now on a positive road and of course I loved and cared for my children any one could clearly see that it was so obvious to the world around us.

In October 2009 I was contacted by a woman from Trafford Council, because Caroline lived in Trafford Borough, who was asked by her Managers to interview me and see me with my family and my home, I assumed she would come and visit with myself and Indi. I thought that when she saw the love and quality of life I was able to provide Indi along with him being such a happy child, and by talking to people who knew me and my family life, that she would look favourably upon the chances of me doing the same for Hari, Kadi and Toba. I knew that if she heard personal friends' testimonies of the depth of love and time I gave to my children and saw the zoo she could see what a wonderful environment it was for children to grow up in.

The woman told me she was "too busy" to come and visit. I could not believe it. I said, "You must come, how else can you see the quality of life I provide for my children?"

"I am too busy, you will have to come down to see me at my office in Manchester."

I had no choice but to comply and travel down to Manchester where it became immediately apparent that I was quite unpopular. I later found out that once a month for a period of six months this lady had been sitting chatting with Caroline about me as she was her social worker and somehow this woman was allowed to be assigned to make an impartial decision over whether I was a good man and a good father. It was not fair but there was nothing I could do.

Suddenly the woman told me someone else was taking part in the interview with me. I could not believe the interrogation I then received, it was like something from a Nazi film – I may as well have had a light shined in my face. There were two people from different angles both berating me with a mass of accusations from which I felt I had to defend myself. The idea was supposedly a way to see the positive qualities of the father but it was nothing like that. It was a complete interrogation which was abusive and tantamount to bullying. On top of this it was sexist in my opinion, two women berating me for three hours.

The subject matter was a bit of a shock to me and didn't really seem to focus on my abilities as a father. I was told amongst other things that I had tried to kill my family when I accidentally missed a turning in America. I countered saying it was odd how they stayed with me for another ten days of the trip if they believed I was trying to kill them. The women were aggressive and intimidating. I walked out shaking. As soon as I got home I wrote and apologised that perhaps I didn't come across as my real self because I was so intimidated. I also had to make a complaint about their methods.

Unsurprisingly there was nothing resolved from my initial complaint, the response was that they had carried out their jobs the way they should have. I later found out via the complaints process that the first woman had contacted Amy and Ben for their opinions about me. She didn't balance it out by asking other people who might give a positive opinion; she only spoke with the two children who had become estranged from me. What then followed remains the worst thing that has ever happened to me and my family.

I had put over twenty years of my life into raising my son Ben and daughter Amy. They were my life, I loved them dearly, sacrificed so much for them and when I worked all the hours God sent it was to provide a great quality of life for my kids and to secure my family's future. I never wanted to become estranged from Amy or Ben but it is the way my life had turned. It was something I had come to accept even if I didn't understand the reasons why. The following information was supplied to me by other family members, confirmed by both my older children at a later stage and not from any official documents and was also revealed to me via investigators into my complaints during a separate and unconnected investigation against Trafford Council and is not intended to breach any rules or legal confidences but to illustrate the desperate and emotionally challenging situation I have been faced with and to assist any reader who may wish to avoid such horrendous scenarios in their lives.

Out of the blue, without me even knowing, Amy made a verbal statement over the phone to the Social Services which shocked me.

She said she was so frightened of me she thought I was going to shoot her. She also mentioned something which had happened, but which was as baffling to me then as it is now. Amy had given birth to a baby that I had never seen and amazingly, she had taken her daughter for her vaccinations at the same time I had taken Indi. I arrived in the doctor's waiting room. There were other people around but when Amy caught sight of me she ran into the toilets screaming. Everyone must have wondered what on earth was happening. I know I did. Amy apparently told the social worker that she ran into the toilet screaming because she thought I was a danger to her and her child. She said that she would never let her daughter anywhere near me because I was so dangerous. Then came the most shocking damnations. Amy, I was led to understand stated she had an absolutely terrible upbringing and that I had been abusive to her as a child – both verbally and in the manner I had neglected her and Ben. Amy concluded that she never wanted to see me again and that Hari and Kadi would be better away from me because I was such a terrible father.

Ben's statement concurred with Amy's, in fact it was almost identical. I was a terrible father, I hit him as a child, I spent no time with them, didn't care about them and he had a terrible childhood. In Ben's opinion Hari should be protected from me and not allowed to see me and that as far as he was concerned he never ever wanted to have anything to do with me ever again and it would be stupid of anybody to allow those children near me. Whilst the words may not be totally accurate because of the second hand nature of the information the picture was the same.

Well I will have to leave it to your imagination as to what then happened as I am not allowed by the Secrecy/Privacy Laws to comment on the content of that report but it doesn't take much imagination to see what the "system" thought of such information given by my own children.

I had no chance to question the comments or counteract, it was merely passed on. This inability to question so called professionals and opinions was by now a familiar story. The "system" I had explained to me, works on the balance of probability and not actual fact.

This was a massive problem for me and from what I read of others in the "system" for any father. Anyone could make the most horrendous accusations which were failed to be corroborated by anyone yet be taken as gospel truth and acted upon. No common sense or corroboration ensued at any stage in order to build a fuller picture.

My own two older children put themselves into the position of whether or not I got to see my children, whether they appreciated the fact or not that is what happened. Their words and their anger at me and Caroline were the precursors to the next 2 years of my life story. There was nothing condemning from Caroline, it had all come from my older children.

I have told you I was forbidden from contacting Caroline in any way. I was told by my advisors that it was stricter than before and if I so much as looked at Caroline I would be put in prison. Tears were flowing freely while this was being said.

I knew that Caroline didn't want this for the children or herself but the "system" with the assistance of my two older children and the people within it had finally broken us, not once at any stage looking for a more beneficial , constructive or less traumatic outcome for our children, which is my criticism of the outcome that no one really did think about the real effects that would be dealt to our children.

I do honestly believe the older two kids reacted this way for me divorcing my first wife, their mother, Alison. I know it is possible for this kind of resentment to simmer under the surface and come out later in life. I obviously didn't help myself by bringing Shelley, Alison Creary and Caroline into the picture one after another but it was still no excuse for the outright lies that my own children told about me to people who had such influence. They destroyed my life and took love and opportunity from my other 3 children.

I was absolutely devastated.

I don't know how I survived those next few hours or the days that followed. I had to go and talk to all my friends to try and purge my feelings. I knew I would never see the kids again – it was a shocking realisation and the only way I kept it together was by talking things through and leaning on my support network. The only child I had left was my baby boy Indi and the ridiculous situation was that I was seen as a great father to him.

At the time I hated Ben and Amy for what they had done. I hated Alison Gill. I couldn't believe that she even kept my name. Why did she want my name when all she felt for me was hatred and disgust? My feeling is that the "system" does not want, or somehow cannot see that a man would give up his life and career for his kids – make so much effort with them and put all his love and time into them. It just isn't the norm, Social Services are used to dealing with deadbeat dads and this is how they place men in terms of society. Anything outside that is anathema to them and they don't know how to deal with it. They certainly crippled my chance of the perfect family when this was all I had ever wanted. It was even worse because it seemed to me that my local Social Services understood the situation far better than Trafford, but they could not intervene as it was under the jurisdiction of Trafford.

I formally complained to Trafford Council about their Social worker and her methods and for a long while nothing happened. I eventually complained about the complaints procedure itself and still nothing happened for an eternity. I told them I would take things much further if they did not take my complaints seriously. Eventually I managed to force a complaints investigation but they simply concluded that they had done nothing wrong. I told them this was absurd and I wanted to take the complaint to Stage 2. This was an internal investigation where they would be investigating themselves. They sent two social workers who were not employed by the Council but appointed by them, to spend a couple of hours with me. They talked about the background to the whole issue but left before they would let me talk about the complaint itself they suggested they may need to return, but they never did. English law can be quite frustrating sometimes. I could not complain about the factual evidence presented, I could only complain about the methodology that had been used. So their report was made without the inclusion of my actual complaint.

I moved onto Stage 3. Once again this was ignored for a long time before, after much persistence and persuasion, there was a panel with three eminent independent people who sat and listened to my case. I won my case against Trafford Council's Children's Services with my complaint being partially upheld in that seven recommendations for change to Trafford Children's Services procedures be made.

The panel agreed the procedure had been biased against me and sexually discriminate in that two women interviewing a man was not fair nor seen to be fair. They agreed it was unfair for the social worker who was allocated to the mother to write the "balanced" report when she had six visits with her and I had none, the conclusion was that anyone who writes a report in the future on two parties must not be associated with one party only to ensure fairness and seen to be fair.

They also agreed that Trafford should have responded much earlier, in fact they were quite angry that this had not happened. I had to make yet another, separate complaint on their advice, against Trafford Social Services. It took over a year for Trafford to even respond. It was patently clear that Trafford were just holding on hoping I would drop the case because it was taking so long. The panel was adamant that the least that was needed was major change to the process and how it is carried out in the interest of fairness. My desired outcome from the complaints process was a real hope that in the future Trafford might not be so detrimental to fathers hoping to win back their kids and be fair to children by treating fathers with fairness. Would Social Services have placed two men in a room berating a woman? Of course not. The world is a one sided, twisted place sometimes and in my experience especially in the world of Social Services and children it needs change and equality.

Indi and I were left alone banned by default from seeing his brothers and sister, and vice versa we had to find a new life a new future and all the time I was finding more and more peace in my heart, tolerance and understanding. It is amazing to me that through all this going on, the business, the family and the emotions, my outlook on life was finding a way to put perspective into things, I learned to accept what I cant change and look for solutions and not battles. Indi became my whole focus and all my love and time was being put into him, I had him full time throughout his first 2 years and without him I do not know how I would have coped with the huge void my other children left in my life. Indi was my saviour and the fact that he was left with me for the majority of the time was the key to me finding my new outlook and contentment with life.

If one positive aspect emerged from the whole court process and losing my entire family life in the space of a few hours, it is that I settled on a desire to make a life in the United States of America. I had long thought that the way to start a new life was to move away and start again in another country. I had actually wanted to live in France; I think it would have worked. For some reason it didn't happen. After attempting to come to terms with the court's decision I started to think seriously about moving to America.

I loved the idea of living in a cowboy town, I felt it was somewhere I would just blend in whereas in Dalton I stood out like a sore thumb and always seemed to attract derision whenever I set foot in the town from people who had no idea about the real me. It is ironic that as I approached my fiftieth year I wanted to take a backseat from standing out. All my life I had wanted to be different and to be noticed. The thing that never crossed my mind when I was younger is that this could be a curse.

Late in 2009 I visited Sumatra once again, for the 11th time since I started my mission to protect the beautiful and elusive Sumatran Tiger. On this visit I took with me my trusted friend Pierre for the first time to the project. Pierre had been sending 5000 Euros a year for a few years to support the local education aspect of the programme, paying for the school teacher's wages and the material in our two schools located deep in the Sumatran jungle. With Pierre came his nephew Julien, he was no ordinary nephew, because Julien Pierre, yes this is confusing as his surname is the first name of his uncle, played International Rugby Union for France, he was a rugby superstar and was twice the size of all of us. This huge mountain of a man had a deep interest in wildlife conservation and had asked his uncle to let him accompany him on our trip. He had a real difficulty fitting in the seats on the plane and didn't speak English much but this only encouraged me to try out my French language skills throughout the trip. We had to visit Dumai on the north eastern coast of Sumatra where one of our teams was based to look after and manage the newly formed Tiger Reserve in the Forest of Senepis Bulahala. To get to this remote part of Sumatra it involves a very tedious eight hour boat journey up the coast line in our "Pom Pom". So called because of loud noise the huge single cylinder petrol engine makes as it turns the propeller, they are common in these Asian countries, very noisy, distinctive and simple of course with little to go wrong. We also had a high speed outboard powered boat for intercepting boats fast, we decided to take the high speed boat to Senepis, it would be half the time but twice as bumpy. About half way along the coast line about a kilometre out to sea the engine stopped, the sea became silent and soon we could hear nothing but waves once our ears got feeling back. Our staff tried in vain to repair the problem that was a simple broken wire but impossible to fix out at sea. So we floated drifting towards shore for a very long time, we knew the "Pom Pom" would be a few hours behind us and we could change boats. However the radios only worked within a few kilometres of each other and we had no idea where they were. Eventually we hit the shore line and got tangled in the writhing branches of a mangrove patch. After much effort we tied ourselves up to the trees and waited, and waited and waited. It seemed like an eternity until we heard the "Pom Pom" beat for the engine of our large boat, even then it took half an hour for the boat to reach us. We jumped aboard the larger boat and got ready for a long slow sail to Senepis Camp. About half an hour into the journey a loud bang and a cloud of smoke and then silence, I could not believe we had a second engine failure. We floated into a river opening and slid to the bank, what happened next amazed me and all who watched as the team took out the huge engine and installed a spare one held in the hold. I took huge strength and power to lift it out and Julien helped out with his hulk. The team were all in underpants and covered in black oil from the events, but staggeringly in the middle of nowhere on the bank of a river estuary in tropical waters we had the welcome noise of the "Pom Pom" once again within a few hours. Whilst there we went for a walk into the forest, only to be staggered by what we saw. Where a year earlier had been pristine diverse perfect forest full of animals, plants, insects and birds there now was a desert, a complete wasteland flat, soil and mud, nothing but dozer tracks and destruction done by one of Asia's destroyers of wildlife and diversity on a huge unimaginable scale. APP, Asia Pulp and Paper have been destroying forests for many years killing thousands of animals including tiger, elephants, rhinos and all sorts of primates in the need to make profits from paper and pulp product. The destruction we witnessed was just a small part of the millions of acres ripped down by this company and others without a care at all for what happens to the animals. It seems like a hopeless task sometimes when you are up against such huge mighty companies who's aim is to destroy everything and ask questions afterwards. We eventually arrived at our destination where the Senepis River enters the sea, we sailed up river a few kilometres before tying up at the old logging camp there. I was feeling very odd and decidedly ill after the journey and wanted to sleep outdoors on the deck of the boat in a sleeping bag. Julien decided to sleep alongside on the deck instead of inside where the temperature was oppressive. I had to get up a number of times in the night as I was sick as a dog and couldn't keep water down. The next morning we set off for a trip deep into the forest to see what illegal logging was taking place accompanied by our trusted guards. I was so sick I could not walk, I lost too much fluid and had to stay behind to try to rest and get some strength from somewhere. This area of Sumatra has a very specific form of Malaria in the local village, it is a type that simple old fashioned remedies work well upon and the teams take a tablet that costs a few pennies a day to take instead of the modern complex tablets such as Malarone in Europe that cost over £3 per day. I wasn't taking any preventative medicine and Julien was taking Malarone. It transpired that on arrival back in France Julien had a Malarial attack and had picked it up whilst sleeping next to me on the boat deck, he got it and I didn't yet he was taking the medicine and I wasn't. The Malaria nearly ruined his international rugby career as it destroyed his health and fitness. The great news is that he worked so hard and fought off the Malaria and eventually got himself back into the French national team to play his part in the Rugby world cup in New Zealand recently. We travelled all over Sumatra on this trip as usual for me and it is a very tiring and demanding trip around the three centres for our teams. The rest of the trip went very well and we achieved all our aims not knowing of course that Julien had the malaria in his blood waiting to erupt and cause so much damage to him. In Way Kambas National Park we trekked through the forest to Kali Biru, a grassland opening in the forest where deer congregate and tigers lurk in the long grass waiting to pounce. But it wasn't tigers that came out this time it was forest elephants. With only around 300 of these creatures left on the planet it is a rare sight to see and I had never seen wild ones before. We walked barefooted across the muddy river bed to a tree that stands out alone in the grassland leaning over the river. Climbing up was difficult with muddy bare feet but once up the view was amazing with 360 degrees visibility. The most gruesome aspect of our view point was that there was blood dripping constantly from my legs to the ground below and it would not stop. The leeches had struck and made my legs a sea of blood that ran onto the branches and then down below, not a sight for the faint hearted I can tell you. Whilst waiting up there , I had done this on many occasions in the past and seen much wildlife, a small group of elephants appeared from the dark cover of the forest. The group became bigger and about 15 elephants came closer to us in the thick grass. It is a fact that the most dangerous animal in the forest is not the Tiger as many may think, but rather the elephant. Elephants do not tolerate humans at all and will charge and get rid of the intruders with a weight and power unsurpassed in the environment they live. A tiger will always run away from any sight or sound of a human except in very rare circumstances. A wonderful and very rare occurrence and one I will always remember. I have seen herds of hundreds of elephants in South Africa but this group was by far more exciting and fulfilling because of how desperately rare they were and how elusive they are to see. That night, camping on a ground sheet in the depths of the forest in a place where tigers are regularly photographed remotely, a tiger walked right by our camp and left his prints for all to see, a close encounter with a magnificent animal that we never knew was there yet it sent a shiver through the camp. I know Pierre was affected by this and will never forget the night where the tiger walked right by his sleeping place. Travel in these countries is always difficult because of the nature of the poverty and lack of infrastructure yet somehow the more difficult it is to get to where I aim to go the more exciting, challenging and rewarding it is.

Chapter 44
A Dream house and
a conservation success

By the start of 2010 I just wanted to get away from it all.

I had been emailing Bev Richard, a Real Estate Agent in Cody, Wyoming and had organised to travel there in February. I had found Bev after seeing an advert while we had been at the cowboy show when I first entered Cody. It must have been fate because I remembered the advert I saw that day and made a note of it later, which was something I would not normally have done. Bev arranged for me to view nine houses in and around Cody.

This time I packed a coat as I knew it was going to be minus 20 degrees Celsius! I combined the Cody trip with a trip to Peru with Indi and Pierre. I had two suitcases – one for Peru with tropical clothing and the other which would see us through a bitter winter in Wyoming. The houses and the scenery were magical. Though it was snowing on and off in Wyoming the sky was a vivid blue with perpetual sunshine. I loved every second. It would cost a fair amount of money but that didn't bother me. I wanted to change my life, to resurrect myself. I believe you only live once and sometimes you need to take the bull by the horns. I had to make a huge leap in my life to change myself and change my future.

Ultimately it was a house in which to relax and switch off from my UK life – it was not a permanent move, more like a holiday home.

There was one house in particular which stood out, and I went back a number of times for another look. The views were stupendous and in terms of location, every box was ticked. Even Bev suggested if there was a house she would buy it would be this one. Once you put an offer in for a house in America it is legally binding. I signed the offer and off it went. Thankfully the offer was accepted and I didn't want to back out. Why would I, the house was beyond my dreams. Twenty acres lying alongside the Shoshone national forest in the Rocky Mountains, "a wood framed house with a porch all around , my heaven" taken from a Trace Adkins song and in exquisite settings. It was my heaven and I viewed it as such from the first day I saw it.

The surroundings in Cody were very 'me'. I have been known for wearing a cowboy hat for many years now and in Cody most people wear one. The first hat I ever wore was a brimmed hat because I have sensitive eyes, which are affected by very bright sunlight. To avoid headaches I found it was best to wear sunglasses and a hat as a buffer. I would wear an Akubra, an iconic Australian hat which was also perfect for when I was in the outback. Soon wearing the hat became part of my character and I would wear it in the UK.

Ever since I have bought hats all over the world, from Brazil to Madagascar, and I have quite a collection. In America I would wear a Stetson, which felt very comfortable and natural. I don't go anywhere without my hat on. If I go out the door I know straight away if I don't have my hat on, it's like not having your underpants on. I feel naked without it – it is a part of me now.

Alison came with us to Peru and we flew down to Los Angeles to meet Pierre. He wasn't arriving until the next day however so I decided to hire a car and drive around the city. This was something that frightened Alison – she couldn't understand how I could just hire a car and drive around LA and Hollywood when I had no idea of the area. It was all part of the adventure to me and it was more baffling to me how she thought it was so unusual. We travelled through the likes of Bel Air, Rodeo Drive and all the way down to Malibu beach.

Once we met up with Pierre we went on to Lima, the capital of Peru. One of the things Pierre and I do is try to visit the local zoos in each country and see if we can be of assistance to them and whether they can join with us in conservation projects. In Lima there are two large zoological collections, Parque de Las Leyendas and Huachipa Zoo, in the past few years we have become friends of Huachipa and have built good relations with them, this is a private zoo. The "city" Zoo is Las Leyendas and on a holiday it is one of the busiest places in Lima. The day we chose to visit was indeed a public holiday and when we arrived in a hot and cramped taxi, we found ourselves in the centre of a huge crowd trying to enter the zoo. I have never seen queues like it, strings of people strung out like a spiders web patiently waiting to see the animals in the Parque. We were taken to one side and pushed through the side gate so we didn't have to queue; it is useful to have connections! It was a major effort just trying to walk around in the intense heat and bright sun. At one point there was a enclosure for the three toed sloth and animal I have a particular liking for, I stopped outside the window, took some photos and was then knocked quite hard in the side and lost my balance. I composed myself and made my way out of the place and found Pierre again. A little later I wanted an ice cream for Indi and myself of course, I put my hand in my pocket to extract my wallet and to my horror it had gone. I searched every pocket ten times over in a panic. Then it struck me, I was pick pocketed in the Sloth area. The push was to distract me whilst my wallet was extracted, the disastrous thing was that all my cash, all my cards and all my financial connections were in that wallet. A sheer desperate vulnerability hit me like a hammer as I realised I didn't even have enough money to take the taxi back to the hotel , I could not get more from the bank without a card and I was only on day two of a 10 days trip in Peru. I could not pay my hotel bill and had no way to contact anyone.

This is when having your best friends with you saves your life, well not literally but figuratively. Pierre stepped into my panic, worry and sense of loss, he agreed to pay all my trip expenses and I could pay him back after the trip. However this didn't seem to allay my feelings, I cannot explain it well but losing the wallet like that was like having my heart ripped out, I hated the idea that someone else had all my cards and my cash my private life in their hands. I managed to get in touch with my office in the UK on the phone and they sent me the numbers for cancelling the cards. This was done immediately and a slight sense of relief was had. I was beginning to feel that Peru and my wallet were not meant for each other because a couple of years earlier I had lost my wallet in the taxi/bus we took from Chiclayo to Chaparri. I could not find it once there, I searched everywhere and finally accepted I had lost it on the bus and the chance of seeing it again with the $200 in it was zero. Heinz our host managed to track down the bus driver and asked him if he had found a wallet, he phoned back later and said he had looked where I said and sure enough down the side of the seat there was my wallet after 7 days. A miracle, but better still the driver brought it back to me and not a single cent was missing from the wallet. This was the most honest action I had seen in an age and gave the gentleman a cash bonus to make him smile and reward his honesty. From Lima we travelled over night on a Coche Cama, this is a luxury bus with seat that convert to a bed a bit like a first class seat on a plane, so you can lie flat as the journey from Lima to Chiclayo is over 12 hours driving. It is excellent and so easy to sleep waking up fresh and at the destination in the dry desert environment of Lambayeque.

We went to Chaparri in northern Peru to visit our projects but this time specifically to the penguin project. Indi was in tow and at just over a year-old he was already starting to recognise the wonderful animals which were always around us, complimenting his life. He smiled throughout the trip as he had done since he was born spending nearly every second of his life in the zoo or on amazing trips around the globe.

We had decided to start the penguin project because just a year before we had been to the north of Peru and in the whole of the north we found just ten penguins. There were supposed to be hundreds, maybe thousands yet they had just disappeared, due to disturbance from the local fishermen. The penguins nest in sand and constant interference from dogs, people and pet catchers had decimated their numbers. After two years of constant lobbying and persuasion The Minister for the Environment in Peru thankfully announced that the area would become a National Conservation Area after we started our project, which was a real coup.

We also instigated a reintroduction project where illegally held or injured penguins could be looked after and then returned to their natural habitat. By now we looked after bears, condors and penguins in Peru. I look forward to visiting every year. It was some trip overall, given I had just bought a house in America and started to introduce measures for the protection of Northern Peru's native penguins. After the immense travelling and the non-stop adventure of the whole trip I turned to Alison with a huge smile on my face as we sat on the plane back to the UK.

"What did you think of that then, pretty good huh?"

Alison turned towards me and said, "David, I'm sorry but your life is too big for me."

I was not surprised at all when Alison said my life was too big for her. I turned to her, and asked her. "What do you mean 'too big for you'?"

"I'm not into this," she said candidly. "I'm not into your conservation, I'm not into your animals, I'm not into your travelling all over, I'm not into that. My idea of a good time is going for a night out with my friends to the pub and you don't do that, you do all of this but I'm not interested."

I knew if I was honest with myself that I had always known this but at the bare minimum I wanted her to see what a fantastic life it was for Indi to be travelling, learning and helping people and animals the world over.

"Surely you can see what a wonderful life it is if you open your mind?" I implored. I thought her ideal life was somewhat limited when the world had so much to offer. I'm sure Alison was picturing Caroline and my kids with me in the house in Cody. I had to admit I was still wondering if it might happen some day. Once again divisions were made as Alison could not deal at all with the fact I had children with Caroline and especially Toba who she had promised me she would never let play with Indi as the anger that was always there still was as strong as ever. As soon as we got home she moved out of the house in Dalton that originally I had bought for her to live in under contract. She only moved about ten doors down the street but the idea for her was to have nothing connected to me.

Of course we still had a son together but Alison had put her own life, work and socialising needs before the commitment to a baby from the beginning with regards to Indi and by now she was almost completely distancing herself, even from her own flesh and blood. She only once invited Indi to stay the night at her new home.

A Dream house and a conservation success

Chapter 45
Returning children and
an avalanche in the USA

A year and seven months after disowning me and disappearing from my life Amy suddenly appeared at the park one morning in February 2010 and we embraced immediately. I came to the conclusion that the negative behaviour with Amy all came from her brother Ben and her association with Barclay Bland – she was like a different person. Her mother's influence was nothing but negative as well and Amy had so much unconstructive pressure on her to conform to their wishes that she had changed, she wasn't the girl I knew.

We decided to take things one step at a time, and the next time she visited she brought my little granddaughter – it was the first time I had seen her. Amy's baby was just two weeks younger than Indi. It seemed I may even manage to reconcile with Ben. He turned up at the park one day not wishing to let Amy make all the running, so I went to speak with him. He was much more tense than Amy and bereft of emotion. There were no hugs or tears; it was a cold calculated decision that things could be worked out. Walking around the park I could have screamed at him several times. He was still playing the grown up, blaming me for everything without a shred of recognition for his part in the matter. Unfortunately it was typical Ben. I bit my tongue a lot in order to keep the peace and it seemed we might just be able to keep a civil relationship. It was soon clear however the reasons that Ben had been so ferocious towards me. Although I had never invited my first wife Alison, whenever I asked Ben to come up to see me, he would always bring her. This went on for months.

One day after becoming fed up with this I took my children to one side and sat them down. I said, "Look, please do not take offence at what I am going to say but I have got to tell you this. I don't mind you bringing your mam, it's your mother, but, remember that I am divorced from her and your mother is my ex-wife and it doesn't work, it is stressful, it's upsetting, it's not working. Please do not bring her unless I invite her."

Ben reacted crazily. He jumped up and said, "I will bring my mother *wherever* I want, *whenever* I want and it's nothing to do with you!"

"Actually Ben it is," I countered, "it is my private property, it's my home, it's my family, I would invite who I want. You are not then entitled to secondarily invite anybody else, that's not the way it works. Wait until you get your own house and your own family and then see. Just imagine if you invited your ex to your house – see what your girlfriend would think. Think about it." Unfortunately Ben wouldn't think about it. Amy however told me afterwards that she completely understood. Sadly within six months this as it happens "false" reconciliation was over and they resorted to their previous positions simply because I asked them to help me to get Hari, Kadi and Toba back in my life. It was a real test of my ability to forgive to allow them back into my life after all they did against me, but my heart was open and it was taken advantage of again. The first time they turned on me was heartbreaking the second time was just plain cruel and it felt cold and the end of the line, a 25 year investment lost because of ?.......I actually don't even know the answer to that which makes it all the worse

In May 2010 when I was signing all of the papers to complete the house deal in Wyoming it was just Indi and I who boarded the flight from Manchester. We met our wonderful Cody neighbours Rick and Sherry. I could only have imagined what beautiful people they would turn out to be – true friends who would keep in touch and look after my house whenever I was in the UK or somewhere else in the world. Rick Adair, an ex-oil industry businessman from Texas, had done exactly the same as I had. He purchased a home in the mountains for a holiday refuge and loved it so much he sold his company and moved up there full time. They have three mules and a dog. Sherry works in Cody out of choice and they have a great lifestyle with roaring log fires in deep winter and long slow rides in the mountains in the summer. They do not have grandchildren and in many ways they treat Indi like their grandchild.

The first night we spent in the house it was freezing cold and snowing outside but Bev and Chan, the real estate agents, along with Rick and Sherry, made sure our house had been fully heated and adorned with bed covers and pillows. It was a lovely touch.

The next day I took advantage of the fact that the Yellowstone National Park had just opened. I bought a yearly season ticket and drove my new car into the parking lot.

I had purchased a big Chevy Suburban to go along with the new house and furniture I was buying in order to furnish the complete new life in America. There had been a lot of snow before we arrived but the road had just reopened. As we were leaving after a fantastic time in Yellowstone that first weekend we learned the road was blocked yet again due to a huge avalanche that had fallen just behind us on our way in over the Sylvan Pass.

The road was blocked for two days. The only way I could get home was to take a 360-mile detour which took about seven hours. It was one way to become familiar with the area, driving through stunning mountain scenery. The wildlife was outstanding; I spotted four black bears and a Grizzly bear during the drive. It was just a little tiring however considering we already had a full day before setting off at 5pm. Indi slept and I just about kept myself awake, falling into the house after midnight.

I went home to the UK for just a month or so and I couldn't wait to return to Wyoming for a summer holiday from the end of June to the start of August. Sadly whenever Alison did come to see Indi all Alison would talk about was Caroline and my new baby Toba. I thought I had Caroline on the brain but it was apparently the same for Alison. She seemed obsessed with just what I was going to 'do' about Toba. She told me she couldn't deal with it. I told her she had no choice, I had to deal with the fact I might never see him and that was bad enough without her adding to the difficulties. After this seemingly never ending conversation, the anger that

Alison held for my baby son Toba and Caroline was just the same if not worse than it ever was.

From early August 2010 Alison suddenly didn't seem to want to see Indi at all, and it took a few weeks before she admitted she was seeing someone else. Much as I did not think it would ever be easy with Alison, much as I still loved Caroline, but it dawned on me that if she wanted someone else I had to accept that and work with it for Indi's sake.

She respects and understands conservation and she has even imparted some of these very special beliefs and teachings to Hari. My son has been involved with dolphin conservation thanks to Caroline's teachings. I was so proud that he can raise money for the protection of dolphins. In fact, following Hari's amazing example I decided that South Lakes Wild Animal Park should not sell tuna. Today the park does not sell tuna and I certainly won't eat it myself.

Caroline takes the kids out for nature walks and on a Friday or a Saturday she won't be found down the local pub getting hammered with her friends in the way Alison does, she will spend time with the kids teaching them the important things in life. Like me, she also loves country music; in fact we have many of the same favourite artists. She even loves wearing a cowboy hat! I believe Caroline and I also share the same vision of the type of life we would want together and with our kids. But that is not something I expect to happen.

Chapter 46
Tiger cub born and a cheeky capuchin escape

We were not just known for breeding rhinos at South Lakes. Ever since the beginning of the Park I had sought to breed Sumatran tigers. After the death of Toba, my first ever tiger, we had been allocated a very young female, who came from Berlin Zoo. We also received another young male. At the time I did a little moving around and sent our then current tigers over to my zoo in Australia. We had hoped to get the tigers breeding within three years but again, as had happened with Toba, nothing was happening. The tigers were mating all the time but still the female would never actually catch. We followed the natural cycle and appropriate dates and times but nothing emerged.

Eventually, on September 7, 2010, as I was packing my bag for Indi and I to go on a trip to our home in Cody Wyoming, I heard the zoo radio blast in my kitchen.

"David, David get out to the tiger house immediately!" It was early morning. I rushed out to the tiger house where I almost knocked the tiger keeper Gavin clean over.

"I think we've got a baby tiger cub," Gavin said. "I can hear it inside and I daren't go in. I don't know what to do."

"Right, I'll have a look," I said, trying to remain calm but feeling immensely excited.

She didn't seem bothered by my visit and I couldn't see a cub though I could hear it. The mother didn't seem bothered, she seemed more interested in us. I brought the female out of the enclosure and walked in to where she had been guarding. Behind the door lying in a pool of urine, cold and almost dead was a tiny tiger cub, yowling out for milk. Unfortunately its mum had no idea what to do and seemingly no interest. A lot of animals experience the same uncertainty and apathy when they first give birth, mainly because they do not know any better. It is no different to many humans in this world, the difference is, we are supposed to be educated.

As I looked at the defenceless little cub I said to Gavin, "Come on, we'll have to get some warmth into it." I fed the tiger some warm bottled milk, cleaned and dried her before putting her back in with her mum. Once again the mother had no interest, she wouldn't sit there for the cub to feed or bond, she just sat away from it. By the end of the day I was exceedingly worried. I called my partners in the Breeding Programme for Sumatran Tigers to ask their advice. "It will be very important genetics this time," they told me. "The mother and father are important and it will be important for the programme if it survives. Can you please rear it because we haven't got that many Sumatran tigers coming on of that quality." Clearly, it was more important to make sure the cub survived, however that might have to be. I decided we would have to play mum. The only problem was I was due to fly to America the next day. It was a tough decision but I decided that my staff had the necessary dedication and expertise to handle such a delicate process. They performed admirably and the cub turned out just fine. I named her Kadi, after my daughter. I had two children named after tigers, Hari and Toba, and now a new tiger named after my daughter to even out the tiger connections in the children.

Indi was the child who benefited the most, not to mention the quickest, from having Kadi in the park. Indi and I were the first people to feed her milk from a bottle and then as soon as Indi and I returned from the US in October the first thing we did was to go and pay a visit to Kadi. She seemed to bond with Indi right away and we would make a daily pilgrimage where we would feed and play with her. Initially she was very similar to a domestic cat, albeit stronger. I found out just how strong when, in early December, the playing became stronger. Up until now it had been strong but safe, though I could sense the tiger's strength was increasing and becoming a potential problem. This particular day as Indi was playing with Kadi, she jumped onto him from behind, and knocking him down. It was clear Kadi was developing her natural skills, which would include eventually the urge to attack and kill. It was time we stopped getting so close to Kadi well before there was any real danger of injury.

Tigers eat small amounts and gradually they begin to grow to the point where they can consume much more food and as they do their strength increases considerably. Their speed of development becomes quite staggering, as much as their power. The claws of even a small tiger are impressive and even when Kadi was just a few months old there is no doubt she could tear a human to pieces. Even the staff would not go in past a certain point in the cub's life. I was not so sensible myself. I played with Kadi for perhaps a little too long. Over the years I have appeared quite often on television and radio and one day I was talking with BBC Radio for a segment, explaining all about Kadi. I was playing with her as I was talking and she caught my lip with her claw causing an instant eruption of blood to seep all over me. It was a mess but I had to keep going as it was a live show. TV would have been far more embarrassing but on the radio, I don't think anyone realised I had just been pulverised by a baby tiger.

At this time at South Lakes Wild Animal Park there was also a problem with a Capuchin monkey. One young male was ostracized from his group by the eldest in the pack. He chased him out with ferocity and purpose and so the poor, smaller monkey had to make a big choice between an electric fence and a shock or being ripped to pieces by the big male and he made the right choice – jumping straight through the fence before escaping. We thought this was probably a one off and caught the monkey before putting him back in with his mates. Of course he couldn't talk to us and explain the problem though I had my reservations that this might happen again. He was once again chased out by the bigger male before we could re-home him. This time he jumped the fence and disappeared before we could catch him.

We then received a call from the police saying someone had reported seeing a monkey running down the side of the road. It was right near a roundabout so myself and a keeper went along to try and find the monkey. Though we had received a very accurate description of a Capuchin monkey there was nothing in sight. We looked high and low but couldn't find the monkey anywhere. There was nothing else to do but wait until there was another report of where the monkey might be seen next.

We didn't have to wait long for a torrent of reports which indicated the Capuchin was now sitting in the middle of the round-about eating bits of litter and discarded food as well as helping himself to drinks from plastic bottles. Yet whenever we turned up at the roundabout to intercept him he had disappeared, even when we were just minutes behind the report.

Next he was seen on the local railway line – it was clearly described but once we had travelled the two-and-a-half miles to the end of the line he wasn't there. It happened a few times and it appeared the monkey was using the railway line as a pathway and marker.

When we received another report I decided it was time to go with restraining and darting equipment. This required special permission from the police as one dart would most likely kill a human in the wrong hands and blowpipes and darts are strictly regulated by the authorities and very few people have the licence to do this kind of work.

Because of the specialist skills involved I was called out by Lancashire Police to a particularly horrendous dog attack in Rishton, Blackburn in early 2011 to put to sleep two huge Pit Bull dogs who had nearly killed their owners friend. That was a frightening day all round but I did what I had to do and returned, community helped and public protected. It is part of my service to the community at large that I volunteer my services to both Cumbria and Lancashire Police for these kind of incidents.

We didn't want to kill the monkey but we certainly had to catch it. The monkey on the loose was a not really a danger to humans – it would not attack a human but it could have, for instance, run into the road and caused an accident. I had the police follow me as we decided to pursue the monkey. Once we caught sight of him we followed him on a wild goose chase, across roads, fields and everything in-between. Day after day we followed him, though we would often lose him and have to start again.

The police thought it was hilarious, one of the most amusing criminal chases they had ever undertaken. Together we all had quite a laugh about the situation, though inside I was worried for the monkey's health and feeling quite under the spotlight as it was my monkey that had escaped from my zoo. By now it was day five and the case was very much public knowledge, appearing in all local media. I was interviewed on the radio to talk about the search and I revealed I was concerned about the monkey's welfare though it was clear he was still eating well enough. He had been seen in a number of horse stables, helping himself to carrots. Eventually we had a call from Green Haume (pronounced Arm) where some poor soul had encountered the monkey sitting on his pigeon loft trying to steal the pigeon feed. Once again we went to catch it, only for him to escape. This time he ran back towards Dalton and was sighted running into the railway tunnel there. This time we had him cornered with a policeman at one end of the tunnel and me at the other. The monkey dashed out in front of the policeman, evading capture once again and shot up a tree near the tunnel.

"It's here," the policeman radioed through to me, "we've got it, it's at the far end, it's up a tree. You have to come round."

The monkey was so wary of people that I couldn't get a clean shot. He then ran onto a Dalton housing estate which meant I could no longer use the equipment, there was too much of a risk for local residents. The monkey ran across the rooftops before heading down into the cemetery. Once again we thought we might succeed here as it was an enclosed area. By now there were six or seven police officers – all in a line attempting to intercept the monkey. I was stood at the front of this amusing 'Keystone Cops' set up with my head keeper Gavin Clunie who was carrying a net while I held onto the gun with immense paranoia. Eventually the monkey slipped out of the cemetery into a nearby field. I decided I would run as fast as I could to try and apprehend him, but I couldn't catch him. He was like lightning. He headed back towards the chapel which sits dormant in the cemetery. The door was open and the monkey let himself right in to the old chapel.

"Great, run, quick, shut the door!" I exclaimed. Suddenly we were trapped in a tiny room, just Gavin, me and the monkey. There were other people in the chapel in the room next door, we could hear them talking. I shouted through,

"Don't worry! Don't come out though. Stay there we have a dangerous animal in here." It was becoming surreal but I was paranoid that they might come in and disturb us or the monkey. We found an old bin with a black rubber lid and tin body. Our new plan was to catch the monkey in the bin. Suddenly I was up close and personal with the escapee and as fast as I could I thrust the empty bin over the top of him before sliding it around and slamming the bin lid over the top.

"Sit on that lid!" I shouted to Gavin, "don't get off it!"

After six days of chasing and complete frustration we trapped the monkey in a dustbin, in a chapel, in a cemetery. It was surreal and ultimately, at least by now, amusing to all concerned.

It was a seemingly fitting end in some way. I spoke with Tony Livesey on Radio Five Live the night of the capture, it must have been midnight. A huge cheer went up in the studio when they learned we had finally caught the little beggar. The best part was, the monkey had a nice little holiday and we, as a business learned a lot about how to work closely with the police on escapes. For the future we worked even more directly with the police, producing new guidelines and strategies for dangerous animal escapes. In the end the whole charade had been a useful tool to improve our joint response and co-ordination. After learning a great deal we had a more specified escape plan for any future Alcatraz hopefuls.

In 2009 I started a huge project to expand the zoo to three times its size. A major job including new car parks, entrance, childrens facilities and many new animal facilities. The process took forever to conform to all the new planning requirements. Unbelievable red tape and cost. The budget £4m a far cry from 1993 and £177,000 to build the zoo.

Chapter 47
Adrenalin, endorphins and free entry

2010 would be a changing year in my life where I was forced to finally take stock of everything I previously held to be true. The years of stress I had experienced were to finally catch up to me. There is no question stress had played a huge role in my life up until this point. A modern life full of stress is a terrible thing and it can cause people to make bad decisions, it certainly did so with myself. Stress can kill people at worst and it can damage your life causing you to not even be able to think straight. From the time I built South Lakes Wild Animal Park, stress was in my life and it seemed to increase year upon year. I have experienced Mount Everest peaks in my life but also the deepest drops imaginable – a great contrast of positive and negative experiences which have caused me huge strain. By now I can recognise the symptoms of when I am feeling stressed. Even if I don't feel that I am stressed my body will let me know otherwise. My eyes will blink a lot and one eye will twitch incessantly.

In September 2010, I took Indi with me to Cody. Things had been worsening with Alison for a long while and she was by now in a new relationship. It was clear her life was going to change completely and I knew this meant the situation with Indi could change. I wasn't sure how it was going to change. I wasn't sure whether Alison would run away or whether she'd come and try to take him off me. I had no idea, but the moment I found out about her new situation my stress levels increased. Still, I had learned a lot from counselling and my past experience. I knew I had to escape the situation and allow my mind to work things out without antagonism, argument, or recrimination. I needed to escape to Cody , my heaven.

As I started to unwind in the magical mountains I quickly saw Alison's moving on as a very positive aspect in my life, as it would leave the door open for Caroline and the kids to potentially come back into my life. It seemed clear the more I thought about it – Caroline left town because Alison was in my life, it was not because she didn't want to be with me. I thought I was able to get through the uncertainty. At the time the expansion with the park was not going to plan. Everything seemed to be going wrong, we were a year behind schedule – every piece of news I received in relation to the expansion was bad news and seemed to cost me more money. I felt very let down by a number of so-called professionals and had another reminder of the appalling quality of these people in the UK who think that because they attended university, had a few letters after their names they could rip people off with un profes- sional work, failure to achieve and quite honestly pathetic results, it was a stark reminder of just how much better things seemed to be when I ran everything directly and could perform all tasks myself.

It was October 17th, Caroline's birthday. I took Indi out for a drive but I was thinking of Caroline a lot – it was unavoidable. Music was playing on the stereo and I was singing along, much to Indi's amusement. I drove over the Sylvan Pass going into Yellowstone when all of a sudden I felt a very strange sensation in my heart and chest. It was such a jolt that I had to pull over as soon as I could. By now Indi was asleep in the back of the car. I felt that I couldn't get my breath and I started to panic. My chest was tighter than my wallet. I was clutching my chest. Though there was a certain thud and quiver to my heart it was nothing like palpitations. Everyone gets those and I had experienced them before. This was far worse – I couldn't breathe.

I knew it was bad news, but I convinced myself it wasn't. I told myself I had twisted something somehow, or it was a bad case of wind. I must have eaten something that didn't agree with me. Whenever I had bad pains in the past it had always been something that would just naturally go away. I decided to carry on driving and take no notice of it. I carried on singing, which somehow didn't wake Indi. All I thought about was Caroline – it was her day. I had sent some money to Hari to get a card and present for her; it was all I was allowed to do.

I had a wrenching pain in my chest but decided I might feel better if we stopped for something to eat – I am always sure to take a picnic whenever we go out for long drives. Once we reached Yellowstone we had a picnic and then walked around for a few hours. As we set off home I was feeling light headed, but mostly light chested, if such a feeling can exist. I felt odd. Normally we would have stopped for something to eat on the way home, usually it would be at a cowboy refuge called Shoshone Lodge, where they had got to know me by now. We drove right past as I thought I would be better getting home to rest. I sat in my house still feeling strange and started to worry seeing as it was just Indi and I. I decided to go down to Rick and Sherry's house. They were watching an American football game and seemed to be engrossed. I felt as if I were gate crashing.

"I just want to tell you that I'm not feeling very well," I said to them both. They told me to come in and sit down. I'd lost my Internet connection at home for some reason but Rick's connection was working so I decided I would do some work and take my mind off things. I started to work on the laptop and suddenly there was a massive thud in my chest – it was a sharp bang and it was painful. I almost dropped my laptop and rolled onto the floor.

Rick and Sherry jumped up. "What the heck's going on here?" Sherry said, alarmed. I explained I had had these pains through the day and that they were getting worse.

"Get to hospital!" she responded, quite understandably.

"No it'll be alright," I said unconvincingly. "I'm sure it's just stress or something like that. I don't think it's anything". I decided not to go to hospital and just went back home, though they were very worried about me.

Once I was home, I seemed to feel a lot better and just went to sleep as normal. The next morning however the same thing happened again – a feeling in my chest of a thousand butterflies crawling around – they were fluttering but there wasn't enough space for them all. I felt as if my heart was not working properly – as if it were beating twice as fast as it should. By now I was becoming paranoid that there was really something wrong. I couldn't thwart Rick and Sherry's logic any longer. They told me now I really should go. So I set off on the twenty-mile drive to the hospital. Rick couldn't leave home that day but Sherry followed behind me in case there were any problems. She had to go to work but told me if there were any problems to call her and she would come.

The hospital took my problem very seriously and brought me in immediately – wired up as if I was attached to the National Grid. After all the tests they performed they revealed that I had a stress attack. It wasn't quite a heart attack but it was close. The results showed a ridiculously high peaking of adrenaline and endorphins in my blood, ironically, the chemicals that give one a feeling of being in love. I had a conversation with my vet when I returned home and he revealed this to me, as well as expressing complete shock at my situation, he lovingly informed me that was very dangerous.

"With animals, if they have too much adrenaline and it does not dissipate quickly their heart can stop because the heart cannot work over a certain level," the vet revealed. "You just go ping and that's it," he continued alarmingly, "it can be as bad as a heart attack."

It startled me because at the time I was in the hospital I didn't believe it was anything too frightening as the staff were concerned, but not panicky. All they told me was that I had to get rid of the adrenaline from my system. The majority of people who have a high level of adrenaline would go off and perform some type of physical exertion to make it dissipate. For some reason I had a very high level of adrenaline, this was happening regularly. The doctors were fantastic; they explained the full extent of my problem and calmed me right down. They told me I needed to find a way of preventing situations or events that would cause the overload of endorphins and adrenalin.

The specialist explained, "One of the biggest problems of people with heart problems is they worry so they make it worse because the more they've got a problem, the more they worry, the more the problem occurs. So, what you've got to have now is a mental treatment, if you will."

"Mental treatment…sounds awful."

"You've got to have a mental image of what the problem is so that your body, your mind can deal with it."

I had a therapist come in and see me, which I thought was some way better than the NHS who may have given me a box of tablets and told me to go home. I was in the place all day and they even looked after Indi for me in a Day Care Centre. Then again, it should have been top class treatment as the final bill was somewhere in the region of $12,000.

I had every test they could possibly have taken and felt that if there was anything wrong with me they'd have found it. Even at the end of the day when they knew I wasn't going to die from a heart attack, they put me on a treadmill test and nearly did give me a heart attack. I was forced to run like a madman as they measured my breathing and heart rate.

Ironically, the test is designed to stress the heart, something in the region of 85% more than its usual beat rate. They take you to the maximum and then measure the recovery rate. Luckily my heart seemed to recover well which meant there was no actual damage to the heart itself.

Physically, that seemed to be an end of the problem but mentally, the challenge was just beginning. I had to examine everything that was overstressing me so that this never happened again.

The conversation with the doctor was the beginning of my changing all that needed to be changed in my life.

"You've got stress in your life and what causes stress in your life?"

"Well, my business."

"Why does your business cause stress? Are you losing money?"

"No the business is doing very well thanks. I'm very profitable."

"So, how does your life stress you?"

I thought about it.

"The people in it," I answered candidly, "some people in my life stress me because they're constantly negative, looking to blame everyone else, arguing with each other, constantly falling out. They bring me stress because I have to go in and deal with it and I want a life that's smooth and easy."

"Ok. Are there particular individuals that cause you stress?"

"Yes."

"So what are you going to do about it?"

"Well, what can I do?"

"Well, you'd better do something about it because you have to get rid of the stress out of your life. So you've got to get rid of the people and things that *cause* you stress." I identified who the people were causing me stress and decided to confront them with a letter when I returned home. I think the people concerned believed they were indispensable but I pointed out this was not the case. No one is indispensable and it was a very stark realisation that my life was worth way more than a particular issue. 'If I die because I didn't deal with this, I'll be annoyed when I go up to heaven,' I wrote with a bittersweet tinge. It worked. I had been advised very literally by the specialists to remove anyone in my life who was causing me problems and stress. It then moved onto my business life, a cornucopia of unrecognised stress and strain which had taken its toll on my near fifty years.

"Who gives you grief in your private life?" I was asked. I named everyone I could think of. They asked me what caused the grief.

"Get rid of them. Get rid of the stress." I suddenly felt powerful and in control of my own future. "Get rid of the potential problems that might occur in my life."

"Who causes stress in your life?"

"My two children, my ex-wife."

The response was as savage as it was with anyone else in my life.

The message was, 'Get rid of them'. I looked in surprise; it was not what I had expected to hear about my own flesh and blood.

'Because, David," the therapist ventured, "what is worth more, having two kids in your life that cause you hell or dying? So you either live or die because of two kids that cause you hell. What do you prefer?"

"Well, living."

"Right, get rid of them, not physically but emotionally."

I'd never heard of this black or white, do or die psychology before in my life. Most people tend to look for cop out solutions in their lives; perhaps even I had done this many times myself in the past. The way the doctors put the situation to me was very clear. It really was do or die. It didn't scare me, in fact it made perfect sense. I had always tried to placate people who caused me nothing but grief; I had always worried about whether people loved me and if they didn't, then why not. But I had a stark realisation that if people could not contribute to my life and show me the same love and respect me as I showed them, then they weren't worth worrying about. I should just erase them from my life and my brain. I knew I had to tell everyone who I felt this way about. From my ex-wife to Ben and Amy, I wrote letters to all those who I needed to separate myself from.

It wasn't a letter of permanent goodbye. It was a letter stating that unless we made strides towards greater mutual respect then I was wiping the slate clean and I would get on with my life. I wouldn't worry about it and that would be the end of it.

There were harsh truths told to my ex-wife Alison and my children in particular but I felt I had by now, earned the right to decide to dispense with negativity after all the years I had yearned for positive solutions.

The flipside was the positive long term, and it wasn't going to kill me. I would only have people in my life that I got on with and who wanted me in their lives.

Suddenly a light was switched on.

I took my phone and deleted an enormous amount of phone numbers. I deleted hundreds of email addresses. It was the only way I could truly have a clean slate in life, it was something I had never done before but it felt extraordinarily liberating.

It is the ultimate irony however that the greatest stress in my life was caused by people who didn't even know me, particularly through the court system. People who made judgments on me based on talking to me for a few hours. It is ironic that certain people look up to me because I have been successful in business yet I couldn't keep my family together. Even after all these years there are few people who know me to any significant degree. The only way you can truly get to know a person is to live with them.

The last six years of my life have been the most traumatic ever but they have spawned tremendous change within me and in the pages of my life. I came to the realisation that half of the time I was attempting to prove to my dad that I could do better than he ever could. He failed to relate to me so much I had to try and prove something in return. I felt he was not a good father to make me feel that way and that I had to outdo him and be something incredible myself. I was charged by the feeling of proving myself. I don't feel that anymore. In fact I don't have anything to prove to anybody anymore – nobody but my children, all I want to prove to them is that I can commit totally, utterly and for the rest of my life.

The work and personal revelations had a wonderful effect on me. Those who were still able to prove themselves to me, as with my business, made the positive effort and change. It lifted a huge burden which I had been carrying with me, life changed for the better and it was then that I decided to write the book you are holding in your hands after being asked to do so many times over.

Maybe the heart scare had scrambled my brain. My management team certainly believed so when I told them of an idea I had to increase business at the park over the winter period of 2010. My idea was to let visitors in for free. Yes, a £12.50 ticket would be waived for nothing. All off my staff looked at me as if finally, I had lost my mind. My logic was that, though they were coming in through the gates for free, they would still have to eat and might also buy something in the shop, or contribute to the conservation fund. Kids would always want to feed the few animals that we can actually charge to feed. The idea worked extremely well, perhaps even better than I envisaged. We would normally have 10,000 people through the gates during the lean winter months. With the free entry enticement over 70,000 people visited the park. I managed to cover all the running costs and keep every member of staff employed where normally a few would be laid off during winter. I had already put an allowance in place whereby every primary school has free entry all year round. If they are coming in for free and they are learning something it is fine with me. I would love just one person a day to change how they see animals – you can change the world by changing people's opinions.

I've managed to expand the ideas surrounding South Lakes Wild Animal Park over the years, particularly at Christmas time. I thought we were all missing the real meaning of Christmas, it is disappearing from society. I didn't want Santa's grotto and a group of elves, I wanted a Nativity where the kids come in and dress up, sitting by the crib, following the story of Mary and Joseph and then linking it to Father Christmas and giving and receiving presents on baby Jesus' birthday. We created a living room of a house with a fireplace, Christmas tree and so on, because most people open their presents at home in their living room. I thought this was more realistic than some seedy grotto, far more homely and traditional. South Lakes also keep our Christmas lights on all the way through the dark winter months.

It would have cost as much to hire a skating rink as buy one so I bought a rink which we also now use every winter. It brings me such great joy to have a full family experience available at the park; it is part of my overall wish for my own life.

Chapter 48
Friends and dreams

I dream of having the perfect family life and a loving relationship once again. From this perspective is just another reason why I admire and in truth, am a little envious of my friend Pierre. He and his wife Elisa have such a beautiful partnership. I have stayed with them many times on our travels around the world. They deeply love each other. One time Pierre and I were in Brazil together. He came down to breakfast one morning and noticed something in the breast pocket of his shirt. It was a note that he pulled out. It read, 'I was ironing your shirt and I was thinking of you and the next time you open the shirt you will be a long way from me. I just want to remind you how much I love you.' The letter wasn't for me but even I nearly cried! I thought about what I would give for that. There was clearly a lot of forethought behind Elisa's gesture.

When we had spent time on the private island in Madagascar I had watched the two of them together frolicking around on the beach. I took some photos which remain some of the most natural, loving photographs I have ever taken or seen. They did not know I was taking them. When they saw them afterwards they were over-whelmed. The sun was shining off the water with the waves and spray of the water frothing up behind them. They are proud of the pictures because they had no idea they were being taken – it was merely their natural behaviour, their natural love for each other that they show every day. That is what I would give anything to have.

No matter what has happened in my personal life, one thing has remained constant – my love for animals. I built South Lakes Wild Animal Park because I love animals and I am still absolutely enthralled by them. To this day, all these years on, the only thing I'm interested in is animals. I do of course love being successful in business but it's the animals that keep me enthused. If it weren't for working with my animals, being able to talk to them, to be around them on a daily basis, I wouldn't do it. I couldn't be a zoo director who sat in an office wearing a suit pushing paperwork around. I am out in the field every day with my wellies on. Many times people do not even realise I am the owner. I am often asked by the public, 'Is the boss in today?' It is ironic and revealing because people do not expect the owner to be out working as hard as his staff, getting dirty. But this is the reason no doubt, for my success. And it is still what I love best. I want to be in the wild, whether it is in the UK or America, and I want animals around me. I am just thankful to the human race for indulging my love by visiting our wonderful park and enabling me to continue.

The park is currently in the midst of a huge expansion that will mean it is more spread out and easier for people to enjoy in larger numbers as our visitors continue to increase. The total investment is between £3.5 and £4 million. This sounds a lot but the majority of zoos in the UK would spend that amount on an exhibit. London Zoo once spent around £5m on a gorilla exhibit, an obscene amount. Yet, it is my long held concepts of trying to do as much of the work myself which has kept the costs down even on a major expansion project. Eventually the park will be three times bigger than when we started and it will cost a fraction of such a development at another zoo because I have designed everything myself and still like to get my hands dirty whenever time permits.

The difference in my working on the park today is that it comes as a second priority in my life; second to my children. I often think about what I want for my children. I want the very best for Hari, Kadi, Toba and Indi. With regard to my older two children Ben and Amy, to the day I write this Ben still insists that he has done nothing wrong and I am the one needing the help. Amy got married and had another child without even having the courtesy of informing me. I don't even know the child's name. It makes me very sad to imagine what my grandchildren will one day think when they realise they do not know me or my zoo. Neither of them seems remotely interested in resolving the problems to allow forgiveness to take its course. Strangely however, Amy and Ben never did show much of an interest in animals which was a real surprise.

I would encourage my children to become the same kind of adults as my good friends Stewart and Christine and Pierre and Elisa – to me that would be a success. I would like them to have the same attitude towards other people – that giving and caring is far more important than anything else. I would love them to follow in my footsteps, but not necessarily in business, rather in my philanthropy which has become one of the most important parts of my life.

Yet I believe the most successful parents are those who allow their children to develop at their own natural pace. Pierre would be a good example of this. Whereas he has his own zoo, his eldest son is an opera singer in Paris. His other son is a landscape architect. There was no pressure to follow in their father's footsteps. His architect son, Francois, has helped Pierre re-design the zoo, so he has been involved with the zoo but on his own terms and is now the Director.

I would love my children to take over South Lakes Wild Animal Park one day but there is no expectation or pressure for them to do so. It is far more important that Hari, Kadi, Toba and Indi grow up respecting other people, valuing money in the right way and learning just how the majority of the world lives in poverty. I want them to see the worst kinds of poverty. I want them to see atrocious ghettos and what most people have to eat on a daily basis. I want them to know not to waste food or throw anything away. There is importance in appreciating just what you have.

Many people believe I am a tight fisted so and so. I will always finish off food that the kids didn't eat. I don't believe in waste, I believe in making the most of everything you have. It is a real dichotomy to most people because they see me as a zoo owner with a Bentley. And yet if I see food left on a plate in my home I will eat it. As shown in the details of my early life, the simple truth is, I was raised this way and it has remained part of my character that has never gone away, despite the material possessions or success from my zoo.

When I was a child you could not leave the table until you finished the food on your plate and therefore, today I don't overfill the plate in the first place! I do have a real bugbear about waste, I hate to see it. I don't think we have a right to waste food when there are people out there dying because they don't have food to eat.

It helped that I came from nothing. I came from a childhood where there was no expectation of anything, where I had to work for everything I had. Everything we had was basic. As a consequence I will not go shopping for food until I have finished everything in the cupboards first. This does mean of course that sometimes I am stuck eating Indian curries every day for a week sometimes but I feel the urge to eat everything I have before restocking. In essence I live a very simple life, despite having a Bentley in the Garage that I rarely ever drive. I drive a Land Rover, I buy my clothes from George at Asda – if it fits and I like it, I will wear it. I wear a one-dollar necklace around my neck which I bought in Colombia.

As many studies point out, your character is formed within the first four or five years of your life. It is an aspect of my character I never want to change.

Chapter 49
Horse Ranch Adventure in Wyoming

In August 2011 the latest adventure in my life was born, the purchase of a Horse Ranch in Wyoming, USA. The UXU Ranch is a holiday 'Dude Ranch' just a short 15 minute drive from my house, towards Yellowstone National Park. It features ten amazing log cabins in the middle of the forest where up to 39 people can be a cowboy for a week. Though the accommodation is luxury they can live a relatively historic Western lifestyle. I have always wanted to be a cowboy and now we can all live the cowboy life, for a few months of the year at least. The place is idyllic, in the middle of wilderness forest and with bears, wolves, elk, moose and deer all around a paradise on this earth. I can't wait to spend our summers riding in the mountains and camping in the back country and seeing my children develop in the wonderful surroundings of Cody, Wyoming. A dream for my family to have the opportunity to live and work in the wild west of the USA and bring smiles and adventure to so many people's lives. I have always loved cowboy films ever since I was a boy when the only thing worth watching on TV was from the Wild West, Alias Smith and Jones, The High Chaparral, Bonanza and many more had a huge influence on me. We dressed and played Cowboys and Indians as children and had great fun in the innocence of not having a clue about the real history. I simply love the lifestyle, the wilderness and the reliance on a trusted horse. I hope I get the chance to enjoy my future years horseback riding in the back country of the Yellowstone region. So I have taken on a new challenge, but this time a relaxing, holiday challenge and one I hope I have to do little work on and just enjoy the whole experience. I just love Cody, Wyoming, the people, the Cowboy town atmosphere and sheer wildness of the place.

The people in and around Cody that I am proud to call my friends are some of the most special people I have ever met, just like when I was in Australia with Maureen and Des Lane and family, our real estate agents "The Richard's" have become "family". A truly wonderful and heart warming feeling of being integrated into a new life style and group of people who do truly love and care for each other. My team at the Ranch as well as my neighbours at our house there are just so positive to be around and it really is contagious. Going 25 miles into town on a Saturday night for a meal and a dance has become an event to look forward to, the atmosphere is so different to the UK, in a cowboy bar eating steaks and doing the two step and jitterbug is such a stimulating environment. I have found that I actually really do like to go out and have fun, something I have not done for over 30 years!

I just recently returned from a horseback ride in the Rocky Mountains around the Ranch in deep fresh snow, with the sun bright and a clear blue sky. With horses that are as one with the rider and trusting in the ability to climb and walk through astounding forest and mountain scenery whilst in deep snow. The day was one of the most exhilarating of my life. 7000 ft up and a feeling of one with nature and my own being.

There were animal tracks in the snow in abundance and the two of us were riding along up a drainage in over a foot of snow when "Stretch", (so named for his long thin body) my Ranch Manager and very experienced western horseman and mountain guide turned to me and said :

"Stop."

"What have you seen", I asked with interest.

"Looky there", he said and pointed at a huge number of tracks in the fresh snow.

"Lots of activity here recently", I said.

We both looked around from the safety of horseback. Clyde my horse was real steady and alert to all around.

"Look over there" Stretch pointed out", what do you think that is?"

I replied "Bear?"

"Yep, a bear has been here a short while ago made a kill of a deer and then buried what was not eaten for later, he will have covered it in snow and soil then peed on it to hide it".

"It isn't very well hidden though now" I said. The carcass was made into a makeshift grave with large sods of grass and mud dragged up from deep under the snow making it stand out a mile in the pristine fresh snow all around.

"The tracks are here", Stretch calmly pointed out.

"It is a big bear", I said looking down at the paw prints like dinner plates with big claws and with an excited feeling of being so close to such a huge wild animal once again in my life.

"Let's move on as he may be still very close and will protect his kill!" Stretch advised with assured confidence.

We urged the horses further up the mountain trail following in the footsteps of the bear as it was our only way to go.

"Did you bring a gun or Pepper Spray?" I asked Stretch suddenly.

"Sure did" he said whilst pulling out his pistol from the holster like John Wayne in a movie.

I had not brought mine making an assumption Stretch would be armed with a side arm as most people are in this country, not to kill the Bear that is totally illegal as they are fully protected under Federal Law, but to frighten it off and for last resort protection. Grizzly Bears are not normally aggressive to humans and prefer to avoid them, but every now and then because of specific circumstances such as being too close to cubs or when they are starving in the spring or fall needing fattening up for hibernation they can be very unpredictable and with such a huge carnivore you need to be aware and protected for that emergency that may never happen.

We rode just a few minutes and then came upon another mass of tracks and messed up snow, this time red with blood and clearly a place where predators had made a kill of a Mule Deer. The body was lying a few feet further down the trail.

"Keep your eyes open around here we have a very awake and active Bear", Stretch said and pointed out the shape of the huge bear in the snow where it had laid to gorge itself on the carcass of the deer.

"What are those other prints all around? They look like Wolf!" I said.

"Sure are and whole mess of them too" said Stretch, It was then obvious that the kill was made by either the wolves and the bear cleaned it up or the Bear and the wolves finished it off. Only a few steps away in the snow there was another Bear burial site so very fresh, so three kills in a really small area in the past 24 hours.

I can honestly say that at that point I suddenly realised that we were truly in the wilderness and wilds of North America and an urge to move forward and away from this activity was becoming urgent in my mind.

" It was very late for a Bear to be active they are usually tucked up in a den and asleep in such deep snow!" I was told " but sometimes they can come out again searching for food and very hungry"

Wolves are the kings of the wilderness once winter sets in , having many advantages over the deer and Elk. I was excited knowing we had stumbled on such a hive of carnivorous predatory activity. We carried on with our ride to ever higher altitude for many hours and eventually came to the top of the ridge where both sides of the mountain were unfolded before our eyes at the top of the tree line the world opened up and the views were of such beauty and clarity they took my breath along with the altitude and freezing temperature.

We had to dismount and lead our horses Clyde and Dillon down the mountain as it was too slippery and steep to ride , making the adventure more stimulating , knowing the pack of Wolves and a seriously big hungry Grizzly were somewhere in those trees.

Breathless, feeling light headed from the altitude and dehydration of the dry atmosphere it was a welcome feeling to put the horses in the coral, sit by a log fire and recall our adventure on the North Fork of the Shoshone river in the Rocky Mountains of Wyoming next to Yellowstone.

Wow, just thinking about it again is uplifting ! I hope that I get many more of those days in our future and with my children by my side because it is these experiences that make life the adventure it is.

Another link to the west is one of my real loves, Country music.

I started to listen to New Country way back in 1995 as I recalled earlier in the book , when we first had a satellite dish installed, there was only about 5 channels then and one was CMT Country Music Television. It was the start of the careers of many a now famous singer, such as Shania Twain, Faith Hill, Tracy Lawrence and many others. I used to put it on every morning before work and became hooked on the melodies, the stories and the real life, down to earth feel of the music. Now after being a Jethro Tull fan and listening to Genesis as a kid the contrast was huge, but it hit a place in me that has kept me entertained ever since and grown. My favourites are without a doubt Tracy Lawrence and Brad Paisley, both of whom I had the pleasure of seeing live in 2011. Tracey Lawrence played with his band at the Park County Fair in Powell Wyoming in July, this was only an hour's drive from our home in Wapiti, Wyoming. Set in the arena where the demolition derby and car racing takes place the next night it was very special, in cowboy country and on a warm sultry night, a dream I never thought I would witness. Every song a gem and driving home with three of my good friends from Cody we sang along all the way back to a CD in the car. In august I returned briefly to the UK and in that window Brad Paisley was playing the O2 Arena in London for one night only. I managed to secure some tickets and took two of my staff as a thank you for working so hard. This concert I have to say without any doubt in my mind was by far and away the best music, atmosphere and show that I have ever seen, Brad was outstanding with his voice and guitar playing for which is so very well known. It still amazes me that one of the highest selling artists in the USA who is a household name there is so barely known over here. Most people still think of Johnny Cash and Tammy Wynette when Country is mentioned but today's country stars produce music of such a varied and broad appeal and with such quality that makes it the most listened to music in the USA by far. I just can't get enough of it.

Chapter 50
Frustration, revelation and reflection

Looking at the future my life can be split into four sections. There is my beloved zoo, my conservation and charity work, the UXU Ranch and home in the USA and my personal life. From the perspective of South Lakes Wild Animal Park, within the next ten to fifteen years I would like to see it change from the somewhat tight and pressured atmosphere that comes on a busy day to be more wide and expansive to allow people to enjoy a more relaxed visit. I hope that the staff I have working with me now continue to stay on the team, for they are a marvellous group of people – dedicated, loyal and hard working. I also consider a number of them very good friends.

I would love that our zoo continue to increase in size and popularity, I would like it to be the flagship attraction for the whole of the Lake District.

In the same way I want my conservation and charity work to increase and improve, in fact I would like the two charities I formed to be twice as successful as they are now, I am currently employing more people to improve it in the very near future. I now have a manager and a scientist behind it because my own passion, desire and ability to travel doesn't necessarily manage projects so well. For the future I want the charities to be better known but still have the same passion and commitment I have put into them from day one. The Ranch and home in the USA are just stunning in every way and the friendships as good, the future I hope will bring success and adventure for my children and myself and give a wider life experience for them.

From a personal point of view I hope my young children can see I have been a good person who loves them and always wanted them to be in my life and that I did not escape them by desire, it has been because of my own mistakes and the mistruths of others. It has been my main dream and goal in life over the last few years to have Hari, Kadi and Toba in my life. It is very painful to look back and realise every single minute of every day I have not been able to talk, hold or look at my children. The court situation turned into something completely out of hand and it is quite ludicrous to think things have got to this stage. All my children ever had from me is love and a desire to secure their future. They are still the reason I live and work each day. It would be the greatest honour of my life if they could one day work in, or even run South Lakes Wild Animal Park. That would be my greatest achievement in many respects.

I turned 50 in 2011 and as I head towards the latter half of my life, it becomes very apparent that not only am I not immortal, but that as time goes on, the ultimate mark of a successful man is to have a loving woman by his side. I would like to settle with my soul mate because towards the end of your life, giving and receiving love is the main thing you should be concentrating upon. Of course I will never give up doing the work that I love but I now approach it from a position of contentment and see the work as an enhancement to my life, not the be all and end all.

I can't see retirement on the horizon, I don't want to vegetate. I still have lots of energy and drive. I have four children under the age of nine to keep me on my toes. Now, however I want to oversee rather than manage, not be involved every day. I don't want work to dictate to me. I do enjoy *not* working now however, which is certainly a recent development. Generally I will pop in to the zoo at least once a day but just recently Indi and I spent the whole weekend gardening and I didn't get involved with the park at all and didn't even feel guilty. Now that's progress! I am still frustrated about the situation I have had to face with the Family Court on behalf of every family who will have the misfortune to enter its grasp. It is not one individual who causes the problems; A Judge is faced with an impossible task. He goes from one case to the next case. He reads papers in between and that's all he has. He doesn't know where I live. He doesn't know my house. He doesn't know the child, whose course in life he is about to determine. All he knows is what is presented by lawyers and so called professionals such as Psychologists and Social workers , many of whom have proven to me over the years to be utterly un professional and have the power to cause hell for families. By failing miserably to ascertain the real facts, real issues and come up with sadly personal biased reports that are then used as factual evidence when they are simply one persons opinion that divide families.

Everyone makes a fortune from the sad inability of parents to work together to the benefit of the child and they don't deserve the extortionate accounts they generate for coming up with factually incorrect sexually biased self important reports when they go home and spend the families hard earned money on their holidays.

The adversarial system for profit has to be changed. Children can never ever be protected by the law when you've got lawyers that are interested only in money, making it worse for families whilst building their for profit business. I have been lucky to have a very understanding lawyer for the past few years who does think of the children first before me which I truly appreciate but I have witnessed very aggressive and damaging lawyers at work, clearly never once thinking of the child or children involved at all, just "winning".

The system is discriminatory in its very core by the unrealistic costs charged by lawyers and the system does not consider the long term financial devastation that Family court inflicts on the families for the rest of their lives. You cannot ever get the best for children when that happens.

The fact is parents involved in Family Law cases in Courts in the UK who have never done anything wrong in their lives will be punished far more than people who break criminal law, steal, drive drunk, commit violent crime and in fact virtually every crime that does not involve a Custodial sentence.

How?

Simple, one court appearance can cost as must as £4,000 and there will be many of them if agreement is not made, no criminal ends up with "fine" like that they get £100 and £65 costs as a man on the TV got today for driving drunk without insurance. The cost of Family Law to me has been over £160,000 to date, it is horrendous and once you elect to enter its doors or you are forced by the other party, you lose control of when you can let go. Your money will be extracted from you in chunk sizes you will find abhorrent and all because two people who once were in love cannot be decent enough or show love enough to their own children. I learned far too late that placing the children's needs first would have avoided this for me. Sadly it is not our choice either, if the other parent decides they are going to argue you are dragged in screaming against your will and better judgement and you will be financially ruined. What justice is this? What positive result does this give families? There has to be a new way of doing this and it has to be radical. in time, things will start to change. They have to.

One of the funniest yet most dangerous things that has happened to me with animals in my life so far happened on a trip to France. I drove over to CERZA a great zoo in north western France to collect a new male Andean Bear to go with our four female bears. Snoopy was allocated to us via the European endangered Species Breeding Programme for Andean Bear and it was to be our first chance to breed these wonderful rare animals. They have the most wonderful enclosure for these bears and we walked around and were impressed with the facilities, I had brought a large crate we normally would use for Tigers and Lions, it was a heavy wooden crate with steel lined sides and roof. It was very heavy and had to be lifted to the Bear housing by 6 men. The crate was set up and then Snoopy was invited to enter it with the temptation of food. Something we would later learn he never ever refuses ! Once inside the door was secured and the Bear was set to move to Cumbria. We enrolled the help of a couple more people and all spaced ourselves around the crate to get a grip and lift.
"Un, deux, trois"
and loud grunts and the crate lifted , it has to be said easier than I expected. We all had hold and I said
"ok Move forward"
" It is stuck" in French of course.
"How can it be stuck?"
"Something is stopping us"

I looked down and to my surprise and then sheer amazement I saw one of Snoopy's feet .

Just like in a cartoon, we had counted 1,2,3 and then lifted and left the floor of the box behind and we were trying to walk off and would have left the bear sat looking at us !

Luckily he was so big and heavy we couldn't walk off and be left with him staring us in the face.

We all dropped the box, missed his toes and all jumped on top of it at once.

It was then and only then , that we had the ability to look at each other and laugh and laugh we did, because I think the realisation , the fear and the way we all ended up piled on top released the energy.

We had to get Snoopy into another crate but this time we got a solid steel crate one with every part welded together, it weighed twice as much and was fork lifted into place. Snoopy slid into it and with a sigh of relief we shut the slide and relaxed.

When we got back to the zoo it was so difficult to get the crate out of the van, but we did and Snoopy took up residence , a bear twice the size of his new lady friends but he clearly felt at home as Mona and Alice, who arrived years earlier from Paris must have greeted him in French !

I had an exact replica made of the crate before we returned it to France so we would never have the excitement of a bear looking at us when the floor fell out ever again, another lesson learned.

When I was in the hospital after my heart scare I had my latest realisation of my own mortality. I realised I could die any second whether it was from heart failure or a car crash or stroke. Something's going to get you eventually; there are a million ways one can die. Strangely, despite all my near death experiences, I had never faced up to this sober, sombre reality before. I started to look at life completely differently when I realised we are all on the slippery slope heading towards death. But in this realisation is a wholesome yearning to appreciate and experience life to its fullest. I might not be here tomorrow. Since then I have learned how to keep perspective in all things and never let something control my thoughts or my happiness. Life is far too short.

As one quote has said,

'Today is the present and that's what God intended it to be, a present, so use it well.'

Indeed, it is called a present, and why? Because it is a gift from God and you should enjoy it. Not tomorrow, not the past, not the future, but the present because if you actually start living your life looking towards the future you'll never enjoy your day. If you are always aiming beyond today you can never enjoy the present and this was a very pertinent realisation from my time in the hospital. Now I feel as if I truly live for today. I want to make myself happy in some part every single day. You cannot always have a happy experience every minute of every day but an inner contentment is a true gift. In the words of George Bernard Shaw, "I rejoice in life for its own sake. Life is no brief candle to me. It's a sort of splendid torch which I've got to hold up for the moment and I want to make it burn as brightly as possible before handing it on to future generations."

People who know me have described to me how they have seen an incredible change in me within the last two years. My contentment is obvious to those who have seen me hit the darkest depths.

It is clear that my determination and sometimes single-mindedness has held me in good stead in terms of achievement within my work. It came at a big price because it destroyed a big part of my family life and the one thing I would do differently is to balance my priorities better. Work does not have to consume you, but it is my persistence and effort that has brought South Lakes Wild Animal Park a very prominent place in the zoo world.

There is always a way to avoid the hardship, the doubts and the difficulties that other people or circumstances place upon you. It does not matter where you start from in life, or where you are. It doesn't matter how many people or circumstances try to block your way, there is always a way around. If you want something you have to work for it, you have to make it happen. Too many people ponder that one person cannot make a difference but they can. Any individual from any background can make a huge difference in this world if they want to and it's about wanting to because you can but you have to want to. You've got to want to change the world and you've got to want to get in there and do it. Not rely on others to do it, but get in there and do it yourself. You have to be willing to cope with people's petty jealousies and insecurities. This has been the bane of my existence but no one has managed to bring me down.

My initial idea with my animal park was to change the world just a little, and to change people's perceptions and beliefs about animals in the wild and how they should be housed in a public setting. I managed this and then have improved way beyond this to provide facilities and benefits to animals, and indeed people, all around the world (see Appendix). I no longer need the recognition I once craved. I've achieved much more than I ever thought I would, so anything else is a bonus.

"Dwell not on the past. Use it to illustrate a point, then leave it behind. Nothing really matters except what you do now in this instant of time.

From this moment onward you can be an entirely different person, filled with love and understanding, ready with an outstretched hand, uplifted and positive in every thought and deed."

It took me twelve years of living with the wrong wiring, to realise exactly what I was doing to my family with my incessant workload and one-track mind to success. Even when the realisation dawned it took another couple of years to truly start to implement the right changes, to become a better person and a better father. It has been an unenviable, hard task to keep my head above water with all of my projects and still try to improve as a person and be calm, positive and pleasant to those around me. If something isn't happening in my business then it will be my charities, or a personal issue. Things never stop with me and it has been a difficult time to try and keep things in perspective.

But I believe perspective is one of the biggest lessons one can learn. What really matters ultimately is personal relationships, not money or status, or business achievements. Today I know this better than ever. We can all spend time focusing on the day-to-day irritants of life but if we realise the true meaning of life is strong family bonds and good friendships we might all live with a touch more positivism. Not to mention contentment.

I'm a long way from perfect but I'm closer than I ever have been before. I have experienced terrible lows and made some very big mistakes but don't we all? I have always strove to be unique, but in the end we are all human and we all have strengths and weaknesses, successes and failures. Mine have just been a little more exaggerated. One thing I have managed to do is take positive lessons from all the tribulations I have been through. If it makes me, not to mention my children, a better person then it was all worth it.

The greatest moments of my life are the things you cannot buy – any time I get to spend with my children hugging them and playing games. True friends are hard to come by and I am blessed with a number of wonderful people in my life and thank God for them and those times together.

The biggest lesson I've learned?

What you want is not always the best thing for you and never do today what is best done tomorrow. Oh, and check weather forecasts before getting in a boat anywhere !

Epilogue

I have spent a few words in this book talking of relationships but when talking about love, trust and deeper emotions it brings me to the very special and unique relationship I have with my herd of white rhinos. Going right back to the start of this book I spoke of the "gift" that I had with animals, the ability to communicate and be at one with them on a level that is not available to many and the "friendship" I have with my rhinos is something that is very difficult to explain and to comprehend by others I am certain. I have had Huubke and Mazungo now for 13 years , they arrived as 2 year old males together and I gained their trust at that point and in fact became their new "Dad" and senior family member. The way we built the trust was simple and based on confidence and knowledge that I was their protector feeder and comforter. The 2 boys grew up fast, eventually becoming near 3 tonne monsters yet because of my consistent love and dedication to them we still have as close a "friendship" together now as ever. The trust they place in me is astounding to experience and to be a family member with access to the space they are in without issue is one of the most amazing feelings any one could ever have with animals. The 2 girls arrived 8 years ago now from South Africa and after a difficult few months of communication with them eventually I built the trust needed to be accepted as close family. They were also very young on arrival and it took a long while to show them the love and commitment I had to them after their long journey from their parents. They were very playful girls and when I went in with them I had to be very alert for years as they would love to just push me around for fun. After 5 years of constant interactions and special relationship building Ntombi and Tala finally were pregnant and because of my close trust and bonds both she and Tala would allow me to check them over each day and closer to the births feel their udders and get up close. This led to a funny event because at this time we were being filmed for weeks by a team from Channel 5 TV and in the final cut for Michaela's Animal Babies I was shown walking round the back of a rhino to feel her teats, the shot however made it look like I suddenly disappeared up the rhinos bum ! A sharp eyed but clearly twisted Harry Hill on ITV picked this up and I appeared on Harry Hills TV burps on Boxing Day 2008 with the comments "Cumbrian man disappears up a rhino's backside" well it surprised me when told by my staff and it did look funny in that context.

In June 2008 Ntombi gave birth to Nyala, the wonderful part is that she allowed me to be with her at the birth, she trusted me with her baby and responded so positively to all my requests of her, I had her with the other rhino's including both adult males within 10 days out on the field with her tiny new baby and all went so well. Tala was similar and now I feel so privileged to be a part of a family of 6 white rhinos where I can walk with them , between them and play , tickle and check their feet over in the middle of the field and with no fear, concern or worry from either me or the rhinos. Ntombi and Nyala actually roll over onto their backs for a tickle on their tum and recently Nyala now 3 years old rolled over and was squealing with delight having a tummy rub when Ntombi her mother ran over to see what was going on and promptly dropped down alongside her, rolled over and asked me to give her a tickle on the tum too, very emotional moments in my animal existence and something I know so few people will ever have experienced in this world. Being accepted as an integral part of their herd is without a doubt the most moving and deepest relationship I have with any animals and I doubt there is anyone else who has this very unique and special ability with rhinos. I can quite happily take my young children in with me to stroke and tickle them even the huge males lift their legs for my 2 year olds to give them a tickle and scratch a very, very special thing to be a part of. I don't take risks and if they are particularly playful or in a mating frenzy then of course I let them get on with dissipating the energy. But out of all the wonderful, dramatic and heart rending experiences I have had the day to day continuing family relationship with my rhinos is still the most special part of my animal life and I hope will continue to be for as long as I can walk on this earth, because they are dependable, totally trusting and they never let me down in anyway, true friends, true family and a privilege to be a part of their family. As I am finishing writing the book another wonderful event occurred in that Ntombi produced her second baby on 17th November 2011. This baby arrived with speed, energy and strength. He got up and walked in minutes and it seemed only right to call it Indiana after my son who has loved and shared with the rhino family since his own birth only 3 years earlier. Having a white rhino named after my 3 year old son and our baby Sumatran tiger named after my 4 year old daughter Kadi seems appropriate as Hari and Toba my other sons aged 9 and 2 respectively are named after Sumatran Tigers we had at the park. So we now have a small herd of seven White Rhinos at the zoo and a dream come true to breed them successfully and contribute to the desperately worrying situation for rhinos on this planet that are still poached and killed in such high numbers for their horn which is simply the same as finger nail. Our additions to this modern dinosaur's numbers are vital in the long term viability of captive populations and the whole future of Rhinos in our modern world. Breeding the rhinos remains the highlight of my work with captive animals and the most fulfilling achievement in my zoo and long may we be successful with these gentle giants who want nothing more than to eat grass and reproduce in the face of mans stupidity and greed attempting to wipe them out for monetary gains.

A very sad development to hit the wonderful life Indi and I shared for his first two years came in November 2010 when from out of the blue his mother suddenly decided she wanted to have full custody of him after I had brought him up at the zoo since his birth with him spending well over 95% of his time with me. In doing so, sickeningly for me, she brought me to the family court system once again. All I have tried to do since this dramatic change in her attitude towards Indi and myself is look for a compromise to provide Indi with two parents while still experiencing his unique and special lifestyle – full of travel, excitement, education and unique life experience. I tried so hard to get Alison to sit around a table to find a solution for Indi but she refused to talk and just seemed to want to fight. The very last place on this earth I would have chosen to go to was the court as you can imagine after the nightmare of the past. Maybe that is why she did thinking she could get the same result.

What is it within parents that drives them to use a child or children to do as much hurt to the other parent as possible? A question I have spent many a long sleepless night pondering upon as the one you claim to love so much is the ultimate loser from the very action they take. A case in point is that every year since 2005 I have visited our wonderful friends, the Plenge family in Chaparri, Peru. Every year I have taken my children with me, Hari visited 4 times with me from the age of 3 along with Amy visiting twice. Indi has previously visited there when he was just 14 months old, yet when I informed Alison that I wanted to take Indi with me to Peru in February of 2011 she just flatly refused to agree. No reason given just no.

The situation then was brought before the court to decide and whilst I cannot divulge any of the proceedings and contents of the hearing I can say she and her desperate and heartless lawyer put everything they had into stopping Indi from travelling to our friend's home and our wonderful wildlife projects. In the end Indi and I did go to Peru for 18 days granted it was a slightly shorter trip than was planned and he had an amazing time with me (some of the photos are included in the book with Bears, Condors and baby macaws) an adventure that no school, playgroup or book could ever attempt to compete with in terms of life experience. This desperate attempt by Indi's own mother to stop his life experience was really surprising as it was obvious that when she went on the trips it was all fine, but now she had chosen a different road and was not going she wanted to stop Indi also. One of the major concerns I have about this kind of conflict is how blatant lies can be told, then proven to be a lie by factual evidence and yet nothing seems to be done about it especially in costs terms the "victim" still has to pay out a fortune to defend themselves from attack. In this case it cost me an extra £3000 in legal fees to fight to take Indi with me, far more than the whole cost of the trip in total. A cost I have no rights to recover, the system is so set up against fairness and who can afford to fight for a simple holiday when it is so easy for a parent to inflict this very selfish action on the child and other parent. The attempt to stop Indi travelling the world didn't stop there though and has continued throughout with Indi being the victim of the need to restrict his opportunities something she always promised myself and Indi to our faces that she would never do?

It is so difficult to be forced to enter into conflict about our son when I have always tried to find compromise and solutions. I fully wanted Indi to have his mother in his life as a fair solution, I know she loves him and that love hopefully would be shown by giving Indi the best possible outcome for him, but sadly even though I worked so hard to find an equal solution for us all it was not accepted, so another frightening waste of money to lawyers and a fight then ensued that had no reason to take place at all if decency and fairness to Indi had been shown.

For any father or mother reading this it must be obvious just how emotionally difficult it is to let your child be with any other man or woman for long periods and have that significant influence on your child. How do you think you would feel if the person your 3 year old son was "forced" to be with had convictions for violence or had spent two separate lengths of time in prison? What if he had two separate convictions and driving bans for drunk driving for instance? With suggested links to drugs, proven regular excessive alcohol drinking, the list seems endless and the thoughts of such things frighten me and upset me that my own son could be influenced by such an example of anti social behaviour in the house he was living. I have no idea what influences Indi will be "forced" to absorb in that new family but all I have experienced before is a clear failure of the system in its ability to apply protection criteria consistently. My requests for Indi to be protected from these negative influences have fallen on deaf ears so I have to have trust and faith that he will be safe in his future simply because the "system" has no consistency or control over the influences a child is subjected to.

I had hoped his mother would come to the realisation that there is only one huge loser from failing to find an amicable solution and that is our son Indi. Especially if she continued to force by legal means his separation from me, the zoo and his life of frequent and exotic travel thus taking away his unique opportunities in this life to please her needs rather than Indi's. Because it is clear that when he is 9 or 10 he will have his own views and if fairness wasn't shown then he will surely want to have the life he should have had and it will all end up in tears as my recent experiences show me.

I have shown consistently that my deep love for him is seen in my need to help him find equality with his parents and a solid start to his life. He deserves this from both his parents. I do not want any more conflict in my life, Alison remarried in July of 2011 and I sincerely hope that she is happy in her new life and that we can parent our son positively and successfully in a friendly way whilst we both enjoy our new futures.

As you are aware I cannot divulge any details of the proceedings but they dragged on for a year and cost me a further £60,000 simply to defend Indi's lifestyle and right to his Dad, his unique life and keep Indi living with me against her desperate need to remove him from my life and take him away from his travel and home in the zoo. The desperation from her was awful and I could not see why Indi would benefit from being forcibly prevented from what he loves the most.

I advocated a 50/50 split of time and responsibility out of court since March 2011 yet that was rejected by her outright at every stage. This time however CAFCASS seemed to get a decent grip on the situation and I felt that for the most part they did see Indiana's needs and opportunities and views of his future for his benefit. It is so sad for a child when one parent decides to try to have a monopoly on them as love is not something that is measured by science but is felt deeply by the child involved and yet often parents only see their own selfish needs and are blind to the child's real need for balance and love from both parents equally. Indi has had a wonderful start in his life with me and I accept without question his right to be with both parents equally, yet that has still cost us emotional heartache, worry and sadly now a ridiculous £60,000 from me and probably around £40,000 for her to pursue this need to remove Indi from me save for a couple of days a fortnight that she offered to me, that money could have been spent on something way better for Indi's future than solicitors and barristers in a negative, adversarial Court system that is so damaging to families for such a long time after. The Court case is now over and I can tell you that Indi will be spending his time 50/50 between myself and his mother after all the horrible arguments and court appearances over a year. A position that was offered by me to her 9 months before, it would have saved both myself and her about £100,000 if she had accepted the mediated settlement then and a lot of heartache.

The only desperately negative thing from Indi's point of view is the fact he has been prevented from travelling on holiday abroad with me in school term time. Now that decision is beyond my understanding or logic because he isn't even at school and wont be for over one and half years nor will he be taking exams for many years to come. Yet it was demanded that he should not travel with me from before the start of the court case. So because of the way the whole situation has ended up Indi is still the main loser in that his life of international travel, wonderful wildlife and natural history experience has been curbed dramatically.

I know that Hari when he was 3 years old, travelled all over the world with me to every continent and his experience was invaluable at school where he excelled in sciences and geography because he had the travel and education I gave him, not only that but the cultural experiences. I have no doubt that in years to come there will be a huge amount of emotional resentment from Indi toward those who prevented his travel and restricted his life experience. I know that Hari when prevented from seeing me and travelling etc. by the Court resented authority and linked anyone with power over him with the "system" that took his Dad away and the loves of his life. Only now is it so apparent the huge mistake the "system" made in taking me and his life from the child to resolve parental issues. I hope that this situation does not stay like this for long and Indi is allowed to travel with me at any time of year so that the same deep resentment does not arise in Indi against those who took his travel away without any reason whatsoever to justify it at all.

In my opinion only a professional teacher who knows Indi should be able to decide on whether travel in school time is detrimental, they never did say that with all my other children because my trips were so educationally positive for them.

I still have no explanation to me for the reason that he is prevented from travel.

I am sickened by the way I was forced to waste £60,000 to end up with what I offered in the first instance and this is why the Court system is so deeply flawed and does not resolve issues but creates even more long term stress in a family as now we both have to pay off the debts for the rest of our lives ?

Take note all mothers and fathers out there that you must do everything possible to find solutions out of the Court system and a solution that puts the children's needs first, because the result of any Court action will leave you wondering what you did it for and why forever. I could never have abandoned my son and never will but I did try to get a balanced and fair solution always.

I have told you this story because it is a lesson to all who read to find other mediated solutions and to avoid Court totally as it will ruin your lives for a very long time to come, find compassion for your child, find the will to give and be fair and drop the urge to win, do this because your children deserve two loving parents who showed their real love by finding a fair solution themselves without a Judge having to make a decision for you.

Whilst I with the help of two women certainly created the impossible situation with them both pregnant with my sons, we are left with a future where we all have to forgive for us all to live in peace. I have no axe to grind, no wish to find fault but I do have a strong need to find a solution that benefits us all in the long run. Lets hope that they all are the benefciary of fairness in the future and they are allowed to have all they are entitled to and to travel widley and often for their benefit and life experience.

As I was coming to the end of writing the story of my life an extraordinarily life changing event happened. The last eleven years have been laid bare for all to see, eleven years in which I have been completely linked with Caroline Jellicoe, from the moment I saw her until now. Whether she knew it or not, Caroline controlled my life.

How?

It was as if I was a radio-controlled toy, though I was sometimes out of range, sometimes without batteries, I was always there and could be influenced by her from anywhere in the world.

Our time together brought us our three children.

I had several "messages" from family that suggested Caroline wanted the kids to be with me. I was even allowed to have some rabbits, which had belonged to Hari, Kadi and Toba. Hari had even called his pet rabbit Indi! I felt certain that, like me, Caroline was waiting for a judge to allow us to find a family love without the workload or other people interfering and free of the courts.

Everything pointed to this, everything showed me it was just a matter of time and I committed myself to our family 100% by investing in the new ranch and applying to the court in June 2011. It was all done to create a safe, loving and secure future for the children.

I thought the process would be easy, because two years had passed without any problems or issues between us, but court is slow, cumbersome and has no feeling for the loss of love and time with children. It took eight months to reach the first hearing to allow the children back into my life, eight more months that can never be replaced.

At this hearing I saw Caroline in the corridor of the Court for the first time in over two years, she smiled at me. We had been negotiating via lawyers for a few weeks and it all came together so well, with a comprehensive joint agreement before we went into the court to let me see the three children. Caroline was helpful and understanding of the children's needs and I was so pleased with the ability to find a very happy situation for us all for our futures. I have to say that I was so emotional, tears streamed down my face throughout. All the restrictions were lifted and it is wonderful to be given the respect of being a responsible parent to them again. I sat in an interview room for half an hour with Caroline alone whilst the lawyers drew up the paperwork, for the first time in over 2 years we had a conversation. My heart jumped and I knew then that all would be fine.

Two days later I found myself driving to Manchester to see Hari, it all happened so quickly. When I arrived outside the house Hari ran excitedly to me and gave me a big hug and a broad smile, he could not wait to be with me and the day started with seeing that he was so tall, over 2 years had added a foot to his height and his accent had changed from Cumbrian to Mancunian, a little surprise for me there. We did everything from play football for hours, ten pin bowling, mini golf and digging over the allotment garden but Hari is a born naturalist and his favoured pastime was pond dipping with a small net and discovering what nature hides in the bottom of ponds. The day passed with much laughter, fun and a natural bond that was never broken between us. Later in the day we returned to their home and I was invited in the house to meet Kadi and Toba, not forgetting I had never met Toba in his 2 years and 2 months of life. The experience was as special as it possibly could be, with Kadi just so excited to be with Daddy again and I was given a guided tour of the house and toys by her with an enthusiastic and proud little voice, she just could not get enough of me. Toba who had been quiet since I came into the house, got up walked over to me and pointed straight at me and said "Daddy" and my heart was sent into a spin. Toba had never seen anything but a photo of me and he knew who I was, Caroline told me to keep my cowboy hat on, as Toba didn't recognise me without one on as his whole experience of me for his 2 years was from photos !

The next weekend I took Hari to his football match and he played so well and they won 11-1 a score never heard of before and Hari was inspired by my presence with him. Kadi and Toba ran rings around me and the whole day in the countryside was beautiful with Caroline and the 3 children. Then the next visit I took Indi down to meet his brothers and sister and it was very special the very first time all 4 children met and played together, the day was full of fun, excitement and love.

I discovered that Hari had been suffering emotionally without me in his life he had become angry that he was not allowed to see me and this affected his schooling and friendships. The decisions made by CAFCASS, psychologists and Social Workers who said they were protecting him back in 2008/9 actually caused him real and clear distress for 2 years, the "experts" who pontificate they know best actually inflicted punishment on my children for 2 years when they didn't deserve it and it hurt them more than it hurt anyone else. I have no respect for the "experts" who voiced their opinions and decisions and inflicted hell on my children and caused them such trauma. I have no training in these matters but common sense said it was obvious that Hari would suffer terribly with the punishment that he received and directly handed down by the "system". They are the worst enemies of families and children and they continue to inflict hell on families every day. We need real care, real understanding and solutions that are positive for families and to move away from negativity and this reliance on so called "experts" who have no idea what they are talking about and are totally protected from criticism by the secrecy and privacy laws that apply.

On October 2nd 2011 it was Kadi's 4th birthday, four years since I got the text message in the middle of the Niger desert. I was invited down to their home and we had a wonderful birthday together as a family. Had a party, lovely cake and a fun day all round but I will remember it for the look on Kadis' face when opening the Rapunzel singing doll I got her. Kadi looked beautiful in her Minnie mouse dress and it was a reminder that love cannot be taken from us by others and my family is still and always has been the most important part of my life.

To have all four of my amazing children loving me, shouting daddy constantly and not wanting me to leave was a day that I shall cherish for the rest of my life

The children were coming more often to my home and wanted me more and more. Just before Christmas I took them all including Caroline to Disneyland Paris as a Christmas present and for 4 days we all had a great time in that place of escapism. I had taken all my children there virtually every year in the winter since 1997. It was especially good to see Toba and Indi so close in age and so close as brothers, they went on so many rides together with me. Kadi was dressed as a princess every day and was the most beautiful one in Disneyland, she had a special time and Hari and I rebuilt the amazing father / son bond we had for so long before we were forced apart. I have made effort to get down the 100 miles to see him play soccer every Saturday as he loves playing for his team in the local league. In fact they have not lost a single game whilst I have been watching from the touchline !

Christmas came and all four of the children were with just me on Christmas Day for the first time ever and I made a full traditional Dinner, although I was the only one who ate it ! We had such brilliant fun and the love and smiles were just special for me after all the years of torment. The photos and videos are treasures.

In the new year of 2012 the children just got closer and closer to me to the point where Toba was running to me as if he had known me all his life and Kadi was just realising what the love of her daddy really felt like and she reciprocated my love with kisses and telling me she loved me when I tucked her into bed. For Hari the whole situation was just flooding back to him and he also had a realisation of what he had been forced to miss because of the decisions of others. He cuddled up to me watching a film and told me how much he had missed me, my family and the zoo. I have to say that at that point I was in tears because we can never replace those two and half years stolen from us by the "system" but we can make up for it .

The future for the children and myself looks bright, they are going to visit the house and Ranch in Wyoming with me and are looking forward to horseback riding and the wildlife surrounding the house in the Rocky Mountains.

I have had some staggering negativity brought into my life but I count my special blessings that surround me in my friends, my work and my children.

One of those blessings of course is my zoo and the wonderful natural events that we witness and the last special birth as I write the end of the book is a very small baby Pygmy hippopotamus another little miracle and this time Indi wanted it to be called Hari ! I am really excited by the opportunities the future holds and I have confidence in the balance I have found in my life.

The last event to happen before finally putting the "pen down" on this first 50 years of my life was a triumph for common sense. The letter arrived in February 2012. Announcing that our appeal against the local council planning refusal was upheld and we can start work on the major expansion and redesign of the South Lakes Wild Animal Park. With a totally different approach to the park by road, new car parks, new entrance and children's facilities, with huge new animal enclosures and expansions of the railway the park is set to be without any doubt the flagship attraction of the Lake District and will give so many new opportunities for conservation throughout the world. A huge personal investment, I had not had to borrow money since 2006 but need to invest to make a change that is essential to the long term future of the park and its aims and mission. It is also proof that the local councillors in the Barrow in Furness Borough Council who are on the Labour group did not make a decision that was right or for the benefit of the community as a whole. When will democracy actually work and councillors actually reflect the views of their electorate? When personal vindictiveness on the part of certain councillors takes over they should not be allowed to have the power they wield. I named certain councillors in the earlier text and the same person was a ring leader to force the appeal that now has wasted Tax payers money once again.

So the next years are going to be as exciting as any of the others, because I have recently also taken a completely new direction in my business life by getting involved in the development of a new dot.com internet company in the USA, watch out for iAuto.net as it is sure to be a fast growing national car sales web site. This is an exciting adventure into the jungle of the internet and the world of computers and communications, a far cry from the jungles that I am used to cutting my way through. Working with friends I have made since buying my home in Cody, Wyoming, five of us have got together to develop this very exciting new product using some amazing young local programming and internet talent, blending that with 3 experienced businessmen from different walks of life who are the investors in that talent. When I think back to the day in 1993 when the guy walked up to me at the zoo when I was building it telling me the internet was the future and I laughed at him, I now feel a bit of a fool, but can laugh at myself !

If I add this new venture to the zoo expansion, huge investment, getting the Ranch successful and operating for the family and developing all the very successful conservation projects even more I certainly have created a world of amazing variety for my children's future.

The good news is there will be no more children ! I have a totally different approach to life, relationships, values and are surrounded by such excellent friends all over the world who are so good at keeping me on the straight and narrow. I am so excited for my children Hari, Kadi, Indi and Toba because their future has the most amazing opportunities to expand and develop what I have started and put their own stamp on it all and take it to even greater heights.

I wish to make it clear that I have no wish to cause any upset to Indi's mother, I have been very descriptive in some of the issues but felt after much thought that it was essential to convey the events that all were tied together to create the situation I was in. I admit openly that my actions by not being honest with myself and her about my true feelings and needs led to the events, whilst this does not excuse them at all it certainly explains them, I want nothing more than to have an amicable relationship with her to ensure our son Indi has the best life possible with the both of us in our new futures and hold nothing against her for the past.

I am not angry at my parents but wish they could have found a way to be a part of my life and regret that we don't have a relationship at all, I am certain my mother yearns to share in my life and my children, I do feel love towards her and a deep wish that it had all been different and that she could have had the strength to do what she wanted and felt with her children and grand children, I really hope that we can find a solution as time we cannot buy. My oldest two children I can only hope see the errors of their ways and find a way to say they are sorry to me and my children for the way they have intervened in our lives and caused so much upset and turmoil. The door is always open to anyone who genuinely acknowledges and is sorry for their actions, just as I am so sorry for the mistakes I have made over the years.

So here I end my book at a point I never thought would arrive, after well over 2 years separation a clear realisation that what I perceived about myself and Caroline was all wrong, a mirage of false images and it was never to be, that I was clinging onto a dream of a family together and not because we were right for each other or that it would make us all happy. After nearly 2 years of being effectively single I have a wonderful future waiting with a new relationship in its infancy but showing me what real true love and trust is and for the first time in my life having the experience, perspective and a knowledge that love is unconditional and the most important of emotions to culture, care for and commit to. I have the love of my young children returning to my life and I value that more than any asset I have accrued.

I have so many things still to do and a knowledge that my family will always come before anything else and nothing will ever take my love from my children again because so many lessons have been learned and it just goes to show that it doesn't matter how dark the clouds get, how impossible a situation may seem the fact is there is light at the end of all tunnels and every cloud has a silver lining and the sun is always there ready to emerge.....

I cant wait to share all my life with them in every way possible and find resolution to all outstanding issues God willing.

"My life is a performance for which I was never given any chance to rehearse."

So why write this book?

Why put my family life in the spotlight?

Why reveal all the major mistakes and disappointments alongside the adventure, success, humour and love in my life?

Simply because I get asked every single day

"How did you start a zoo? " and

"How did you get to where you are today?"

In real life, there are always ups and usually equally dramatic downs. To tell the success side without illustrating the mountains I had to climb and depths I fell into and the emotions I had to live through would be like looking at a negative of a photo without all the true colour. I only have one reason for laying my life bare for all to read and that is a deep desire to help other people who may find themselves in similar situations. To have a warning before they make the same mistakes I did, to avoid the nightmares and disastrous emotional and financial consequences of Family courts and lawyers and look as deep inside themselves as possible to find solutions for their children between parents for the sake of the kids. To realise that when the darkest clouds seem to be all around there is ALWAYS light at the end of the tunnel and what seems impossible one minute can in fact be real in your life in time. If I can change one family's life by helping them to avoid courts then I feel it is worthwhile, if I can help children to appreciate their parents love, hard work and dedication to them through their childhood and have tolerance for them then it is worth it and if I can enthuse people to appreciate the quality of life we live compared to most in this world and get them to give towards helping the poor and needy whilst conserving nature and all its wonderful wildlife then it certainly has been worth it. This is my reason for telling all and sacrificing my private life to help other families and wild animals, it is a sacrifice I willing make and hope that my family will have understanding, compassion and support for my wish to make other people's lives better by learning from my failures and getting inspiration from my successes in life.

Most of all be inspired you never get to a destination without making the journey and it can be an amazing adventure if you choose the right roads !

A new life with my family starts...continuing the journey and maybe another book.

"It is good to have an end to journey towards, but it is the journey that matters in the end."

Appendix A

You've read my story and have experienced the highs and the lows. Here you can see just how much I was working during my personal experiences.

History of South Lakes Wild Animal Park

1993: November, construction starts. No fences, roads, electric, water or trees on site, everything built from scratch.

1994: 28th May 1994 opens to the public. Wallabies, antelope, guanacos, raccoons, coatis, parrots, pheasants and ducks held the stage. Projected 10,000 visitors a year.

1995: 55,000 visitors. Antelope facilities and lemur enclosures developed this year. Free ranging lemurs became a feature of the park.

1996: 101,000 visitors. Tigers arrive. Sumatran Tiger, Toba, took up residence on 1st April. Hari followed close behind. In August Amur tigers, Igor and Nina arrived. Fund raising started for Tiger conservation in the wild - it truly was the "Year of the Tiger".

1997: 150,000 visitors. The start of the Australian experience, with the introduction of the largest collection of kangaroo species outside of Australia. Cheetahs arrived and small cat areas created for Ocelot, Margay and Geoffroy's cats.

1998: Rhinos arrived March and the "Africa" section begins.

1999: 220,000 visitors. Primate House and facilities completed with ground breaking fencing and open environments that give the primates a unique facility. Top Attraction in the Lake District awarded for 1999.

2000: Giraffe facilities were completed: Giraffe, rhinos, zebra and antelope all feature together. Top Attraction in the Lake District for 2000.

2001:   New developments for lemurs, cats and other species.

2002:   Spectacled Bears - unique to the UK - arrive along with a pride of lions.
        Top Attraction in the Lake District for 2002.

2003:   Female rhinos arrived. New groups of lemurs, marmosets and monkeys, along with a troop of baboons mixing with the rhinos and giraffes.

2004:   First breedings of Rodriguez Fruit Bat, Agile Wallaby, Siamang and Babirusa, all significant advances for the park and its programmes.

2005:   Penguins, Mandrills, and Hippos arrive. The first walkway opened enabling visitors oversee the Giraffes. Top Attraction in the Lake District for 2005.

2006:   Sees the biggest change in the whole history of the park. A major investment results in fantastic new African style restaurant, themed gift shop and walk through aviary. Vultures and Condors arrive. New bat aviary opens. Attempt to tarmac car park causes local disruption and controversy.

2007:   A record-breaking year with an extra 48,000 visitors. New aerial walkways and viewpoints around the bears and tigers. Progression in the international breeding programmes included rare births, the arrival of a male Spectacled Bear and White Rhinoceroses pregnancies announced. Santa and Rudolf drop in for a truly spectacular Christmas.

2008:   Another record-breaking year. June and September saw the most important event in the park's history with the births of two White Rhino calves, Another first in the park's history were births from all eight lemur species. Capuchin, Squirrel monkeys, Scarlet Ibis, Alpaca, Reindeer and Donkeys are amongst the new arrivals. Top Attraction in the Lake District for 2008.

2009:   New arrivals include Flamingos, Glossy Ibis, Scarlet macaws. Free roaming troops of Capuchin Monkeys and Cotton Topped Tamarins are introduced.

2010:   The park bid farewell to the Macaques but welcomed a whole host of exciting new arrivals including: Sloths, Giant otter, Black howler monkeys, Prairie marmots and Jaguars. First Sumatran tiger birth.

2011: New Gift shop, new extension to restaurant, new toilet facilities all constructed. Changed most heating systems to renewable Air source heat pumps from oil and gas. New major extension begins. 3rd Rhino birth.

When I look back at the start of building the zoo and compare it to now it is amazing to me. I had a proposed total annual budget of £30,000 in 1994 and it staggers me that we now have an annual budget of £3m, a hundred times greater. I have a full-time staff of almost 50 people with extra seasonal staff. In all there are well over a hundred employees, a far cry from the husband and wife tandem which started the park!

In 1994 I was thinking and hoping to change the world and today I can fulfil that dream, providing these ways in so many active and successful ways and contributing over £200,000 a year to conservation projects around the world.

The future looks so bright, with an expansion of the park to three times its present size with all new facilities and car parking consolidating South Lakes Wild Animal Park as one of the best attractions in the north west of England and certainly one of the most proactive conservation zoos in the world.

All of the park managers are 'home grown'; starting at the park and working up to the responsibilities they now have, keeping my philosophy going and giving an experience to visitors that is unique in the world.

Appendix B

CONSERVATION PROJECTS
The following are projects which I have funded and worked towards constructing. They are all ongoing concerns and continue to take up much of my time and air miles!

CHAPARRI ECOLOGICAL RESERVE
Andean Bear conservation, Peru
Created in 2001 to protect 34,412 hectares of dry forest, the area is exceptionally rich in endemic and threatened species and is home to at least 194 species of birds, 15 mammals, 4 amphibians and 21 reptiles. Chaparri is the refuge of two emblematic species, the Spectacled Bear and the Andean Condor. Working with Heinz and Ana Plenge who are the people behind the project.

Activities:
- Management of the reserve with the local community Santa Catalina of Chongoyape.
- Rescue and reintroduction centre for Andean Bears confiscated by the government
- Reintroduction of other endemic wildlife,
- Ecotourism
- Education & awareness.

Support:
Initial sponsorship of "Milagros" a young bear rescued to the project from 2002.

In 2005 I signed a five-year agreement, along with Bioparc, Zoo de Doue la Fontaine to fund this project, the agreement has since been extended to run a further ten years.

CHAPARRI ECOLOGICAL RESERVE
King Vulture & Andean Condor conservation, Peru

Chaparri is the refuge of two emblematic species, the Andean bear and the Andean condor. Flocks of king vultures and Andean condors used to fly in large numbers over the Chaparri ravine. Today they are only seen occasionally, endangered due to habitat loss, hunting & persecution. They have been forced to live elsewhere due to a lack of carrion (food).

Activities:
- The Wildlife Protection Foundation (the charity I founded to fund wildlife conservation) & South Lakes Wild Animal Park fund a feeding station that provides food on a weekly basis to encourage condors and vultures back into the area. Feedback has been positive and condors and vultures are starting to be seen more regularly.
- As well as caring for wild birds, we also take in birds that have been mistreated, with a view to rehabilitating and reintroducing them into the wild. In order to do this, we built a huge flight and release aviary, with a 12m high release tower. The first birds into the aviary were two king vultures and an immature male Andean condor that was confiscated by INRENA after a Yawar fiesta - the illegal practice of tying a condor to a bulls back – symbolising the ancient feud between the Spanish colonists (bull) and the Incans (condor).
- Scientists and bird lovers use the Ecolodge to visit and observe the birds of Chaparri.

Support:
One of the projects funded under Tu Tierra (a new foundation in Peru, I am a founding trustee) South Lakes Wild Animal Park has in 2011 extended its commitment to further long term support.

PROYECTO TITI (PROJECT TAMARIN)
Cotton Topped Tamarin conservation, Colombia

Cotton topped tamarins are on the brink of extinction, with as few as 1,000 left in the wild. Cotton topped tamarins are only found in the tropical forests of North West Colombia. 98% of original forest cover has been lost in the last seven years. The biggest threat to these animals is forest destruction and capture for the pet trade.

Santa Catalina near to Barranquilla, is the last remaining contiguous forest suitable for Cotton tops. This forest – 960 acres – is for sale but could also be cleared for agriculture at any time. Buying the forest is the only option to secure the future for this tamarin.

Activities:
• Working to purchase the forest
• Working with local communities
• Alternative sources of income
• Sustainable use of the forest
• Education & Awareness
Support:
Since 2005 South Lakes Wild Animal Park and our charity The Wildlife Protection Foundation have supported this project and now we are attempting to buy Santa Catalina in order to save a whole species.

ASGN (ASSOCIATION TO SAFEGUARD THE GIRAFFES OF NIGER)
Giraffe conservation, Niger

Just 100 years ago, thousands of Peralta giraffes roamed all over West Africa. Since then, their numbers have been decimated due to hunting, poaching and loss of habitat. By 1996 there were only 41 giraffes left in the region of Dallol Bosso near Niamey, the capital of Niger. The Peralta giraffes of Niger are the last giraffes in West Africa and are critically endangered.

The ASGN (Association to Safeguard the Giraffes of Niger) was created to protect the giraffes and their habitat, whilst improving the lives of the local communities. Due to their hard work and dedication the giraffe population is increasing annually. In 2010 250 giraffes were recorded in Niger!

Niger is one of the poorest and hottest countries in the world, working directly with the local population has been the secret to the astounding success for this project.

Activities:
- Development, protection and management of the giraffe and its habitat
- Environmental education and awareness, re forestation of desert.
- Working with local villages to Improve quality of life, providing fresh water wells, medical assistance etc.

ANTONGIL CONSERVATION
Lemur conservation, Madagascar

Madagascar is the fourth largest island in the world, located in the Indian Ocean 250 miles off the southern east coast of Africa. A biodiversity 'hotspot' full of unique animals and plants Madagascar is the only place where lemurs live naturally in the wild.

Established in 1999 the projects goal is to conserve the Antainambalana Forest in Antongil Bay North East Madagascar. The forest, the largest lowland tropical forest left on the island, is full of endemic fauna and rich in palms & orchids. Clearing the forest for rice cultivation, illegal logging and hunting all put the future of the forest, and all that live in it, under threat.

For centuries the villagers have used the forest's resources in their daily lives. They destroy the forest to grow food for their families and cut down the trees to sell the wood to earn an income. An unsustainable utilisation of the natural resources has resulted in over 90% of Madagascar's forests being destroyed, leaving lemurs literally clinging onto survival.

Because the forest is a vital resource for villagers and its destruction would make their situation even more difficult, Antongil Conservation is managed by a team of fourteen Madagascans working to get locals involved, providing solutions to local development and local problems.

Activities:
- Protection of the rainforest Farankaraina forest is under our direct management and control.
- Development of ecotourism to the region
- Transfer of management of forest plots to villagers
- Environmental awareness and education
- Scientific monitoring of fauna and flora
- Technical support research and conservation
- Support for local development

TAMBOPATA CONSERVATION
Macaw conservation, Amazon basin, Peru

Macaws are an endangered species in the wild. Their tropical rainforest habitat is being destroyed leaving them homeless. They are being killed for their feathers, meat and poachers are stealing the babies to sell as pets. All this together with the fact they have low reproduction rates means that if something is not done then most of the world's macaws could disappear forever!

The Tambopata research facility established in 1990 lies deep in the heart of the Peruvian Amazon rainforest, it's purpose – to study macaws in the wild and to try to conserve them.

Activities:
• Dietary research
• Macaw Satellite Telemetry: using technology to help parrot conservation discover the flying habits and territorial activity of Macaws.

Support:
Since 2005 The Wildlife Protection and South Lakes Wild Animal Park have funded this project which has been led by Dr. Donald Brightsmith.

PENGUIN CONSERVATION
The last penguins of Northern Peru

The Humboldt Penguin is a native species of Peru and Chile, in danger of extinction and in decline on the Peruvian coast. Its presence is limited mainly to some protected zones of the Peruvian southern coast. Fishing and the extraction of guano have resulted in the alteration and disappearance of several nesting places. The progressive disappearance of the Humboldt Penguin represents a true loss for the world and the Peruvian natural heritage. The Illescas hill, Media Luna, and its beaches are the last sites, in the north of the country where you will find this endangered species, and one of the last few sites in Peru where they can be appreciated in the wild.

The coastal sites of The Media Luna and of Illescas were chosen for their wealth of wildlife

Activities:
The two sites complement each other perfectly. The first one, Media Luna, is dedicated to the rescue of the Humboldt Penguin. Being very close to the towns and accessible, it is ideal for education and to show coastal biodiversity and conservation actions for tourists. The Reserve of Illescas, on the other hand, is a protected site with natural barriers

(peninsula surrounded by mountains, cliffs, sandy coasts, dunes) and allows an effective protection of the wildlife and flora. Different zones will be defined: zones of complete protection and zones for tourist visits and activities of fishing. The Reserve represents thus the ideal place for the rehabilitation of the Humboldt Penguin.

Illescas Objective: Protection & Release
- Penguin reintroduction site
- Penguin research centre and collection of works relating to the reintroduction.
- Protection and management of the site working with the community

ECOSANTAFE
Red Howler Monkey Conservation, Colombia

Colombia is the second most diverse country in the world with 10% of the world's biodiversity, which means that one out of every ten plant and animal species is found there. Habitat loss, poverty and a thriving wildlife trade are just a number of threats Colombia's wildlife face.

Red Howler Monkeys are the most trafficked animal in Colombia; the parents are often killed so that the poachers can sell on the cute babies into the illegal pet trade.

To combat this Environmental authorities have dramatically increased their confiscations of wildlife but there is no national plan to rehabilitate and reintroduce them into the wild and zoos have become holding stations. People who made a living trading in these animals have to be found an alternative source of income. Fundacion Ecolombia, now Ecosantafe, was set up in 1999 to organise these activities.

Activities:
- The project rescues, rehabilitates and where possible, returns the monkeys to the wild.
- Education and awareness
- Alternative sources of income for local people, providing employment.

Support:
South Lakes Wild Animal Park through our conservation charity The Wildlife Protection Foundation have proudly supported this project since 2002.

THE SUMATRAN TIGER TRUST
Sumatran Tiger Conservation Programme, Indonesia

In the last century the world tiger population has declined by 95% and four out of its eight sub-species are now extinct in the wild. The Sumatran tiger is now classed as being critically endangered, with just and estimated 350 wild Sumatran tigers left on the planet. The Sumatran Tiger Trust Conservation Programme (STTCP) is the largest tiger conservation project in Indonesia, the largest Sumatran tiger conservation project in the world.

Activities:
- Anti-poaching teams
- Handling of human/tiger conflict
- Monitoring of wild Sumatra tiger
- Education and awareness
- Healthcare activities
- Working with local communities

Support:
The project costs over £120,000 per year to run. Whilst The Sumatran Tiger Trust and South Lakes Wild Animal Park are committed to providing all of this funding each year, Zoo De Doue have contributed towards the costs of the teacher at the schools and provision of a health visitor. We have provided consistent funding for this project for the last fifteen years, which amounts to more than £1,000,000 – making us the largest single fundraiser for Sumatran tigers anywhere in the world. I have been funding and running this project since 1996.

TU TIERRA :
Organisation Overview:
Meaning "Your earth" . Northwest Peru is the southern limit of the Pacific equatorial dry forests ecosystem. This ecosystem spreads itself from north to the south, to the northwest of Peru, alongside the coast of the Pacific, the zone is known as the Tumbesian region. The climate of the region is controlled by two oceanic currents: the cold current of Humboldt and the hot equatorial running from the north.

The dry forests of the Tumbesian region are considered a biodiversity hotspot and one of the main priorities of conservation.

65 types of birds, of which 21 are threatened species, nine types of mammals, of which six are threatened, numerous amphibians and reptiles are endemic. Because of the human population expansion, development of the road networks, extension of the cultures, it is estimated today that only 4% of the original forest remains intact.

Activities:
At this moment in time the foundation brings together three conservation projects:
- The Ecological Reserve of Chaparri (1)
- Conservation of the coastline and development of Media Luna (2)

and Illescas National Reserve (3)

Aims:
- Area Protection
- Actions to rehabilitate the fauna
- Scientific monitoring of fauna and flora
- Enhancing of the sites through eco-tourism
- Environmental awareness and education
- Support local development

Support:

I am a founder board member of the foundation Tu Tierra and fund a majority proportion of the budget for this new organisation.

Acknowledgements

Many people have helped me throughout my life both in a personal and business sense. I would like to express my gratitude to them and especially the following people for their support, great love and friendship.

Karen King, my younger sister by thirteen months, has been my closest ally in my family throughout the years. Though we were like cat and dog in our early years, we have grown closer and closer throughout our lives until today she and her husband John are by far the strongest supporters of me and my own family whilst being family themselves. I love my sister and thank her for her steady support; John is my brother in every sense of the word, always there with good advice and words of encouragement when needed.

Karen sees the real me, the me that others sometimes do not wish to see and she has always been there through thick and thin in my life. I also have been particularly close to their children Katie and Emily, with Emily and I having a very close uncle/niece relationship that has always been special to me. All my seven nieces have been loyal to me and have stuck by me throughout the situation and it has been a great feeling knowing all the other children in the wider family have stuck by me and supported me fully and with love.

My life was absolutely transformed by Keith and Janet Howson and I would like to express my warmest thanks for the opportunity they presented me all those years ago when they changed me from a town lad into a country boy. Keith was a true father figure to me, something I dearly needed at this time of life and an aspect I did not have in my home life. Janet was instrumental along with Keith in giving me a clear moralistic direction in my life and showing me love when I needed it most. I will always be indebted to the two of them for the love and care they showed to me – they have, without question, helped make me the person I am today.

As soon as I met Stewart Lambert I knew he was a person of integrity, loyalty and commitment. In the past 28 years Stewart and Christine have been a solid rock for me, always there when I needed them, with support, care and a useful outlook on all of my issues. They have always shown perspective and patience and to this day are the first people I turn to for guidance and opinion. They don't always agree with me and yet always have found patience and understanding for me when I needed it the most. Thank you.

In just seven years Pierre Gay and I have accomplished so much together for conservation. Yet the greatest and truest achievement is in our enduring friendship. Pierre is someone I look up to, especially for his ever positive outlook on life. He is ten years my senior yet I hope I have his life energy in ten years time. I enjoy every minute I spend in the company of Pierre and his wondrous family. He has helped me to see greater compassion and understanding for both people and animals. He has also endured tragedy and emerged triumphant, still smiling, brimming with positivism, always achieving more. Pierre has taken my natural passion for animals and conservation and helped tune it in. We have been a perfect team for these past defining years of achievement. I consider Pierre and Elisa my 'family' and feel honoured to be their close friends.

In 1995 I met Ian Collings and his wife Gaye for the first time. Ian approached me in the zoo whilst I was building the then new small cat facilities and asked me questions about zoos and other zoo directors. I knew he was very knowledgeable. From then on they were regular visitors with their two girls and we built a friendship that has lasted the following sixteen years. Ian has been a strong supporter of the zoo and the charities, being a trustee of both the STT and WPF. He has also visited the Sumatran Tiger Project with me twice to see first hand the work we do. In all these years Ian and Gaye have seen my life develop, change and have witnessed many of the ups and downs in my family life. They have been true friends, who listen but don't necessarily always agree. They have given good advice and support whenever the need arose. I have to thank them for listening to me when I needed to talk.

I wish to thank my dedicated staff, many of whom have been with me for many years now. Thank you for your time, your care and your will to carry on with the mission of the park now and in the future, you are very much appreciated. I cannot name you all here but I do wish to publicly acknowledge the fact that I could never have done it without you.

Finally I have to thank Caroline Jellicoe for walking into my life in her white blouse those many years ago, for loving me and for having our children. Most of all she has blessed me with three of my most precious achievements: Hari, Kadi and Toba, all of whom I treasure. I will always be forever grateful.

Online Resources:
South Lakes Wild Animal Park
www.wildanimalpark.co.uk

For more information on **conservation** projects and to **donate** –

Sumatran Tiger Trust –
www.tigertrust.info

The Wildlife Protection Foundation - www.wildlifeprotection.info

The UXU Ranch, Yellowstone Highway, Wapiti, Cody, Wyoming USA. To book a Western Riding holiday contact
www.uxuranch.com